L'Académie de droit international de La Haye

honorée du prix Wateler de la Paix (1936, 1950), du prix Félix Houphouët-Boigny pour la recherche de la paix (1992), de l'ordre du Rio Branco, Brésil (1999), et de la médaille de l'Institut royal d'études européennes, Espagne (2000)

The Hague Academy of International Law

awarded the Wateler Peace Prize (1936, 1950), the Félix Houphouët-Boigny Peace Prize (1992), the Order of Rio Branco, Brazil (1999), and the Medal of the Royal Institute of European Studies, Spain (2000)

ISBN 978-90-04-52898-7

Imprimé par/Printed by Triangle Bleu, Maubeuge, France

The Quest for World Order and Human Dignity in the Twenty-First Century

Constitutive Process and Individual Commitment

General Course on Public International Law

(Second Edition)

ACADEMIE DE DROIT INTERNATIONAL DE LA HAYE
THE HAGUE ACADEMY OF INTERNATIONAL LAW

The Quest for World Order and Human Dignity in the Twenty-First Century

Constitutive Process and Individual Commitment

General Course on Public International Law
(Second Edition)

W. Michael Reisman

BRILL | NIJHOFF

2022

Leiden/Boston

TABLE OF CONTENTS

BIOGRAPHICAL NOTE

W. Michael Reisman, born on 23 April 1939 at Philadelphia, Pennsylvania, United States of America.

Myres S. McDougal Professor of International Law at the Yale Law School where he has been on the Faculty since 1965 and also Honorary Professor in the City University of Hong Kong. Has been a visiting professor in Tokyo, Hong Kong, Berlin, Basel, Tel Aviv, Paris and Geneva.

Fellow of the World Academy of Art and Science and a former member of its Executive Council, the President of the Arbitration Tribunal of the Bank for International Settlements, and a member of the Board of the Foreign Policy Association.

Has been elected to the Institut de droit international.

Formerly, was also Vice-Chairman of the Policy Sciences Center, Inc., President of the Inter-American Commission on Human Rights of the Organization of American States, Vice-President, Honorary Vice-President and Honorary President of the American Society of International Law and Editor-in-Chief of the *American Journal of International Law*.

Was President of the OSPAR arbitration and a member of the tribunal in the Eritrea/Ethiopia Boundary Dispute and in the Abyei (Sudan) Boundary Dispute.

PRINCIPAL PUBLICATIONS

Books

The Art of the Possible: Diplomatic Alternatives in the Middle East (Princeton university Press, 1970).
Nullity and Revision: The Review and Enforcement of International Judgments and Awards (Yale university Press, 1971).
Puerto Rico and the International Process: New Roles in Association (American Society of International Law Studies in Transnational Legal Policy, West Publishing Co., 1973); reprinted in 11 *Revista Jurídica de la Universidad Interamericana de Puerto Rico* (1977).
Toward World Order and Human Dignity: Essays in Honor of Myres S. McDougal (Free Press, 1976) (co-edited with Burns Weston).
Folded Lies: Bribery, Crusades, and Reforms (Free Press, 1979). (Spanish translation, *¿Remedios contra la corrup-ción?* (Cohecho, cruzadas y reformas) (Fondo de Cultura Económica, Mexico, 1981); republished in the same publisher's series *Biblioteca Joven*, 1984; Japanese translation, *Iwanami Shoten*, Tokyo, 1983; Russian translation, Moscow, 1988.)
International Law in Contemporary Perspective: The Public Order of the World Community (Foundation Press, 1981) (co-edited with Myres S. McDougal).
International Law Essays (Foundation Press, 1981) (co-edited with Myres S. McDougal).
Power and Policy in Quest of Law: Essays in Honor of Eugene Victor Rostow (Martinus Nijhoff, 1985) (co-edited with Myres S. McDougal).
Jurisprudence: Understanding and Shaping Law (New Haven Press, 1987) (co-edited with Aaron M. Schreiber).
International Incidents: The Law that Counts in World Politics (Princeton University Press, 1988) (co-edited with Andrew R. Willard).
Regulating Covert Action: Practices, Contexts and Policies of Covert Coercion Abroad in International and American Law (Yale University Press, 1992) (with James E. Baker). (Japanese translation, 2000.)
Systems of Control in International Adjudication and Arbitration: Breakdown and Repair (Duke University Press, 1992).
Straight Baselines in International Maritime Boundary Delimitation (St. Martin's Press, 1992) (with Gayl Westerman).
The Laws of War: A Comprehensive Collection of Primary Documents on International Laws Governing Armed Conflict (Vintage Press, 1994) (co-edited with Chris T. antoniou).
International Commercial Arbitration: Cases, Materials and Notes on the Resolution of International Business Disputes (Foundation Press, 1997) (co-edited with W. Laurence Craig, William Park and Jan Paulsson).
Law in Brief Encounters (Yale university Press, 1999).(Chinese translation, *Shenghuozhongde Weiguan Falu (Microscopic Laws in Life)* (Shangzhou Chubanshe, Taipei, 2001).
Jurisdiction in International Law (Ashgate, 1999).
International Law in Contemporary Perspective (Foundation Press, 2nd ed., 2004) (co-edited with Mahnoush H. Arsanjani, Siegfried Wiessner and Gayl S. Westerman).
Foreign Investment Disputes: Cases Materials and Commentary (Kluwer Law International, 2005) (co-edited with R. Doak Bishop and James Crawford).
Guojifa: Lingwu Yu Goujian (Understanding and Shaping International Law: Essays of W. Michael Reisman) (Law Press; China (2007).
The Reasons Requirement in International Investment Arbitration: Critical Case Studies (Martinus Nijhoff Publishers, 2008) (co-edited with Guillermo Aguilar Alvarez).

Stopping Wars and Making Peace: Studies in International Intervention (Martinus Nijhoff Publishers, 2009) (co-edited with Kristen Eichensehr).

L'école de New Haven de droit international (A. Pedone, 2010).

Fraudulent Evidence Before Public International Tribunals: *The Dirty Stories of International Law* (Hersch Lauterpacht Memorial Lectures) (with Christina Parajon Skinner) (Cambridge University Press) (2014).

Selected Articles

"The Role of the Economic Agencies in the Enforcement of International Judgments and Awards: A Functional Approach", 19 *International Organization* 929 (1965).

"Revision of the South West Africa Cases", 7 *Virginia Journal of International Law* 1 (1966).

"Rhodesia and the United Nations: The Lawfulness of International Concern", 62 *American Journal of International Law* 1 (1968) (with Myres S. McDougal); reprinted in 2 *International Lawyer* 721 (1968).

"The Enforcement of International Judgments and Awards", 63 *American Journal of International Law* 1 (1969).

"Sanctions and Enforcement", in 3 *The Future of the International Legal Order* 273 (Cyril E. Black and Richard A. Falk, eds., 1971); reprinted in *International Law Essays* (Myres S. McDougal and W. Michael Reisman, eds., 1981).

"Procedures for Controlling Unilateral Treaty Termination", 63 *American Journal of International Law* 544 (1969).

"Private Armies in a Global War System: Prologue for Decision", 14 *Virginia Journal of International Law* 1 (1973); reprinted in *Law and Civil War in the Modern World* 252 (John Norto Moore, ed., 1974); and *International Law Essays* (Myres S. McDougal and W. Michael Reisman, eds., 1981).

"Compacts: A Study of Interstate Agreements in the American Federal System", 27 *Rutgers Law Review* 70 (1973) (with Gary Simson); reprinted in *Law in the United States of America in Social and Technological Revolution* 459 (John N. Hazard and Wenceslas J. Wagner, eds., 1974).

"Accelerating Advisory Opinions: Critique and Proposal", 68 *American Journal of International Law* 648 (1974).

"Recognition and Social Change", in *Toward World Order and Human Dignity: Essays in Honor of Myres S. McDougal* (Burns Weston and W. Michael Reisman, eds., 1976 (with Eisuke Suzuki).

"Who Can Terminate Mutual Defense Treaties" (Pts. 1 and 2), *National Law Journal*, 28 May 1979 (with Myres S. McDougal).

"The Regime of Straits and National Security: An Appraisal of International Lawmaking", 75 *American Journal of International Law* 48 (1980).

"The Legal Effect of Vetoed Resolutions", 74 *American Journal of International Law* 904 (1980).

""International Law-making: A Process of Communication", Lasswell Memorial Lecture, 75 *American Society of International Law Proceedings* 101 (1981).

"Critical Defense Zones and International Law: The Reagan Codicil", 76 *American Journal of International Law* 589 (1982).

"The Plaintiff's Dilemma: Illegally Obtained Evidence and Admissibility in International Adjudication", 76 *American Journal of International Law* 736 (1982) (with Eric Freedman).

"The Tormented Conscience: Applying and Appraising Unauthorized Coercion", 32 *Emory Law Journal* 499 (1983).

"The Struggle for the Falklands", 93 *Yale Law Journal* 287 (1983).

"Coercion and Self-Determination: Construing Charter Article 2 (4)", 78 *American Journal of International Law* 642 (1984).

"Has the International Court Exceeded Its Jurisdiction?", 80 *American Journal of International Law* 128 (1986).

"Old Wine in New Bottles: The Reagan and Brezhnev Doctrines in Contemporary International Law and Practice", 13 *Yale Journal of International Law* 171 (1988).

"Harnessing International Law to Restrain and Recapture Indigenous Spoliations", 83 *American Journal of International Law* 56 (1989).
"War Powers: The Operational Code of Competence", 83 *American Journal of International Law* 777 (1989); reprinted in *Foreign Affairs and the US Constitution* 68 (Louis Henkin, Michael J. Glennon and William D. Rogers, eds., 1990).
"The Breakdown of the Control Mechanism in ICSID Arbitration", 1989 *Duke Law Journal* 739.
"International Law after the Cold War", 84 *American Journal of International Law* 859 (1990).
"Sovereignty and Human Rights in Contemporary International Law", 84 *American Journal of International Law* 866 (1990).
"Moving International Law from Theory to Practice: The Role of Military Manuals in Effectuating the Law of Armed Conflict", in *The Law of Naval Operations* 1 (US Naval War College, International Law Studies Series No. 64, Horace B. Robertson, Jr., ed., 1991) (with William K. Lietzau).
"The Concept and Functions of Soft Law in International Politics", in 1 *Essays in Honour of Judge Taslim Olawale Elias* 135 (Emmanuel G. Bello and Prince Bola A. Ajibola, eds., 1992).
"Obviating Affirmative Action", 39 *Yale Law Report* (Spring 1993); reprinted in 1 *Discrimination and the Law in South Africa* 256 (Christof Heyns, Johann van der Westhuizen and Tshidi Mayimele-Hashatse, eds., 1994).
"The Constitutional Crisis in the United Nations", 87 *American Journal of International Law* 83 (1993); reprinted in *The Development of the Role of the Security Council: Peace-Keeping and Peace-Building* 399 (René-Jean Dupuy, ed., 1993).
"Hachlata Mishpatit Ki-hachra-ah Chevratit" ("Legal Decision as Social Choice") 18 *Eyunei Ha-Mishpat* 611 (1994) (Isr.).
"The Raid on Baghdad: Some Reflections on Its Lawfulness and Implications", 5 *European Journal of International Law* 120 (1994).
"The Inter-American Commission on Human Rights", *Conference on the Inter-American Human Rights System: Defending Human Rights, 1959-1994*, Regional Meeting of the American Society of International Law, American University (April 1994).
"Protecting Indigenous Rights in International Adjudication", 89 *American Journal of International Law* 350 (1995).
"Legal Responses to Genocide and Other Massive Violations of Human Rights", 59 *Law and Contemporary Problems* 75 (Autumn 1996).
"The Supervisory Jurisdiction of the International Court of Justice: International Arbitration and International Adjudication", 258 *Recueil des cours* 9 (1996).
"The Lessons of Qana", 22 *Yale Journal of International Law* 381 (1997).
"El Control y Vigilancia de Guardianes Corruptos: ¿Reformas Eficaces o Simples 'Cruzadas' de Distracción?", 7 *Revista de Derecho Público* (1997) (Colom.).
"The Quest for an International Liability Regime for the Protection of the Global Commons", in *International Law: Theory and Practice: Essays in Honour of Eric Suy* 469 (Karel Wellens, ed., 1998) (with Mahnoush H. Arsanjani).
"Stopping Wars and Making Peace: Reflections on the Ideology and Practice of Conflict Termination in Contemporary World Politics", 6 *Tulane Journal of International and Comparative Law* 5 (1998).
"Toward a Normative Theory of Differential Responsibility for International Security Functions: Responsibilities of Major Powers", in *Japan and International Law Past, Present and Future: International Symposium to Mark the Centenary of the Japanese Association of International Law* 43 (Nisuke Ando, ed., 1999).
"The United States and International Institutions", 41 *Survival* 62 (November 1999).
"Unilateral Action and the Transformations of the World Constitutive Process: The Special Problem of Humanitarian Intervention", 11 *European Journal of International Law* 3 (2000).
"The Incident at Cavalese and Strategic Compensation", 94 *American Journal of International Law* 505 (2000) (with Robert D. Sloane).

"The Regime for Lacunae in the ICSID Choice of Law Provision and the Question of Its Threshold", in *Essays in Honor of Ibrahim F. I. Shihata*, 15 *ICSID Review* 362 (2000); reprinted in *Liber Amicorum Ibrahim F. I. Shihata: International Finance and Development Law* (Sabine Schlemmer-Schulte and Ko-Yung Tung, eds., 2001).

"Scenarios of Implementation of the Statute of the International Criminal Court", in *The Rome Statute of the International Criminal Court: A Challenge to Impunity* 281 (Mauro Politi and Giuseppe Nesi, eds., 2001).

"Unratified Treaties and Other Unperfected Acts in International Law: Constitutional Functions", 35 *Vanderbilt Journal of Transnational Law* 729 (2002).

"Assessing Claims to Revise the Laws of War", 97 *American Journal of International Law* 82(2003).

"Aftershocks: Reflections on the Implications of September 11", 6 *Yale Human Rights & Development Law Journal* 81 (2003).

"The Use of Friendly Settlements in the Inter-American Human Rights System", in *Man's Inhumanity to Man: Essays on International Law in Honour of Antonio Cassese* 741 (Lal Chand Vohrah, Fausto Pocar, Yvonne Featherstone, Olivier Fourmy, Christine Graham, John Hocking and Nicholas Robson, eds., 2003) (with Susan Benesch).

"Indirect Expropriation and Its Valuation in the BIT Generation", 74 *British Year Book of International Law* 115 (2003) (with Robert D. Sloane).

"Why Regime Change Is (Almost Always) a Bad Idea", Manley O. Hudson Lecture, 98 *American Journal of International Law* 516 (2004); also printed in 98 *Proceedings of the American Society of International Law* 290 (2004).

"The Question of Unilateral Governmental Statements as Applicable Law in Investment Disputes", 19 *ICSID Review* 328 (2004) (with Mahnoush H. Arsanjani).

"The Law-in-Action of the International Criminal Court", 99 *American Journal of International Law* 385(2005) (with Mahnoush H. Arsanjani).

"The Democratization of Contemporary International Law-Making Processes and the Differentiation of Their Application", in *Developments of International Law in Treaty Making* 15 (Rüdiger Wolfrum and Volker Röben, eds., 2005); reprinted in 2 *Transnational Dispute Management* (June 2005).

"The Past and Future of the Claim of Preemptive Self-Defense", 100 *American Journal of International Law* 852 (2006).

"Holding the Center of the Law of Armed Conflict", American Journal of International Law 100 (2006).

"No Exit? A Preliminary Examination of the Legal Consequences of United States' Notification of Withdrawal from the Optional Protocol to the Vienna Convention on Consular Relations", in *Promoting Justice, Human Rights and Conflict Resolution through International Law/La promotion de la justice, des droits de l'homme et du règlement des conflits par le droit international — Liber Amicorum Lucius Caflisch* 897 (Marcelo G. Kohen, ed., 2007) (with Mahnoush H. Arsanjani).

"What Is the Current Value of Signing a Treaty?", in *Human Rights, Democracy and the Rule of Law: Liber Amicorum Luzius Wildhaber* 1491 (Stephen Breitenmoser, Bernhard Ehrenzeller, Marco Sassòli, Walter Stoffel and Beatrice Wagner Pfeifer, eds., 2007) (with Mahnoush H. Arsanjani).

"On the Causes of Uncertainty and Volatility in International Law", in *The Shifting Allocation of Authority in International Law: Considering Sovereignty, Supremacy and Subsidiarity: Essays in Honour of Professor Ruth Lapidoth* 33 (Tomer Broude and Yuval Shany, eds., 2008).

"Acting before Victims Become Victims: Preventing and Arresting Mass Murder", 40 *Case Western Reserve Journal of International Law* 57 (2008).

"International Legal Dynamics and the Design of Feasible Missions: The Case of Afghanistan", in 85 *International Law Studies: The War in Afghanistan: A Legal Analysis* 59 (Michael N. Schmitt, ed., 2009).

"Inversión Extranjera, Desarrollo Económico y Arbitraje Internacional", in *Diálogos Sobre la Justicia Internacional* 26 (Bernardo Sepúlveda, Coordinator) (2009).

"Interpreting Treaties for the Benefit of Third Parties: The 'Salvors' Doctrine and the Use of Legislative History in Investment Treaties", 104 *American Journal of International Law* 597 (2010) (with Mahnoush H. Arsanjani).

"The Changing Relation of National Courts and International Commercial Arbitration", in 21 *The American Review of International Arbitration* 5 (2011) (with Heide Iravani).

"Provisional Application of Treaties in International Law: The Energy Charter Treaty Awards", in *The Law of Treaties beyond the Vienna Convention* (E. Cannizzaro, ed.) 86 (2011) (with Mahnoush H. Arsanjani).

"What Constitutes an Investment and Who Decides?", in *Contemporary Issues in International Arbitration and Mediation. The Fordham Papers 2010 50-70* (Rovine, ed.), (2011) (with Anna Vinnik).

"Reflections on the Cogency of Fragmentation: Statutes of Limitation and 'Continuing Violations' in Investment and Human Rights Law", in *Coexistence, Cooperation and Solidarity: Liber Amicorum of Rüdiger Wolfrum* 265-280 (2012) (with Mahnoush H. Arsanjani).

"Investment and Human Rights Tribunals as Courts of Last Appeal in International Commercial Arbitration", in *Liber Amicorum en l'honneur de Serge Lazareff*, pp. 521-530 (A. Pedone) (2011).

"Tribunals and Courts: An Interpretation of the Architecture of International Commercial Arbitration", with Brian Richardson, in *Arbitration – The Next Fifty Years: 50th Anniversary Conference, Geneva 2011* (ICCA Congress Series No. 16) (van den Berg (gen. ed.), pp. 17-65 (2012).

"The Diversity of Contemporary International Dispute Resolution: Functions and Policies"," in *Journal of International Dispute Settlement*: 10.1093/jnlids/ids015, pp. 47-63 (2012) (Vol. 4, No. 1, March 2013).

"Humanitarian Intervention: Politics and Prudence: The James G. McDonald Distinguished Lecture on Humanitarian Intervention" (New York University School of Law, 27 September 2012), in *Foreign Policy Association* (2013). Republished in *In Pursuit of Peace: Conflict Prevention and World Order*, Noel V. Lateef (ed.), pp. 71-84 (2016).

"'Case Specific Mandates' versus 'Systemic Implications': How Should Investment Tribunals Decide?: The Freshfields Arbitration Lecture", in 29:2 *Arbitration International*, pp. 131-152 (2013).

W. Michael Reisman, *Reflections on the Judicialization of the Crime of Aggression*, 39 *Yale J. Int'l L. Online* 66 (2014), available at http://www.yjil.org/docs/pub/o-39-reisman-reflections-on-the-judicialization-of-the-crime-of-aggression.pdf .

"Canute Confronts the Tide: States versus Tribunals and the Evolution of the Minimum Standard in Customary International Law", in 30:*3 ICSID Review-Foreign Investment Law Journal*, pp. 616-634 (2015) and also in 109 *Proc. Am. Soc'y Int'l L.* 125-141 (2015).

"Babel and BITs: Divergence Analysis and Authentication in the Unusual Decision of *Kiliç* v. *Turkmenistan*" (with Mahnoush H. Arsanjani), in *Practising Virtue: Inside International Arbitration* (D. Caron *et al.*, eds.) (Oxford University Press, pp. 407-424, (2015)).

"Negotiating Investment Treaties: Mechanisms for Anticipating and Controlling Textual Drift" (19 April 2016), Yale Law & Economics Research Paper No. 546, available at SSRN: https://ssrn.com/abstract=2789796 or http://dx.doi.org/10.2139/ssrn.2789796.

"The Empire Strikes Back: The Struggle to Reshape ISDS" (16 February 2017), available at SSRN: https://ssrn.com/abstract=2943514.

"Legal Decisions and Their Implementation in International Law" (with Mahnoush H. Arsanjani), in *The International Legal Order: Current Needs and Possible Responses: Essays in Honour of Djamchid Momtaz* (Crawford, Koroma, Mahmoudi and Pellet, eds.), Brill 2017, pp. 149-161.

"The Past and Future of the Great Compact: White & Case International Arbitration

Lecture" (Lamm Lecture, University of Miami School of Law, 9 February 2017)", in 33:1 *ICSID Review*, pp. 56-66 (2018).

"Will a Policy of Preemptive Self-Defense Make us All Safer?", available at SSRN, https://papers.ssrn.com/sol3/papers.cfm?abstract_id=3162033. Also published as "Will a Policy of Preemptive Self-Defense Make Us All Safe?", in *America in the World: Visionaries Speak* (Noel Lateef, ed.) Foreign Policy Association Centennial Series 2020, at pp 63-80,

"Meddling in Internal Affairs: Establishing the Boundaries of Non-Intervention in a World without Boundaries", in *Resolving Conflicts in the Law: Essays in Honour of Lea Brilmayer* (Giorgetti and Klein, eds.) (Brill Nijhoff 2019), p. 98.

"Negotiating and Maintaining Investment Treaties: Mechanisms for Anticipating and Controlling Textual Drift", 6:1 *Journal of International and Comparative Law*, pp. 75-85 (June 2019).

PREFACE AND ACKNOWLEDGMENTS

This second edition of the General Course goes to press as the major international institutions are beset by aggression, genocides, and massive human rights violations, all amidst global warming. The book is not a call for lamentation but a summons to international lawyers to mobilize the resources of the world community to reinforce international law's arrangements or, if need be, to adapt them to a new reality. I hope that the intellectual tools of the New Haven School will prove useful for these tasks.

I should like to acknowledge the assistance of David Younghoon Moon who reviewed the manuscript, Mahnoush Arsanjani, who made many useful comments, the Yale Law Library and especially Lucie Olejnikova who helped track down the most obscure citations and, once again, Cina Santos, my assistant, who managed the entire process with her usual skill and good humor.

W. Michael Reisman
New Haven, Connecticut
18 May 2022

"A decade into a new century, this old architecture is buckling under the weight of new threats."

Barack Obama[1]

"Il vecchio muore e il nuovo non può nascere: in questo interregno si verificano i fenomeni morbosi piú svariati."

Antonio Gramsci[2]

1. Barack H. Obama, Nobel Peace Prize Acceptance Speech. http ://www.white-house.gov/thepress-office/remarks-president-acceptance-nobel-peace-prize.
2. 1 Antonio Gramsci, Quaderni del Carcere, page 311 (1975).

CHAPTER I

BREAKING OUT OF ALICE'S LOOKING-GLASS: AN INTRODUCTION

> "When Law comes to take on the form most familiar to us, that of authoritative rules and doctrines expressed in their own queer, technical language, gaining precision from the operations of technical specialists at work in their own peculiar context of technique, the Law becomes a world of its own. It is a world like Alice's Looking-Glass – both difficult to break into, and difficult, once one has become acclimated to it, to break out of. Beside the layman who does not know anything about Art, but does know what he likes and is mildly apologetic about insisting on what he likes, there stand a hundred of his brethren who do not know anything about Law, but do know what is right and who insist without any apology at all that they ought to have it. They are baffled, frustrated, angry, if Law and right persist in being different. But they do not see what to do, nor how to take hold. They cannot break in."
>
> Karl Llewellyn and Adamson Hoebel [3]

Law is an important part of the way every society organises and conducts its affairs; international law, no less, is an important part of the way that the world organises itself and conducts its politics and economics. To any thoughtful person, law and the legal process are challenging concepts. But compared to other legal systems or their specialised parts, international law is far more difficult to understand and to practise. Alexis de Tocqueville, the renowned nineteenth-century French observer of the United States, famously said that "[t]here is hardly a political question in the United States which does not sooner or later turn into a judicial one" [4]. That observation certainly reflects the way that American lawyers think about law and, indeed, the way that American legislators make it. Indeed, in most developed legal

3. Karl N. Llewellyn and E. Adamson Hoebel, *The Cheyenne Way: Conflict and Case Law in Primitive Jurisprudence*, 1941, at p. 41.

4. Alexis de Tocqueville, *Democracy in America*, eds. J. P. Mayer and Max Lerner, trans. George Lawrence, Harper & Row, 1966 (orig. 1840), at p. 248. Oliver Wendell Holmes, in one of his most famous apothegms, said that "the practice of law is nothing more pretentious than the prediction of what courts will in fact do" and that the only relevant institution is one which will apply nothing but those legal texts. But even in the United States, the context in which Holmes was writing, focusing only on what courts are likely to do is too narrow: many other institutions and informal procedures may be the actual crucibles of decision. In international law, a focus only on courts and tribunals is perilous, for they are, in all but a few sectors, contingent, and episodic forums for effective decisions.

systems, the lawyers who practise in them and the scholars who write about them conceive of the application of law essentially as the work of courts.

The premise that there can be a meaningful description or analysis of international law solely by reference to the familiar institutions of domestic legal systems has little purchase on reality. In the international legal system, there is no single hierarchical legislature; as for international courts and tribunals, they are contingent and often marginal decision-making institutions. Consequently, even in periods of relative stability, international lawyers and scholars face uniquely formidable intellectual challenges in addressing many of the legal questions presented to them. Their domestic counterparts may confine their application of juridical skills to interpreting what the relevant legislature has decreed and the competent courts have interpreted. But without anything corresponding to an international "legislature", the international lawyer, operating in unorganised arenas, must first glean, from a vast and shifting polyglot cacophony, the *operative* normative expectations against which the various feasible options will be appraised and implemented. Instead of simply repairing to a court with compulsory and reliably effective jurisdiction, confident that an ensuing judgment will be implemented, the international lawyer must identify the likely or potential applier (or, as is often the case, appliers) from a much more complex and continuously changing process of application, in which courts and tribunals in many instances will figure only marginally or contingently.

Matters are further complicated by the fact that in international law, more than in domestic systems, many different types of appliers may be operating simultaneously or sequentially for the same matter. If these are the essential characteristics of the international legal system in periods of relative stability, how much more difficult is the task of the international lawyer in periods of rapid and radical change?

At the normative level, legal systems purport to run their respective writs, based on consistent general principles of law, to every natural and legal person in every corner of their respective realms; in this normative conception, "fragmentation" or differential treatment in different sectors is a legal failing which must be corrected. In practice, however, except for those systems which are completely totalitarian, legal reach is patchy. As a consequence, a disengaged observer, who was scanning a legal system, could describe each legal system of, let us say, a State in archipelagic terms, with an "island" in which the

State's law, in its conventional understanding, is applied comparatively effectively; "offshore" zones in which such conventional legal application is sporadic and is done more often on a case-by-case and policy-sensitive fashion; and zones in which, whatever their formal claims, critical actors will behave, as if, for all intents and purposes, the zones are either anomic or governed by a substantially different code, made and processed by a different set of actors.

International law is more "archipelagic" than many other legal systems. In normative terms, international law is global, the writ of its general principles purporting to run to the furthest reaches of its planetary and near-space realms. Viewed in terms of predictable effectiveness, international law is dramatically, sometimes maddeningly, archipelagic. Much of the literature on and about international law concerns itself with the islands and ignores the "offshore" zones; some of the islands can boast highly developed legal ecologies with effective sanction components approximating those of an idealised domestic law model; some of these islands have been intensely cultivated by scholars. These lectures do not ignore the islands but are particularly concerned with the "offshore" zones, how to act lawfully in them and how, if possible, to progressively "normatise" them. Including, as they do, issues such as the constitutive structure [5], lawmaking, law-applying and the use of force, the offshore zones are, at once, a large part of the reality within which international lawyers have to operate. But, by contrast to their domestic counterparts, the zones must also be viewed as pathological conditions which international lawyers must seek to repair. Lawyers will be unable to change them if they do not acknowledge their existence and nature.

These lectures acknowledge and try to address parts of the offshore zones of international law but reject the notion that there are areas or sectors of international life in which *lawful* decisions which are contextually meaningful and yet realistic are not demanded and cannot be designed. I shall address, in these lectures, the questions of identifying when a classical juridical method is appropriate and when a goal-oriented and contextual method is appropriate and lawful.

* * *

These lectures are concerned, *first*, with understanding and assessing the aggregate performance of the constitutive structure of the

5. See *infra* Chapter IV for discussion of constitutive structures in international law.

international legal system, at present and in some projected scenarios in a number of key areas; *second*, with enquiring into ways it can be made better; *third*, with providing a set of intellectual tools to enable the organisations as well as individual participants in the world community to be more effective; and, *fourth*, with accomplishing these objectives in accessible and comprehensible language. In his critical study of Oswald Spengler, H. Stuart Hughes remarked drily that "[i]n Germany, a book that is not hard to read is scarcely considered worth reading" [6]. I reject as false the purported equation of obscurity and profundity.

These lectures were prepared in the first decade of a new century. In focusing on the future, I claim no gift of prophecy. Rather I wish to emphasise that all law, despite its apparent veneration of the past, its concern with precedent and its almost obsessive quests for the ultimate "sources" of authority, is really about making decisions for the future; about maintaining an appropriate constitutive structure within which all decisions are taken; about maintaining and hopefully enhancing minimum order; within those constraints, about identifying the most efficient ways of shaping the productive processes of social life; and about the ways of sharing their fruits within a sustainable ecology.

I hope to accomplish my objectives by elaborating a framework that can enable not only practitioners but all who participate in and all who are affected by international law (1) to locate themselves in the evolving and unstable decision processes that constitute international law, whether in the normative islands or offshore zones, by means of a set of legal tools and a mapping schema; and (2) especially in the offshore zones, to perform the essential tasks of identifying the factors influencing decision so that they may better anticipate probable outcomes, influence them and thereby improve the aggregate performance of the international legal system. Thereafter I propose to examine some of the salient trends and their future projections in a number of key areas of international law in the twenty-first century [7].

Throughout these lectures, I will try to distinguish the operative from the mythic (but nonetheless significant) parts of the international legal process and to link them to the current social, political and economic contexts in which they operate; to articulate and appraise, at a meaningful

6. H. Stuart Hughes, *Oswald Spengler: A Critical Estimate*, 1952, at p. 66.

7. When the lectures were delivered, I tried to cover many major features of contemporary international law. Within the space limitations prescribed by the Hague Academy, this published version is perforce selective and will confine itself to a few aspects of world public order.

operational level, international law's goals; and, insofar as there is a discrepancy between those goals and actual achievements, to propose realistic and *feasible* alternatives that can recommend themselves for their practicability and not only for their moral appeal. In the many instances in which no alternative solutions are apparent to me, I can only set out the challenges lawyers in the twenty-first century will face in their pursuit of the relevant policy goals.

I am not suggesting that the approach taken here is the only one that is available to the student of international law. As I elaborate in Chapter VI, legal theories are no more than tools; different islands and zones, and the varied legal functions performed within them, present very different problems and types of "law jobs", for which different tools and even toolboxes may be required [8]. For example, the contemporary international lawyer who sits as judge or arbitrator in a case concerning the application of a provision of a treaty or the practitioner who argues before them is part of a very special species of law-application, in one of the normatively rigorous islands in international law's archipelago. Participants there are bound by prescribed law, professional ethics and personal honour to apply the rules, principles and other specific prescriptions which the parties expect to be applied to the dispute in accordance with an expected juridical method. For practitioners in these islands, a toolbox stocked with the usual juridical methods may suffice; a monographic synthesis of prior judgments and awards into a codification of rules will be useful. Other information – what those on these islands often call "political factors" – which might be relevant to different but equally authoritative international appliers, such as members of the UN Security Council, may be inappropriate for the international judge or arbitrator whose jurisdiction is confined to the consent of the litigating parties. Such information may be, as the law of evidence puts it, "inadmissible". Indeed, good reasons may exist for imposing these sorts of blinders on the people performing certain types of judicial and arbitral law jobs [9].

Codifying rules for international judges and arbitrators who inhabit international law's legally developed islands is an important and entirely respectable law job. Moreover, its aesthetic dimension can make it peculiarly enchanting to some. (When I was a student, one

8. The term "law jobs" is borrowed from Karl Llewellyn, "The Normative, the Legal, and the Law Jobs: The Problem of Juristic Method", *Yale LJ*, Vol. 49 (1940), p. 1355 *et seq.*, at 1373-1375.
9. See *infra* Chapter VI.

of my professors rapturously described Hans Kelsen's *Stufentheorie* as "beautiful".) I do not question the utility of codification as such, a task which I have undertaken on occasions for which a textual and rule-based method is proper, but I do argue that it is inappropriate for law jobs in the offshore zones of international law which require a contextual methodology and for which codification methodologies are ill-tooled. In an earlier publication, I recounted"the familiar story of a man, out walking one night on a street in Vienna, who happens on another well-dressed and plainly sober citizen who is crawling about on all fours in the light cast by a street lamp. Naturally, the first fellow stops to find out if there is something wrong. When the man on the ground explains that he has lost his watch, the passerby offers to help him find it and asks exactly where it fell. 'Back there', the man on the ground motions, pointing into the darkness on the other side of the street. 'Then why aren't you looking there?' the first fellow asks in exasperation. 'Because', the man on the ground explains as if it were perfectly obvious, 'it's dark over there and I can't see. But here it's light'" [10].

* * *

A word about those to whom international lawyers provide legal services. In the past, the international lawyer's actual or hypothetical client was the "Prince" or, put in more prosaic terms, a Government, however it might have been organised. That is no longer true. To the extent that they are equipped with an appropriate jurisprudential frame, all people in the twenty-first century are able to participate, whether directly or through the mediation of groups and with, of course, varying degrees of effectiveness, in some of the functions of the transnational decision-making processes which affect their lives. To that extent, they have the potential of functioning as the "Prince" or as John Austin's "political superior" [11].

That is not a platitude. I mean that ordinary folk now *really* participate as opposed to contributing in some small way to the formation of "public opinion". The possibility of meaningful participation in key functions of international decision is increasingly within the reach of more and

10. W. Michael Reisman, "International Incidents: Introduction to a New Genre in the Study of International Law", in W. Michael Reisman and Andrew R. Willard (eds.), *International Incidents: The Law that Counts in World Politics*, 1988, p. 3 *et seq.*, at 14.

11. W. Michael Reisman, "1995 Siebenthaler Lecture: A Jurisprudence from the Perspective of the 'Political Superior' ", *N. Ky. L. Rev.*, Vol. 23 (1996), p. 605 *et seq.*, at 605.

more people who are not affiliated with Governments. Economical electronic communication devices permit an unlimited number of private actors to evade many governmental controls, to present their versions of facts and to urge their recommendations directly to a mass audience, rendering the age-old political requirement of physical proximity and face-to-face contact redundant. The availability of a global communications network now allows the constant formation, reformation and mobilisation of like-minded individuals dispersed all over the planet into more effective interest groups. While some Governments have had – and presumably will have – some success in managing this electronic network and adapting it for the purposes of State control, its net effect (no pun intended) is a significant shift of power, for better or worse, to non-State entities.

The aggregate of all of these new non-State actors, international civil society, is not always civil, and it is not necessarily morally superior to every one of the Governments against which its members may range themselves. Thanks to technologies of communication, however, civil society is effective to a degree unimaginable in the past. Even contemporary Government lawyers can no longer confine themselves to dealing solely with their counterparts in other Governments. They must also take account of these latter-day "Princes" and "Princesses", whether they are multinational enterprises (MNEs), non-governmental organisations (NGOs), religious institutions, gangs, militias, terrorist organisations or other entities or groups of people in civil society who form enduring or evanescent coalitions in order to pursue their particular values.

Members of all of these groups – State and non-State – are staking treasure and life in pursuit of their particular objectives and many of them routinely seek advice from international lawyers. Some of these people may feel compelled, for moral reasons, to comply with what they are advised is "the law". (I believe you will find that, even for those people who have internalised such moral imperatives, the moral commitment is ultimately contingent on "the law" having a minimum congruence with their core values [12].) Others may not use terms like "law" or "international law" or may entertain doubts about its relevance to their immediate concerns, even contending that "international law doesn't exist". But these actors will inevitably learn to appreciate, as have some avowedly "realistic" advisers to a recent US President, that

12. See *infra* Chapter III.

the extent to which others perceive their objectives and their methods for achieving them as lawful becomes an ineluctable factor in the costs of pursuing and the ultimate success or failure of achieving those objectives. Participants in the international community must ultimately take account of what other people think is – to paraphrase Llewellyn in the epigraph to this chapter – the "right" way of doing things for *pragmatic* and not only moral reasons. They turn to international lawyers for guidance as to what those right ways are.

International lawyers themselves are among the groups seeking counsel. One of the questions I will address at the conclusion of these lectures is the responsibility of international lawyers when their Government or client – whether a person or legal entity – is violating international expectations of right. I will ask more generally whether international lawyers, by virtue of their training, understanding and location, can and should act as a critical part of the vanguard of the global community.

But then, what are the expectations of the right ways of doing things? How are they shaped in this inimitably complex global community? How are they applied in concrete cases? How are those expectations changed? In understanding and advising on these questions, the international lawyer in the twenty-first century must deal with a universe different, more complex, more unstable, even more volatile than that encountered in previous eras [13].

It is this particularly challenging set of tasks which a group of scholars, many of whom were taught by Myres McDougal and Harold Lasswell, have been addressing. In doing so, we aspire to what we call a "theory *about* law" rather than a "theory *of* law" [14]. By that we mean, even as actors within the legal process, we try to look at international law from a vantage point outside of it; operating from that vantage point requires a different set of jurisprudential conceptions, some of which will be elaborated in these lectures.

It is a truism that all law is policy, in the sense that every legal arrangement, however humble, procedural or "technical" it may seem, has been designed in order to achieve some preferred social or economic

13. Prosper Weil, "Le droit international en quête de son identité: cours général de droit international public", *Recueil des cours*, Vol. 237 (1992), p. 11 *et seq.*; Erik Suy, "The Status of Observers in International Organizations", *Recueil des cours*, Vol. 160 (1978), p. 75 *et seq.*, at 102.

14. Myres S. McDougal, Harold D. Lasswell and W. Michael Reisman, "Theories about International Law: Prologue to a Configurative Jurisprudence", *Va. J. Int'l L.*, Vol. 8 (1968), p. 188 *et seq.*

objective, including "constitutive" objectives about the structure of the decision-making process itself. A "policy-oriented approach" is proposed not merely to map the complex and changing international decision processes but also to project the range of probable outcomes and to enhance the skills necessary for influencing them so that preferred outcomes ensue. This is something that all persons involved in making or trying to shape any part of their own social environments must learn to do, no matter what they may think their theory of law is.

But we are not norm-neutral. We aspire to go beyond those concepts and tools by assuming the responsibility of seeking to *improve* the structure and performance of decision processes and to enhance the capacity of individuals to achieve outcomes promising an improved world order. This necessarily involves a careful assessment and, where it is found wanting, a critique of current processes, institutions and practices as a prerequisite to the invention of alternatives.

* * *

Where, then, does the international lawyer fit in all this?

As I noted, we often think of the practice of international law as going to court or arbitration to argue a case, and we frame our legal concepts and methodological tools for that particular task. Images of a court and the tools appropriate for it are so deeply embedded in our minds that in academic enquiries we hypothesise problems or conflicts as if they were going to be resolved by a court – even when no court or tribunal is in sight. Evaluating a difficult international legal problem through the eyes of a fantastically neutral judge can be a useful technique for teasing out "purely legal" issues and assessing them thoroughly. Yet it reinforces the deeply held notion that law and courts go together to the point that law cannot exist without courts. But in the archipelago of international law, in contrast to an imagined well-organised municipal system, few of the most important issues and disputes are going to be resolved in one of the normative islands presided over by an international tribunal. A significant part of the professional tasks that fall to international lawyers occur in one of the offshore zones, and they will never see the inside of a courtroom. Their *lawful* resolution may require a different method of advocacy and decision from the usual textual and rule-based methodologies applied in a legal enclave; *lawful* resolution may not be as tidy as the simple application of a rule. The point of emphasis is that just because an international dispute is not resolved in a formal legal institution should not mean that it should not and cannot be resolved lawfully.

Consider, for a moment, some of the sorts of professional problems likely to be encountered, offshore, by international lawyers in the twenty-first century:

- The Secretary-General of the United Nations has sent you, as her Special Representative, to a country lacking internal order and wracked by a high level of violence to restore sufficient order to enable international aid supplies to resume and to make arrangements for such aid to be delivered and distributed in an orderly and equitable way.
- The Director of the International Monetary Fund (IMF) has ordered you to develop, with ten States in a region, a "bailout" plan for another State in that region.
- The International Atomic Energy Agency has sent you to a lawless region to stop the smuggling of weapons-grade plutonium from former Soviet republics.
- The Secretary-General of the North Atlantic Treaty Organization (NATO) instructs you to form a coalition of willing Member States to provide military protection for the civilian population of a country in which internal protest is being violently suppressed.
- The European Union has dispatched you to a country in North Africa in which citizens have risen against a dictator to facilitate a restoration of order by arranging for the safe departure of the dictator.
- Mass murder is taking place in State X but the Security Council, which is debating a resolution authorising States to intervene and arrest the murderers, has been blocked by the veto of a permanent member.
- As a member of the International Law Commission (ILC), you are charged with producing a code for comprehensive international environmental protection for the twenty-first century.
- As a lawyer in the United Nations Office of Legal Affairs, you have been asked to prepare for the Secretary-General a report appraising and, if warranted, restructuring UN peacekeeping operations.
- As Legal Adviser of the US Department of State, you have been asked to advise the President of the United States as to whether to intercept and board, on the high seas, foreign flagged vessels believed to be carrying nuclear components to a terrorist organisation.
- As a lawyer for the World Bank, you have been tasked with devising a code and system for assessing the transparency and honesty of the administrative processes of States receiving bank loans.

- The Organisation for Economic Co-operation and Development (OECD) has asked you to devise a study of whether bilateral investment treaties are promoting desirable economic and social development in capital-importing States and, if not, how to adjust them or replace them with something better.
- As lawyer to an MNE, you have been charged with securing the release of corporate personnel who have been taken hostage by insurgents in a civil war.
- As a legal adviser to a coalition of concerned States, you have been asked to evaluate internationally lawful alternatives for dealing with a putsch by pro-Al-Qaida officers in a nuclear weapons State.
- As a professor of international law, you assume that one of your responsibilities is to conduct an ongoing appraisal of the quality of work of those who perform the tasks in the preceding examples.

Take the first of these examples: the Secretary-General of the United Nations sends you to a failed State which has descended into chaos to restore sufficient order to allow a flow of international aid to stem the high mortality and to arrange for its delivery and distribution.

With whom do you deal? With the Government? If there is one, what if it is barely functioning or its ineffectiveness is the predicate of the problem? Do you go to a local court and seek an injunction? Do you turn to the regional organisation? If it were able to resolve the problem, the United Nations would presumably not be involved. The local scene may be controlled by combinations of competitive private groups in fluid, shifting alliances; private armies of tribes or clans and of criminal gangs; mercantile groups trying to find profit in the situation who may have to rent the services of one or the other of the private armies or pay them for "protection"; local or foreign smugglers; MNEs, some trying to protect their investments, others trying to secure concessions or long-term opportunities or, at the very least, to block competitors from exploiting the situation; foreign Governments, their militaries or corrupt elements in them seeking political or economic benefits and perhaps arming or financing some of the local armies; religious leaders who enjoy some influence over their respective flocks and seek to augment their influence; NGOs trying to operate in the failed State; and international terrorist groups for whom the chaotic situation provides a safe haven for training and a base for mounting foreign operations and who, accordingly, have an interest in perpetuating the chaos.

Whether you decide to meet, let alone deal with any or all of these groups (and that in itself is a sensitive question with implications for international legal policies), you must, at least, be able to identify them, understand their leaders and their goals, their relative influence or power and what it is based on, their internal decision arrangements, how they operate, how they network with other groups and how their behaviour can be changed in ways advantageous or at least neutral to your objectives. Bright-line rules are unlikely to provide meaningful guidance as to lawful options and decisions. You must ultimately determine a meaningful course of action by reference to the possibilities the situation actually allows and the application of many different authoritative policies. These situations are not the limit of law. They are the ultimate test of law.

Is this not, *mutatis mutandis*, a microcosm of many extensive offshore zones of the global process, what international law is attached to and what it purports to regulate? Even in international law's legal enclaves where tribunals may operate relatively efficiently, how do you determine whether existing law is achieving its social and political objectives? How do you devise and promote new law? How do you terminate existing law?

The way you characterise these kinds of problems, the intellectual tools you use to research them and the information you think relevant for answering them will all be determined by your conception of law and your commitment to its application. Your conception will influence the role you assume, the methods you use, the professional ethics you adopt and the outcome.

In the international political process, there are many situations in which radical political and legal change is not proceeding in the institutions (if any such exist) that are supposed to be making those decisions. In contexts in which the power to make choices meaningful depends not on an effective institution, such as you would find in an idealised developed legal system, but rather on securing (which may mean compelling) agreement between actors in shifting coalitions with different power configurations and different interests and in situations in which those actors are trying to innovate or terminate law, international lawyers operate at their peril and at the peril of those they represent if they proceed as if they were before a court, relying on inherited legal texts. They disserve those who have entrusted their lives and treasure to them if, like the proverbial economist on a desert island with nothing but a can of beans who "assumes a can opener", international lawyers assume constitutive arrangements when there is no court with the power to give effect to them and the arrangements in those legal texts have no remit in that situation. Yet international lawyers betray international law if they simply assume that a lawful decision cannot be made in each unique situation.

It is important to emphasise yet again, as I shall do in Chapter VI, that exclusive reliance on texts may be appropriate before certain formal legal appliers; their personnel are expected to address a particular event exclusively in terms of certain formal expectations of authority, to which the parties before them have consented. In that setting, predictions based on the assumption that only certain authoritative texts will be applied is a reliable method for proceeding. International law has such islands, but they are only part of a much bigger and more varied archipelago with diverse offshore zones.

It is vital that international lawyers know where in the archipelago they are operating, which functions of decision they are performing, and which tools and legal conceptions are appropriate for the task at hand. International lawyers should certainly be committed to the application of formal authority and its enhancement and extension. But it is irresponsible to make predictive statements to those seeking legal advice, who will then risk treasure and life in reliance on it, when prediction is based only on texts of formal authority uncorrected by verification that formal authority will be effective in that situation. Is professional responsibility properly discharged by an opinion based on a precise statement of the law of an "island", with predictions of its likely eventuation, uncorrected by a realistic assessment of what is really going to happen in its offshore zone? What is the likelihood of success devising new institutional arrangements without taking accurate account of the social and economic setting in which they will be embedded? Practical success no less than responsible discharge of one's professional duty requires a set of intellectual tools and a richer contextual conception of relevant decision processes, which can correlate, with contextual sensitivity, formal authority with effectiveness and which can essay projections of future decisions under *varying* conditions.

And it is important to emphasise, yet again, that lack of correlation between authoritative prescriptions and their effective application in particular sectors should not be taken to mean that there is no role for the international lawyer nor space for lawful decisions. The contribution of the lawyer in such circumstances is all the more urgent.

It would be lovely if every problem in the international legal process were simply the Jessup Moot writ large, if all the challenges which the international lawyer will confront in the twenty-first century were susceptible to a quick fix, such as an amendment to one of the major architectonic documents of the twentieth century or the creation of some new institution or dreaming up a novel legal argument for an international tribunal. Unfortunately, things are often more complicated, as the hypothetical tasks show. As we will see in Chapter II, the world to which international law is attached – in its physical, social, economic, ecological and technological dimensions – is one which is rapidly changing and one in which formal institutions are only a part and, in some cases, a *marginal* part of the much larger process that is making and applying international law. In this new environment, the international lawyer requires additional sets of concepts and tools in order to understand, shape and use international law effectively in every part of its archipelago.

The traditional juridical skills serve us well in formal settings, especially when they are judicial or quasi-judicial; these are, of course, skills familiar to any lawyer. They do not serve in non-formal settings, nor in decision functions such as intelligence-gathering, promotion or appraisal, even when these functions take place in familiar formal decision settings. If lawyers aspire to use their professional skills to help fashion a world order of human dignity, a toolkit containing a range of skills and approaches is even more urgent. Some of the conceptual tools of such an approach will be considered in these lectures.

* * *

When I began my academic career, even the most visionary internationalists of the time operated with what now seems to be an exceedingly modest conception of the scope of international law. In retrospect, it is hard to believe that a creative innovator such as the great Sir Hersch Lauterpacht could write in his magisterial *Function of Law in the International Community* that

> "the scope of matters governed by international law is on the whole confined to the regulation of the external relations of States. It does not and cannot aim at regulating the lives of the members of the international community in the same intensive and pervading manner as municipal law does. It is mainly adjective law. It is, more than any other kind of law, a regulation of competencies . . . At present international law is more static than any other law not only because of the absence of an international legislature,

> but principally because it regulates relations which are not in themselves liable to be affected in a decisive manner by economic and other changes" [15].

Nowadays international law is, if anything, as Wordsworth put it, "too much with us". In comparison with what it aspired to a century ago, the collective enterprise of international law seeks in the twenty-first century, beyond the maintenance of minimum order, to induce and manage change over a broad spectrum of human rights *within* States, to protect the environment, to facilitate development and productive enterprise, to reduce poverty, to protect public health, to limit violence, murder and mayhem, to rehabilitate failed or feckless States and to induce everywhere better domestic governance, among many, many other things. The fact that these aspirations have emerged as authoritative goals of international law in the twenty-first century is itself a remarkable achievement, and much has been achieved. However, the very installation of goals generates a continuing indictment for each failure to achieve them and renews challenges to international lawyers in the twenty-first century.

Practising law effectively requires the cultivation of realism, but realists are susceptible to a lethal occupational disease: they can become jaded and cynical. Insofar as lawyers lose their sense of indignation at injustice and the violations of human dignity and cease to criticise because "that's just the way things are" or because "those are the limits of law", they are less effective lawyers. But criticism without reference to carefully formulated goals and without a search for better means for their achievement is a sterile intellectualism and a cheap catharsis; at worst, it is nihilism. Criticism *with* reference to goals and *with* the passionate search for alternative means for their achievement is a necessary step in amelioration. I insist that it should be an indispensable part of the vocation of the international lawyer in the twenty-first century.

15. Sir Hersch Lauterpacht, *The Function of Law in the International Community*, 1933, at pp. 249-250.

CHAPTER II

WHAT IS INTERNATIONAL LAW ATTACHED TO: THE FACTS OF INTERNATIONAL LIFE

> "[A]t no time has it been so important, as it is today, that we should see the facts of international life as they really are, and not as they come to us reflected in false or outworn theories."
>
> James Brierly [16]

Professor Thomas Reed Powell was wont to say to his students, "If you can think about something attached to something else, without thinking about what it's attached to . . . you have the mind of a lawyer" [17]. That admonition, whether or not intended facetiously, is actually sound advice if you choose to understand law as a closed and internally consistent system of rules. If so, Professor Powell's conception authorises you to exclude everything outside that logical system which might distract you from contemplation of the rules. Legal jobs are then performed by logical exercises. "New" law is logically derived from prior rules or principles. The criterion for determining whether a decision is "good" is simply the extent to which it complies with "higher" rules, a pattern of conformity called "legality".

Professor Powell's conception is not the only way to approach law. You may start from an entirely different assumption: all legal arrangements – including those continuing, "constitutive" processes that establish and maintain the milieu for creating and implementing all more specific legal arrangements – are artefacts, which have been consciously fashioned by people operating in political processes. Those artefacts are designed to facilitate and regulate ways of producing and distributing, widely or selectively, the things that people want: opportunities for influencing the decisions that will affect them, opportunities for producing and acquiring wealth, knowledge, skills, health, opportunities to enquire about and practise religious belief and cultivate meaningful relations with others – in sum *all* the things that people, in the aggregate, pursue. If this is your approach, then trying to

16. James Brierly, "The Basis of Obligation in International Law", in Sir Hersch Lauterpacht and C. H. M. Waldock (eds.), *The Basis of Obligation in International Law and Other Papers by the Late James Leslie Brierly*, 1958, p. 1 *et seq.*, at 2.
17. See T. W. Arnold, *The Symbols of Government*, 1935.

think about "the law" without thinking about the "what-it's-attached-to" will defeat your purpose.

Your purpose will also be defeated if, instead of evaluating the extent to which a legal arrangement is actually facilitating the particular purpose for which it was created, you confine your appraisal of that arrangement to the extent of its conformity to prior legal decisions. If, as an international lawyer, you do not know what is actually happening and what you want to happen, you will be unable to appraise existing legal arrangements or to design new ones to achieve specific outcomes.

So before we begin to take up and assess some of the key structural arrangements of international law, let us select and consider, necessarily in the most abbreviated fashion, trends in eight of the particularly critical dimensions of what is a multidimensional global ecological, social, economic and political process. That process is, in the broadest sense, the context in which international law is produced and in which those practising it have to operate, and which, in turn, they are trying, in various ways, to direct, adjust and regulate. It is what international law is attached to.

Each of these dimensions is abstracted from an integrated whole and each is interactive and interdependent with the others, so it is impossible in dividing them to avoid some repetition. Because gains in one dimension may have to be secured by losses in another, "trade-offs" are, as we will see, reflected in antinomies in the international legal arrangements which have been built upon them.

Section 1. The demographic dimension of the world community

The explosion of the numbers of our species and their reorganisation in many different territorial and non-territorial communities is a new dimension of international politics with ramifying consequences for international law. On 11 July 1987, Earth's human population reached 5 billion, and the United Nations observes this historic milestone annually on 11 July as "World Population Day" [18]. By 2020, our planet had 7.8 billion inhabitants. Barring natural or man-made disasters, demographers were projecting 9.8 billion inhabitants by 2050 [19] and it

18. UN, "World Population Day", https://www.un.org/en/observances/world-population-day.
19. UN Department of Economic and Social Affairs, "World Population Projected to Reach 9.8 million in 2050, 11.2 Billion in 2100", 21 June 2017, https://www.un.org/development/desa/en/news/population/world-population-prospects-2017.html.

would be a considerably older population. But in 2021, demographers noted a trend reversal almost everywhere with the exception of Africa and the Middle East and they "now predict that by the latter half of the century or possibly earlier, the global population will enter a sustained decline for the first time" [20].

In place of a small number of relatively efficient if not benevolent imperial organisations among whom a much smaller number of inhabitants was distributed, the far greater numbers of inhabitants now live in some 200 territorially organised communities, which vary widely in their resource bases, political stability and the efficiency of their internal organisation. Some of the territorial units are densely populated. The city-State of Singapore has a population of 20,502 per square mile. Bangladesh has a population of 164.6 million in an area of 51,700 square miles. Other States, such as the United States, with a population density of 92 per square mile, are essentially underpopulated. The effect of the demographic dimension varies. In the Middle East, populations are expected to increase from 20 per cent to 40 per cent. The populations of sub-Saharan Africa are expected to increase by almost 25 per cent.

Increases and decreases in population have significant implications not only for the political and economic systems of the States concerned but also for the transboundary movements of peoples, the disruptions that can attend them and the stresses on and heightened competition for natural resources as a consequence of ever more spoons (and chopsticks) in the planet's rice bowl. Pressures also mount as expanding rural populations, unable to sustain themselves on the land, migrate to cities which lack sufficient infrastructure and are unable to provide minimum services. Correlatively, some cities and even some regions are experiencing drastic depopulation.

Absent major calamities, urbanisation could be the dominant form of habitation in the twenty-first century. "From a demographic standpoint, not only do dense settlements have greater capacity than rural areas to absorb large populations sustainably, but urbanization itself is a powerful factor in fertility decline." [21] Beneficial results from increased urbanisation will depend upon planning and installing appropriate legal arrangements. Without such arrangements, the prospects of unplanned urbanisation for the world order could be destructive: "The urbanization

20. Damien Cave, Emma Bubola and Choe Sang-Hun, "World is Facing First Long Slide in its Population", *New York Times*, 23 May 2021, pp. 1 and 17.

21. UN Population Fund, State of World Population 2007: Unleashing the Potential of Urban Growth, 2007, at p. 55.

is jolting mentalities and subjecting them to new influences. This is a historical situation. And now one of the ways for people to reorganize themselves in this urban world is to associate themselves with new or strong, fundamentalist religion" [22].

The consequences of demographic pressures are not limited to shifting masses of people from the countryside to cities within States. Demographic pressures, as noted, also lead people to migrate from poorer to more developed countries, fleeing desperate circumstances and seeking enhanced life opportunities. Throughout the history of our species, migration has been a survival strategy, but its scale has often been limited by natural barriers and primitive transportation. Now, modern modes of transportation allow sudden, virtually unpredictable, mass movements with the possibility of stressing the very economic and other opportunities that make certain States magnets for immigration. In many instances, however, demographic movement may simply shift problems to new locales.

There are other inducements to massive emigration. The revolution in communications, which has been a key girder of the globalising political-economic process, broadcasts images of wealth, intensifying and adding urgency to the demands and expectations of those who have not enjoyed any of the promised benefits of the global market. The migratory pressure increases as people become aware of just how desperate their lives are. And desperate they are! While there is more wealth than ever before, 783 million people live below the World Bank's international poverty line of $1.90 a day. Nearly 10 per cent of the world's workers live with their families on less than $1.90 per person per day [23]. Billions of people do not have clean drinking water or sewage. One third of the world's population – 2.6 billion people – have no decent place to go to the toilet; more than 1 billion drink, wash and work with water polluted by human or animal faeces.

Thanks to the often idealised media presentations of life in developed countries, those who live in abject poverty, unlike their predecessors, keenly appreciate that their condition is not an immutable "fact of life". That realisation becomes a factor pressing for local change; when it is stemmed, it leads to desperate efforts causing local unrest and survival outmigration.

22. See Daniel Howden, "Planet of the Slums: UN Warns Urban Populations Set to Double", *The Independent*, 27 June 2007.

23. UN Sustainable Development Goals, Goal 1: End Poverty in All its Forms Everywhere, https://www.un.org/sustainabledevelopment/poverty/.

Migration is often resisted by the migration magnet States. Yet threats of political explosions at the source of the outflow – which, thanks to tighter interdependencies, now also import international disruptions – can be further exacerbated if the magnet States, in defensive mode, try to close themselves off.

Another feature of the demographic dimension of the global process relates to world health. The movement of people about the planet, thanks to a global transportation network, can facilitate the rapid diffusion of diseases – some currently incurable – that, in the past, would have burned themselves out in isolated corners of the planet. Transnational epidemics and pandemics recur.

Section 2. The ethnocultural dimension of the world community

A community requires a minimum of shared perspectives among politically relevant actors: common identities, common images of past and future, and common demands. With the enormous increase in the number of politically relevant people, these requisites of community are increasingly under stress due to national, regional, class and religious differences [24]. The global community manifests some convergence of perspectives, but it is also marked by divergences in narratives and demands among the tens of thousands of territorial and non-territorial groups of which it is composed. Within each group, these divergences are sustained by the intergenerational transmission and celebration of mythologised historical triumphs, defeats and group traumas. The implications of these chiastic developments for international law in the twenty-first century will be taken up later in these lectures.

During the imperial era, significant numbers of elites and mid-elites shared common perspectives on many issues critical to world order. How much greater is the stress in the world community of today. The Ethnologue lists 7,117 "known living" languages [25], each a medium of communication as well as a repository of group experience – including attitudes towards members of other groups – and ideas and distinct images of the past and the future [26]. At the moment, English has emerged as the *lingua franca* and provides some of the features of

24. See *infra* Chapter XI, Section 4, for discussion of multiple nationality.
25. See Ethnologue, "About", http://www.ethnologue.com/.
26. At the same time, many of the languages spoken by smaller or peripheral groups are dying, some by neglect, some through inundation of mass communications in another language or dialect and some by intentional suppression in programmes of cultural genocide.

a common focus, but different projections of alternative futures could make other languages either serious competitors or replacements for English, regionally, if not globally [27].

The inner lives of the peoples of the world, which provide complex images of the past and the future, of divine and human agency and of social demands, vary enormously. Just under a third of the world (31.4 per cent) are Christians of varying and not necessarily reciprocally amiable sects. Nearly a quarter (23.2 per cent) are Muslim, again of varying and not necessarily reciprocally amiable sects. Fifteen per cent are Hindu [28]. There are no figures for those who are secular and profess no religion, nor are there figures for purely nominal adherents to the various sects. Much of the violence and destruction of human history has been and continues to be the result of conflicts between exponents and under the banner of different religions, a phenomenon which gives no indication of abating.

The international flow of goods and services in the contemporary world has been so amply documented that its mention alone will suffice to confirm interaction and interdependence. But the extent to which this largely beneficial flow of goods and services exacerbates cultural conflicts is less appreciated. Every manufactured object and economic service – and not simply films and books – which crosses a boundary has some cultural effect and that effect often involves the displacement of a local cultural feature. A McDonald's in Changsha displaces local cuisine and traditional dining patterns which may have reinforced family and interfamily alliances. Jeans in Kuala Lumpur displace traditional dress and may affect cultural notions of modesty, female subordination and sexual autonomy.

Thus, the seeds of change are carried by all sorts of unlikely hosts. As they propagate themselves about the planet, they also create their own resistances. One seed is the partial homogenisation of global culture. As global, regional and dominant national languages reinforce their status, they necessarily displace and challenge local languages; traditional language and thought systems are disappearing as rapidly as other endangered species. This is often resisted by trying to install legal arrangements, often in the arena of international trade law, to protect extant cultures for people who benefit from them. These efforts

27. See *infra* Chapter XV for discussion of the design of alternative constructs of the future.

28. See Central Intelligence Agency, The World Factbook, https://www.cia.gov/library/publications/the-world-factbook/geos/xx.html.

at "cultural conservation" or "economic protectionism", depending on one's perspective, rarely staunch the cross-border avalanches of new cultural forms; in a global science-based and scientific civilisation, change cannot be arrested.

Many extol change itself as an ultimate value; indeed, one which should be addressed with audacity. But the human cost of change cannot be ignored and should, itself, be a part of international planning. The more supple, resourceful or gifted members of declining and disappearing cultures and strata may make the leap to the newer, more inclusive cultures with their promises of comparatively greater life opportunities. Less adaptable people may slip into an anomic reality as the social and economic conditions that sustained their traditional kinship units disintegrate, to be replaced by markedly different ones. Those who cannot adapt may respond with a fierce rejection of the global values and practices in favour of what they believe to be renewed "nativist" or "tribalist" values, sometimes justifying extreme violence for the preservation of what are deemed traditional values.

Thus, a rapidly changing world community is prone, at many levels, to conflict between contrary forces, as individuals and groups who desire change press for still more, while those who feel threatened – politically, economically or morally – resist. In certain critical sectors, this has led not only to increasing demands for the use of violence as a political technique for achieving either stasis or change but the elaboration of ideologies in which the use of violence is accorded a central and sacramental status [29].

Yet one notes in some sectors significant homogenisations of culture. Along with goods and services, the exchange of ideas across cultural "boundaries", at one time restricted to human carriers, is more rapid and, in the longer run, may prove even more influential. In the most enduring sense, the significance of physical distance has been the limits it places upon the potential of human experience. The electronic media explosion, the creation of a social appetite for "news", in its broadest sense, the wider participation in its production, dissemination and consumption, and the growth of an infrastructure for marketing it are reducing the political effect of physical distance. In so doing, they may also be changing the perceptual apparatus and psychosocial organisation of the individual.

29. Paul Kahn, *Sacred Violence*, 2008, at pp. 91-101.

The ease of ideological transmission has resulted in a massive, continuing cultural interchange. Many non-European elites have concluded that the power and wealth they seek can only be acquired by adopting certain "Western" methods. European culture, formerly a self-appointed exporter of these methods, is also being influenced by some of the life patterns and styles of its former colonies and is constantly weighing the relevancy of other cultures to its own existence. World history is, indeed, as Adda Bozeman wrote, a history of transnational cultural exchange [30].

Section 3. The historical dimension of the world community

"The past", one of William Faulkner's characters muses, "is never dead. It's not even past" [31]. Although every legal arrangement and the legal enterprise as a whole are always concerned with the future, they are rooted in an historical context which has shaped expectations and demands and which international lawyers ignore at their peril: "Those who cannot remember the past", Santayana counselled, "are condemned to repeat it" [32]. But Santayana apparently believed that there was *a* single, verifiable past. The problem with remembering "the past" in the international context is that no group and no country can claim a monopoly on historical narratives. Each cultivates its own narrative, celebrates its own triumphs, while nursing its own calamities, its own suspicions and its own grievances. Often, one group's triumph is another's tragedy. Those who would appreciate the weight of the past on contemporary behaviour need to understand the historical narratives of the diverse groups which together comprise the world community.

As for the larger picture, on whose broader trends most agree while differing on the evaluation of their legal significance, the changes have been radical and disjunctive. Just over a hundred years ago, in 1907, most of our planet was controlled by great empires: the British, the French, the Dutch, the Belgian, the German, the Austro-Hungarian, the Italian, the Portuguese, the Russian, the Spanish, the Ottoman, the Persian, the Japanese and the Chinese. The United States, having consolidated control over its North American landmass and the remnant of its indigenous population, was then in the midst of its own imperial

30. Adda B. Bozeman, *Politics and Culture in International History: From the Ancient Near East to the Opening of the Modern Age*, 1994, at pp. 1-14.
31. William Faulkner, *Requiem for a Nun*, 1951, at p. 92.
32. George Santayana, *Reason in Common Sense*, Vol. 1 of *The Life of Reason or the Phases of Human Progress*, 2nd ed., 1924, at p. 284.

expansion. It had just wrested the Philippines, Cuba and Puerto Rico from the Spanish Empire and had "detached" Panama from Colombia. The "scramble for Africa", twenty-five years earlier, had been a comparatively orderly distribution among the European empires of the territorial and human spoils of almost an entire continent. It had not, however, sated imperial appetites. Many of the empires were poised to dismember and absorb parts of Imperial China in a process that promised to be a far less orderly scramble. Indeed, the great empires of that moment would likely have done so but for the "Open Door" policy, initiated, albeit for less than altruistic reasons, by the United States. On a smaller scale, European States were jockeying to pick off parts of the Ottoman Empire in the Balkans while Italy was setting its sights on the vilayet of Tripolitania [33].

Each of the powerful and expanding behemoths of the time earned the then coveted title of "empire" by virtue of the fact that it controlled and directly governed significant territories geographically separate from its metropole and inhabited by significant numbers of peoples who were racially, ethnically or religiously distinct from its own populations [34]. Whenever it served their own interests, these various empires routinely suppressed indigenous cultures and their aspirations for self-governance. In place of the indigenous arrangements which they had found upon their arrival, the empires tended to impose their own institutional practices and values, ostensibly to fulfil their self-appointed and self-defined *mission civilisatrice*.

The struggles to gain and keep control were violent and are, sometimes, still unresolved: to mention only a few examples, the Boxers in China, the Moslems in Mindanao, the Mahdi in the Sudan or the hero of Somali resistance, Mohammed Abdullah Hassan, whom Europeans dubbed the "Mad Mullah" [35]. Many current political and

---

33. Christopher Clark, *The Sleepwalkers: How Europe Went to War in 1914*, 2013.

34. "Empire", now pejorative, was then a positive term. The so-called Martens Clause in the Preamble to the 1899 Hague Convention II with Respect to the Laws and Customs of War on Land provided that "populations and belligerents remain under the protection and empire of the principles of international law, as they result from the usages established between civilized nations, from the laws of humanity, and the requirements of the public conscience". Convention with Respect to the Laws and Customs of War on Land, 29 July 1899, 32 Stat. 1803, TS No. 403, 26 Martens Nouveau Recueil (ser. 2) 949.

35. It is sobering to reflect that had the Mahdi or the Mad Mullah lived in the latter years of the twentieth or the beginning of the twenty-first centuries and had the benefit of rocket-propelled grenades and National Liberation or Third Generation war tactics, each might have wrested control of Sudan or Somalia from the imperial power.

military conflicts have their roots in (and cannot be understood without reference to) earlier confrontations such as these.

To regulate their relationships *inter se*, the empires adapted those international law arrangements which were congenial to their common interests. In their version of the *corpus juris gentium*, they were the *gentes*, the actors or "subjects" of the law, and they determined who else might join their august ranks. They took for granted that their races, religions and cultures were superior and were to be bestowed upon backward peoples and territories [36]. War was an honourable part of statecraft, conquest was its prize, and, not surprisingly, the inhabitants of the imperial lands (lands which could be and were deemed worth conquering) were, for the most part, assimilated to their flora and fauna. The last one hundred years have witnessed the collapse of almost all of these empires and their replacement, in the diverse territories they had controlled, by independent or nominally independent States governed by indigenous elites. The most recent to topple was the Czarist Empire, which had morphed into the Soviet Union and belatedly self-destructed in the waning years of the twentieth century. Nor can it be said that the process of imperial necrosis has run its course.

Revulsion at the depravity and destruction of the First and Second World Wars led to major efforts at constitutive innovations in international law. The UN Charter, building on the detritus of the League of Nations, was the major international legal architectural undertaking of the period, and, consistent with the political reality from which it emerged, it featured a Security Council with five permanent members as its centrepiece. Assigning the primary security responsibilities to the most powerful States had seemed a natural "fit", as it would ensure that the Council's decisions would be effective. But the fit was quickly stressed by the Cold War, in which the two superpowers of the Council were ranged against each other, all but paralysing the Council's fulfilment of the responsibilities which the Charter had assigned it.

The Cold War, one of the major events of modern times, did not re-enact the mass slaughters and genocides of the preceding twentieth-century conflicts. But in terms of lives affected, wealth consumed, geographical reach and long-term environmental consequences, it is one of the critical conflicts of human history. The Cold War was marked by continuing high expectations of violence, but, unlike the

36. Sir Mark Frank Lindley, *The Acquisition of Backward Territory in International Law: Being a Treatise on the Law and Practice Relating to Colonial Expansion*, 1926.

great conflicts of the past, it secularised the word "Armageddon" by making, in a plausibly secular and non-religious sense, the prospect of the complete annihilation of the human species entirely credible. The two antagonists were engaged in ceaseless mobilisation and detailed planning for war and their alliances and hegemonic relations in their respective spheres involved almost all the States of the world. Most of the globe was deemed to have some strategic value so that any change in alliance might be viewed as a *casus belli*. The Cold War threatened more people than ever before, for some of the most destructive weapons systems were incapable of distinguishing between combatants and non-combatants.

The Cold War pitted two mutually incompatible ideologies or "contending systems of world public order", each deriving, curiously, from the same cultural and historical sources [37]. Each ideology viewed the other in Manichaean terms and disseminated or inculcated its message intensively in its own sphere. One was intent on "containing", if not "rolling back", its adversary, the other bent on "burying" its opponent. At the height of the Cold War, there were two distinct worlds on the planet between which trade and other human contact were drastically reduced. Similarly, for many purposes, there were two systems of international law and two systems of world public order.

Within each of the adversaries, the anxiety generated by the anticipated conflict infiltrated and shaped many sectors of life. In varying degree, each of the superpowers acquired some garrison-State features. In the West, the effects were felt in ordinary democratic processes, civil and human rights, school curricula, literature and art, environmental protection, individual health, economic distortions, the allocation of vast public funds for weapons development and the maintenance of a large standing military – indeed, in almost every sector of life. In the East, the ideology was overtly totalitarian; millions of people were subjected to high degrees of control and deprived of accurate information about what was occurring elsewhere. Larger and larger proportions of the national wealth were diverted to military and security matters. Though the elites of neither superpower could have taken any pleasure in developments that would poison the environment for generations and increase the incidence of certain diseases among their own children, the threshold of "acceptable costs" and "acceptable

37. Jacob L. Talmon, *The Myth of the Nation and Vision of Revolution: Ideological Polarization in the Twentieth Century*, 1991; see also Jacob L. Talmon, *The Origins of Totalitarian Democracy*, 1955.

risks" for the maintenance of security through weapons development and testing was pushed higher and higher [38].

The Cold War was not a "hot war" because the introduction and constant symmetrical refinement of nuclear weapons established a "balance of terror". While that balance prevented overt military conflict between the superpowers, its precariousness aggravated the general sense of anxiety. The few incidents in which the adversaries faced one another "eyeball-to-eyeball" [39] were traumatic experiences for practically everyone on the planet. The balance of terror, however, did not deter either side from conducting localised yet very lethal "proxy" wars, overt and covert interventions, and to experiment with what came to be known as "low-intensity, protracted conflict". If the big war never eventuated, the expectation of violence and violence itself – in one form or another – never abated.

The Cold War inevitably shaped much of the body of traditional international law that had developed over centuries to facilitate and regulate political, economic and other human relationships across national boundaries. The independence and rights of choice of smaller States were restricted by larger neighbours acting in their own interest and, it was often avowed, in the interest of systemic security. The slow effort to centralise authoritative coercive force and to restrict the freedom of unilateral action, the hallmark of civilised political arrangements and the major acknowledged deficit in international law, was impeded by an institutional international security system that accorded a veto power to each of the major adversaries. That veto ensured the survival of the institutional system by averting decisions that could have led to the withdrawal of one or another bloc, but it also condemned the system to frequent ineffectiveness. Even the freedom of the oceans, one of the most venerable struts of the international system, which had preserved five-sevenths of the planet as a public highway for exchange, was periodically attenuated to facilitate weapons development and testing by the major powers [40]. As soon as outer space became accessible, it, too, became part of the military arena [41].

---

38. David E. Hoffman, *The Dead Hand: The Untold Story of the Cold War Arms Race and Its Dangerous Legacy*, 2009.

39. The memorable phrase is Dean Rusk's. See James G. Blight, Joseph S. Nye, Jr. and David A. Welch, "The Cuban Missile Crisis Revisited", *Foreign Affairs*, Vol. 66 (1987), p. 170 *et seq.*, at 170.

40. Myres S. McDougal and Norbert A. Schlei, "The Hydrogen Bomb Tests in Perspective: Lawful Measures for Security", *Yale LJ*, Vol. 64 (1955), p. 648 *et seq.*

41. Myres S. McDougal, Harold D. Lasswell and Ivan A. Vlasic, *Law and Public Order in Space*, 1963.

Formal prohibitions on unilateral uses of force were skirted by exceptions for the so-called "wars of national liberation", which, in turn, generated and sustained counter-exceptions for "freedom fighters". Symmetrical doctrines of selective intervention – Brezhnev or Reagan – were developed and vigorously applied by each of the adversaries [42]. The *jus in bello*, which historically had sought to reduce the savagery of war and to maintain a distinction between combatants and non-combatants, had suffered serious damage from the application of modern industry to warfare in World Wars I and II. It was dealt an additional blow by the nuclear weapons of the Cold War. By their nature, these weapons cannot be made to discriminate between belligerents and non-combatants or meet any meaningful test of proportionality. Yet, paradoxically, assurances of an umbrella of protection by the nuclear powers restrained further proliferation. As for the notion of necessity, one of the traditional cumulative criteria of the lawful use of armed force, it, too, was drained of meaning by elective strategic doctrines such as "Mutually Assured Destruction". That doctrine worked, in the sense that it deterred nuclear conflict, but the moral implications of such a "defensive" strategy could not but have corrosive effects on other aspects of international and domestic public orders and the sense of personal insecurity of the hundreds of millions of "beneficiaries" of the doctrine.

Espionage and covert actions to influence domestic events in the internal arenas of each adversary were conducted with virtual impunity [43]. A new quasi-legal category of "rules of the game" developed, but the use of the word "game" – like its predecessor, the "Great Game" of the nineteenth century – was macabre. As for the word "rules", it was an oxymoron, for these rules were in fact euphemisms for reciprocally tolerated violations of verbally accepted international law. The level of good faith in international treaty morality sank to an all-time low in arms control agreements; terms such as "national means of verification" were an explicit acknowledgement and acceptance, as part of the treaty regime, of the parties' reciprocal belief in the infinite capacity for misrepresentation and perfidy of their respective treaty partners. Happily, the Cold War, in macro-conflict terms, remained and ended

42. W. Michael Reisman, "Old Wine in New Bottles: The Reagan and Brezhnev Doctrines in Contemporary International Law and Practice", *Yale J. Int'l L.*, Vol. 13 (1988), p. 171 *et seq.*

43. W. Michael Reisman and James E. Baker, *Regulating Covert Action: Practices, Contexts, and Policies of Covert Coercion Abroad in International and American Law*, 1992.

"cold", to be replaced briefly by a unipolar, then, a multipolar and an emerging bipolar international political system.

As the twenty-first century advances, a concatenation of political and technical developments has commenced a transformation of this dimension, whose profundity is appreciated, if its features and implications are not understood. Some of the national and international legal infrastructure of the earlier periods continues, shaping, to some extent, contemporary actors at all levels. In this respect, "the past is not past". But the contours of various possible futures remain indistinct.

Section 4. The economic, environmental and resource dimension of the world community

By the end of the Second World War, the great imperial trading systems, which had practised, in various forms, protectionist mercantilism, had yielded to an increasingly inclusive world economic system pressing national elites to undertake progressive reductions in tariffs, subsidies and other non-tariff barriers. At the same time, claims of sovereignty notwithstanding, those parts of their political economies that Governments have been able to immunise from explicit or functional regulation by this global system have narrowed. The installation almost everywhere of forms of capitalism and, for the present, the eclipse of anti-capitalist economic and moral theories have served to reinforce these globalising economic trends. At the same time, the increasingly acute competition for resources has revived some mercantilist practices by some major actors. Much will depend on whether the US's championing of an inclusive international economic system will resume after what will have proved to have been a short hiatus.

These same trends have ruthlessly demanded that virtually every entity constantly make itself more competitive, a process that has set off, within both developed and developing States, rapid and often disruptive social changes. The resulting extension of a single, inclusive science-based and technological civilisation over great parts of the planet has further generated and diffused new technologies and opportunities for the more resourceful individuals. It has also, as noted above, put great stress on traditional moral and religious doctrines, disrupting the inner lives of those for whom these doctrines are central to their existence.

The scale of globalisation is unprecedented: "$2 trillion worth of currency now moves cross-border every day, roughly 90 per cent of which is accounted for by financial flows unrelated to trade in goods and services"[44]. No State, indeed, no international institution, is able to regulate these daily movements, despite their impacts. If, as Jeffrey A. Frieden observed, "[P]ost-1945 Western nations chose a little bit of integration and a little bit of social reform, but that proved to be only a temporary solution"[45], the institutions produced by those reforms seem less and less able to address the challenges of the twenty-first century. Increasingly, constitutive decisions for the wealth process are taken by *ad hoc* coalitions of the public and private financial institutions of powerful economies; who is powerful has become relative and fluid, with the G7 expanding to G20 and perhaps contracting to a smaller integer. These shifting coalitions are, themselves, composed of factions which prove to be fluid.

Power and wealth have always been reciprocal modes of influence, so it is no surprise that the economic institutions established in the aftermath of World War II reflected the prevailing distribution of power. As wealth is redistributed in very different patterns in the twenty-first century, those institutions are adjusting to reflect the extant power context. The emergence of sovereign wealth funds of smaller States as significant factors in global investment is only one dimension of this shift[46]. "Centre and periphery" continues to be a widely used metaphor in the world economy, but who is near the centre and who near the periphery is often a function of vantage point.

The rise of MNEs and international banks has transformed the economic and resource dimension radically. The largest of the MNEs have bigger budgets and engage more people than many States in the United Nations. Some are owned by vast aggregates of equity shareholders, though they are managed by a small, essentially self-perpetuating elite. Samsung Group, a South Korean multinational, is South Korea's largest *chaebol*, and the revenue of just one of its affiliates, Samsung Electronics, accounts for 14 per cent of South Korea's GDP[47]. As of December 2017, Samsung Electronics generated

---

44. Benn Steil and Robert E. Litan, *Financial Statecraft: The Role of Financial Markets in American Foreign Policy*, 2006, at p. 3.

45. Jeffry A. Frieden, *Global Capitalism: Its Fall and Rise in the Twentieth Century*, 2006, at p. 476.

46. José E. Alvarez, "The Once and Future Foreign Investment Regime", in Mahnoush H. Arsanjani, Jacob Katz Cogan, Robert D. Sloane and Siegfried Wiessner (eds.), *Looking to the Future: Essays on International Law in Honor of W. Michael Reisman*, 2004, at p. 607.

47. Eleanor Albert, "South Korea's Chaebol Challenge", Council on Foreign Relations, 4 May 2018, https://www.cfr.org/backgrounder/south-koreas-chaebol-challenge.

more than $220 billion, had 320,671 employees and operated in seventy-three countries [48]. Other MNEs are privately held. Cargill, a US privately held conglomerate, generated more than $115 billion in 2018 and had 155,000 employees across seventy countries [49].

Entities such as these are created under national law, in the form of corporations or other forms of business units, but they are only partially and contingently dependent upon and subject to national regulation. Operating transnationally, the managers of these entities are able to move their *siège* of administration and management and even their productive facilities from country to country in their quest for economic opportunity in changing environments. Thus, they may maximise their wealth-creating potential while manifesting less and less loyalty, in a traditional civic sense, to a particular State or set of States.

At the same time, however, such entities are sometimes advocates of international order in that they appreciate the utility of maintaining and enhancing a stable transnational economic environment that makes planning feasible and enables their various enterprises to flourish.

The implications for the Westphalian theory are drastic. In the aggregate, all of these entities and all who participate in the global economy constitute a transnational force before which even the most powerful nation-States must sometimes yield. Privately held for-profit entities that are or have persuaded Governments that they are "too big to fail" apparently cannot be unwound by State action. A collective decision of the transnational market may view a national statute to deal with a legitimate national concern as less conducive to profitable enterprise than arrangements and corresponding opportunities in other available venues and lead to a rapid flight of capital; this, in turn, may force the national legislature to review its enactment and to adjust regulatory practices that it had considered vital in order to accommodate the wishes of all or part of the aggregate transnational market. Within this new environment, counter-elites seeking transformations at the national or regional levels find opportunities to operate in innovative and effective ways.

Obviously, a world of this sort will be generating, over time and in a jagged fashion, new principles and governance structures, as the older principles and institutions decay in a similarly staggered fashion.

---

48. Samsung, "Fast Facts", https://news.samsung.com/global/fast-facts.

49. Cargill, "Cargill Reports Fiscal 2018 Fourth-Quarter and Full-Year Results", https://www.cargill.com/2018/cargill-reports-fiscal-2018-fourth-quarter-and-full-year-results.

Consider the once hallowed doctrine of economic self-determination, which was an article of faith in the 1970s and lives on as such in political rhetoric but for all practical purposes is now moribund. While some scholars and politicians still speak reverently of sovereignty and the sanctity of domestic jurisdiction under the UN Charter, extraordinary and unprecedented transfers of national competences to international institutions and public-private partnerships have occurred. The Bretton Woods institutions, reinforced by a network of international and regional trade organisations, specialised agencies, and powerful market forces, tried to install macro-economic policy standards for even large and strong States. Yet other more powerful global forces can reduce the influence of even those formidable financial agencies.

Shifts of wealth do not necessarily lead to shifts in all other values. As more and more of the planet has become part of a single global market, technologies and skills have diffused at a differential pace. While the transfer of relatively rudimentary medical technology has led to population explosions in some parts of the world, with its implications for the demographic dimension, it has yet to be matched by a corresponding transplantation of more advanced social and economic arrangements that would enable women to achieve equality and, as a lifestyle choice, elect to limit their fecundity.

Capitalism, with its "frenzy of increase", in Elias Canetti's vivid phrase, must consume ever more natural resources; synergising with the demographic explosion, that economic model is putting an additional unprecedented stress on the environment [50]. Economists have drawn attention to "peak resources", a concept which emphasises the productive interdependence of oil, water, steel, food, and so forth, all of which are needed to yield more of each unit of those resources. The implications for inter-State conflicts are ominous.

Traditional international legal modes of allowing and protecting the right of capture of resources or of simply allocating them will hardly suffice for what may be the increasingly acute natural resource conflicts on the horizon [51]. Large zones of the oceans have been assigned to coastal States that should now have an incentive to maintain the sustainability of those fish stocks which have become their property. But 64 per cent of the oceans are still high seas. A study in 2010 found

50. Elias Canetti, *Crowds and Power*, trans. Carol Steward, Continuum Press, 1998 (orig. 1960), at pp. 51-52.

51. See Michael T. Klare, *Resource Wars: The New Landscape of Global Conflict*, 2001.

that of forty-five high seas fish stocks, 69 per cent were either depleted or overexploited [52]. The oceans themselves are stressed, with ecological balances in danger.

As for global warming and the aggregate consequences of climate change on the survival of island States, coastal areas of many other States and maritime boundaries, the facts are so well known as to require little recapitulation [53]. Every part of the planet itself has always been in a process of change; continents break apart and drift into others and tectonic plates shift beneath oceans and landmasses. Changes in climate are also part of the history of the planet, as temperate regions undergo desiccation, while frozen areas become temperate. But the current climate change stands out because of the speed of change. The Intergovernmental Panel on Climate Change (IPCC), which was convened by the UN, reported that if greenhouse gases continue to be emitted at the current rate, there will be severe consequences due to climate change as early as 2040 resulting ultimately in $54 trillion in damages [54]. The 2015 Paris Agreement committed nearly every State to reduce emissions [55]. Lamentably, the US, one of its principal architects, withdrew and after a hiatus re-joined, but the Protocol's non-binding targets, even if met, would not evade the consequences envisaged by the IPCC. Accelerated climatic changes in the twenty-first century bode to challenge many legal arrangements and exacerbate many latent conflicts.

Section 5. The war system dimension of the world community

The Charter of the United Nations opens with a determination "to save succeeding generations from the scourge of war". But, paradoxically, one of the enduring and most problematic dimensions of the world to which international law is attached and in which the United Nations is

52. Sarika Cullis-Suzuki and Daniel Pauly, "Evaluating Global Regional Fisheries Management Organizations: Methodology and Scoring", Fisheries Centre, Univ. of British Columbia, Working Paper No. 12, 2009, ftp://ftp.fisheries.ubc.ca/fCWP/fCWP 2009-12_CullisSuzukiPauly.pdf.

53. UN Department of Economic and Social Affairs, World Social Report 2020: Inequality in a Rapidly Changing World, 2020, https://www.un.org/development/desa/dspd/world-social-report/2020-2.html; UN, The Sustainable Development Goals Report, 2020, https://unstats.un.org/sdgs/report/2020/.

54. Coral Davenport, "Major Climate Report Describes a Strong Risk of Crisis as Early as 2040", *New York Times*, 7 October 2018.

55. Paris Agreement to the United Nations Framework Convention on Climate Change, 12 December 2015, TIAS No. 16-1104.

embedded, is a self-sustaining "war system". Exacerbated by conflicts for power and resources, considered above, widely shared expectations of violence sustain the war system; tangible evidence of violence (whether personally or vicariously experienced) sustains and reinforces those expectations. The system incorporates within its myth and folklore a cosmology of conflict which extols the necessity and virtue of sacrifice for the good of the group as well as the morality of the application of violence against outsiders when it is deemed necessary for group security or survival [56]. The level of crisis which it generates may vary within States and wax and wane between different groups, but it is sufficient to ensure that the system is continuous.

In different geographical locations and at different social levels, various factors, other than the obvious sources of conflict, feed into and drive the war system. Factors such as exposure to and collective recollection of traumatic crises in the past, cultural and religious conceptions [57] and even geographic location may inter-stimulate to maintain the system [58]. Anthropological data indicate that, in primitive groups, where intergroup conflict is an avenue through which poor but enterprising youths may acquire property and other forms of wealth, wives, prestige and power within the tribe or clan, members will insist on the continued prosecution of conflict with other groups – even in the face of severe costs to their own group.

Nor is this a phenomenon limited to so-called primitive societies. Eisenhower's valedictory condemnation of a "military-industrial complex" in the United States (a critique applicable to many of the other most developed political economies of the time) drew attention to the extent to which economic concentrations concerned with the preparation and resupply of the wherewithal of war may become so important to a civilian peacetime political economy that all domestic participants, including both capital and labour, come to perceive an urgent interest in sustaining the war system. "We must", he counselled, "guard against the acquisition of unwarranted influence, whether sought or unsought, by the military-industrial complex" [59].

Specialists in violence have a similar interest in the continuation of those conditions which make their skills indispensable to the group

56. See W. Michael Reisman, "Private Armies in a Global War System: Prologue to Decision", *Va. J. Int'l L.*, Vol. 14 (1973), p. 1 *et seq.*

57. See *infra* Chapter III.

58. See Charles Hill, *Trial of a Thousand Years: World Order and Islamism*, 2011.

59. Dwight D. Eisenhower, Farewell Address, 17 January 1961, https://www.eisenhowerlibrary.gov/research/online-documents/farewell-address.

they serve or wish to serve. In many societies, military castes promote the virtues of the Spartan life, of struggle, and of the mystique of the supposedly purifying effects of battle.

The application of science and technology to the military arsenal has made new generations of weapons available to a much wider range of users. Now leaders and would-be leaders of a great number of hitherto unorganised and suppressed groups with their own images of past and future and with specific demands can take advantage of the development and proliferation of miniaturised, highly mobile weapons and innovative military tactics. Together, these can introduce a rough parity between otherwise unequal antagonists. The development of universally accessible communications technologies has facilitated the mobilisation of peoples who previously were only passive members of latent groups.

Groups committed to transformative ideologies aggravate war systems. Any political movement that views itself as an agent of change with respect to external arenas and to non-group members sustains the expectations on which the war system is based. Whether it is socialism, communism, proselytising religions or, as Carl Schmitt argued, liberal democracy, a system of public order which prides itself on tolerance [60], the self-authorised mission to change parts or all of the public and civic order, including those whose members do not wish to be changed, reinforces the war system.

A war system is sustained at the psycho-personal level by pervasive individual anxiety for both individual and group security. Fear or apprehension of severe injury to the self is, of course, a primary human experience and is crucial for individual survival, for it alerts the self to those aspects of the environment which, entirely plausibly, may threaten it with injury or death. Anxiety, fear which exceeds the actual threat and sustains and reinforces itself, becomes a crucial element of a group's own narrative and serves as a basis for mobilising individuals in political organisations against other organisations.

The credible threat of war and the conviction of the probability of aggression upon the nuclear and extended self sustain the political symbols of anxiety: the need for "self-defence" is ever present. It is axiomatic that one must fight wars to maintain security; to this end, one must maintain cadres of specialists in violence who are prepared, at any

60. Carl Schmitt, *The Crisis of Parliamentary Democracy*, trans. Ellen Kennedy, 1988 (orig. 1923), at pp. 22-33.

time, to fight for the group. These specialists are supposed to increase security by deterring wars, for is it not obvious that if a group is to minimise the possibility of wars without sacrificing security, it must be prepared to fight wars? Yet, paradoxically, the presence of specialists in violence and the public celebration of their past and prospective sacrifices actually provoke and confirm anxiety and insecurity within the groups they are supposed to protect while triggering other groups to mobilise in defence against them.

The result of the interaction of all of these factors is a constant process of mobilisation of populations under the supervision of security experts who serve as "anxiety managers". The objective or promise of this process is security, but the inevitable result is the exacerbation of anxiety and the reinforcement of personal and group insecurity, as each group's preparation for attack stimulates comparable preparations in other groups.

The manipulation of anxiety is a standard technique of social control, used politically, theologically and educationally to induce certain preferred patterns of behaviour. I use the term "anxiety manager" to refer to those whose role, whether political or theological, is specialised in making group members sufficiently aware of the threats to security, from within and without, so that they can be readily mobilised. The technique is simple: the manager, with "unique" intelligence which cannot be revealed lest it expose the necessarily secret sources which are themselves vital for security, testifies to the external danger, in order for group members to contribute to defence against it.

Anxiety managers and specialists in security are not necessarily charlatans. They may believe that there are external dangers for which worst-case contingency plans must be developed or that resources vital for community survival are about to be seized by rival States or groups. And there may, indeed, be external dangers, yet they must be exaggerated to ensure that a passive, even sceptical rank and file continues to be willing to allow the diversion of resources from other interests to contribute to preparation for defence. So the most remote worst-case contingency, even the "one percent case"[61], becomes the operative projection. Plans for high-consequence but low-probability calamities shoulder in alongside plans for low-consequence but high-probability calamities, additional "defensive depth" is needed to reinforce existing "defensive depth" and soon there are efforts to mount

61. Ron Suskind, *The One Percent Doctrine: Deep Inside America's Pursuit of Its Enemies Since 9/11*, 2006.

defences for every imaginable contingency. Because all of these efforts and sacrifices stimulate comparable responses in security specialists and anxiety managers in other groups, from which protection was being sought in the first place, their efforts do not assuage but further exacerbate the anxieties that feed them.

Ironically, the extension of democracy and the need for substantial contributions to security by all group members means that more and more strata of the population become active participants in the war system and, at the same time, economic beneficiaries and supporters of it. And before one indicts caricatured "merchants of death", "weapons mongers" and "war profiteers", one should not exclude trade union leadership in liberal democracies. Their members may junket to meetings of the "Socialist International", only to return home to join their political representatives in agitating against the decommissioning of local weapons, submarines and munitions factories because their constituents will lose jobs and their communities will lose a source of revenue. The "military-industrial complex" includes a labour auxiliary.

New transnational patterns of loyalty which might have seemed to promise a moderation of the war system may actually perpetuate it. As States and smaller, traditional social units prove unable to ensure security and the other benefits for which their members look to them, desperate searches for new identifications are ignited. Candidates for these loyalties are not necessarily members or even adherents of the State system. While some of such groups lack the benefits of a territorial base, neither do they operate under the constraints that such bases impose.

Some global trends present new opportunities for devising and executing actions that threaten public order. As noted, weapons, including those with the capacity to wreak massive destruction with unprecedented speed, have become more miniaturised, mobile and accessible. Non-territorial groups with ambitious global objectives can, thus, operate with greater lethal efficiency than they could before, further aggravating the anxiety which drives the war system.

International law is inextricably attached to this, at once, functional and dysfunctional system. Yet while some of its prescriptions seek to prohibit the use of force, to minimise and to confine its violence when it is used and to establish institutions that are supposed to obviate it, others actually sustain the war system [62]. Alas, the inability of international

62. See *infra* Chapter XIII.

institutional arrangements to persuade those who might be dependent on them that the international institutions can provide security means that people still turn to and support their own or allied security specialists; those specialists, in turn, justify and provoke their opposite numbers in potential adversaries. The perception that key values are at stake induces further reliance on exclusive means of protection. In turn, this induces mirror-like reactions in any other group viewed as a latent adversary.

In this volatile context, insecurity at the personal level is exacerbated by the ongoing expectation of violence and the perception that "peace", as the normal state, is actually a fragile and eroding *entr'acte* between major crises [63]. Rather than facilitating rationally deliberated *collective* choices for survival, expectations such as these lay the groundwork for further conflicts with other groups for they only reinforce parallel perspectives there.

In its quest for world order, international law will have to address the need for the management of the anxiety of individuals at the national and subnational levels as part of an integrated programme for transforming the war system.

Section 6. The scientific and technological dimension of the world community

The sheer number of exchanges between territorial communities that characterises the present era is the result of scientific and technological developments which began centuries earlier. These developments have had profound effects on the political organisation of the planet, as political and economic elites acted diplomatically and militarily to ensure access to resources and markets. The advent of the "hydrocarbon age" at the beginning of the twentieth century led the elites of the time to restructure the State system in entire regions. Providing for the economic resource requirements of territorial communities has become a critical factor in the current international political arrangements and the evolving arrangements for the exploitation of the resources of outer space [64].

Each new technique of communication – from Guttenberg's movable type to the present – has had profound and often transforming effects on politics, economics, military strategy and practice, and on the psycho-

63. Harold D. Lasswell, *World Politics and Personal Insecurity*, Free Press pbk. ed. with new intr., 1965 (orig. 1935), at p. 57.
64. McDougal, Lasswell and Vlasic, *supra* footnote 41.

personal organisation of the individual. But compared to devices like the telegraph and the telephone, the cybernetic revolution has had more far-reaching consequences in every sphere of activity. All of these technological innovations have led to social, economic and, above all, psycho-personal changes whose radical character and implications for world order are not entirely understood.

The increasingly accessible Internet has had manifold political and economic consequences and implications. The social media have become a tool in national politics and an instrument by which Governments can influence the outcome of elections in other countries. Another consequence, the sharing economy, has changed the way consumers participate in the market. The widespread dependence of these tools has created a new type of vulnerability for State and non-State entities alike as they struggle to repel cybersecurity interventions from State and non-State actors.

The re-emergence of integrated economic networks throughout much of the planet in the latter half of the twentieth century created interdependencies which affect every level of social organisation, from global to subnational. Until now, episodic man-made and natural crises have not reversed this trend. The COVID-19 pandemic of 2020 may lead to a rollback of many heretofore global networks and supply chains.

The quicker and cheaper movement of peoples about the planet, in contrast to the more measured, generational migrations and assimilations of previous eras, have transformed the most efficient territorial communities (the targets for in-migration) from the largely tribal States which they were into more heterogeneous communities. Many of the inhabitants of these heterogeneous communities have complex identity systems in which loyalties are now shared with the "host" State and other territorial and non-territorial communities [65]. The "heterogenising" of many States and the internal reactions to it is a development with potential consequences for many of the dimensions of the world social process.

Section 7. The dimension of interdependence of the world community

The interactions of individuals worldwide – whether face to face or through electronic communications – have become such common and subtle features of our existence that their magnitude and full

65. See *infra* Chapter XI.

import in every dimension of the world social process are sometimes unappreciated. To maximise their wealth, their skill, their understanding, their religious goals and even their prestige, people now cross national boundaries in unprecedented numbers and regularity.

Interdependence, the by-product of sustained global interaction, has made the lives of more and more individuals dependent upon numerous factors operating beyond their local and national boundaries. In no sector is the fact of interdependence more manifest than in the pursuit of wealth. No contemporary State can achieve or sustain a desired level of economic activity on an autarchic basis. The production of wealth has come to require resources, skill, labour, goods and markets beyond a State's own borders. The quality of a harvest in Argentina affects the commodities exchange in Chicago; a rail strike in Sweden disrupts or debilitates rail traffic in France and, in turn, throughout Europe. A copper strike in Chile closes factories in the United States while a suspension of the export of rare earths from China closes factories in Japan which, in turn, disrupts supply chains for manufacturing a wide variety of products and components in many other countries. That leads to unemployment in still other countries, labour unrest and epidemiological consequences. An outbreak of E. coli in Germany disrupts the agricultural sector in Spain. A collapse of an exchange in Shanghai brings down stocks in New York, London, Paris, Milan, Frankfurt and Tokyo. A popular uprising in Libya may send the price of oil skyrocketing, aggravating recession in downstream countries. A suspension of gas transmission in Russia affects the economies and politics of Europe and the world market. The mismanagement of one national economy can bring down banks around the world and undo inter-State political and economic arrangements.

Business planning everywhere routinely concerns itself with labour relations not only in a given city but in mines in other countries from which vital raw materials come, the maritime and transport unions of States which participate in distribution and national marketing unions at many different points of final consumption. The goods must meet the standards and tastes of a variety of official and functional regulators. A breakdown of any sector of this global economy can be felt everywhere.

The interdependence of peoples in relation to values such as personal well-being and respect is more subtle but no less decisive. The cumulative impact of personal and cultural interchange leads to a broadening of identifications, even as crises lead to their retraction, further exacerbating crisis. Despite the persistence of national and ethnic parochialisms, many peoples of the world demand – and acknowledge the fundamental right of others – to the minimum conditions for a dignified human existence.

Section 8. The "sovereign" state dimension of the world community

In traditional theories of international law, the sovereign State is presented as the dominant actor. And, indeed, many of the goals of contemporary international law cannot be realised without a system comprised of robust States; many of the so-called "failures of international law" are actually internal failures of States. But when we look at what international law is now attached to, it is clear that in an increasing number of its sectors, the transnationalisation of civic activity is rendering the corresponding parts of the State's governmental apparatus insufficient for the protection of national public order. Whether one looks at efforts to maintain viable national economies and to protect health and control the spread of disease, crime, economic monopolisation, immigration or the protection of intellectual and material property, a single State's Government, be it a superpower or a micro-State, can no longer accomplish what is expected of it without locking itself into increasingly complex and durable intergovernmental arrangements – each of which promises some palpable gains, while requiring the yielding of some national competence. There are no exceptions to this phenomenon. The continuing search for alliances even by the strongest States, along with the limits on national action inevitably imposed by such arrangements, generates and exacerbates anxiety in others who must, in turn, seek counter-alliances. The quest for national security in an interdependent world has ramifying effects on the global war system.

Yet if the conception of national security is taken to include the prevention of the proliferation of nuclear and biological weapons, stemming the transnational transmission of disease, protecting the environment and assuring the stability of the value of currency, financial institutions and external markets – to mention only a few commonly accepted priority items – the subordination of the putative sovereign State to international arrangements seems inescapable.

The growing networks of intergovernmental arrangements that these changes have necessitated may well enhance the political and economic security of those who participate in them, but they also lead to ambivalences and insecurities at many political levels. Robert A. Dahl has written:

> "A country's economic life, physical environment, national security, and survival are highly, and probably increasingly, dependent on actors and actions that are outside the country's boundaries and not directly subject to its government. Thus the members of the demos cannot employ their national government, and much less their local governments, to exercise direct control over external actors whose decisions bear critically on their lives." [66]

If Europe, as a regional laboratory, is any harbinger, centralised transnational bureaucracies are making more and more decisions that penetrate deeply into the fabric of national and local life. Not surprisingly, this trend has already generated counter-forces: the broad spectrum of anti-Maastricht reaction in Europe, the increased influence of far-right political parties on many continents and the recrudescence and, more surprisingly, legitimisation of isolationism in the domestic politics of erstwhile superpowers. In Europe, even the promise of deference to local decision, the so-called "subsidiarity" principle, has not moderated the reaction.

Rational responses to this increasingly "global" fact of life seem to require and involve the creation of still more alliances and more transnational governmental and non-governmental arrangements, which further minimise opportunities for collective and individual participation in the policy decisions that affect one's life. Globalisation of the world to which international law is attached, for all its benefits, has a darker underside that exacerbates, at many levels, a sense of personal insecurity or even inessentiality. These experiences drive some to revert to the narrowest identity systems, providing fertile soil for proponents of authoritarian systems.

An urgent function of international law becomes the containment of demagoguery that incites and exacerbates anxiety and, more generally, the social management of anxiety, all this accomplished in ways compatible with systems of freedom of expression. In a world comprised of territorial communities manifesting all of the cultural, ethnic and historical variations reviewed earlier, the management and containment of anxiety is a formidable challenge.

---

66. Robert A. Dahl, *Democracy and Its Critics*, 1989, at p. 319.

It is, in the end, the impact of these eight dimensions of global interaction to which international law is attached on the lives of individual human beings that is most significant for the future of international law. The numerous roles played by individuals in the intersecting groups and communities which they inhabit increasingly partake of international involvement. Occupational activities – in business, politics, the law, the sciences, the media, religious institutions, and so on – are daily more international in focus, in audience and in impact. The broad category of professional intellectuals in each society, whose function is to make sense of it all for their audiences, can no longer comment pertinently or creatively on any aspect of a domestic scene without an appreciation of the comprehensive global arena which affects and is affected by its component parts. Citizens, a role common to all, may resist the fact that, for better or worse, events beyond their territories affect their quotidian existence and that international arrangements are critical to orderly and satisfactory life in their own communities, but they cannot ignore it.

In sum, the world to which international law is attached is vastly different from the landscape in which many of the basic postulates of international law were fashioned and installed. In the next chapter, we will posit some basic propositions that can serve to locate key features and their trends in the international legal system to which the world is attached.

CHAPTER III

SOME PROPOSITIONS AND CONDITIONING FACTORS

"There is nothing so practical as a good theory."

Kurt Lewin [67]

Definitions of law which focus on particular institutions abound but, understood most comprehensively, law refers to the authoritative processes through which persons who are politically relevant with respect to each other establish and maintain arrangements for securing order, allocating the opportunities, benefits and burdens of life, and providing for modes of resolving differences – all in ways that serve their perceived interests. These processes may be based on agreements or understandings which those persons call "legal". These processes and the arrangements they produce may not be explicit and, indeed, may operate at levels of consciousness so deep that many of those involved are unaware of them or simply assume that they are part of a natural order of things. Such processes and arrangements relate at one level to how these legal arrangements themselves are established, applied and amended. The process that establishes, maintains and adjusts these constitutive arrangements may be called the "constitutive process" [68]. Constitutive arrangements may include institutions as well as informal arrangements.

Apart from the constitutive process, other arrangements address all the "who gets whats" of life: who gets power, wealth, enlightenment, skill, well-being, affection, respect and rectitude [69]. These arrangements may be referred to as the "public order".

"Agreements" in the constitutive process and the public order are often a euphemism. Rather than the result of a happy and spontaneous or carefully negotiated consensus of all of the persons who are to be affected by them, some "agreed" arrangements may be based on "offers that cannot be refused". Other arrangements are the result of authentic agreement but only between *some* persons who are then able to impose

67. Kurt Lewin, *Field Theory in Social Science: Selected Theoretical Papers* (New York, NY: Harper & Row 1951) on p. 169.

68. See *infra* Chapter IV for further discussion.

69. Harold D. Lasswell and Myres S. McDougal, *Jurisprudence for a Free Society: Studies in Law, Science, and Policy*, 1992.

them on others who are handicapped by having less knowledge and information, influence, access, manipulative skill, organisation or tools of violence and the skill in and appetite for using them.

Section 1. The organised and unorganised character of international processes

Many legal theories emphasise the State as the centrepiece of a legal system, with State and law reflecting two parts of the same entity. In this view, "law" means only those written arrangements which have been made and applied by specific organs of the State or those private arrangements which are recognised and given the force of law by those State organs. In some sectors of social space, the most critical legal arrangements may be made and applied by organs of the State. But it is important not to overlook the myriad exchanges that take place continuously *between* groups and individuals without regard to the arrangements of State organs.

Identifying the State with law is particularly ill-suited for enquiries about international law. There is no "global State", though there may be global or near-global arrangements. Pretending that the Security Council or the G20 is the embryonic executive branch or executive committee of a "world State", that the General Assembly is its legislature, that the IMF and the World Bank are its central bank and that the International Court of Justice (ICJ) is its supreme court may serve some unifying and reassuring mythic purposes [70]. But assuming that all international decision is so organised will ignore many of the processes (1) in which expectations of politically relevant actors about what policies and arrangements are lawful are shaped and (2) in which actions taken with regard to those expectations are lawful.

Section 2. Symbols of authority

In every type of interaction, some arrangements are characterised by distinctive modes of communication: one of them is the "language" of the law. Formal "legal" statements are expressed in the imperative or subjunctive mood: "do or refrain from doing something" or "do something in a particular way and secure a certain benefit or suffer a certain loss". But it is not the grammatical form that makes statements such as these controlling. Legal communications are distinguished

---

70. See *infra* Section 6 of this chapter on the functions of myth systems in international law.

from the daily bombardment of "you shoulds" and "you oughts" by the fact that they are accompanied by (1) symbols of authority along with (2) commitments to make those communications controlling. Together, signals of authority and control serve to mark the communications they attend as legally meaningful and effective.

Symbols of authority are designed to indicate to their intended audiences that the arrangements which they accompany are "law" and to enhance respect for and to trigger predispositions to comply with them. Symbols of authority, themselves, are a factor that contributes towards compliance. So is the content of an arrangement; the more its content is perceived as being in an actor's interest, the more that actor will support the arrangement, even in the absence of a symbolic authorisation or the demonstration or application of external compulsion [71].

Meaningful symbols of authority will vary with the audience to whom they are addressed; the symbols may import, for example, endorsement by a divinity, derivation from utterances attributed to a charismatic leader or his successor or derived from a venerated text of divine or secular origin, or the supposed emanations of the *vox populi*, "the will of the people". The effectiveness of those symbols of authority in legal arrangements depends upon the cohesiveness of the audience's culture, class and religion. If all of its members do not share in the same authority or belief system, the symbolic component for sustaining the arrangements will be less effective, and the symbol used may even prove to be a negative factor for particular strata or groups. For example, the use of the word "crusade" to characterise a legal arrangement in a multi-ethnic State – let us say, a national campaign against corruption – may have a powerful authoritising force for some Christian audiences, evoking at deep levels of consciousness images of heroism and self-sacrifice *ad majorem Dei gloriam*. It will have exactly the opposite effect for an audience of Muslims. In parallel fashion, the ascription of the word "jihad" to that arrangement may evoke a powerful positive emotion for many Muslims, with the converse effect for Christians.

The selection of the situationally appropriate symbols of authority in lawmaking and law-applying has especially urgent implications for multi-ethnic audiences in which there are few or only incipient and weak transethnic identifications. It is an especially daunting task in the

71. Nicholai S. Timasheff, *An Introduction to the Sociology of Law*, Transaction Publ. ed. with new intr. by A. Javier Treviño, 2002 (orig. 1939), at pp. 3-19.

extraordinarily diverse world community, which we considered in the previous chapter. One of the ongoing challenges of governance in such environments is the crafting, cultivation, inculcation and reinforcement of common authority symbols that are compelling enough to evoke inclusive identifications and to counter symbols evoking more exclusive identifications.

Section 3. Commitments to support arrangements

Legal arrangements must also include credible commitments to invest the resources necessary to make them effective; the expectation that there are such commitments and that they will be applied in the event of deviance from the arrangement is an important factor in compliance. The less advantageous the content of an arrangement is to politically relevant actors and the less compelling its symbolic component, the more the arrangement must depend upon the credible commitments of effective actors to invest their own resources to uphold it. Where an arrangement takes the form of an institution, endowed with sufficient resources and adequately skilled personnel charged with taking the steps necessary for making the arrangement effective, those to whom the arrangement is addressed will expect that it will be sustained. That anticipation, itself, is likely to lead to adjustments in behaviour to conform to those arrangements. An arrangement taking the form of a weak institution will depend for its effectiveness on one of two factors: either on the self-interest of those to whom the arrangement is addressed, leading to voluntary, seemingly spontaneous compliance or on the resources of other participants who commit to deploy them in support of the arrangement. Effective *institutional* arrangements are plainly to be preferred over *ad hoc* support, for the ability and willingness of other participants to continue to invest their own resources may prove less than constant, whether because of a change in interest, a willingness to see the arrangement, which they had theretofore supported, adjust, change or terminate, or a diversion of their resources to competing interests which they have come to deem more important.

This is one of the challenges of contemporary international law. At the constitutive level, institutional arrangements have been established, but many of the most ambitious of them lack sufficient resources and a sufficient number of adequately skilled personnel to accomplish the tasks assigned to them. This is not the result of an accident or an oversight: many actors in international political processes – and not only those of major States – are, in fact, ambivalent about constituting independently effective international institutional arrangements. Yet, paradoxically, the consequent reliance on other participants to make the arrangements effective when international institutions prove unable to do so runs counter to a widely affirmed constitutive policy of confining the right of forceful implementation to the most inclusive institutions [72]. When other participants with sufficient resources decide to apply them in a specific instance, their actions may sustain that arrangement. At the same time, however, they undermine the more general goal of the constitutive arrangement.

Truly international symbols of authority are insufficiently inclusive to support many institutional arrangements and the decisions which they take. The design and dissemination of such symbols remain challenges for international law. Until there are such symbols, self-interest becomes an even more important factor in securing compliance with international arrangements.

Section 4. The practicality of the common interest

At any level of social organisation, people will defend constitutive legal arrangements against those who wish to replace them with other arrangements as long as the defenders believe that the existing arrangements serve their interests. Actors who do not believe that the conception and institutional expression of particular shared interests adequately accommodate their own purposes will be disinclined to support those arrangements and indeed may actively agitate against them. Incentivising – as opposed to coercing – diverse actors to support a legal arrangement requires more than the invocation of legal symbols. It requires crafting or adjusting the terms of that arrangement so that a sufficient number of politically relevant actors are persuaded that their own interests have been incorporated as part of the formulation of the *common* interest. The more the arrangement encompasses the interests of those affected by it, the less enforcement is required.

Moral arguments may be easily marshalled in support of arrangements that encompass the interests of all relevant actors. Designing arrangements which actually incorporate the interests of all politically relevant actors must be pragmatic. This political imperative is often ignored

72. See *infra* Chapters IV and XIII for discussion of this dilemma.

by those who are the momentary beneficiaries of an indulgent and apparently stable legal system whose arrangements generally work to their advantage. Such beneficiaries are prone (as long as they benefit) to mythologise the arrangements as "the Law", thinking of them as naturally majestic, enduring and self-sustaining to which obedience is universally owed simply because it is "the Law", whatever the content and distribution of benefits actually effected by the arrangements.

Expressions such as "Pillars of the Law", "Grandeur of the Law", "Majesty of the Law", and so on, which are routinely repeated in post-prandial bar association speeches and international discussions of the "Rule of Law", import an inherent permanence to legal arrangements simply because they are represented as "the Law". "Though the notion of a 'rule of law' may be the moral background of revolt", Thurman Arnold wrote, "it ordinarily operates to induce acceptance of things as they are" [73]. By contrast, those who view themselves as excluded from, insufficiently indulged, or victimised by specific legal arrangements tend to view and often just as eloquently characterise "the Law" and the institutional practices it supports as an artefact of alien power and oppression – until they themselves gain sufficient power to share in redefining what will henceforth constitute the common interest. At that point, the erstwhile iconoclasts become zealous apostles of the Law's "Majesty", "Grandeur" and "Permanence", and of the "universal" duty of obedience to it.

The function of such rhetoric is to reinforce respect for and obedience to legal arrangements without regard to their content. For some audiences and for some time, such elevated language and commanding symbols may contribute to the fulfilment of this function, but it is the perception by actors that specific arrangements are also in their interest that accounts for willingness to support and contribute resources for their continuing implementation. Participants who succeed in getting everything they want in a specific arrangement to the exclusion of what their competitors are seeking may actually be winning pyrrhic victories because the arrangement will generate opposition whose intensity varies directly with the arrangement's perceived inequity. To that extent, the arrangement will be unstable and will require of its beneficiaries greater resources for its "enforcement".

73. Thurman Arnold, *The Symbols of Government*, 1935, at p. 34.

Section 5. The volatility of international law

Historicist theories would have us believe that institutions and practices perpetuate themselves automatically from generation to generation. They do not. No matter how skilfully the rhetoric of legal grandeur is deployed, both the content and procedures of legal arrangements in complex societies (and bear in mind that the world community is *the* complex society) are inherently volatile, even when they seek to express and implement an interest common to all participants. This volatility is owed to a number of factors [74].

Para. 1. Diversity

The first volatility factor is pervasive class and religious and cultural diversity. If all politically relevant actors shared the same perspectives, identifications, images of the past and the future, and demands, the common interests of all of these actors, once identified and expressed in a legal arrangement, would be universally shared, stable and enduring. Indeed, even if some discord crept in, the fact that all the participants in such a process resonated to the same symbols of authority would act to support the arrangements. Even if actors' perspectives did not coincide, but they believed their interests were served by a common constitutive arrangement, in which each and every actor believed in his or her place in an interlocking set of subordinations and superordinations, the legal arrangements produced in this constitutive context would be stable. Such arrangements, which may have achieved their most refined philosophical endorsement in Confucianism, are commonly espoused in regimes that invoke a divinity as one of the bases of authority. This is by no means an exclusively Asian value. In an earlier version of the Anglican Book of Common Prayer, the catechist undertakes to "submit myself to all my governours . . . and masters . . . and do my duty to that state of life, unto which it shall please God to call me" [75]. This was a most convenient pledge for those at or near the apex of the social pyramid.

---

74. By volatile or unstable, I do not refer to the deconstructionists' contention that language is inherently imprecise. I mean, rather, that the *content* of both constitutive and specific arrangements is constantly under political stress to change and that changes in the context of the arrangements will be registered in adjustments in the content of those arrangements.

75. Rev. Rowland Smith, *The Church Catechism Illustrated by Parallel Passage from the Book of Common Prayer*, 1845, at p. 20.

Other than in charismatic systems (which endure as long as the charismatic leader), congruence of perspectives and effective deference to a single symbol of authority are not permanent features of political communities. It is certainly not the situation in the international community, comprised as it is of peoples who subscribe to radically different narratives of past and future and hold different assumptions about human and divine agency. As described in Chapter II, the international community is made up of individuals who belong to different religions, classes and cultures and are distributed in territorial and non-territorial communities at various levels of development, each with its own authority system. The communities or the parts or strata of those communities which they inhabit exhibit different levels of minimum order and varying expectations of violence.

Not all of the relevant communities to which people owe loyalty are territorial or governmental. Some are non-governmental, ranging from corporate entities devoted to the maximisation of wealth, to religious entities, to private armies and to transnational criminal organisations. All of these entities generate their own symbols of authority and, indeed, their own "legal" systems [76]. Those symbols and legal systems need not recognise the superordination of another authority even if their members take into account the potential application of its prescripts as an occupational hazard. Many of these groups are effective transnational actors, and some may insist on participating in the definition of the common interest; the operations of others may be incompatible with any notion of common interest.

There have always been some actors *within* the international system who do not merely aspire but actually seek to transform the world to comport with their own idiosyncratic visions, whether they be secular and materialistic – a world of liberal democracies or a world of capitalism or of communism – or divine – a world of a particular creed of Christianity, of a particular sect of Islam or of any other confession.

The pursuit of these various visions puts stress on existing legal arrangements, increasing the volatility of international law. Were any one of these visions to be realised, it would, at least for the short term, stabilise international law. But none has yet prevailed. Even the international human rights movement, which claims to be universal, is far from it; while its code is *universalisable*, in the sense of holding itself out for and being capable of application to everyone without regard to

76. Leopold J. Pospisil, *Anthropology of Law: A Comparative Theory*, 1971.

race, religion, ethnicity or gender, if it is universally *accepted* (which is debatable), it would be the case only at the most general level. In sum, in a world of diverse images of past and future, of radically different demands, of sharply demarked identities and of jagged distributions of political power, it is difficult to agree upon, establish and maintain, over time, stable legal arrangements.

Para. 2. The dialectical character of law

A second factor accounting for instability is the dialectical character of all legal arrangements. Every legal arrangement is born of political bargains and compromises. Each, reflecting the prevailing allocation of power as well as the prevailing calculus of fairness or justice, inevitably discriminates, to some degree, in favour of some and against others. So the moment a legal arrangement is struck, it coalesces latent opposing coalitions who demand its adjustment, amendment or replacement. The demand may be for formal amendment within the system, or it may be expressed through non-compliant behaviour that tests and stresses the particular arrangements, if not the constitutive arrangement itself. This dynamic dialectic of law accounts for its vitality – what Rudolf von Jhering called its struggle – and its volatility [77].

Thanks to this dialectical dynamic, at every moment, the arrangements that comprise the corpus of any body of law, include (1) some inherited arrangements whose support is declining, while other inherited arrangements overcome or accommodate challenges; (2) new arrangements which are displacing existing ones; and (3) surviving arrangements that continue because of a common interest or disinterest in them. This last group of arrangements, sometimes described as historical or path-dependent, may seem natural and inevitable, but their duration, too, is uncertain.

Para. 3. Justicial anachronism

A related reason for the volatility of all law, and of contemporary international law in particular, is to be found in the phenomenon of "justicial anachronism"; that is, the ceaseless changing content of the term "justice", accompanied by a demand for the retroactive application

77. Rudolf von Jhering, *The Struggle for Law*, trans. John Lalor, 2nd ed., 1915 (orig. 1872).

of the newer conception [78]. Within the formal institutions of some of the islands of international law, *tempus regit actum*. Thus, the ICJ declared that "[t]he compatibility of an act with international law can be determined only by reference to the law in force at the time when the act occurred" [79].

In offshore zones, however, the Court's dictum holds no sway. There, self-selected leaders of groups that were hitherto unorganised or ineffective try to "raise" in others a consciousness of their shared identity and of the deprivations which they believe they have suffered on account of their membership in that group. As soon as the would-be leaders can organise and mobilise a constituency, they agitate for legal adjustments in the arrangements that will ameliorate their situation. The new arrangements they seek are not only *pro futuro*; they often demand retroactive adjustment as well. Thus, they may seek compensation for deprivations which, though lawful in the moment in the past when they were implemented, would be unlawful by reference to the newly demanded or newly installed arrangements.

This is a worldwide phenomenon. Whether we speak of Germans expelled from Upper Silesia or Sudetenland, African Americans seeking compensation for the deprivations of slavery, indigenous peoples demanding restitution of land "legally" alienated in the past (i.e. in terms of the legal system of the then dominant group) or for the deprivations of colonialism after "decolonisation", or Palestinians seeking return to lands from which they were expelled or fled more than half a century ago, we are encountering manifestations of the phenomenon of justicial anachronism. Common to all of these examples is the insistence, on the basis of the application of contemporary or evolving notions of justice, that past practices which violated them but were accomplished under arrangements then lawful, be re-characterised *nunc pro tunc* as unlawful and be requited by a meaningful remedy.

Justicial anachronism has become a recurring feature of contemporary law because of the dialectical dynamic we considered earlier, the shifting power relations of different classes and groups, as well as variations in the professions from which agents of change are recruited. Of particular importance is the catalytic role of specialist groups of lawyers, moral

78. But cf. Rudolf Stammler, *The Theory of Justice*, trans. Isaac Husik, 2000 (orig. 1925), which does not use the term in a retroactive sense. I am grateful to Megumi Kanayaki for this insight.

79. *Jurisdictional Immunities of the State (Ger. v. It.: Greece intervening)*, Judgment, 3 February 2012, ICJ Reports 2012, p. 99, at 124, para. 58.

entrepreneurs and professional agitators who see opportunities for moral satisfaction, profit and/or personal advancement in the promotion of new notions of collective social responsibility.

The phenomenon of justicial anachronism is not limited to the islands and offshore zones of international law. Yet, even when apparently internal to a particular territory, those applying it do not hesitate to invoke whatever international legal symbols promise to serve to advance their demands.

When justicial anachronism transcends the boundaries of an efficiently organised State, it becomes particularly complex and conflictive because the remedies may then entail adjustments affecting the so-called "acquired rights" of actors in other States. Yet the international legal arrangements for the orderly and fair termination of existing arrangements, optimistically called "peaceful change", remain underdeveloped.

Para. 4. Intellectual revisionism

Other reasons for the volatility of international law are shared with various intellectual disciplines. Although a key part of the study of history is ostensibly a verification and assembly of objective facts from the past, historical narratives or meditations on past events are constantly being rewritten and reinterpreted upon that palimpsest in terms of the perspectives and values of the culture, class, gender and crisis experience of successive historians. Major events or leaders who might have been viewed affirmatively, neutrally or even ignored by one generation may be appraised in radically different ways by a subsequent generation whose evaluations will be shaped by its own perspectives. In some cases, successive reinterpretations can be quite rapid.

Comparable revisions occur in international law [80]. In its heyday, the era of imperialism and colonialism was glorified by the principal States of the day. On the basis of and consistent with that era's fundamental

80. Thus, to cite an acute international legal example, when Israel, in a lightning aerial raid, destroyed the Osiraq reactor in Iraq, its action was roundly condemned as unlawful by the Security Council and by much of the media. Ten years later, with the Saddam regime condemned for its effort to seize and annex Kuwait, the Israeli action was re-evaluated and viewed quite differently by many actors with a retrospective relief. Fifteen years later, as Iran persisted in developing the wherewithal for a nuclear arsenal and the United States and Israel were reported to have begun to consider pre-emptive actions akin to the 1981 destruction of Osiraq, fears of the consequences of such a prospective action in a new context occasioned a further re-evaluation of the Osiraq incident.

legal arrangements, long-term rights and duties were established. In current international law, imperialism and colonialism are viewed as pathologies, and many of the institutional arrangements and private rights, in particular, which were legally established and transmitted through time in that era, are being terminated or adapted to a new set of values as part of the phenomenon of justicial anachronism.

Para. 5. Incomplete knowledge at the time of judgment

Instability in judgments about international events is also caused by incomplete knowledge of those events and the factors that gave rise to them. Assessments of lawfulness in international law, as in all law, are in the first instance fact-determined.

In some critical cases, facts and their contexts which could have a major impact on the assessment of lawfulness will become known only years later. While the policies underlying the principle of *res judicata* may insulate judicial decisions from revision in the light of new information, no comparable principle insulates general assessments of the lawfulness of other legal events after authoritative decisions about them.

Para. 6. The dynamism of a science and technologically based civilisation

Our civilisation of science and technology introduces a further factor that causes volatility in the law. Participants in such a civilisation are locked in a relentless process of research and a frenzied, competitive drive to apply the results wherever they promise enhanced productivity and profit. Each innovation stimulates further innovations which stimulate still further innovations *ad infinitum*. Thanks to legislation's characteristic deliberative and measured methods, the installation of legal arrangements that would regulate the innovations often lags behind them. The result is that there are intervals in which the validity, relevance or applicability of inherited legal arrangements becomes uncertain.

Section 6. The law's myth systems and operational codes

Yet another phenomenon contributes to the uncertainty of international law and makes the role of the international lawyer particularly challenging and, in some circumstances, perilous: a multiplicity of inconsistent normative codes. Drawing upon the seminal work of Eugen Ehrlich, Roscoe Pound usefully distinguished between the "law-in-the-books" and the "law-in-action" [81]. The law-in-the-books, according to Pound, presents a very complete picture of apparently authorised arrangements, including how disputes about them should be processed. But that image does not always correspond, point for point, with the actual flow of decisions taken by various authoritative institutions. Pound called the latter flow of decisions the law in-action.

International law is rife with glaring discrepancies between the law-in-the-books and the law-in-action. Consider the puzzled reaction of one legal scholar:

> "[T]he massive increase in international legislation during the last quarter of a century, particularly in the environmental field, has not created a new world order. In fact, the gap between law in books and how states act may now appear wider than at any other time in history – the more rules there are, the more occasion there is to break them. After years of active standard-setting, global and regional organizations stand somewhat baffled in front of a reality that has sometimes little in common with the objectives expressed in the inflated languages of their major conventions and declarations." [82]

Some jurists might assume that whatever is not consistent with the law-in-the-books is and must be unlawful. But Pound's genius was to appreciate that what was *actually* done might well be lawful, even if it was inconsistent with the law-in-the-books. Hence, he employed the word "law" for both. Yet he was far from content with the departure of the law-in-action from the law-in-the-books. At heart, he believed that the law-in-the-books should always be accepted as the "real" law. He viewed the discrepancy between the law-in-the-books and the law-in-action as a deficiency that could easily be remedied, if only lawmakers would exercise discipline and realism in enacting legislation.

Discipline and realism are certainly desirable traits for legislators, but the discrepancy between the law-in-the-books and the law-in-action

---

81. Roscoe Pound, "Law in Books and Law in Action", *Am. L. Rev.*, Vol. 44 (1910), p. 12 *et seq.*, at 15.

82. Martti Koskenniemi, "New Institutions and Procedures for Implementation Control and Reaction", in Jacob Werksmann (ed.), *Greening International Institutions*, 1996, p. 236 *et seq.*, at 236.

derives from reasons more complicated than legislative incontinence or fecklessness. Legislation is sometimes enacted simply to affirm a value or placate a constituency without an intention or expectation of making it effective. On its face, the exercise is legislative, but the product is simulated law or *lex simulata*, in the sense that the process is a simulation of lawmaking in which the key actors appreciate that they neither intend to nor actually install an operative prescription. In some circumstances, political mediation between contending groups produces legislation which vindicates one group's claims but is designed to be unenforceable because it is inconsistent with other legislation demanded by equally powerful (or more powerful) groups. Sometimes legislation is enacted without a specified or sufficient sanction, or its sanction is rendered unenforceable by underbudgeting or understaffing. The process of arriving at the apparent prescription is familiarly legislative or, one might better say, "legislatistic", but the product of the exercise is and was intended to be genetically ineffective: *lex imperfecta*.

Jurists whose perspective of law is internal to the system and who operate with a theory *of* rather than a theory *about* law fail to grasp the function of *lex simulata* and *lex imperfecta*. They assume, like Pound and his notion of law-in-action, that an imperative juridical task is to correct the failure of a presumed feckless legislator by transforming simulated and imperfect legislative efforts into effective law. That misses the point; paradoxically, the intention and function of this type of inoperative legislation is precisely to be inoperable, thereby serving as a technique of political accommodation and stabilisation.

Whatever may be the short-term benefits of simulated legislation and the enactment of imperfect laws, the net result of these varied phenomena is the existence, at every moment, of significant and persisting discrepancies between certain parts of the formal legal system and the way decisions are actually going to be made. Such discrepancies do not mean that there is no "law" in those sectors in which practice deviates from formal law. Indeed, while some deviation from the law-in-the-books may be violations, some discrepancies may conform to a different "code", based on another set of normative expectations and demands. But these latter codes are different from the many normative formulations that are routinely ignored, in that these are effectively, though usually informally, sanctioned.

Thus, those actors who must actually make and contend with decisions encounter two relevant normative systems: one that is *supposed* to apply continues to enjoy public deference by elites and is presented to the relevant community at large as the law and another, different one that is expected to be applied and *actually* is applied. To complicate matters further, different arenas or application agencies in international law's archipelago may apply one or the other of the codes in question: normative islands may hew to the myth system, while in offshore zones operational codes reign.

In other work, I have called the norms of the official but largely unapplied normative system the "myth system" of a given group [83]. Parts of it may be operational and may indeed provide the appropriate code of conduct for many group members in normative enclaves; for all those members of a community who are not actually or actively engaged in the decision process, most of the myth system may be their normative guide, even if it involves decisions in which they do not participate. But there are enough discrepancies between this myth system and the way things are actually expected to be done by key officials or effective actors to warrant reserving another name, the "operational code", for the unofficial but nonetheless effective code of behaviour in those discrepant sectors.

Myth system is different from "legal fiction". The latter is an authoritative statement whose patent falseness is, by convention, scrupulously ignored. Such statements occur in legal systems in which veneration for existing prescriptions is great or formal amendment procedures are cumbersome or politically expensive or easily blocked by a small minority. The device of the fiction enables those charged with making decisions to abrogate existing law without formally changing it, a function usually beyond their formal competence. (In judicial forums, a comparable function is performed by irrebuttable "presumptions", judicial creations which effectively change the law that applies.)

Virtually all who use a particular legal fiction know it for what it is: a device for circumventing a norm that is obsolete. Yet the costs of its formal abrogation are believed to exceed the benefit of such open termination, or the decision-maker lacks the authority to abrogate it. By contrast, the myth system is *not* widely appreciated as consciously false. It does not express values that are obsolete but rather affirms values that continue to be important socially and personally. Though not applied within the zone or "jurisdiction" of the operational code, the myth system may yet influence decision.

83. W. Michael Reisman, *Folded Lies: Bribery, Crusades, and Reforms*, 1979.

Precisely because discrepancies between myth system and operational code can erode the credibility of the former, maintenance of belief in the myth system is a dynamic process requiring ongoing contributions from many participants. Conversely, those who practise the operational code try to obscure it from the general public. But there is an almost symbiotic relationship between myth system and operational code: the latter provides a degree of suppleness and practicality that the myth system could not achieve without changing much of its content and procedures of application.

Members of a community who are not privy to its operational code may, at one level, view operational code activities as unlawful. Yet there may also be a certain uneasy toleration or a desire for and cultivation of ignorance. A fascinating example of this double-thinking may be found in the reaction of the "invisible college of international lawyers" to NATO's bombardment of Serbia as a result of Serbia's actions in the province of Kosovo [84]. The bombardment, which was not authorised by the Security Council, was clearly against international law's myth system, yet it was an action which the collegium nonetheless felt was the right thing to do [85]. A number of sociologists have studied the phenomenon of so-called "dirty work" in society – things which a community requires to be done in order for it to function, but which cannot be done in accordance with the community's formal law – and have noted the way that social ignorance is cultivated when such work must be performed. [86]

An operational code, it must be emphasised, is a code. As such, it prohibits some things, permits others and prescribes *how* those things are to be done. It does not permit *any* behaviour. Actions deviating from the operational code will remain unlawful and are expected to be effectively condemned. It is the operators who know that some discrepancies from the myth system are licit and will be tolerated, while others, either generally or in certain circumstances, will not. Where myth system and operational code coexist, determining the socially proper course of behaviour in a particular setting necessitates a much wider enquiry than the simple consultation of a single rule in the authoritative processes of

84. Oscar Schachter, "The Invisible College of International Lawyers", *Nw. U. L. Rev.*, Vol. 72 (1977), p. 217 *et seq.*

85. W. Michael Reisman, "Acting *Before* Victims Become Victims: Preventing and Arresting Mass Murder", *Case W. Res. J. Int'l L. Rev.*, Vol. 40 (2008), p. 57 *et seq.*, at 68-72.

86. See e.g. Everett C. Hughes, "Good People and Dirty Work", *Soc. Probs.*, Vol. 10 (1962), p. 3 *et seq.*

formal law. To make matters even more perilous for decision-makers and their advisers, it is never certain that the best judgement exercised at a critical moment and even acknowledged, at that moment, as the "right thing" to do in terms of the operational code, will not later be reappraised in terms of the myth system and be penalised in its name.

It would be as naive to assume that operational codes, for all the suppleness they afford legal systems, persist only because they benefit the system as a whole as it would be to assume that all legal arrangements benefit everyone equally. Operational codes provide flexibility to the myth system component of law, but many parts of the code, if not the code itself, are not necessarily good for the community at large. Every norm of the operational code need not contribute to the commonweal any more than every rule in the law-in-the-books does. In terms of the goals expressed in the myth system, much of the operational code may be profoundly dysfunctional, serving only to protect the entrenched position of elites or particular groups, for example, allowing rewards to be granted on the basis of "old-boy" crony contacts or class, gender, caste, tribal or ethnic ties rather than the performance merit prescribed by the myth system.

Those who apply and benefit from the operational code have a continuing interest in sustaining it. When purges of operational code practices are conducted in the name of the myth system, the "operators" or practitioners of the operational code will often stand together and try to thwart the effort. Even if sanctions are imposed and new prescriptions are enacted to prevent the practices, indeed, even if the old operators are purged and replaced by new operators, practices will continue if those who control them conclude that they are necessary for managing the collective enterprise or – exploiting that justification – that such practices are convenient for the operators. We need only reflect on the sad incident of "oil-for-food", a programme rife with self-dealing by scores of the very Governments who were critical to its implementation. Multiple investigations and reports produced a few prosecutions but no change in the essential arrangements that made such a scandal possible.

The distinction between myth system and operational code has practical as well as theoretical significance. The advice and guidance which international lawyers give about expectations of authority is vital to those making decisions and those affected by them. Many legal formulations in international law establish prescriptions that express aspiration, but those who understand the current capacities of actual international decision processes know that they are not likely to be implemented. Those who are about to risk life or treasure are entitled to be informed of the difference between legal formulations that are *likely* to be effective and those that *should* be effective. To make the distinction, it is important to have a framework of enquiry that permits the identification of the full range of those expectations which are *actually operative*.

Yet even then the myth system may prove a potentially significant factor. International lawyers who are privy to the existence and terms of an operational code run a risk in following it. Reformers, political opponents or counter-elites may belatedly prosecute actions that were consonant with the operational code as defections from the myth system. Reformers may do this in response to popular outcry about deviations from the myth system or to provoke such an outcry and then to demonstrate their own courage and skill in protecting the myth system's integrity. The defence of compliance with the operational code is unlikely to prevail against these deferred prosecutions.

These perils underline the fact that the myth system is never irrelevant. Key values of a community are expressed in its myth system; one of the *goals* of a legal system may, as Pound urged, be to secure greater and greater realisation of many of those values. Before that goal is achieved, however, the operational code cannot be ignored.

The cultivation and elaboration of the myth system is particularly fascinating in international law. Consider the UN Security Council, a body formally endowed with apparently unlimited competence and with the theoretical capacity to compel Member (and non-Member) States to comply with its decisions, even if their compliance in a particular case might require violating some of their existing treaty obligations. Merely read the UN Charter and you must conclude that international law is an effective system. Yet who does not know that, as a practical matter, the Council is often unable to act in precisely those critical events for which it was created? On the celebrated occasions when it proves itself capable of acting – for example, in imposing economic sanctions against a recalcitrant State – its decisions are often so bland as to amount to exercises in *lex simulata*. Even permanent members pressing for a meaningful decision in a specific instance will often accept an anodyne compromise, elevating the illusion that the Council is making a decision over the reality that the decision cannot accomplish its purported objective, other than maintain the myth that this part of international law is indeed working. Yet there may be times when the Council can and *does* make a meaningful decision or at least may render itself a significant factor in instituting or preserving an arrangement. When the Council proves entirely unable to act and a State or coalition of States acts, the assessment of the lawfulness of its action may vary depending upon whether it is assessed according to the myth system or operational code; it is often likely to end by being condemned, especially if it fails spectacularly.

The very transposition of key concepts and technical terms of organised domestic legal systems to international law often has the consequence of embroidering the latter's myth system. Many of those domestic concepts presuppose an omnipresent hierarchical enforcement mechanism. Indeed, positivism insists that such a structure is the essential indicator of law. Consider the concept of "duty" in a developed legal system. By contrast to the notion of "duty" in moral discourse, the legal concept rests on the presumption that there are effective institutions to compel performance of a given duty. Thus, a "duty" in a domestic legal system not to cause harm to the environment may be made meaningful. The willy-nilly transposition of such terms to international law whose context and many of whose institutional articulations are radically different creates an idealised image of a legal system that may bear little correspondence to the actual processes of decision and to the real intellectual challenges lawyers face in making different parts of international law effective. This is not to say that international law "is not law", that it cannot be enforced or that it is a negligible factor in international politics. But those who would be effective in understanding and shaping international law must distinguish between its myth system and operational code.

The myth system and operational code of international law, along with the factors causing its volatility, present formidable intellectual and professional-ethical challenges to the international lawyer. These challenges are made even more stark by the operation of the variable of power, to which I now turn.

Section 7. Power

Power is the capacity of one party to a relationship to influence the behaviour of another party to that relationship. Power is authoritative when it is applied in accordance with the expectations of authority or rightness of the relevant community and for the achievement of authoritative objectives. When power is used without regard to those expectations of authority and their legal arrangements, we refer to it as naked power. Some arrangements which are exercises in naked power dress themselves in the raiment of high legal language to conceal it. International law documents and pronouncements frequently indulge in this sort of cultivated hypocrisy. Professor D. W. Meinig writes:

> "[T]he modern reader of Indian treaties is saved from choking on the clotted hypocrisy of those solemn assurances – 'perpetual peace and friendship'; 'protect against all disturbance'; 'a permanent home . . . which shall, under the most solemn guarantee of the United States, be and remain theirs forever' – if it is understood to be the language of Empire, drawing upon the standard vocabulary of diplomacy, the formal etiquette of adversaries, of the rhetorical disguise of actual power relations and feelings between the two parties." [87]

Power is an indispensable component of any effective legal arrangement. Purported legal arrangements without sufficient power remain semantic exercises, whether they were only intended to be girders of the myth system or whether they originated in a real effort to install an arrangement but failed of their purpose because they could not mobilise sufficient power. Because power in the service of legal arrangements must be built into those arrangements, the need for sufficient power to make arrangements effective is a factor in determining the content of arrangements; the arrangements may require adjustments in their content in order to mobilise sufficient support. The point of emphasis here is that it is a mistake to assume that law and power are inherently and always incompatible.

Yet for many students of international law, power is not simply a professionally irrelevant word; it is virtually obscene. The scholar who dares mention its relevance and attempts to deal with it is likely to be viewed as cynically denying meaningful law or as acting as the covert agent of some powerful State, seeking to justify that State's disregard for the legal arrangements demanded by others.

Much as denial at the personal level is a mode of ego defence, denial at the international legal level is a way of defending an amiable but mythic image of international law from the political reality within which it must operate. The peril inherent in this sort of denial at both the personal and the legal levels is that of the proverbial ostrich: it

87. D. W. Meinig, *The Shaping of America: A Geographical Perspective of 500 Years of History*, 1993, at p. 188.

prevents both the denier and the ostrich from dealing efficiently with a life-threatening and unyielding part of reality. To be sure, no moral fault attaches to a person retreating into a more pleasant private reality and accepting the personal consequences. But surely it is morally wrong for a person purporting to advise others or acting on their behalf to ignore reality.

For many of their professional roles and for the performance of many decision functions in international law's archipelago, international lawyers require a way of mapping and then either mobilising or neutralising the power process. Consider lawmaking [88]. To support and implement them, normative arrangements require power. In a developed State with an effective political and legal system, formal enforcement institutions are usually (but not always) relied upon for implementation. That is not the case in many zones of international law, so the would-be international lawmaker must either adjust or dilute the content of a prescription to win support or assemble coalitions to buttress the preferred content. Similarly, in law-application, one of the requisites of *effective* decisions is that they be crafted to win the support necessary to make them meaningful. In many of their roles, international lawyers must understand the power variable and learn to be adept in mobilising it in support of public order.

Alas, there are no simple and easy metrics for assessing power, for it is always *relational* and *contextual*. The statement that "A is powerful" is meaningless. A is not a bodybuilder admiring his physique in a mirror. The statement can be made meaningful only when it is contextually specific: A is powerful in relation to some B in a particular context and with respect to particular matters. If B associates with C and D to counter A in that same context, A may cease to be "powerful" with respect to those matters. If B should devise or acquire novel ways of counteracting A's power, A ceases to be powerful in a meaningful sense; the power relationship is reversed, and B is powerful in relation to A for those contexts and matters. If A is a composite actor, some of whose politically critical allies are ill-disposed to exercise the potential influence of A *vis-à-vis* B, preferring it to be applied, for example, against C or D, or preferring it to be reserved or directed to the achievement of internal goals, A is not powerful with respect to B.

88. See *infra* Chapter V on lawmaking.

Thus, while power is invariably relevant to legal arrangements, it is not a fixed factor in particular contexts but a variable one, subject to possible adjustment and manipulation by other actors – *if* the actors' frame of reference includes ways of identifying and influencing power constellations. The statement that A, the bodybuilder, is powerful is meaningful only insofar as others allow it to be self-fulfilling; that is, that others, unequipped with a way of thinking about and influencing power relationships or unable to shape the power variable and irrationally fearing A's bulging biceps, yield to him.

Power preponderance in international politics is not measured by the number of missiles, bombs, tanks or men and women under arms [89].

---

89. Power is never entirely immune to authority since shared expectations of authority can be a form of power which can be manipulated by those who understand its potential. Consider the fascinating role of celebrities who use their bases of respect and affection held by their audiences to influence political leaders. Bono, the lead singer of U2, has campaigned, through highly publicised personal meetings with Western leaders, to increase aid for and secure forgiveness of debts of African States. In an interview with the American network, National Public Radio, he explained his method:

> "*Question.* Can I ask if you've had a meeting with any leader at this summit that you feel is not keeping a promise there?
>
> *Answer.* Well, we met with the Italian Prime Minister, Romano Prodi, and to be fair to the situation, the United States under-promised and has over-delivered; Italy overpromised and is really under-delivering. And it was a very, very tense meeting and we weren't sure we were going to get anything. We got up to leave and they said, 'Stop, just please wait', and we said, 'We've got to go to meet the president of France', and they said, 'Please, please wait and we think we have something'. They disappeared around the corner, came back with a proposal which may turn Italy around. Now, you may think that's absurd. You know, what does an Irish musician have anything to do with that? But actually, they're not afraid of me; they are afraid of our audience, and they're afraid of this movement that I'm trying to tell you about. And that's not about a photo op; that's about a man putting his credibility on the line with the Italian public. And I think we might have got some movement. We then had to explain to the president of France why we were late; we just said, oh, it's the Italians – (laughter).
>
> *Question.* And he was fine with that, I'm sure.
>
> *Answer.* And he just, you know, he rolled his eyes and smiled. And then we got into hammering France. We're hammers here.
>
> *Question.* Just to understand how you believe this works: are you saying that you think you have power because there are people in Italy who know who you are, maybe like your music, and would be unhappy if you told the world that Italy was not keeping its promises?
>
> *Answer.* Of course, we have power. You know that – you don't have to ask me that question. We don't have political power, but people who like our music vote. I mean, it's just that simple."

"Bono Presses G-8 Leaders on African Aid", NPR (orig. Associated Press), 8 June 2008, https://www.npr.org/templates/story/story.php?storyId=10830589. And the results Bono achieves prove him correct: as he says, of course, he has power. It is neither unlimited nor protean, but no form of power is; each is relative to context and objective. Just as each weapon in an arsenal is not effective for every objective and

Nor can power be assessed by a measure such as gross domestic product, number of people in a population, number of universities, and so forth. Consider the "trophy" indicators of power, such as nuclear weapons or the enormous ballistic missiles of the Soviet era which were traditionally hauled, like great phallic symbols, through awed crowds massed in Red Square each May Day. Such weapons are frequently neutralised by the comparable arsenals of an adversary, arsenals whose ready deployability ensures that the initiation of the use of these particular weapons would be self-destructive. The effect of such weapons may also be neutralised by the invention and refinement of new asymmetrical weapons and techniques. Insignias of power they may be, but are they meaningful?

Even in situations in which such ultimate weapons of mass destruction are not available to an actual or latent adversary and, as a result, are theoretically operative, a distinction must be drawn between what sociologists call "fate control" and "behaviour control". Many of the weapons commonly assumed to indicate ultimate power enable an entity to annihilate its adversary but do not necessarily enable it to control the adversary's behaviour. Insofar as annihilation has ceased to be a legitimate, beneficial or practicable objective, the critical test of the adequacy of an arsenal is whether it can control an adversary's behaviour.

The myriad network of relationships that comprise modern international politics contain many shifting power relationships. Any of the values comprising the resources of different parties or the community as a whole may serve as components in a power relationship: wealth, enlightenment, skill, well-being, affection, respect and rectitude. The resources which will prove effective and serve as means of influence in a particular situation will depend on the context, the interrelated dependencies of the participants concerned and the relative abilities of each of those participants to understand and to mobilise internal resources for that particular relationship. Since, as explained in Chapter II, the technologies of our science-based and technological civilisation are constantly changing and being adapted to new purposes, a useful instrument for the exercise of power in a particular setting will continue to change as a function of many variables.

context, each form of power is effective for some objectives and contexts and not others. The point is that any quantitative metric of power must also be correlated with authoritative decision processes, which can enhance, limit or even neutralise it.

The role of power in making and applying legal arrangements in global politics affects the volatility of the international legal system. And the presence of contending symbol systems means that different people may view the same set of events as either self-interested exercises in naked power or functionally lawful exercises of power in defence of world public order.

CHAPTER IV

THE WORLD CONSTITUTIVE PROCESS AND ITS DECISION FUNCTIONS

> "An institution is in first instance a set of ways of living and doing. It is not, in first instance, a matter of words or rules . . . . An institution of major size, then, our working constitution embraces the interlocking ways and attitudes of different groups and classes in the community – *different* ways and attitudes of *different* groups and classes, but all cogging together into a fairly well organized whole."
>
> Karl Llewellyn [90]

Every legal system, from the most evanescent encounter of two persons to the most comprehensive international one, includes a flow of decisions, whether express or implicit, which establishes the way all other decisions are taken [91]. This constitutive process and its constitutive decisions must be distinguished from the rest of the flow of specific decisions about the what-it's-attached-to, all of those quotidian who-gets-what decisions which the institutions and procedures established for that purpose are constantly making. These latter decisions determine the public order: how resources are allocated and developed, and wealth produced and distributed; how human rights are promoted, allocated and protected or deprived; how enlightenment is encouraged or retarded; how health and well-being are fostered or neglected; how rectitude and civic responsibility are nurtured or blighted; and so on, through the whole gamut of values which people demand. The constitutive process establishes and maintains those public order decision-making institutions.

Many legal systems purport to describe their own constitutive processes in a document called a constitution. Even at the moment of its creation, the document may not have been an accurate picture of the constitutive process; it may have been a product of the myth system with scant correspondence to actual constitutive decisions. Moreover, even when a documentary constitution starts as an accurate description and a practicable prescription of how decisions are to be made, it is still

90. Karl Llewellyn, "The Constitution as an Institution", *Columb. L. Rev.*, Vol. 34 (1934), p. 1 *et seq*.

91. See W. Michael Reisman, *Law in Brief Encounters*, 1999.

subject to law's dialectical dynamic discussed in Chapter III, Section 5, Paragraph 2. Under stress and counter-stress, it may adapt itself, whether by formal amendment or informal adjustment. The constitutive process begins to drift from, edit and elaborate the snapshot taken at the moment of drafting of the written constitution [92].

Indeed the constitutive process may not only vary from a written constitution which is venerated by strata of the community; it may even violate the constitution. One dramatic example, drawn from the United States, whose written Constitution is almost the object of veneration of a secular religious cult, should suffice to make the point.

In 1982, at the height of the Cold War, the National Security Council of the United States was concerned about a possible nuclear attack and its effect on the highest level of civilian command. President Reagan had announced that in the event of an attack, he would not abandon the White House for the safety of a bunker, but he did authorise a secret directive to ensure Government continuity [93]. As David Hoffman recounts in his study of the Cold War arms race:

> "[T]he Reagan planners realized that a President might not make it to these bunkers in time. They devised a plan to dispatch three teams from Washington to separate, secure locations around the United States. Each team had to be prepared to proclaim a new American 'president' and assume command of the country, according to author James Mann. If the Soviet Union was able to hit one team with a nuclear weapon, the next one would be ready. 'This was not some abstract textbook plan, but was practiced in concrete, thorough and elaborate detail', Mann said. Each time a team left Washington, usually for several days of exercises, it brought one member of Reagan's cabinet who would serve as the successor 'president'." [94]

James Mann writes of this practice:

> "The Constitution and the Twenty-fifth amendment make the vice president the successor if the president dies or is incapacitated, but they do not establish any order of succession beyond that. Federal law, most recently the Presidential Succession Act of

---

92. See *supra* Chapter III, Section 5, for discussion of the volatility of international law.
93. National Security Decision Directives, 14 September 1982, at p. 55.
94. David E. Hoffman, *The Dead Hand: Reagan, Gorbachev and the Untold Story of the Cold War Arms Race*, 2010, at p. 45.

> 1947, establishes further details: If the vice president dies or cannot serve, then the Speaker of the House of Representatives becomes president. After him in line of succession are the president pro tempore of the Senate (typically the longest-serving member of the majority party) and the members of the cabinet in the order in which their cabinet posts were first created, starting first with the secretary of state, followed by the secretary of the treasury and then defense.
>
> Reagan's secret program set aside these constitutional and statutory requirements under some circumstances; it established its own process for creating a new American president, ignoring the hierarchy of presidential succession established by law." [95]

Hoffman observes:

> "The entire program – intended to be carried out swiftly, under extreme stress and amid the potential chaos of impending nuclear war – was extra-legal and extra-constitutional. It established a process of presidential succession, Mann pointed out, that is nowhere in the Constitution or federal law." [96]

The point of the example is not to enquire whether this arrangement did, in fact, violate "the law" or the "Constitution". It was certainly "illegal" in the sense in which that term was defined in Chapters II and III. Nor is the point to assess whether it was "lawful" in the sense of implementing the fundamental policies of the polity. Rather, the point is that as long as it was in effect, it was a fundamental and effective, though contingent, constitutive arrangement, supporting the decision process of the United States; it replaced an arrangement in the Constitution with a different arrangement.

Anyone trying to understand, operate within or influence a system requires a framework of enquiry that allows such arrangements to be identified and appraised, for it is the nature of constitutive arrangements that they have a profound effect on other public order decision-making.

To understand and influence them, constitutive processes must be described in detail: the full range of those who actually participate in them; their background conceptions and explicit and latent objectives; the arenas in which the process takes place and the characteristics

95. James Mann, *Rise of the Vulcans: The History of Bush's War Cabinet*, 2004, at p. 141.
96. Hoffman, *supra* footnote 94, at p. 45.

of those arenas; the bases of power that participants deploy and the strategic ways they deploy them; and the aggregate of outcomes of the process.

The world's constitutive process is complex and dynamic. Its mythic representation is "Westphalian": sovereign and equal States as the exclusive participants, concluding treaties against a backdrop of custom derived from their practice and subject to the application of international law only upon their consent [97]. The reality is a vast and variegated cast of actors, ranging from Governments and individuals and groups within them, intergovernmental organisations and their secretariats, NGOs, corporations and other wealth-maximising entities, religious organisations, criminal organisations and individuals. And, unlike Westphalia, very concerned with how power is exercised *within* States.

A detailed exposition of the world constitutive process will be presented in Chapters VIII and XI. This chapter will enquire, with broad brushstrokes, into successive transformations of the world constitutive process and its impact on assessments of lawfulness for one of the major issues in contemporary international law: unilateral military action conducted without the authorisation of a formal international organisation.

Four types of constitutive configuration assist in understanding how lawfulness is determined at the constitutive level: first, constitutive processes without hierarchical institutions of decision; second, constitutive processes in which there are hierarchical institutions which are manifestly ineffective; third, constitutive processes in which the hierarchical institutions are generally effective in some prominent islands of international law's archipelago but prove to be ineffective for the application of particular prescriptions in offshore zones; and fourth, constitutive processes in which hierarchical institutions are highly effective.

In each of these configurations, the competence to deploy high levels of coercion is allocated differently; as a consequence, those who are operating within each configuration view unilateral actions taken without prior institutional approval differently. In the first three configurations, actions taken without the authorisation of the formal institutions may have an uncertain legal valence, with their lawfulness depending on

97. Leo Gross, "The Peace of Westphalia 1648-1948", *Am. J. Int'l L.*, Vol. 42 (1948), p. 20 *et seq.*

a variety of contextual factors. In the fourth type, unilateral actions will simply be characterised as "taking the law into one's own hands"; for this reason alone, unilateral action will be viewed as delictual, no matter the explanations and contexts and no matter how passionate the justifications invoked.

Let us consider each of these types of constitutive arrangement briefly.

Section 1. Unorganised and non-hierarchical constitutive structures

In legal systems whose constitutive processes do not have or do not operate through hierarchical institutions for making and applying law, unilateral action is perforce the method for making decisions; the unilaterality of a coercive action, in itself, is not a relevant consideration in the assessment of its lawfulness. Participants within the legal system may lament the absence of organised decision-making arrangements whose existence would have obviated the need and justification for unilateral action; some may even struggle to install such arrangements at the constitutive level. But until effective arrangements and institutions are brought into operation, unilateral action is perforce the lawful mode of decision.

By their nature, unorganised and non-hierarchical systems mirror the power process, in which the quintessential *Grundnorm* is Thucydides's "The strong do what they will and the weak suffer what they must" [98].

Section 2. Ineffective constitutive structures

In the panorama of the world's domestic formal legal systems, some are essentially semantic: they are furnished with sometimes grandiloquent paper constitutions, along with corresponding paper institutions adorned with elaborate legal procedures, which together purport to be their legal and political systems. Yet the institutions they describe have no power. Actual decisions are made by a shadow process, which may converge with the formal "legal" system, but that shadow process operates on the basis of an entirely different value calculus. In some circumstances, the formal system will issue the actual decisions and outsiders may attribute them to the "legal" process. But insiders – operators, who understand the "operational code", in the sense in which

98. Thucydides, *The Complete Writings of Thucydides: The Peloponnesian War*, trans. Richard Crawley, The Modern Library, 1951, at p. 331.

we used the term in Chapter III, Section 6 – know that it is fruitless to seek specific decisions from the formal process if they have not first been certified by the actual power process. For example, in so-called "telephone justice" regimes in some contemporary dictatorships, a formal legal system replete with an appropriately costumed judiciary exists, but its judges ignore it when the political elite instructs otherwise.

Ineffective political and legal systems abound, as we saw in Chapter II. Rogelio Perez Perdomo has produced a rich study of *caudillo* States or *caudillajes* in nineteenth-century Latin America [99]. Ernst Fraenkel analysed the phenomenon in his classic study of the *Doppelstaat* [100]. In my experience as a member of a regional human rights oversight body, I found this to be a situation common enough such that, for all of its offensiveness to the values of orderly lawful decision, one hesitates to ignore its prevalence and significance by minimising its prevalence with the adjective "abnormal".

At some level of consciousness, all who read these lectures have, at some moment, entertained the existentially disturbing possibility that the legal system to which they turn in a particular situation may be only semantic. Yet for those who have been enculturated and work within largely effective legal systems, each confrontation with semantic systems, even when recognised as such, still generates a type of "cognitive dissonance" [101]. We have been conditioned to respond affirmatively to the symbols of the law. Even if they are only the symbols of a legal system, without an effective system behind them, the influence of those symbols still makes any action – whether taken by others or ourselves – that has not been pre-authorised by what we know to be its paper institutions seem unlawful and further corrosive of the law. This sense of corrosive unlawfulness is felt even when we think that, on balance, the unauthorised action that was taken may have been, in the circumstances, the "right" thing to do.

Section 3. Partially effective constitutive structures

There are legal systems that are only partially or episodically effective. Ineffectiveness in particular sectors over extended periods may occur because of a lack of coordination of political power and

99. Rogelio Perez Perdomo, *El Formalismo Juridico y sus Funciones Sociales en el Siglo XIX Venezolano*, 1978.
100. Ernst Fraenkel, *The Dual State: A Contribution to the Theory of Dictatorship*, trans. E. A. Shils, 2006 (orig. 1941).
101. See Leon Festinger, *A Theory of Cognitive Dissonance*, 1957.

political authority. In other circumstances, it occurs over time but only for specific matters. This phenomenon is more common than may be generally appreciated, for ineffective law, rather than a failure of legal drafting or a lapse of legislative continence, is, as we saw in Chapter III, a technique, used intentionally, to mediate between the incompatible aspirations of different classes and interest groups: recognising legislatively the validity of claims while ensuring that their legal promise will neither be enforced nor otherwise fulfilled [102]. In other circumstances, the phenomenon occurs, not because of an intentionally designed incapacity but because of a particular, unanticipated stress on the system or because of a crisis.

Many legal systems which purport to monopolise the competence to make coercive decisions contain contingent *exceptios* allowing for unauthorised unilateral action which will fill a gap for those important matters for which there are clear substantive standards and prescribed procedures but temporarily insufficient power to take them or, having taken them, to make them effective. In modern international law, the prime example of the *exceptio* is the so-called right of self-defence [103]. This contingent power, which the UN Charter allows its State parties, is not, it should be emphasised, a relic from an earlier period of law, as the rather archaic naturalist language of the French version of Article 51 of the Charter "(droit naturel de légitime défense)" would suggest. It is an intentional *exceptio*, for there was no "right" of self-defence prior to the Charter's installation of a prohibition on the use of force. Until that time, States, as a manifestation of their sovereignty, were entitled to wage war, whether to defend existing rights or to change them; in such a constitutive arrangement, a "right" of self-defence was redundant [104]. Despite the word "inherent" in the English version or "droit naturel" in the corresponding French version of Charter Article 51, the provision was designed to function as an *exceptio* to the general assignment of the right to use force that had been made to the Security Council.

Section 4. Effective constitutive structures

When a legal system's constitutive process has installed hierarchical decision institutions that are reliably effective such that they can meet

102. See Thurman W. Arnold, *Folklore of Capitalism*, 1937; see also Arnold, *Symbols*, *supra* footnote 73.

103. See *infra* Chapter XIII, Section 2, for more detailed discussion.

104. See Robert Y. Jennings, "The Caroline and McLeod Cases", *Am. J. Int'l L.*, Vol. 32 (1938), p. 82 *et seq.* on the early efforts to transform this form of unilateral action into a "right", henceforth subject to legal regulation.

the demands of participants, there are no justifications for unilateral action. Hence virtually all unilateral action in this constitutive setting is delictual. The sanctioning agents may sometimes appreciate that a particular unilateral action is different from ordinary delicts that are occasioned by negligence or criminal negligence, or animated by an intention to self-enrich. Moreover, those applying the sanctions may be conscious of the moral arguments that may have been marshalled to justify the particular unilateral action.

Nevertheless, the action will still be condemned and sanctioned, lest this constitutive process cease to be effective and degrade to the third type. In constitutive processes that have established and maintained effective structures, we then encounter unique oxymorons such as "*civil* disobedience" and complex multi-referential terms such as "vigilantism".

A term such as "civil disobedience" is invoked by the unilateral actor, who acknowledges the authority and effectiveness of the decision process he or she is disobeying and, in some theories, the propriety of punishment for the "civil disobedience"[105]. "Vigilantism" is an equally complex term used by decision-makers in this constitutive process; it at once condemns the unilateral action taken and insists that penal sanctions be applied, yet, in abstaining from attaching the term "criminal" to the action, implies some understanding of the reasons it was undertaken: usually because of the inability or refusal of the political and legal system to address, through either timely lawmaking or effective application of the law, the vigilante's demand.

Each of these four types of constitutive configurations views the category of events that we call unilateral action differently. Only in the last three of them is unilateral action a "legal" problem; in the second and third, the uncertainty with regard to the lawfulness of unilateral action arises from the cognitive dissonance caused by the realisation that the institution of the constitutive process to which the prerogative of action has been assigned is either generally or momentarily unable to implement rights which were supposedly guaranteed. In the fourth configuration, the problem is one of control, as the constitutive process is effective, so unilateral actions are unnecessary to vindicate rights and are unlawful, yet even in the last type of constitutive structure, particular unilateral acts, and unilateral action in general, may be viewed

105. See W. Michael Reisman, "The Tormented Conscience: Applying and Appraising Unauthorized Coercion", *Emory LJ*, Vol. 32 (1983), p. 499 *et seq*.

as unlawful by only some participants. Standpoint and its perspective may influence assessments of lawfulness.

National foreign policy specialists often operate simultaneously in a national constitutive process that is of the fourth type and the international constitutive process that is of the second or third. At some level of consciousness, they may transpose the expectations that are accurate and cogent in the national constitutive process to the international one.

Section 5. The succession of constitutive processes in international law

Until the early twentieth century, international law approximated the first constitutive structure: there were no hierarchical institutions and decisions were perforce taken unilaterally unless Governments found it in their interest to participate in an *ad hoc* bilateral or multilateral action. Lawmaking was largely accomplished by custom, which advanced by unilateral acts that made new law by violating previous law, so that, in an ironic but accurate inversion of the maxim *ex delicto non oritur jus*, the maxim of international law that applied to every successful change in customary international law was *ex delicto oritur jus*. As for law-application, the usual method was perforce by unilateral act: a State that felt it was entitled to certain rights had no alternative but to secure them itself by what was inelegantly but accurately called "self-help". If a particular State lacked the power to self-help, there was no institution to which it could turn; in consequence, it was simply unable to vindicate its rights; over time, moreover, they might cease to be conceived of as "rights" and degrade to "claims".

A discussion of the lawfulness of unilateral action would have been meaningless in this constitutive structure. After 1899, efforts were mounted to change the constitutive process by establishing hierarchical institutions to which States were supposed to assign decision competence while surrendering the "rights" of unilateral action they would otherwise have enjoyed. But these efforts were clearly perceived as *de lege ferenda.*

The creation of the League of Nations in 1919 and its entry into force in 1920 brought into being a constitutive arrangement of the second type [106]. An apparently hierarchical structure had been established, but

106. See League of Nations Covenant, Article 1.

if one read the fine print, it was clear that its functioning depended upon the voluntary actions of the powerful States that were party to the Covenant; if those actions were not forthcoming, there was no effective sanction, and one would have expected a regression to the first constitutive structure. But with the conflation of two constitutive processes, one allowing unilateral action, the other purporting to incorporate competent institutions authorised to make decisions that would obviate unilateral action, the lawfulness of unilateral actions in international law became ambiguous and began to generate cognitive and moral dissonance. Nonetheless, some came to reassess their assumption that a legal system necessarily imported a centralisation of power and monopolisation of the use of force; many intergenerationally stable systems which they encountered had neither but perforce assessed lawfulness by reference to the conformity of outcomes to substantive principles rather than to the propriety of the procedures by which those outcomes were achieved. Georges Scelle used the insight available from comparative studies to coin the term "dédoublement fonctionnel" as a way of describing a system characterised by the unilateral actions of its members. The term was especially useful for comprehending the actual operation of a legal system when there were few, weak, hierarchical institutions [107].

The creation of the United Nations in 1945 was the culmination of efforts to establish a constitutive process approximating the fourth ideal type. The State representatives who designed the organisation wanted a constitutive structure that would address their basic security needs. Accordingly, a general prohibition on the threat or use of force was installed, and, other than a short-term right of self-defence pending the response of the Security Council, the Council was assigned the exclusive right to use force to respond to "threats to the peace", "breaches of the peace" and "acts of aggression" [108].

Contemporaneously, this seemed a realistic formula: in the political environment of the time, if the five permanent members of the Security Council, on whose agreement its operation depended, concurred that an armed attack against the political independence or territorial integrity of a State were a real threat to the international order which served

107. Georges Scelle, "Le Phenomène juridique de dédoublement fonctionnel", in Walter Schätzel and Hans-Jürgen Schlochauer (eds.), *Rechtsfragen der Internationalen Organisation*, 1956, p. 324 *et seq.* Sir Hersh Lauterpacht rejected this notion in *The Function of Law in the International Community*, 1933.

108. Charter of the United Nations, 24 October 1945, 1 UNTS 16 (hereafter UN Charter), Chapter VII.

their shared interest, they had the wherewithal to stop it. Henceforth, violations of these widely accepted norms no longer had to be resisted unilaterally but would be resisted by the collective action of the United Nations. Many matters, on the law of which the permanent members would likely have disagreed, were deemed to fall within a sphere of "domestic jurisdiction", a normative zone that was insulated from international concern. In this period, then, unilateral action would have been deemed unlawful.

The high-minded language of the Charter ignored the persisting competitive strategic interests of the permanent members of the Security Council. But with the advent of the Cold War, those submerged interests bounded to the surface. The constitutive structure created by the Charter remained in place, but, in practice, it quickly degraded from what had been intended to be the fourth type of constitutive arrangement to the third. The veto power of the permanent members effectively paralysed the Council in circumstances in which the Charter regime had been designed to operate. Alternative, essentially unilateral techniques for addressing the security concerns of the Governments that had established the system developed, but efforts were still made to shelter such practices under the authority of the UN Charter. Expansive and at times patently forced interpretations of Article 51's right of self-defence were invented. A new term, "countermeasures", was minted in order to fill a vacuum created by the broadly formulated prohibition of the threat or use of force and the intervening ineffectiveness of the constitutive structure that had been assigned the exclusive competence to use force in support of public order [109]. Even the ICJ, while condemning unilateral uses of force, still allowed the State resorting to them to enjoy some of their fruits [110].

In the course of this period, participation in the constitutive process expanded rapidly and the relative effectiveness of the various categories of participants began to shift in ways quite different from the conceptions of classical international law. The latter had deemed States the only category of "subjects" of international law. Non-State participants in international legal processes were hardly an innovation. For centuries, wealth elites had operated effectively through "charter companies" and directly on Governments. Long after it had ceased to

109. See *Case concerning the Air Services Agreement of 27 March 1946 Between the United States of America and France*, Decision, 9 December 1978, 18 RIAA 416.

110. *Military and Paramilitary Activities in and Against Nicaragua (Nicar.* v. *US)*, Judgment, 27 June 1986, ICJ Reports 1986, p. 14 (hereafter *Nicaragua*).

have a territorial base, the Holy See was acknowledged as one of a few *sui generis* participants in the international legal process by even the most positivist of doctrinalists. Now, as we saw in Chapter II, thanks to developments in communications, many new non-governmental entities began to operate directly in the international legal process while more and more private individuals began to play increasingly effective roles in decision functions such as promoting, prescribing, invoking and applying the law [111]. Thus, in a relatively short period of time, an international decision process essentially comprised of representatives of States operating severally and later collectively in the United Nations and other informal arenas, with access formally restricted to State representatives, had been incorporated into a contemporary international decision process, which also included, in its aggregate, intergovernmental organisations, NGOs and, in no small measure, the media. All the actors, who assess, retrospectively or prospectively, the lawfulness of international actions and whose consequent reactions shape the flow of events, now constitute, in sum, the international legal decision process.

The transformation of a system that was largely managed by State elites into the contemporary international legal process has coincided with the virtual enfranchisement of a new international "Fourth Estate", the transnational electronic mass media, operating independently of Governments in many parts of the world. The media have proved able to play a role in invoking international decision by presentation of graphic descriptions of human rights violations and insistence that a remedy be provided; we shall consider this phenomenon in more detail in our discussion in Chapters VI and VII of the invocation and application functions in international law.

Non-State actors' increased influence has correlatively reduced the influence of many of the more traditional State-based actors and the theretofore organisations composed of States. The political objectives of the multitude of non-governmental participants are not homogeneous, but they are essentially different from those of the elites managing the affairs of nation-States [112]. To be sure, State representatives still control formal access to many of the organised arenas of international law, but non-State actors have proved able to co-opt or circumvent them. To a limited extent, they can initiate and participate in them, as the

111. See *infra* Chapters V and VII.
112. See *infra* Chapter XI.

Legality of Nuclear Weapons opinions showed [113]. Some theorists resist the notion that this phenomenon is a legal process, let alone *the* legal process that now decisively shapes expectations of authority about international behaviour [114]. However, Heads of even the most powerful States, delegates to intergovernmental organisations, members of international secretariats, legal advisers, corporate elites and, indeed, even mid-level officers planning targeting for military campaigns have learned that they ignore the operation of this phenomenon, whatever they may call it, at their peril.

The installation of the international human rights code as part of modern international law and the establishment of oversight institutions that purport to regulate the techniques by which Governments control their populations are largely results of the agitation and growing influence of non-governmental participants in the expanded international decision process. After all, few State elites are likely to initiate an external process that is authorised to limit their own freedom to deploy the ruthless time-tested methods of management and control of people. But thanks to the ability of State elites to protect their interests, the human rights norms that had been prescribed in formal documents have remained, in significant part, aspirational rather than effective, on the order of a "standard of achievement" [115], the Universal Declaration's functional equivalent of the US Supreme Court's "all deliberate speed" formula [116]. Binding instruments have been laced with critical reservations, understandings and declarations. Institutions established at the universal level were either firmly controlled by Governments and subject to their political interests or, sad to acknowledge, only inconsistently effective even when composed of independent experts.

The end of the Cold War and the disintegration of the Soviet Union seemed to signal the apparent restoration of the consensus among the five permanent members of the Security Council. As this had been the precondition for the operation of the Charter system, it appeared, for a short time, that the world community had returned to the fourth type of constitutive structure. This impression was reinforced by

113. *Legality of the Threat of Use of Nuclear Weapons*, Advisory Opinion, 8 July 1996, ICJ Reports 1996, p. 226 (hereafter *Legality of Nuclear Weapons*); see esp. at p. 330 (Dissenting Opinion of Judge Oda).

114. See *infra* Chapter V.

115. Universal Declaration of Human Rights, 10 December 1948, GA Res. 217 (III) A, UN Doc. A/RES/217(III), Preamble.

116. *Brown* v. *Bd. of Educ. of Topeka*, 347 US 294 (1954), p. 301.

the Security Council's response to Iraq's invasion of Kuwait[117]. But the impression of effectiveness was only partially accurate, for the consensus never went beyond responses to manifest violations of an international boundary and seizure of the territory of another Member of the United Nations (unless the seizure was effected by a permanent member). It had not extended to human rights violations within a State. Authoritative international scrutiny of violent techniques by which some State elites control their populations continues to be spotty. At least one of the five permanent and veto-franchised members was a dictatorship that could not comply meaningfully with the international human rights standard without weakening or transforming itself, while another was in a process of transition whose ultimate outcome could not be predicted with any confidence.

The introduction of human rights into international law and the opening of international decision processes to broad and increasingly effective non-governmental participation has had a surprising effect on the legal status of unilateral action. Recall that the absence of consensus on human rights was of little consequence for the operation of the Security Council as long as those rights were considered to be matters falling within domestic jurisdiction and neither the responsibility of the United Nations nor assigned to the Security Council. Now, however, key actors in the contemporary world constitutive process have taken the Universal Declaration of Human Rights' normatively uncertain "standard of achievement", refashioned it into a programme known as the "international protection of human rights" and elevated it to an international legal imperative level. Indeed, some of its norms are increasingly characterised as *jus cogens*, a term currently used in ways quite different from its denotation in Roman law or in the Vienna Convention on the Law of Treaties (VCLT).[118]

In the Convention, a *jus cogens* deprives other, inconsistent treaty obligations of legal effect. In human rights discourse, *jus cogens* has been shaped into a type of super-custom or Law of Nature, based on trans-empirical sources and hence not requiring demonstrations of State practice for its validity. This new and radical understanding of *jus cogens* purports to render national law that is inconsistent with it devoid of international and national legal effect, such that national

117. See e.g. SC Res. 678, 29 November 1990 (implicitly authorising use of force against Iraq).

118. Vienna Convention on the Law of Treaties, 23 May 1969, 1155 UNTS 331, Article 53.

officials who purport to act on the putative authority of that national law may now incur direct personal international responsibility [119].

But meaningful law, as explained in Chapter III, requires the availability, in case of non-compliance, if not of implementation then of the imposition of a meaningful cost; that is a function assigned in the Charter to the Security Council alone. Yet the members of the Council cannot discharge it, for they do not share a consensus on human rights norms. In a decision process in which lawmakers and law-appliers are identical, non-enforcement of norms over time would render them caducous, but as the norms in question – international human rights norms – derive from a decision process that is broader than the body assigned to enforce the norms, the broader decision process sustains the authority of norms and seeks alternative modes for their implementation.

In the fourth type of constitutive process, the decision to use force – the *ultima ratio* of legal arrangements – is taken from the individual State and assigned exclusively to the Security Council. As remedies for grave human rights violations may require the application of coercion against a non-compliant State, they, too, fall within the competence of the Security Council. But the absence of consensus on human rights means that remedial action, requiring, as it does, agreement of all the permanent members of the Council, is unlikely.

Yet the international legal process's demand for a remedy for grave violations of human rights can become so intense that democratic Governments with the wherewithal to effect a remedy can be pressed by their constituencies to act unilaterally. Hence, for purposes of enforcement against grave human rights violations, a constitutive process of the fourth type then reverts to the third type: enforcement through the Security Council if it can be achieved but enforcement unilaterally if it cannot.

Thus, we encounter an anomalous constitutive regime, which has begun to reserve different legal treatment for different types of unilateral actions, based principally on the purpose or objective of the actions concerned. For jurists who assume that an ineluctable feature of law is generality of application, this constitutive regime can engender normative cognitive dissonance and can, as we will see in Chapter XVI, cause acute moral dilemmas.

---

119. See *infra* Chapter XV for further discussion.

CHAPTER V

THE INTERNATIONAL LAWMAKING FUNCTION

> "The legislature is not the only group enacting legislation; whoever makes policy is legislating."
>
> Harold Lasswell and Abraham Kaplan [120]

Section 1. Prescribing as a process of communication

Every community, every group, is a communications network. Lawmaking, the prescribing of policy as authoritative for a group, is an integral part of that communication. It involves the mediation of policy statements, couched in the imperative or subjunctive mood, accompanied by symbols of authority and communications of control intention. When it is successful, the intended audience receives and incorporates the message in the form of a set of expectations about the right way of doing specific things in specific circumstances. Those expectations are supposed to guide behaviour and to activate community enforcement responses when deviations from the prescribed behaviour are deemed to threaten public order.

The research problem for the international legal scholar is how to fashion conceptual tools for understanding, collecting and processing relevant data about the lawmaking which occurs in the widely varying circumstances of the world community. The additional practical problem for the international lawyer is how to apply the skills of the jurist to influence the lawmaking process so as to secure desired outcomes: law in support of world public order.

Harold D. Lasswell reduced the essential heuristic to a series of questions: Who? Says what? In which channel? To whom? With what effect? The operational difficulty in applying this to the international political arena is the very richness of the contemporary global communications processes to which international law is attached. The enquiry was simpler in periods when a limited number of elites concentrated power in their hands and communications media were rudimentary. The "Prince" we discussed in Chapter I communicated

120. Harold D. Lasswell and Abraham Kaplan, *Power and Society: A Framework for Political Inquiry*, 1953, at p. 196.

with his counterparts, either directly or by means of his own diplomatic agents; content, channel and audience analysis was comparatively simple and manageable. But after the innovation of Guttenberg in Europe, then the perfection of the simultaneous coordinated mediation of images and sound over great distances, and, most recently, the installation and diffusion of the Internet, the sheer quantity of communications through time and across boundaries has been growing at a dizzying pace. With satellite communication, the planet's potential as a complex yet comprehensively integrated communications unit are increasingly realised. More and more human beings live in and are influenced by a state of global electronic simultaneity.

While an elite monopoly of prescriptive communication is still jealously guarded in many parts of the world by means of direct control of the media, intimidation, censorship and jamming, the proliferation of broadcast and narrowcast media and the potentiality of rapid transborder mediation of signs and symbols through the Internet provide enhanced opportunities for wider non-official and counter-official participation. An aged cleric's speeches taped on cassettes, a carefully staged and skilfully videotaped military action or gruesome murder, a terrorist raid conceived as guerrilla theatre or a self-immolation in a public square can now have enormous direct and indirect impacts on the expectations of members of politically relevant groups around the globe, despite the efforts of elites to suppress them. Expectations of what is right may be conveyed in a more indirect fashion, often without any explicit lawmaking intention. Even the exchange of goods and services in mass society may have a politically relevant effect on the expectations and demands of those who enjoy them and those who conclude they will never have access to them.

Formal and informal lawmaking have increased as a function of global interaction and its integrated communications network. An explosion of official channels with specific political and international lawmaking relevance has paralleled the burst of interstitial channels of communication. The traditional diplomatic conduits, by which territorial-based elites communicated and clarified their common interests, continue to be important, but many other international conference and parliamentary arenas have come into operation. Janet Levitt has shown how communications between mid-level administrators in different Governments generate expectations and demands and serve as functional international law [121]. In both formal and informal arenas, non-official actors participate in direct or indirect fashion. And the ever-present private media of the world rapidly monitor, interpret and diffuse what they believe is occurring and its consistency with authoritative expectations.

Along with the extraordinary increases in the variety, number and range of channels in international political communication, there has been a comparable increase in the size, complexity and nature of the audience. Except for those who voluntarily and successfully retreat into fantasised private realities, virtually everyone in the world is at some point a member of the international lawmaking audience, though the significance and importance of different members will vary as a function of their interests and political relevance.

Not everyone has viewed this democratisation of prescription favourably. From the nineteenth century on, initially as a way of discrediting popular politics after the French Revolution, then as a convenient conception of Leninism and, ironically, consumer-oriented capitalism, large audiences were often referred to as a "mass". The term implied the passivity and characterlessness of a *tabula rasa*, waiting to be moulded, inscribed and triggered into action by a charge of agitprop from an elite vanguard. Unquestionably, human beings can be manipulated, in varying degree, by signs and symbols. "You can", as Abraham Lincoln put it, "fool some of the people all of the time and all of the people some of the time". But communication is not a one-way flow: the audience also communicates, drawing on its collective experience and ascribing expectations about authority and control even to the communicators themselves.

Expectations about appropriate behaviour, some explicit, some at levels of consciousness so deep that people are unaware of them, are shaped in all of these processes of communication. If one is to understand and influence international lawmaking, let alone identify the operative international prescriptions, plainly one must address the process in its rich totality.

The communications model of lawmaking poses formidable research challenges but it liberates the enquirer from the insistence that, "yes, these processes may create expectations, but *real* law is *only* made

121. Janet Koven Levit, "Bottom-Up International Lawmaking: Reflections on the New Haven School of International Law", *Yale J. Int'l L.*, Vol. 32 (2007), p. 393 *et seq.* See also Anne-Marie Slaughter, "A Liberal Theory of International Law", *Am. Soc'y Int'l L. Proc.*, Vol. 94 (2000), p. 240 *et seq.*, at 240-241 (discussing the idea that the fundamental actors in international politics are individuals and private groups).

by the legislature" or "real international law is only made by States through treaties or through *their* practice". Viewed through the lens of communications theory, it is clear that while some law may indeed be made by specialised lawmaking institutions, any communication between elites and politically relevant groups which shapes expectations about appropriate future behaviour and about its effectiveness is functional lawmaking. As such, it may provide the normative expectations operative in informal arenas where, before a particular event, they will be relevant in opting for a course of action and, after the action has been taken, for assessing its lawfulness. Understanding how and where this occurs underscores the importance of determining when and what law has been prescribed and for intervening and influencing prescriptive trends. It is useful to conceive of this ongoing process in terms of six concurrent enquiries:

1. the range of communicators and audiences – including international and national officials and non-official elites in every value process;
2. the subjectivities that animate these actors – including their identifications, the matter-of-fact expectations of past and future that comprise their inner worlds, and their demands for values. (Manifest demands may be described as objectives; more latent demands, sometimes held at levels so deep that communicator and audience are unaware of them, must also be explored);
3. the different situations, varying from value process to value process, in which subjectivities are mediated, in word and deed, and expectations about authority and control are shaped;
4. the resources and other bases of effective power and authority which all communicators and especially would-be prescribers employ to give weight to their words and deeds;
5. the different modalities and strategies of communication in different elite and target audience constellations;
6. the shared expectations about appropriate future behaviour that are the outcome of the process.

The first enquiry, communicators and audiences includes international and national officials at different levels of their respective bureaucracies, the elites of MNEs, the media, many NGOs and interest and pressure group leaders. For some norms, the relevant audience may comprise large numbers of people; for others, effectiveness may be achieved if a comparatively small number of elites comes to expect them.

The second enquiry, the subjectivities of participants in the communications process will vary from those identifying with a global system to those identifying only with most exclusive groups; demands will vary from those for world order and justice to those of exclusive self-interest; expectations vary in terms of their realism.

It is commonplace that international law is prescribed in a wide range of settings, varying from the most formal and specialised arenas, for example, a lawmaking conference, to the most informal, unorganised and unauthorised, for example the behaviour of two naval commanders in a maritime fishing dispute. It is equally commonplace that the events in these settings sometimes do not produce prescriptions but only legislatistic communications: *lex simulata* and *lex imperfecta*[122]. Modalities of communication exhibit a similarly wide variety, in terms of instrument and degree of persuasion or coercion. But for these processes to culminate in effective lawmaking, they must generate expectations entertained by politically relevant groups that certain policies are authoritative and controlling.

All communication involves the mediation of messages. What is distinctive about prescriptive or lawmaking communications is that rather than transmitting a single message, they carry simultaneously *three* coordinate communication flows in a fashion akin to the coaxial cables of telephonic communications: the policy content, the authority signal and the control intention. Unless each of these flows is present and effectively mediated to the relevant audience, a prescription does not result. Equally important, even if the three components are initially communicated, *they must continue to be communicated* for the prescription, as such, to endure; if one or more of the components should cease to be communicated, the prescription undergoes a type of desuetude and is terminated.

Let us consider each of these communication flows in more detail. The content of a prescription, the norm – the injunction that one ought to do or refrain from doing something or, writ large, the policy about the production and distribution of some value – is obviously an indispensable component. In statutes and various forms of written agreements, the policy content is express, though not necessarily complete or unambiguous. But beware the fallacy of elevating form over substance. Explicit content does not automatically equal prescription. Bear in mind that not all communications in prescriptive form are

122. See *supra* Chapter III, Section 6.

intended to be prescriptive. Only some carry lawmaking intention. Some are pageantry, expressions of aspiration or *vœux*, affirmations of values with neither intention on the part of the communicator nor expectation on the part of the audience of their being realised in fact.

Indications of an absence of prescriptive intent may be subtle and ambiguous. Consider, for a moment, the General Assembly's adoption of the New International Economic Order's (NIEO) "Charter of Economic Rights and Duties of States". At one phase, the Assembly was invited to adopt the Charter "as a measure of codification and progressive development" of international law. Because of opposition, this description was abandoned when the NIEO's Charter was submitted to the General Assembly for vote. But the legislatistic form of the Charter was retained. Some contended that the insistence on deleting any reference to codification and progressive development meant that part of the majority did not believe that they were making law. Conversely, as Oscar Schachter wrote, "even nonbinding agreements can be authoritative and controlling for the parties. There is no *a priori* reason to assume that these understandings are illusory because they are not legal" [123]. Moreover, a communication in the form of a legal instrument which was not intended to be law may not become law if it later acquires, in addition to its authority symbols, indications of control intentions. Communication is an ongoing process and much as a prescription may cease to be law if it loses its authority and control, a communication may become law if it acquires them. The decline of the Charter of Economic Rights and Duties of States may be compared, in this regard, to the ascendance of the Universal Declaration of Human Rights, from a similarly ambiguous procedural origin.

Where prescribing takes place behaviourally with its content embedded in and inferred from the situation, it may be subject to different reasonably plausible interpretations. While formal *legislation* sometimes suffers from unintended ambiguity (so-called "constructive ambiguity" is intentional), normative ambiguity is one of the recurring transaction costs of informal prescription.

Consider a mundane example. In what appears to the actors within it to be a novel situation, a mother asks her child to refrain from doing something. When the child persists, the mother says, "Stop it or I'm going to tell your father". Ignoring the fact that two or three decision

---

123. Oscar Schachter, "The Twilight Existence of Nonbinding International Agreements", *Am. J. Int'l L.*, Vol. 71 (1977), p. 296 *et seq.*, at 304.

functions – prescription, invocation and application – are being performed here, what is the policy content of the norm the erring child has violated? Both mother and child in that particular case know the specific offending behaviour which must stop if the child is to evade application by the father. They also implicitly know the content of what Kelsen called the "dynamic" norm: "obey your parent". But mother and child may not know or may differ in understanding the policy content of the general norm applicable in future situations, in which context and contingency are likely to be quite different.

Consider a situation in which the coastguard of State A insists on escorting the fishing vessels of State B from waters that B's fishermen have plied for generations [124]. What A's coastguard is doing in that example is utterly clear; its prescriptive policy content is not. A's acts may signal a permanent closing of areas theretofore open to international maritime users, or a brief closure for naval exercises, or a short-term conservation measure or a pollution-control effort, or the establishment of a new security zone, or a signal of displeasure with the B's Government over an unrelated matter that simply uses the presence of B's fishermen opportunistically to send a message. Some in A may themselves be unsure of the policy content of that communication and the extent of its control intention. By contrast, a bilateral agreement between the Governments of A and B establishing a conservation zone would make the legislative purpose clear.

The function of the second communication flow in prescription may be illustrated by a hypothetical. Imagine four thugs sitting in a bar and deciding, meticulously following *Robert's Rules of Order*, that all shopkeepers in the district will henceforth pay them 10 per cent of gross receipts for "protection" [125]. Have they prescribed or made law? There is certainly a clear policy content, and they may have the capacity to "enforce". But whatever the expectation of effectiveness, few would say, at least initially, that they had made law. Interestingly, if a parliament in a well-run State had said *exactly* the same thing, few would gainsay that a prescription had been created.

It was Augustine who remarked that a bandit is a little king and a king a big bandit [126]. Missing in both Augustine's observation and the farce enacted by the thugs is the "authority signal", a communication which

124. See e.g. *Guyana* v. *Suriname*, Award of the Arbitration Tribunal, 17 September 2007, 47 ILM 166.
125. Henry M. Robert III *et al.*, *Robert's Rules of Order*, 3rd ed., 2020.
126. Saint Augustine, *The City of God*, 4:4, trans. Marcus Dods, 2009.

attends the communications of policy content and control intention and which signals to the relevant audience that the communicators are the appropriate lawmakers: they have the authority to prescribe.

The base of authority from which a particular authority signal draws may vary, from the divine or monarchical to the constitutional and democratic. It may be formal and derivative or personal and charismatic, and, as such, it may be patently contrary to formal law: a charismatic religious leader may declare "That is the law, but I say . . ." or he may skip intermediate steps and say, as Mansur al-Hallaj said, "Ana al-Haq", "I am the law" [127]. There may be a single base of authority or, as in heterogeneous and pluralistic systems, multiple bases requiring complex authority signals, going through several steps or phases, each component of which is directed at a different constituent group. Recall in Chapter III, Section 2, the benefits and perils of using powerfully evocative words such as "jihad" and "crusade" when addressing heterogeneous audiences. Authority may be explicit, as when agents-plenipotentiary scrutinise each other's authorisations, and it may be implicit, as when the son-in-law of a president purports to speak on behalf of the State. And authority changes: witness, for example, changes in the UN General Assembly's assertions of a general prescriptive competence. It has no basis in the Charter but, in some contexts, participants and observers may infer a lawmaking authority for specific matters. Whatever its source, the point of emphasis is that an indispensable component of the complex communication that is a prescription is some attendant authority signal which distinguishes demands backed up only by credible threats – the demands of the thugs in our example – from law.

The authority signal is more complex and variable than the communication of policy content. A text does not degrade, but its authority may. Moreover, while the command of *what* to do is essentially unilinear, the communication of authority is a closed loop. It is the audience, whether or not all of its members realise it, that endows the prescribers with the authority that renders their communications prescriptive. The composition of the audience, the relative influence of its members and their own perspectives may change. Non-authoritative practices that endure may become prescriptive. Hence the search for authority, rather

127. Herbert I. W. Mason, *Al-Hallaj*, 1995; Massimo Companini, "Ḥallāj, al-Ḥusayn ibn Manṣūr al-.", in John L. Esposito (ed.), *The Oxford Encyclopedia of the Islamic World*, Vol. 1, 2009, at p. 289.

than confined to a documentary universe, must be empirical in a broad *and* continuous sense.

The third communications flow is the control intention. Lawmaking is not a polite ethical conversation, a search for truth, a dialogue requiring only content and authority, the latter derived from the cogency of the former. Lawmaking, though often regulated by law, is a political process and, as such, depends upon power, the capacity and willingness to ensure that a preferred policy is effective.

Control intention is not synonymous with the concept of sanction. All prescriptions contain a sanction, either a threat of deprivation for non-compliance or a promise of reward for compliance. But the fact that the drafter includes a formal sanction does not mean that the decision-makers whose jurisdiction will be invoked when there is a departure from the norm have the capacity or the will to enforce the norm. It is delusory and sometimes dangerous to call a statement in the subjunctive mood a prescription or law if it is not accompanied by a credible communication that those prescribing it intend to – and can – make it controlling. Moreover, the communication of control intention must be continuous throughout the life of the prescription. In the dialectic of law considered in episodic violations of a prescription have, among other things, a testing function, initiated by those members of the community who wish to amend or terminate it; they push and probe to see whether its control intention has waned and whether the prescription may henceforth be violated with diminished likelihood of sanction, if not with utter impunity [128].

Nor is control intention synonymous with potential power. Recall our discussion of power in Section 7 of Chapter III. In many cases, a State elite that has, in an arithmetical sense, adequate power bases to enforce an unpopular norm, will find it inexpedient to do so if that application or power would alienate allies or internal constituencies or undermine processes for decision-making in which the elite recognises a continuing interest. Where, however, the vicious use of power is an elite group's cachet, it may seek opportunities to convey control intention in a superfluously brutal fashion as a way of reinforcing the terror on which it bases its regime.

Control intention for specific prescriptions does not require unanimity or even broad consensus, only enough to support the norm in question.

---

128. See *supra* Chapter III, Section 5, Paragraph 2, on the dialectical character of law.

As was discussed in Chapter III, Section 6, norms are prescribed as law because they promote policies which part of the community does not voluntarily or spontaneously support. They become effective because some elites have sufficient interest to devote the resources necessary to make them effective. They continue to be meaningful norms only so long as some are able and willing to make them effective. Elite objectives change, support for a prescription may wane, or proclamations of unqualified support for a prescription may conceal a limit.

For those who undertake to advise others as to the law, determining whether control intention is sufficient to support particular prescriptions in specific circumstances is no simple task. It requires a comprehensive survey of the power process and the interests of those on whom the effectiveness of the prescriptions depend: which groups, official or non-official, constitute the effective power in the specific situation in which the norm is to be implemented, the objectives of members of the elite constellation, the importance its members attach to maintaining the norm in present and projected contexts, and the actual investment those elites are willing to commit to sustain the prescription. Sometimes only a few States may be critical to the effectiveness of the norm.

It is the coordination of these three message flows – policy content, authority signal and control intention – that indicates a prescription or, in popular parlance, law. Demands on others that are backed up only by threats, only by control intention communications, may well shape the aggregate behaviour of the target audience, so long as the demanders are willing to deploy the power which they threaten. But it would be improper to designate their commands as prescriptive or “law”, though they may ultimately acquire authority and become such.

Demands rich in authority signals but without adequate communications of control intention may produce, for some members of the community, compelling expressions of what is morally right. But it would be improper to call such expressions law – and perilous to rely on them – unless, in the hypothetically possible but extremely rare case, the target audience is so enthralled by the particular authority mystique that control intention is obviated. The exact mix of authority signal and control intention required to prescribe varies from context to context. In groups in which there is a high sense of collective purpose, in which common interests have been internalised by its politically relevant members and the application of the prescription in question entails minimum deprivations of key values, authority signals alone may, indeed, be sufficient to create prescriptive expectations. In aggregates in which inclusive identifications and perceptions of common interest are low or merely rhetorical, the need for communications of credible control intention increases.

The text carrying the policy content may seem as permanent as the proverbial decrees of the Medes and the Persians. It is not. Viewing lawmaking as a form of communication comprised of policy content, authority signal and control intention exposes that every prescription is a *continuous* process. In determining international law for particular matters and in specific contexts, the critical question is the *actual* expectations of politically relevant individuals and groups. These expectations will be sustained or will be adjusted by streams of communication about the authority and credible control intentions of those whose support is needed for the prescription's efficacy. Changes in global authority structures, changes in the power process or reassessments by effective elites of the degree of their prospective interest in continuing to invest resources to support particular prescriptions may signal the waning of a prescription or its termination even though it continues on the books. As we will see in Chapter VII, the dynamic character of the process means that judges, arbitrators and other decision-makers may find themselves in situations in which their actions can contribute to the consolidation of a desirable policy into an effective prescription, only then acquiring an adequate authority and control base.

Section 2. Soft law

The term "soft law" has come to refer to diverse phenomena related to international lawmaking. The products of lawmaking can be soft in all three of its dimensions. The normative content may be expressed in very general terms and be contextually variable as opposed to highly specific and narrowly drafted, affording no discretion to those applying it [129]. The authority signal may be clear and unequivocal, as, for example, when the Security Council discharges its primary responsibility to maintain peace and security under Chapter VII of the Charter with respect to a matter designated a threat to the peace, breach of the peace or act of aggression. In customary prescription, the authority signal, inferred from the *opinio juris* of many States, may be blurred and a matter of inference, for example when the General Assembly passes, by large majority including some of the permanent members of the

129. See W. Michael Reisman, "Canute Confronts the Tide: States versus Tribunals and the Evolution of the Minimum Standard in Customary International Law", *ICSID Rev. – Foreign Inv. LJ*, Vol. 30 (2015), pp. 616-634.

Security Council, a resolution that is couched in formal lawmaking terms, or when the ICJ renders an innovative advisory opinion by a large majority. And commitments of control intention may be soft when powerful actors whose support is indispensable cannot be counted on to support the prescription in different scenarios.

The concept of soft law alerts us to the fact that "normativity" is nowhere monolithic, unidimensional or static [130]. At every level of modern social organisation, the individual, whether operating on his or her own behalf or on behalf of a group, is bombarded with communications framed in the subjunctive mood and indicating, with varying degrees of authority and control, that the person to whom the normative communication is directed ought to do or refrain from doing something. The individual neither perceives nor respects each of these norms equally. Some are readily associated with the threat of severe sanctions whose probability of application is high. Some are associated with severe sanctions whose probability of application is relatively low or intermittent to the point where violation of the norm may become a rationally calculated "business" risk or even be part of a programme to replace the norm. Some norms are associated with sanctions that involve immaterial deprivations, such as respect, in contexts in which such deprivations are sufficiently meaningful to require serious calculation before the norms are violated. Some norms are associated with sanctions that may involve ostracism. Some norms may entail no sanctioning deprivations whatsoever. Some norms may have sanctions, but their incidence may vary according to legal or contextual factors, such as the identity or social location of the norm violator: *quod licet Jovi, non licet bovi*.

Those who use the term "soft law" often associate it with specific institutions. The assumption is that *everything* that emerges from certain institutions is real or "hard" law, while *anything* that emerges from other sources is not. We have encountered the "institutional fallacy" in enquiry about and practice of international law from the very outset of these lectures. If the question is not the source of a prescription but its probable degree of authority and control, then much apparently "real" or "hard" law may be exposed as ineffective, while much "soft" law may be quite effective. Recall Oscar Schachter's acknowledgement of the effect of "non-binding" agreements.

---

130. Prosper Weil, "Towards Relative Normativity in International Law?", *Am J. Int'l. L.*, Vol. 77 (1983), p. 413 *et seq.*

Popular perceptions of the conduct of an MNE in terms of media-transmitted conceptions of law, which perceptions then express themselves as spontaneous consumer boycotts, may be far more likely to force the managers of the MNE to comply with those normative standards than would a prescription deemed to be hard law simply because of its institutional provenance. The corporation would be even more prone to ignore the prescription if it knew that the prescription had been intentionally assigned to a bureaucratic unit with an insufficient budget, and, as a result, the probability of actual enforcement was low and the penalty minimal.

In the ongoing effort to optimise their interests, actors will assess how a prescription is likely to affect them in particular situations and the *likelihood* of its application to them in a concrete case. But likelihood of application cannot be understood only in terms of the cost of the prescription's specific sanction. At every level of social organisation, lawyers, among other decision specialists who advise others on the lawful ways of achieving their objectives, calculate and assess the relative costs of strategic options in terms of these sanction probabilities. The costs may range from high to low likelihoods of going to jail; of being penalised by fines ranging from a contextually manageable to onerous amounts; from suffering respect deprivations which may, in projected contexts, be insupportable. The likelihood of the sanction being applied is another calculation. Sanctioning is expensive and Governments have to live within their means. Because enforcing every violation of a prescription could exceed an enforcement budget, the official charged with the task must exercise discretion and sanction selectively. Hence the nominal severity and projected incidence of published sanctions is not, of itself, a reliable indicator. Sanction severity and incidence of application are points on a sliding scale and turn on many variables. The application of the prescription – how it will be applied, if at all – depends on contextual possibilities at the moment of application.

Sanction incidence may, itself, serve policy purposes. A totalitarian system, as its name imports, seeks to regulate every facet of social process, and its prescriptions are accompanied by severe sanctions. Liberal and democratic systems prescribe with more restraint but, for philosophical reasons, severely sanction only those matters that are deemed indispensable for the protection of public order. The remaining social sectors are supported by mild sanctions which are not applied by the State [131]. The distinctions between degrees of control intention and

131. Reisman, *Brief Encounters*, *supra* footnote 91, at pp. 15-16.

severity of sanction range along a continuum which is more inflected than can be described by the dyad "hard" and "soft".

Section 3. State-made law and media-made law

The functional term "prescription" permits us to encompass all the effective normative arrangements, whatever their origin, that bear upon actors and decision-makers and not only the prescriptions legislated by States. Functional terms can bring into focus effective prescriptions of a non-State origin and reveal the role of "civil society" in shaping prescriptions [132]. In this latter sense, it empowers the individual to the dismay of State elites who wish to retain control over lawmaking procedures.

The approach has also been resisted by some scholars because the old signposts of law – ratified treaties and custom verified by State practice – have been jostled from centre stage by the novel products. Prosper Weil, in his seminal essay in the *American Journal of International Law*, took note of the proliferation of types and levels of normativity in contemporary international law and registered his regret over the jurisprudential loss of analytical precision. "We find ourselves", he lamented, "in ever widening circles of increasing uncertainty". Yet, ever the disciplined scientist, Weil acknowledged that what he called "pre-normative acts do create expectations and exert on the conduct of States an influence that in certain cases may be greater than that of rules of treaty or customary international law" [133].

Many factors account for the democratisation and expansion of private sector international lawmaking. The technological revolution, considered in Chapter II, which installed the communications infrastructure that has empowered non-State actors, has facilitated non-State participation in international lawmaking. Coincident with the new communications opportunities has been the phenomenon of "privatisation", the voluntary withdrawal of the State apparatus from activities that were previously deemed to be inherently "public" and the collapse of public services in others. These far-reaching changes have coincided with the increased opening of national markets to foreign investors who demand the minimum standards of international law. The rapidity of

132. International judges and arbitrators who are directed to consult a limited number of "sources" of law are not supposed to take account of the broad conception of law. We will consider this when we turn, in Chapters VII and XV, to international judge and arbitration roles specialised to the application of law.

133. Weil, "Towards Relative Normativity", *supra* footnote 130.

change, characteristic of a science-based and technological civilisation, has, in itself, required national lawmaking institutions, unable to keep up, to yield some of their legislative competence to informal lawmaking by the often transnational economic sectors concerned.

The modalities through which international law is being prescribed now range over a wide spectrum. At one end, we find treaties and other international agreements, the classical form of international lawmaking. Close to it we find the growing network of agreements between international governmental organisations and, to an extent, agreements between those organisations and NGOs. We then find delegated lawmaking, the pre-eminent example of which is the Security Council when it operates under Chapter VII of the Charter; incipient developments may also be detected in some regional environmental treaties. Arrangements reached informally by corresponding levels of Government in different countries, especially in economic matters, constitute an important part of the prescriptive web. Beyond that is an area in which expectations of authority on particular courses of right behaviour are established and supported by informal sanctions. The dynamic international process of communication allows a wide range of non-State actors to play critical roles in the shaping and sustaining of expectations of right behaviour. It is these actors who have sustained the general demand for human rights and the general intolerance of cruel and violent behaviour.

Thus, we encounter in contemporary international law two broad types of international lawmaking: one essentially oligarchical, restricted to the representatives of States and couching its products in the traditional language of public international law, the other more democratic but not necessarily egalitarian and not denying the validity of the first. While there is an interplay between the two forms of international lawmaking, they are often distinct in their outcomes. In the dynamic process, some of the law production is unsuccessful or evanescent, though it may nonetheless exercise some influence on decision-makers. At the Land Mines Conference or the Rome Conference [134], the influence of

134. Convention on the Prohibition of the Use, Stockpiling, Production and Transfer of Anti-Personnel Mines and on Their Destruction, 3 December 1997, 36 ILM 1507; Rome Statute of the International Criminal Court, 17 July 1998, 2187 UNTS 90 (hereafter ICC Statute). See also Richard Price, "Reversing the Gun Sights: Transnational Civil Society Targets Land Mines", *Int'l Org.*, Vol. 52 (1998), p. 613 *et seq.*; Fanny Benedetti and John L. Washburn, "Drafting the International Criminal Court Treaty: Two Years to Rome and an Afterword on the Rome Diplomatic Conference", *Global Governance*, Vol. 5 (1999), p. 1 *et seq.*, at 21-23.

NGOs on the formal lawmaking process was manifest and, at some moments, even dominant. But the outcome of that process was still a classical instrument of international law. Not surprisingly, the two types may produce different and sometimes inconsistent results due to the different policy objectives pursued by States in treaty-making and in public international organisational decision-making on the one hand, and the range of non-State actors in their prescriptive endeavours on the other.

Modern international law thus prescribes in different settings and for a range of different institutions and audiences. The law that will be applied in courts and other formal institutions of international law, which operate under explicit choice-of-law regimes, continues to be largely treaty and custom, for whose identification classical international law prescribes traditional procedures. International tribunals, such as the ICJ, have governing law provisions that direct those tribunals to these "sources" [135]. This stream of international lawmaking is "State-made law", produced in arenas to which only State representatives are supposed to have formal access. As a result, it reflects the minimal shared concerns of a majority of Governments. (As explained above, even here functional analysis reveals some infiltration of non-State actors.)

At the same time, a much larger and more open lawmaking process, which is transmitted through multiple electronic and print channels and operates directly on the politically relevant strata of the world, is continuously shaping expectations and demands as to what is right and wrong and, more urgently, which wrongs require some legal remedy. Call this, for convenience, "media-made law". (This is not the most felicitous designation, for it takes its name from the channels through which the communications are delivered rather than the diverse range of groups and individuals who, acting through the channels, shape and reinforce expectations.) Given the different casts of actors in State-made and media-made law, it is no surprise that the expectations shaped by these two lawmaking streams are not always congruent. Lack of congruity becomes especially problematic when decision-makers and decision institutions, relying on one form of international law, are called upon to review activities that were taken under the "authority" of another form of international law. Striking examples are

135. W. Michael Reisman, "Unratified Treaties and Other Unperfected Acts in International Law: Constitutional Functions", *Vand. J. of Transn'l L.*, Vol. 35 (2002), p. 729 *et seq.*

to be found in the United Kingdom House of Commons review of the lawfulness of NATO's actions against Yugoslavia and the cases about the bombardment of Serbia in which the ICJ was invoked against a number of NATO countries against whom jurisdiction was thought to lie [136].

The difference between State-made law and media-made law is most dramatic in their respective characterisations of certain grave violations of human rights and the specification and implementation of their remedies. The international protection of human rights programme operates case by case, but its overall effect is the internationalisation of the standards by which the actions of national elites are appraised. Hence significant differences emerge here between characterisations and demanded legal responses in State-made law and media-made law. The great human rights instruments, which are State-made law, though justly celebrated, are cautiously drawn, as many of the Governments that create and ratify them are wary of installing international regimes that could constrain their techniques of governance.

By contrast, media-made law, emanating from non-governmental sources, has no such interest. Hence, its characterisations of events and its remedial components, based on the expectations and demands of those who have been shaped by this form of lawmaking, are not held back by the remedial restraints of State-made law. But while the prescriptions of State-made law are framed in terms of general application, media-made law's characterisation of legal violation and demand for remedy may vary from population to population and case to case. A majority of the American public, who were bombarded with massive amounts of words and images by nationalist media, felt that the US invasion of Iraq in 2003 was lawful, while the European public, deriving its information from other media, viewed it as unlawful. These differences expose a problematic feature of media-made law as international law. The remedial component of State-made law tends to caution, acutely aware of the difficulties and costs of enforcement; the remedial component of media-made law demands immediate satisfaction, and its sense of political possibility is not tempered by experience.

---

136. See UK Parliament Foreign Affairs Select Committee, Fourth Report, Session 1999-2000, http://www.publications.parliament.uk/pa/cm199900/cmselect/cmfaff/28/2802.htm. See also ICJ, "Yugoslav Applies to the International Court of Justice in a Dispute with the Member States of NATO in Respect of the Threat of Use of Force by NATO", Press Release No. 1994/11, 21 March 1994, https://www.icj-cij.org/public/files/press-releases/3/10343.pdf.

Because of the capacity of media-made law to characterise events as grave human rights violations, the managers of democratic Governments are compelled to assume that in more instances than in the past they will be pressed to use governmental resources to respond to grave human rights violations, despite the fact that their intervention has not been authorised by State-made law or would not be compatible with the national interest. This may generate acute tensions within domestic legal institutions in which the lawfulness of the action driven by media-made law may be challenged, as well as in international institutions, such as the International Criminal Court (ICC). The personal consequences for international lawyers will be considered in Chapter XVI.

Thus, the contemporary international system makes law through multiple processes and in multiple settings. Moreover, as we will see, the international system applies international law in multiple arenas. The practical problems created by this prescriptive multiplicity are formidable, and a workable method of accommodation has yet to emerge. The democratisation of international lawmaking, while fulfilling a goal of power-sharing, has increased uncertainties about the application of international law in view of the disparities between the applications of the formal legal institutions and other arenas. In circumstances in which the formal legal institutions of State-made law must review the lawfulness of decisions of the other institutions – for example, NATO's bombardment of Serbia over the latter's action in Kosovo – or other actors – for example, French action in Côte d'Ivoire – the discrepancy may undermine the effectiveness or credibility of one or the other institution.

The discrepancy also poses technical and ethical challenges for those who advise actors as to what the law is. From a methodology based on a careful analysis of texts and judgments, the intellectual task becomes one of trying to anticipate and influence decision, based on a complex analysis of the factors bearing on different decision-makers for particular cases. Thus, we may anticipate a world in which assumptions about what decision-makers will do will turn in varying measure on *who* the authoritative decision-makers are, the context of the case or incident and especially the degree of popular approval or disapproval. The comparative predictability of State-made law may yield to the fickleness of *vox populi*.

The rapid growth of these many types of international lawmaking looks to be a relatively long-term fixture. Those who bemoan it may frame their criticisms in terms of defective, excessive or relativised normativity, but they must come to terms with it, much as lawyers and diplomats in small or weak States come to terms with the prescriptive force of "rules of the game" and other effective norms established largely on the basis of power.

Criticisms of soft law come mostly from custodians of the legal establishments of the First World. For them, part of the problem appears to be that much of this type of law is being made in settings in which the older and wealthier States find their effective power is offset in the international parliamentary arena in which power, which prevails in unorganised arenas where "clubs are trumps", by the votes of a numerically large but otherwise politically weak group of States and non-governmental entities operating in parliamentary arenas or in other "soft forums". The undesirable result of the coexistence of hard and soft law is inconsistent normativity to the point where, in critical matters, international law may become a camera whose shots are double exposures.

Given the increasing polarity of the international political system, the prevalence of these different types of lawmaking may be systemically beneficial insofar as it channels political agitation for change into a demand for lawmaking and, at least over the short term, reinforces international authority symbols. Over the longer term, however, it could prove deleterious, for the failure to requite expectations that have been stimulated and validated by international prescriptions may well undermine belief in the efficacy of international law.

The professional tasks of international lawyers would be simpler if the lawmaking system were unitary or, at least, more organised. But a lawmaking process must serve the needs of the actual community of which it is a part and not the convenience of its factotums. The world community, as we have seen, is diverse in identifications, value demands and narratives; it is geographically dispersed with many different levels of development. Yet the need for lawmaking is enormous. No single legislative process could possibly encompass this system, accommodate the diverse and often conflicting demands of its many participants or satisfy its needs. The creaky time-consuming process of treaty-making and ratification will continue to have its place, but it would border on fantasy to imagine that it can be juiced up to become the principal lawmaking modality of contemporary international law. Nor can the modality of customary lawmaking, based on State practice accompanied by inferences about subjective perceptions of law itself, fill the need. But media-made law, for all its increased participation, is far from a satisfactory substitute. In a context of rapid technological change, the crafting of normative arrangements that take account of the aggregate effects of innovative practices on human beings and their environment should precede rather than follow from practice.

CHAPTER VI

TWO MODES OF PRINCIPLED DECISION-MAKING

> "Philosophically the apportionment of the field between rule and discretion which is suggested by the use of rules and of standards respectively in modern law has its basis in the respective fields of intelligence and intuition."
>
> Roscoe Pound [137]

Section 1. Multiple modes of decision-making

The previous chapters referred to the intellectual tools necessary for making and applying international law to the what-it's-attached-to. The word "tools" was used because theories about law and their concepts are essentially instruments used by decision specialists in the tasks assigned to them. The words "tools" and "tasks" are pluralised because international lawyers are charged with many different tasks for which different conceptual tools and toolboxes are necessary.

Consider an example: Colonel Smith, a legal officer in the US Army's Judge Advocate General Corps, currently has two major assignments. He chairs a court martial that has been convened to try an alleged violation of the law of war concerning cyberwar. But he also leads a working group which has been assembled by the Judge Advocate General as part of the army's updating of its codification of the law of war with respect to the emerging practice of cyberwar; should the colonel's working group find the current codification ill-adapted to what it anticipates will be the future contours of cyberwar, it is instructed to propose feasible recommendations for its amendment.

Isn't it clear that in his function as a judge in the court martial, Smith is expected to limit his focus to the text of the legal code, as it exists, in light of prior judgments in which the code was applied by higher courts and to apply it in strict conformity to maxims such as *nullum crimen, nulla poena sine lege*? Isn't it equally clear that in his assignment to appraise the adequacy of the inherited law of war as it confronts the techniques of cyberwarfare, Smith and his working group will be looking through different lenses at a range of facts, policies and

137. Roscoe Pound, *An Introduction to the Philosophy of Law*, 1922, at p. 70.

political processes that go far beyond what he may properly address in his role as a judge in a court martial? In both of his roles, Smith will be functioning as a lawyer who is acting in a principled fashion if he does it correctly. But in each, he will be expected to deploy a different set of concepts and intellectual tools.

In most general terms, persons performing law jobs use two entirely distinct modes of making principled decisions: a textual-rule-based mode and a contextual-policy-based mode. The modes correspond respectively to the terms *lex lata*, what the law is, and *lex ferenda*, what the law should be. The legitimacy of decision-making depends upon using the right mode and its tools for the right job. In his role as a judge in a criminal case, Smith may not decide to use the contextual-policy-based mode because he personally thinks the law should be changed or because he thinks policy analysis is intellectually superior and "rule-crunching" humdrum. Conversely, Smith will not accomplish much in his second assignment if he uses the textual-rule-based mode to appraise the adequacy of an area of the law that is new and different, for which it may be necessary to imagine new situations and to invent and promote new law to replace the *lex lata*.

In most general terms, the textual-rule-based mode of decision requires the persons applying it to approach the issues before them through the prism of rules. In this mode, a central question is *which* rules apply. Great emphasis is placed on the origin and validity of the rules and whether they are properly derived from higher rules. The principles of interpretation of texts and other verbal formulations which lay claim to some authority are revered as virtual articles of faith. The primary focus is on a text: even the word "context" in Article 31 VCLT, the authoritative statement of international law's rule-based methodology, means "text" [138]. When the text proves to be unclear, this mode does not authorise the applier to break out of the text into the domain of policy; rather it directs the applier to the records of the process that produced the text! A valid decision in this mode is "legal" to the extent that it identifies and correctly applies the relevant rules and is consistent with prior decisions that applied those rules. Derivational logic plays a critical role and is extolled as a means of finding truth. Above all, the introduction of the decision-maker's personal political or even policy

138. See Mahnoush H. Arsanjani and W. Michael Reisman, "Interpreting Treaties for the Benefit of Third Parties: The 'Salvors' Doctrine' and the Use of Legislative History in Investment Treaties", *Am. J. Int'l L.*, Vol. 104 (2010), p. 597 *et seq.*, at 604.

preferences is deemed improper. The range of permissible operations of the decision-maker in this mode of decision is bounded; actions that go beyond those bounds are considered an *excès de pouvoir* and a ground for setting aside the decision.

The contextual-policy-based mode of decision, by contrast, requires decision-makers to approach the issues before them through the prism of policy and the contexts in which the values of that policy are produced and distributed. Rather than the question as to which rules apply, the questions underlying the contextual-policy-based decision-making are (1) what ought to be the goal values of the community with respect to the values concerned; (2) which practicable arrangements will most efficiently optimise the production and distribution of those goal values in short-term and longer-term projected contexts; and (3) how those arrangements can be installed.

The tasks involved in answering these questions include, at a minimum, (1) the clarification and specification of community policy; (2) the examination of the extent to which that policy is currently being achieved in ways compatible with other relevant policies; (3) the identification of the factors that account for achieving or failing to achieve the policies; (4) the extent to which existing arrangements are likely to realise the policies in various imagined futures; and, if the prognosis is that the policies are unlikely to be secured, (5) the invention of alternative arrangements which are more likely to realise the policies. Instead of compliance with rules, the decision-maker operating in this mode is concerned with assessing the production and distribution of values in preferred ways.

The examination of rules and authoritative texts are not excluded from the scope of the contextual-policy-based mode of decision. Rules in extant legal arrangements will be examined, but rather than the grammatical and syntactical examination of the textual-rule-based mode, the rules are now considered in terms of the extent to which the social and economic consequences of their application will approximate the value goals of the relevant community. Alternatives may certainly include new rules designed to be applied by other decision-makers who use the rule-based mode. These new rules are instruments for achieving particular policies, but rules, as such, neither guide the contextual-policy-based enquiry nor determine its outcome. In place of the veneration of logic and the intricate syntactical analyses of the textual-rule-based mode, the contextual-policy-based mode, especially when it turns to inventing alternatives, may resort to associational methods that go "beyond the noise of logic" [139]. Where the environing system is democratic, the contextual-policy-based mode may include consultations, through diverse sampling methods of the views of relevant communities. These techniques are anathema to the textual-rule-based approach. Can one imagine Colonel Smith lawfully condemning a defendant on the basis of a sampling of the momentary national mood?

The outcome of the textual-rule-based mode is a conclusion as to whether a rule has been violated; it may take the form of a judgment or award. If it confirms the violation, it may specify a penalty or remedy. The outcome of the contextual-policy-based mode varies according to the decision function for which it is deployed. If, for example, the decision function is the gathering and processing of *intelligence* to be used in other decision functions, the outcome is the assembly and provision of data or relevant information. If the function is the *promotion* of new law, the outcome is a proposal, which may take the form of a bill or *projet-loi*. If the function is *prescription*, the outcome is a law, decree, regulation or some other informal way of expressing an authoritative normative arrangement. If the function is *termination*, the outcome is the abrogation of an authoritative arrangement and may also include transitional regimes. And if the function is *appraisal*, the outcome is the assessment of the degree of achievement of a specific arrangement in terms of the policy goals for which it was installed and, where appropriate, recommendations for its adjustment or replacement.

As observed in Chapter I, much legal education focuses on refining skills in the application of the textual-rule-based mode, taking it as the quintessential "legal" approach and teaching the apprentice to "think like a lawyer". And that is correct because for certain tasks in certain forums, the textual-rule-based mode is expected and demanded by those directly engaged in that decision process as well as by the community of which they are part; its presence as the exclusive decision mode is an element of the legitimacy of the outcome. For example, in an arbitration of an international investment dispute, both the State and non-State party expect not only that the governing treaty or, if relevant, the national law of the State party, will be rigorously and impartially applied by the tribunal to the issues before it and that the reasons accompanying the decision will demonstrate that rigour and

---

139. James Agee, "Sonnet XXII", in Robert Fitzgerald (ed.), *The Collected Poems of James Agee*, 1968, at p. 47.

impartiality [140]. By contrast, the legitimacy of the contextual-policy-based mode of decision depends upon the design, through impartial and transparent methods, of arrangements that produce and distribute the values at stake in the common interest.

Colonel Smith must apply the textual-rule-based mode when sitting as a criminal judge, as must his judicial counterpart on the ICC. But the Prosecutor of the ICC, under Article 15 of the Rome Statute, presumably focuses on more. When the UN Security Council is seised of an incident involving the use of force, it is not expected that the Council, in discharging its mandate, will use the textual-rule-based mode of decision. Its mandate is to restore the peace; everything that it does will be dictated by that critical policy in the context in which it is presented [141].

The idea that the textual-rule-based mode is the only legitimate legal decision mode would be correct if the application of the law to events in formal settings, such as by courts or tribunals, were the only *legal* function. A moment's reflection will show how unfounded such a belief is. Making the "law" which is being applied is also part of the legal process. Lawyers engaged in lawmaking are not deploying the textual-rule-based mode. If they were, the content of the law would be a closed circuit, constantly replicating itself. Nor is Colonel Smith applying the textual-rule-based mode when gathering information about cyberwarfare or assessing, in projected scenarios, the aptitude of existing legal arrangements for dealing with a new mode of conflict or proposing new legal arrangements for dealing with it. Whatever they call their *modus operandi* and however well or poorly they perform it, those engaged in pre-lawmaking and lawmaking functions are using the contextual-policy-based mode of decision.

Lawmaking, which we considered in the previous chapter, and law-applying are only two parts of the activities encompassed in legal

140. W. Michael Reisman, " 'Case Specific Mandates' versus 'Systemic Implications': How Should Investment Tribunals Decide?: The Freshfields Arbitration Lecture, *Arbitration International*, Vol. 29 (2013), p. 131 *et seq.*; Guillermo Aguilar Alvarez and W. Michael Reisman, "How Well are Investment Awards Reasoned", in *id.*, *The Reasons Requirement in International Investment Arbitration: Critical Case Studies*, 2008, p. 1 *et seq.*

141. This is one of the reasons why it may be anomalous to assign to a body such as the ICC the determination of whether certain behaviour constituted an "act of aggression". W. Michael Reisman, "Reflections on the Judicialization of the Crime of Aggression", *Yale J. Int'l L.*, Vol. 39 (2014), p. 66 *et seq.*, http://www.yjil.org/docs/pub/o-39-reisman-reflections-on-the-judicialization-of-the-crime-of-aggression.pdf.

decision. If we take the word "decision" and deconstruct it, we will see, as briefly noted above, that it comprises seven component functions:

1. *intelligence*, the gathering, processing and dissemination of information relevant to making social choices;
2. *promotion*, the processes by which individual or collective awareness of a discrepancy between a desirable state of affairs and one that is or is about to eventuate leads to a demand and agitation for some type of community intervention and regulation;
3. *prescription*, including conventional lawmaking, which occurs when actors, with varying degrees of authority, select and install certain policy preferences as community law. This may be accomplished by the enactment of a legislature or some other organised lawmaker but is also, and especially in international law, largely accomplished in unorganised processes whose outcomes are generally referred to as "custom" or "soft law";
4. *invocation*, the provisional characterisation of a certain action or a state of affairs as inconsistent with a prescription, accompanied by agitation for a community institution to apply the appropriate prescription to it;
5. *application*, the organisation of the facts of a particular dispute, the specification of the prescriptions that apply and their implementation. When a court is the agency of application, the outcome is a judgment; in international law, most applications occur in informal, unorganised situations;
6. *termination*, the abrogation of existing norms and the social arrangements based upon them, the development of transitional regimes, including the design of compensatory programmes for those who have made good faith value investments on the expectation that the arrangements made under now terminated arrangements would continue [142]; and
7. *appraisal*, the evaluation of the aggregate performance of all decision functions in terms of community requirements [143].

Ordinarily, the textual-rule-based mode of decision is expected to be used in the invocation and application functions [144]. In developed

142. This function corresponds to what textbooks call "Peaceful Change".

143. See Myres S. McDougal *et al.*, "The World Constitutive Process of Authoritative Decision", in *id.*, *International Law Essays: A Supplement to International Law in Contemporary Perspective*, 1981, p. 191 *et seq.*, at 267-286.

144. But when the Prosecutor of the ICC, out of concern over her limited resources, exercises "discretion" as to which of a number of possible violations within her

domestic legal systems in which the process of abrogation of law is regulated by prescriptions, the textual-rule-based mode may be deployed in the termination function as well; that is especially the case when termination involves no more than abrogating the obsolescent. But because the abrogation of any operational legal arrangement, on which myriad interlocking good faith value investments have been made, is likely to precipitate secondary social disruptions and resistance, the contextual-policy-based mode will also be deployed. In the other component decision functions, participants do not utilise the textual-rule-based mode, irrespective of the mode of decision the participants may think they are deploying.

Section 2. The textual-rule-based mode

I do not minimise the intellectual challenges involved in properly using the textual-rule-based mode. Some scholars liken the application function in legal arrangements to the decisions of a referee or umpire in a sports match. But the notion that application in this mode involves simply applying a rule in some artificially confined and mechanical fashion – for example, to use a baseball analogy, calling a runner sliding into home plate "safe" or "out" – grossly oversimplifies an extremely complex decision function. Consider the following sequential components of any application:

1. the applier must explore the facts, including the precipitating events, within their larger factual context and assemble a provisional factual picture;
2. the applier must explore the prescriptions invoked by the relevant parties which they have asserted are engaged by the provisional factual focus and then assemble a provisional picture of the relevant prescriptions;
3. the applier must make a determination of the facts;
4. the applier must specify the prescriptions directly relevant to those facts as well as other authoritative policies which may be relevant;
5. the applier must formulate the substance of the decision;
6. the applier must determine, as distinct from the preceding phase, the content and mode of promulgation of the decision;
7. the applier must enforce the decision; and

jurisdiction she will prosecute, she is using the contextual-policy-based mode of decision.

8. other appliers must review the decision for its conformity to the procedural and substantive standards of the relevant application process.

Now it should be clear that each of these phases involves, in all but unique applications, complex intellectual operations for which the relevant rules may provide no clear guidelines. Moreover, relevant authoritative policies may vary greatly depending on the decision-maker who is engaged. The UN Security Council, for example, using the contextual-policy-based mode of decision, may be legally bound to look at a different set of facts and policies from those made available to an international judge or arbitrator, a point to which we will return below. But there are also commonalities among all authoritative appliers. For example, in all application, whatever its mode, the tensions between internal cameral deliberations and the content and modes of promulgation of the actual decision often require trade-offs between interests in effectiveness and transparency, the latter of which is one of the factors contributing to the legitimacy of both the textual-rule-based and contextual-policy-based modes [145].

In some circumstances, legal prescriptions of the textual-rule-based mode are designed to allow relatively little or even no contextual adjustment by the person designated and authorised to apply them. To take an extreme example, the sergeant sitting in a silo housing intercontinental ballistic missiles (ICBMs) is given the strictest instructions about the circumstances under which he is to flip a switch and send the missiles in his charge hurtling towards their target. Those who have established the rules (and indeed all the rest of us) do not want the sergeant to do any contextual-policy-based appraisal, even less to undertake a Jacques Derrida-style deconstruction of his commands. He is expected to confine himself to a drastically limited normative universe in which one and only one relevant rule contains a single binary choice which is to be made on the occurrence of one and only one specified contingency.

Or do we really want the sergeant to be confined to that binary universe? In the mid-1970s, a malfunction occurred in the Soviet nuclear alert system, the counterpart to the contemporaneous US system in which the sergeant in his silo was a cog.

145. See *infra* Chapter XV, Section 2, on these principles.

> "An erroneous message was automatically transmitted from the top down to the command posts of all rocket divisions: go one step to a higher alert. Most duty officers in the command posts failed to obey. 'People didn't believe it', Yarynich said. [Valery Yarynich was a high-ranking officer in the elite Strategic Rocket forces.] 'We were not at war'. Instead of summoning troops from their barracks to combat sites, they began telephoning their superiors to find out if the message was genuine. Only a lone duty officer, a lieutenant colonel, actually put his unit on alert. The incident revealed a great deal of reluctance in the rocket forces to push any buttons. The duty officers knew, Yarynich said, that 'one could not act blindly'." [146]

Life as we know it may have survived because the Soviet officers did not do what they had been trained and ordered to do in accordance with the textual-rule-based mode of decision which governed them [147].

In some circumstances, treaty drafters or a legislature may frame their respective prescriptions in a more open-textured fashion. A bilateral investment treaty, designed to refer to a range of phenomena which cannot be known in advance, may require a tribunal to determine whether a measure taken by the host State's Government against a qualifying investor or investment constituted "fair and equitable treatment". Then the implication is clear: the persons assigned to apply that sort of prescriptive formula in the textual-rule-based mode are authorised and required to make certain adjustments in their application so as to ensure that the policies animating the prescriptions are given effect in that particular situation. In these latter circumstances, the appliers, whether judges or arbitrators, must view the prescriptions which they are called upon to apply not as black-letter rules, as would the sergeant in the silo, but as authoritative communications conveying information about (1) the policy or policies to be achieved as well as (2) an indication of the type and range of circumstances in which those policies are to be applied.

Where lawmaking institutions are unable to operate or they abdicate their responsibility, appliers who are expected to decide according to the textual-rule-based mode have no choice but to deploy the contextual-policy-based mode. Even then, the legitimacy of their decisions depends on their fidelity to the textual-rule-based mode so they may go

146. Hoffman, *Dead Hand: Untold Story*, *supra* footnote 38, at p. 148.
147. See *infra* Chapter XVI on the issue of making such choices.

to great lengths to present their decisions in this fashion. The Appellate Body of the World Trade Organization (WTO) or the ICJ sometimes produces decisions that can be described as androgynous. Although the policy content of such decisions may be defensible, they suffer from a legitimacy deficit precisely because the ostensible mode of deciding that was used is unpersuasive. Forced and tortured logical elaborations are usually an indicator of an attempt to conceal that a contextual-policy-based mode of decision was actually employed.

Where a rule formulation with little room for applier discretion is the vehicle chosen for the achievement of a policy and the rule proves ill-adapted to do so in a particular case, whether because of the anachronism of the rule in the face of subsequent social changes or the idiosyncratic character of the factual situation, the appliers operating in the textual-rule-based mode must consult and apply the policy, but it is the policy of the rule-giver, the drafter or its authoritative successor. They must, as the ICJ put it in the *South West Africa* cases, engage in *actualisation* [148].

A conception of textual-rule-based application which tries to model itself for all purposes only on the sergeant in the silo and to insist upon strict application of the rules is likely, in these circumstances, to produce anachronistic decisions at odds with the contemporary objectives of the legislature. Sensitivity to the policy *animating* a prescription – its "object and purpose" – as well as to the language formulating it is also important in complex cases and not inconsistent with the textual-rule-based mode. Unlike academic exercises, real controversies rarely engage a single law, rule or, indeed, policy. As a result, the textual-rule-based applier, whether judge or arbitrator, may have to make some adjustments in the accommodation of a policy to shape the package of remedies to be awarded so that they approximate *all* the policy objectives of the legal system which are engaged in that case. Again, however, not every application is complex; when it is, the consultation of policy or policies is to those of international law.

Consider Colonel Smith in his role as a judge or his counterpart on the ICC. Two key features of their lawful applications in the textual-rule-based mode are the scope of authority to decide assigned to the applier and the fidelity of the applier to the relevant prescriptions. In principle, one would wish high achievement quotients in each of these dimensions. But given the complexity and instability of the

148. *Admissibility of Hearings of Petitioners by the Committee on South West Africa*, Advisory Opinion, 1 June 1956, ICJ Reports 1956, p. 73.

contemporary international legal system, incorporating, as it does, a wide range of formal and functional appliers and the variegations in international lawmaking which we considered in the previous chapter, the formal authority accorded to particular appliers may vary greatly. As observed earlier, a member of the Security Council enjoys an explicit authority to make decisions for the maintenance or restoration of minimum order. But the discharge of this function cannot rely on a few detailed prescriptions or rules in the textual-rule-based mode; it must, instead, revert to the most fundamental policies of the international system, applied with full sensitivity to the context *and* to the consequences which alternative decision options will have for all of those policies.

Judges of the ICJ have an explicit authority to decide matters properly submitted to the Court, but, by contrast to the Security Council, the judges are supposed to be confined to the specific prescriptions, whether decided in advance by the parties or itemised in the Court's choice-of-law clause, Article 38 of its Statute. Both the Security Council and the ICJ are "legal" decision-makers, and both will apply international law. Yet they may produce quite different though equally "lawful" decisions in the same or similar cases, each using a different yet equally principled mode of decision.

A national court or arbitration tribunal using the textual-rule-based mode will assess damages entirely in terms of the injury which the claimant suffered. By contrast, a decision-maker using the contextual-policy-based mode is likely to take into account the possible political consequences on the respondent in order to avoid "Versailles" effects. Same victims, same injuries, different decision-makers using different modes of principled decision, different, but equally lawful decisions.

Section 3. The contextual-policy-based mode

By contrast to the textual-rule-based mode, the contextual-policy-based mode has three defining characteristics. First, it is contextual rather than textual so that it can identify and map all the features of the social process of immediate concern. This is all the more urgent for situations in which decisions must be taken *outside* of formal institutions or in an offshore zone, as they often must in this mode. Second, although it uses many of the methods of pure research, unlike the ethic and praxis of *wertfrei Wissenschaft*, the contextual-policy-based mode has to identify and solve a specific problem and not merely to pose and answer "interesting" questions. Third, instead of relying on derivational logic, as in the textual-rule-based mode, it is methodologically eclectic, applying whatever methods promise to best perform the decision function at hand and not committing itself to a single method.

Let us consider each of these briefly.

Contextuality is critical because the comprehensiveness and realism with which those deploying the contextual-policy-based mode conceive their major focus of attention – how they locate relevant processes of decision in the community or communities which they affect and are affected by – will influence how they conceive every part of their investigation, their framing of problems and their selection of tools for enquiry.

The second of these lectures (Chap. II) undertook a brief foray into the "what-it's-attached-to" in order to draw attention to the scale of the challenge which the purposes of contemporary international law present: the degree of achievement of those purposes is the basis for appraising the performance of international legal decision. A comparable, but more detailed, contextual method is implicit in every non-judicial and non-arbitrable problem to which international lawyers turn their attention. Few of the international lawyers' assignments which we hypothesised in Chapter I and none of the non-adjudicatory decision functions can be discharged without a way of mapping the social process that enables the international lawyer to take vast amounts of "data" and to organise and interrelate them in ways that render them useful "information". When engaged in contextual-policy-based exercises, we always think we have a sense of the context. But unless disciplined by some framework of enquiry, our picture of the context is likely to be incomplete. The map which is deployed for identifying and organising data must also be able to focus on those parts of the context which are indispensable to the effective discharge of the lawyer's tasks.

Wertfrei Wissenschaft certainly has its place. But in this mode of decision, problem-orientation is necessary to avoid enquiries into questions that are undertaken only because they are "interesting" or "difficult" but that expend resources and energy without a corresponding contribution to the improvement of the arrangements whose dysfunctions are provoking injuries for which an alternative legal arrangement is demanded.

Methodology must be eclectic because the integrality of phenomena, goal-achievement discrepancies and feasible solutions involve many different features of the context. A multiplicity of analytical and remedial methods is required. In reviewing the what-it's-attached-to of international law, it was clear that the different dimensions which were summarised for purposes of illustration inter-stimulate, such that the selection of a single method that only addresses one dimension – no matter how powerful the intellectual tools it brings to bear – is prone to ignore factors that may be critical to correctly perceiving the problem and fashioning an effective solution. Attempting to solve problems by methods which are neither contextual nor multi-method increases the probability of engendering unintended – and undesired – consequences.

Now it is clear that the application of a contextual, problem-oriented and methodologically eclectic approach as a mode of decision requires the performance of a series of distinct but interrelated intellectual tasks that are not part of the textual-rule-based approach. These tasks, which are often performed intuitively, are a matter of common sense, but their specification is important because each is an indispensable part of an ensemble and the quality with which all of them are performed will determine the utility and relevance of any enquiry and the aptness of the solutions it proposes. The critical intellectual tasks include the following:

1. clarification of the goals of decision relevant to the problem being addressed;
2. description of the trends towards or away from the realisation of those goals;
3. analysis of the constellation of conditioning factors that appear to have affected past decision;
4. projection of a range of possible future developments, assuming no decision is taken; and
5. assuming that the most probable projections indicate that goals will not be achieved, the formulation of alternative strategies that can contribute, at minimum net cost and risk, to the realisation of preferred goals.

Although these tasks are a common sense praxis, brief comments on some of them will be useful.

Goals: Purposive behaviour requires a clarified objective. For the performance of some roles, the objective is relatively clear and constant: the litigator is committed to winning the case for the client, while negotiators seek to achieve as many of their principal's objectives as they can. The legislator is concerned with fashioning a legal instrument which will secure as many constituent political goals as possible.

International lawyers who are deploying the contextual-policy-based mode in various decision functions are discharging unique professional and citizenship roles [149]. Appraising and making recommendations for the improvement of the international legal system requires a set of goals as comprehensive as the system itself.

Trends and conditions: Anyone bent on achieving a particular objective will attempt to understand the extent to which that or similar objectives have been achieved or failed of achievement in the past. Lawyers applying the textual-rule-based mode are especially respectful of certain types of past trends. Past decisions may be useful indicators, but the lawyers' search for precedents errs when it assumes that past decisions will be replicated in the future. The potential wisdom to be gleaned from past precedents is adulterated if the decisions which they made are taken out of context. The point is that past decisions were not made in a vacuum; they were conditioned by a constellation of contextual factors that accounted for why they were taken and for the extent to which they succeeded or failed in terms of those factors. Many of those factors are not recited in the recitation of the decision; indeed, those making the decision may not have been explicitly conscious of them. If those factors are not operative in future situations, the lessons to be gleaned from the past decisions may be missed. A past decision may, indeed, be an indicator of how decisions will be taken in the future but only if the factors that accounted for that past decision are taken into account.

For example, human rights lawyers, keen to demonstrate that the "Responsibility to Protect" (R2P) has been accepted by the UN Security Council, might be inclined to cite the Council's decision in 2011 authorising States to take "all necessary means" to protect civilians in Libya as a decisive "precedent", showing that R2P has been accepted [150]. But that optimistic conclusion would overlook the unique conditions that accounted for the resolution, not the least being the general disenchantment and overt dislike of the Qaddafi regime, the Arab League's endorsement of international action, the European fear of a migratory outflow of refugees, and so on. Considered in the context

149. See *infra* Chapters XIV and XV.
150. See Alex J. Bellamy and Paul D. Williams, "The New Politics of Protection? Côte d'Ivoire, Libya and the Responsibility to Protect", *Int'l Aff.*, Vol. 87 (2011), p. 825 *et seq*.

of all the factors that attended it, the Security Council resolution might be seen as unusual, even aberrational, rather than a reliable predictor of future decision [151].

Projections: Routinely, people speak of "the future", which they often assume to be an uninterrupted continuation of that fragment of the "present" of which they are aware. But there is no such thing as "*the* future"; there are, at any moment, many possible futures, any one of which may eventuate depending on what actors do in a constantly eroding "present". The eventuation of a particular future is contingent on contemporary behaviour. The intellectual task of projection involves the generation of alternative imagined futures, ranging from the most utopic to the most dystopic. The constructs of alternative futures serve to indicate what steps are likely to increase the probability of the eventuation of a preferred future while minimising the likelihood of the eventuation of undesirable ones.

Alternatives: If the execution of the preceding intellectual tasks indicates the probability that a particular goal will not be achieved or the probability of the eventuation of an undesirable future, those deploying the contextual-policy-based mode undertake to invent and promote alternative strategies for increasing the probability of achieving goals [152]. The invention of alternatives does not exclude adjustments of goals or the timetables for their achievement.

A common international legal response to the perception of discrepancies between goals and projections is simply to draft a new treaty or establish a new institution, especially a court or tribunal. This is often undertaken without a prior contextual examination of the reasons for discrepancies between past and projected trends and goals and the role of existing legal arrangements themselves in that discrepancy. Consider the Robert Jennings and Arthur Watts's appraisal of international lawyers' response to the prospect of environmental accidents.

> "[T]he whole matter raises a serious legal question whether the international community can afford to go on attempting to deal with those problems by adapting, and supplementing by treaty, a legal system based essentially on establishing the delictual liability of certain respondents and assessing appropriate compensation. This, by itself at least, seems an inadequate way of tackling what is basically a question of public order, and accidents are likely to

151. See *infra* Chapter XIV.
152. See *infra* Chapter XIV.

have results not compensatable by damages. A delictual system is hardly designed to deal with things that ought not to be allowed to happen at all." [153]Solving a problem in the contextual-policy-based mode involves closing the gap between preference and projection. Concluding a new treaty or creating a new institution (especially a court) is often gratifying, and it certainly generates new jobs for lawyers. But such initiatives often do no more than add another layer of bureaucracy to an arrangement which has already demonstrated its ineffectiveness, while failing to address the actual reason for it. Sometimes a contextual examination of trends, conditions and projections may reveal that the problem can be traced to particular personnel or their performance rather than institutional design. Those responsible will often try to deflect it by blaming "the system". Sometimes the reason for the discrepancy is systemic, but especially then the creative invention of alternatives will require a richer palette of colours than more treaties, courts or commissions. Designing effective alternatives requires a map of the social process that sets out all the contextual features that can be manipulated.

Section 4. Mapping

The international lawyer, operating in the contextual-policy-based mode, needs an explicit frame of reference for mapping the relevant processes. The New Haven School has adapted, with a number of adjustments, a schema of cultural anthropology, in which any social process is described systematically in terms of those who engage in it (the participants), the subjective dimensions that animate them (their perspectives), the situations in which they interact, the resources upon which they draw (which include authority and power), the ways they manipulate those resources (their strategies) and the aggregate outcomes of the process of interaction.

The participants in any decision process include those formally endowed with decision competence, such as lawmakers, executives and judges, as well as all those other actors who, though not endowed with formal competence, may nonetheless play important roles in influencing decision outcomes. In international decision, depending on the problem addressed, the lawyer may have to examine (in addition to formal international institutions), State officials, NGOs, pressure

153. Robert Jennings and Arthur Watts (eds.), *Oppenheim's International Law*, 9th ed., 2008, at p. 415.

groups, the elites of multinational corporations, interest groups, gangs, militias, terrorist organisations and, of course, individuals, who act on behalf of other participants as well as on their own [154].

The inventory of participants, however comprehensive it may be, will not prove to be of much use if it does not take into account the subjectivities – the inner worlds – of these various actors. Such perspectives include their specific patterns of identification (and disidentification), their matter-of-fact expectations of past and future and the values they demand. In a complex and richly cross-cultural arena, the perspectives of the various participants actually playing a role in decision often diverge in critical ways, as was noted earlier [155].

The term "situations" refers to *where* decisions are actually being made. Conventional legal analysis generally looks to courts, secondarily examining the work of executive branches and legislatures. For some islands of the international legal archipelago, a focus confined in that fashion will suffice; for many offshore zones, it will not. The New Haven School uses an approach which focuses on the range of centralised and decentralised settings in which decisions are actually taken, their varying degree of organisation and formality, the extent to which they are specialised and the extent to which they are continuous or episodic. It is also important to examine the extent to which participants in a particular situation perceive themselves to be in a state of crisis, a situation in which values they view as critical for their survival are at stake. In crisis, actors, under stress, are prone to actions they might otherwise eschew. Widening the aperture of relevant situations is indispensable if one is to depict the archipelago of international law and identify all the varying zones in which contemporary international law is made and applied.

The resources on which participants draw to influence outcomes, their "bases of power", include all forms of effective power as well as symbols of authority. The ways in which resources are manipulated, or the strategies used by different participants, involve the management of bases of power with a view to securing preferred outcomes. Strategic modalities include military, economic, propagandistic and diplomatic techniques and are deployed in varying combinations.

Simply defining the outcomes of the process in terms of who "wins" and who "loses" is of limited utility for appraising the aggregate

---

154. See *infra* Chapter XI.
155. See *supra* Chapter II.

consequences for the entire community. Outcomes are more usefully measured in terms of all values: the allocation or reallocation of power, the production and distribution of wealth, well-being, enlightenment, skill, affection, respect and rectitude.

The frame of reference's mapping device of this sort of phase analysis, along with the basic concepts considered earlier, permits those trying to influence decision in the contextual-policy-based mode to orient themselves contextually in the relevant processes. A tool such as this may seem mechanical, but neurological studies have demonstrated the non-contextual character of observation [156]. Even without those scientific insights, lawyers know the perils inherent in the tendency to focus on matters that "seem" of primary importance at the moment and regularly rely on "checklists" to avoid overlooking important factors.

Contexts vary enormously and there can be no single one-size-fits-all map for every problem. Thus, the participants who will be relevant for a problem involving international security may include the major powers and their antagonists, those who can support or work against them in that context (whether State or non-State entities and whether within or outside them) and the international organisations or other institutions which may be relevant for some of the decision functions. For a problem involving international investment law in a particular context, the critical participants are likely to be the States concerned, factions within the Government, the opposition, productive and financial MNEs involved in a particular investment, religious leaders, labour and other interest groups in civil society, and the public and private institutions specialised to making and applying law for the transnational wealth process. For a currency crisis, the critical actors are likely to include, in addition to the IMF and the World Bank, the Bank for International Settlements, the European Central Bank, the Federal Reserve Bank and the national banks of the major economies, and the major private financial institutions. If you are trying to organise a failed State or install critical arrangements within it, the most relevant actors may include clan and tribal leaders, the leaders of private armies and criminal organisations. The point of emphasis is that this sort of functional approach enables the international lawyer, applying the contextual-policy-based mode of decision, to operate with a contextual and realistic sense of the relevant processes.

---

156. David Eagleman, *Incognito: The Secret Life of the Brain*, 2011, at p. 220.

CHAPTER VII

THE INTERNATIONAL LAW-APPLYING FUNCTION

> "Though the prevailing juristic science applies the term courts only to the state organs for the administration of justice with which it must concern itself professionally, the sociology of law when it defines the term court is concerned only with the question whether or not the institution involved performs the general functions of a court."
>
> Eugen Ehrlich [157]

Section 1. The scope of international application

Application is the decision function which puts prescriptions into effect in specific instances. Legal theories which identify law with courts and tribunals and the outcome of application as some form of judgment confine attention to a small number of formally authorised appliers: international courts and arbitral tribunals and a few other domestic tribunals which, thanks to the power of their States, sometimes operate as functional international tribunals. These are only part of the application function in the archipelago of international law. Effective appliers of international prescriptions function in all sectors and at all levels of the world social process.

In the broadest sense, every effective response to a cognitive association of some particular action or behaviour to an authoritative prescription contains some of the elements of an application. Indeed, where large numbers of individuals, each acting alone, respond to the same events in a similar way, we encounter a "market" phenomenon in which the aggregate of uncoordinated individual choices may, in certain contexts, constitute an effective application. The actions of those individuals are triggered by a perceived violation of what they believe is right, such that their uncoordinated but collective response is, with varying effectiveness, an application of law, though one lacking the procedural safeguards of a judicial or arbitral process. For much as the market "speaks" through the voices of large numbers of its members, an aggregate of participants of the international community, responding

157. Eugen Ehrlich, *Fundamental Principles of the Sociology of Law*, 1936, at p. 121.

to incidents involving international prescriptions its members deem critical to their interests, may, thus, make decisions.

Formal constitutions do not take account of such spontaneous and unorganised modes of application, but their constitutive *processes* often do. When political leaders solemnly refer to the actions of the "market" and adjust their own programmes to accommodate them, they are – without formally acknowledging it – treating the aggregate of uncoordinated individual choices as an essentially authoritative application. Where such mass yet uncoordinated responses are responding to an authoritative prescription which supports public order goals, we encounter events that are of significance to law. And where such mass responses can be provoked by invocation of international prescriptions, they acquire significance for the practice of international law.

The insistence on identifying the full range of informal as well as formal appliers in international law does not mean that all are equally authoritative. Nor is every informal application necessarily controlling, even less does each meet the procedural fairness criteria which are common to developed legal systems and are rooted in customary international law and contemporary human rights instruments. But process deficits – as lamentable as they are – do not necessarily mean that the applications are not perceived by those affected by them as authoritative.

International legal texts conceive of a much narrower range of application modalities. Article 33 (1) of the UN Charter provides:

> "The parties to any dispute, the continuance of which is likely to endanger the maintenance of international peace and security, shall, first of all, seek a solution by negotiation, enquiry, mediation, conciliation, arbitration, judicial settlement, resort to regional agencies or arrangements, or other peaceful means of their own choice." [158]

The imperative mood notwithstanding, all of those modalities are optional and depend on the consent of the States concerned. By contrast, Chapter VII of the Charter contemplates imposed settlements by the Security Council – through military means if the Council should deem them necessary – for events which the Council itself determines, on the basis of very general criteria, to be threats to the peace, breaches

158. UN Charter, *supra* footnote 108, Article 33, para. 1.

of the peace or acts of aggression. But for disputes which do not rise to that level and for whose peaceful resolution the protagonists do not consent, the Charter allows for their continued *non-resolution*. In the interdependent world to which international law is attached, this relic from an earlier type of constitutive process is unsatisfactory both as a framework for enquiry and as a policy. Unresolved bilateral disputes may now impose serious costs – "collateral damage" – on other States. There have been, as we will see, subtle but nonetheless far-reaching changes with respect to this pillar of international law.

Article 33 is far from a complete map of international application. A contextual focus reveals a much wider range of contemporary international appliers, from institutions *within* international organisations, such as the Security Council, the General Assembly, especially when it purports to exercise its "secondary competence", subordinate bodies created by international and regional organisations, specialised agencies, public-private partnerships, MNEs, banks and other private financial institutions and their associations, national officials, international courts and tribunals to which States have repaired and national courts, and the media and shifting congeries of unorganised participants whose reactions and demands function, in the aggregate, as a type of informal jury of international law.

In the development of national legal systems, the centralisation, monopolisation and professionalisation of application in public sectors, rather than its democratisation, is deemed positive. An urgent policy question is whether increased participation in the international *application* function should be encouraged, even though it is achieved at the cost of other important applicative policies, often summarised under the rubric of "due process". Or, alternatively, whether informal international application can somehow be made to approximate the key procedural standards, compliance with which international law demands of its formal appliers.

Section 2. The invocation function

Application, it will be recalled, is initiated by a prior decision function that we call invocation: it consists of processes which make provisional characterisations of certain behaviour inconsistent with relevant legal arrangements and demand that those authorised to perform application undertake it and, if it proves warranted, fashion an appropriate remedy. Non-State actors, in particular NGOs and individuals operating through the media, have become important participants in international invocation: a major newspaper, a television network, a widely read blog or a private cell phone photo that goes "viral" and exposes practices in secret prisons or violent repression of public demonstrations in authoritarian or dictatorial systems. These are all invocations, inasmuch as events are brought to the attention of politically relevant strata and are provisionally characterised, whether explicitly or implicitly, as inconsistent with what is legally required, and an application of those legal requirements is demanded.

More formalised invocations are effected by bringing a matter to the Security Council, by submitting a notice of arbitration under a bilateral investment treaty or the General Agreement on Tariffs and Trade (GATT) or by initiating suit in a national court whose jurisdiction extends to events that involve international issues. Given the availability of electronic communications to more and more people and the operation of what Malcolm Gladwell has nicely termed the "tipping point" phenomenon [159], the possibilities of invoking international decision have undergone a process of democratisation parallel to the one which we tracked in our examination of contemporary international lawmaking. A wider range of groups and individuals in the international political process can participate in invocation.

International invokers who are passionate about an issue frequently mimic the language of application, but invocation is distinguished from application because, at its core, invocation does not involve a thorough investigation and does not culminate in an effective decision involving the specification of policy to a rigorously confirmed set of facts and its implementation; many invokers lack the wherewithal of effective appliers and can only draw attention to an alleged violation and try to provoke a process of application.

If successful, an invocation initiates an application which then puts into effect the prescriptions which have been invoked. Many invocations fail to trigger an application and many international legal applications, which were successfully invoked, still fail to produce an authoritative and controlling application. In some instances, the failure occurs because it is later determined that the invokers were incorrect in their provisional assessments or failed to persuade appliers of either the facts or law on which their invocation was based. In other instances, the invocation may have been factually and legally well founded but the

---

159. Malcolm Gladwell, *The Tipping Point: How Little Things Can Make a Big Difference*, 2000.

application will have failed to proceed because the putative international applier found itself without jurisdiction or without the power or other resources necessary to follow through.

Section 3. Differing scopes of authority

Three recurring issues in lawful application are the scope of authority of the applier, the fidelity required of the applier to the relevant prescriptions and the use of the appropriate mode of decision-making, textual-rule-based or contextual-policy-based. In principle, one would wish high quotients in each of these dimensions. But given the complexity and volatility of the international legal system, incorporating, as it does, a wide range of formal and functional appliers, the formal authority accorded to particular appliers may vary; nor is it always clear which mode of principled decision-making a particular applier is actually applying.

The UN Security Council enjoys an explicit authority to make decisions for the maintenance or restoration of minimum order. But, as noted in the previous chapter, the performance of this function does not involve the mechanical application of a few prescriptions or rules; deploying the contextual-policy-based mode of decision, the Council must, instead, fall back on the most fundamental minimum order policies of international law, applied with sensitivity to the potentialities and limitations of the context *and* to the aggregate consequences which alternative decision options will have on those policies. Judges of the ICJ have explicit authority to decide matters properly submitted to the Court but, by contrast to the Security Council, the judges are supposed to confine themselves to specific prescriptions, whether decided in advance by the parties or itemised in Article 38 of the Statute, the Court's choice-of-law clause. Both the Security Council and the ICJ are "legal" decision-makers, and both apply international law. Yet, as explained in the preceding chapter, they may produce quite different though equally lawful decisions in the same or in cognate cases.

Only consider a paradigmatic situation like that encountered in the *Wall* opinion: the Council was seised of a matter under its Chapter VII competence, while the General Assembly, under its own Charter authority and animated by a different view of events, petitioned the ICJ for an advisory opinion [160]. The Court confirmed that the question which the Assembly had submitted was within its competence and then

160. *Legal Consequences of the Construction of a Wall in the Occupied Palestinian Territory*, Advisory Opinion, 9 July 2004 ICJ Reports 2004, p. 136 (hereafter *The Wall*).

it purported to apply Article 38 of its Statute to the matter. Yet because of the different modes of principled decision-making which these various entities used, it was possible for the Court to issue an opinion different in content from the decisions taken by the Council in the same matter. Yet each would be an authoritative application of international law.

In circumstances in which the Security Council finds that there has been a threat to the peace, breach of the peace or act of aggression, extraordinary powers are assigned to it. In the discharge of all of its security functions, the Council is expected to take account of the widest context, the goals and policies of the international community which the dispute before it engages and then to fashion a decision that promises to secure as great an approximation as possible of the minimum and optimum order goals of the international community. In discharging this function, the Council's decision may, in accordance with Charter Article 103, supersede existing treaty obligations of the parties. Indeed, it may, by intentional inaction, even supersede a decision of the Court. For when the Council is called upon to enforce a judgment of the ICJ under Article 94 (2), far from serving as the bailiff of the Court, drafters of the Charter assigned a broad discretion to the Council.

Given the inevitable discretion in critical sequential phases of any application, normative arrangements usually prescribe how and for what purposes that discretion is to be exercised. For judges of the ICJ, for example, a solemn declaration is made upon assuming their posts. International arbitrators do not ordinarily take oaths on commencing their duties, but in most systems they sign a declaration at the time of appointment, which functions as its equivalent. Paradoxically, those persons who serve in the Security Council, the most powerful international applier, make no comparable declaration. Indeed, the Charter provides no normative instructions to individuals as to how the powers of the Council are to be discharged. This reflects an unresolved tension in contemporary international law. The most powerful States are indispensable to the operation of the collective security mechanisms of the world community but are not normatively proscribed from using the powers to promote national interests [161].

Section 4. Are there constitutional limits?

Given the multiplicity of appliers and the likelihood of inconsistent applications for the same matter, is there an international applier "of

161. See *infra* Chapter XVI.

last instance"? If so, is it the Council or the Court? Or neither of them?

Article 25 of the Charter obliges Member States to "accept and carry out" Chapter VII decisions of the Council, and the Charter explicitly superordinates Council decisions taken under Chapter VII over other treaty obligations. But the Charter provides no indication as to whether the Council, acting under Chapter VII, has been empowered to ignore or contravene principles of customary international law or even *jus cogens*. Were the Council to decide, in a particular case, to act in violation of a principle of customary international law, are there guards to guard them?

In some municipal constitutional systems, some courts have been assigned or have assumed that type of competence with respect to the other branches of Government. In some advisory opinions, the ICJ has been requested to assess the lawfulness of an action taken by another organ of the United Nations, but it has never found a violation. In the *Lockerbie* case, in the exercise of its contentious jurisdiction, the Court danced around such a possibility. Some separate opinions in *Lockerbie* addressed the constitutional issues more directly, but, whether in concurrence or dissent, seem to have done little more than intimate a position in favour of a limited constitutional review role. The mood of oddly resigned judicial detachment was best captured by Judge Shahabuddeen in his separate opinion:

> "Are there any limits to the Council's powers of appreciation? In the equilibrium of forces underpinning the structure of the United Nations within the evolving international order, is there any conceivable point beyond which a legal issue may properly arise as to the competence of the Security Council to produce such overriding results? If there are any limits, what are those limits and what body, if other than the Security Council, is competent to say what those limits are?
>
> If the answers to these delicate and complex questions are all in the negative, the position is potentially curious. It would not, on that account, be necessarily unsustainable in law; and how far the Court can enter the field is another matter." [162]

162. *Questions of Interpretation and Application of the 1971 Montreal Convention arising from the Aerial Incident at Lockerbie (Libya* v. *UK; Libya* v. *US)*, Provisional Measures, 27 February 1992, ICJ Reports 1992, p. 140, at 142 (Separate Opinion of Judge Shahabuddeen).

Judge Shahabuddeen concluded his recital of provocative questions by remarking that they were important but could not then be examined.

In the international effort to restrain Salafist terrorism, the Council, basing itself on its Chapter VII authority, has installed asset-freezing programmes which cut deeply into domestic legal arrangements, some of which derive from hard-fought and jealously guarded judicial protections in international law [163]. National and regional courts have reviewed those Council arrangements and, in some instances, have held them to violate important human rights [164].

Now some of the Security Council's freezing arrangements clearly raise serious (but potentially remediable) human rights questions which the Council itself had failed to address adequately. At the same time, the effectiveness of the Council and, more generally, the security function of the United Nations would appear best served by requiring that Council decisions under Chapter VII be treated as insulated from review and non-implementation by the organs of Member States. Whether the *Kadi* cases are part of a testing process that will lead the Council belatedly to make meaningful adjustments in its freezing arrangements or whether they signal an undoing of the authority of the Council under Chapter VII and a fundamental constitutive adjustment remains to be seen.

Section 5. Consent as a prerequisite for application

A growing network of international courts and standing and *ad hoc* tribunals enjoy competences assigned to them by the treaties which created them or by special agreements between litigating States or between private parties *inter se*.

These institutions have a more restricted applicative competence than the principal organs of the United Nations. They all purport to apply the textual-rule-based mode of decision and to operate within the islands of international law, and their procedures are expected to adhere to international standards of due process. In theory, their jurisdiction is based on consent, but here the tectonic plates of the system have been shifting subtly.

---

163. See e.g. SC Res. 1973, 17 March 2011 (Libya); SC Res. 1929, 9 June 2010 (Iran); SC Res. 1844, 20 November 2008 (Som.); SC Res. 1636, 31 October 2005 (Leb.); SC Res. 1591, 29 March 2005 (Sudan); SC Res. 1572, 14 November 2004 (Côte d'Ivoire); SC Res. 1718, 14 October 2006 (N. Kor.); SC Res. 1596, 3 May 2005 (Dem. Rep. Congo); SC Res. 1521, 22 December 2003 (Liber.).

164. *Kadi and Al Barakaat International Foundation* v. *Council of the European Union*, Joined Cases C-402/05 P and C-415/05 P, 2008 ECR I-06351, para. 353.

As long as jurisdiction is based on consent, relatively few cases will be brought to the formal applicative modes of adjudication and arbitration. In general, it is difficult for democratic Governments to make decisions, requiring, as they do, the approval of many ministries and departments, not to speak of stakeholders outside the formal governmental structure. In the modalities of negotiation, mediation and conciliation, a Government need not accept a proposed result if its costs exceed the hoped-for benefits from resolution of the dispute. By contrast, submitting to arbitration and adjudication imports a prospective decision that will be either a clear win or loss. If the law is not clear, as is often the case in a system as dynamic and dialectical as international law, or if the judicial or arbitral institution in question cannot be trusted to confine itself to application by means of the textual-rule-based mode, a State may not only lose its case, a risk which can be assessed and contingently accepted before it agrees to adjudicate, but it may be presented with a decision exceeding the downside risk which it had originally estimated and discounted. This may outweigh the prospective advantages of resolving the dispute.

In the light of considerations of this sort, States have insisted that jurisdiction for those "win-or-lose" third-party decisions be based on their prior consent. For a long time, tribunals were disposed to respect that condition. In *Mavrommatis Palestine Concessions*, Judge John Bassett Moore said famously:

> "The international judicial tribunals so far created have been tribunals of limited powers. Therefore no presumption in favour of their jurisdiction may be indulged. Their jurisdiction must always affirmatively appear on the face of the record." [165]

This oft-repeated statement notwithstanding, one can detect, in the law-in-practice, a gradual trend towards "compulsorisation" of judicial and arbitral jurisdiction in key areas. This is transpiring in five ways.

First, in a number of cases, the ICJ has simply ignored Judge Moore's dictum. Consider, for example, the jurisdictional phase of *Qatar* v. *Bahrain* and contrast it with the Court's earlier holding in the *Aegean* case [166].

165. *Mavrommatis Palestine Concessions (Greece* v. *UK)*, Judgment, 30 August 1924, PCIJ (Ser. B), No. 3, at p. 60.

166. Compare: *Maritime Delimitation and Territorial Questions between Qatar and Bahrain (Qatar* v. *Bahr.)*, Judgment, 1 July 1994, ICJ Reports 1994, p. 112; with: *Aegean Sea Continental Shelf (Greece* v. *Turk.)*, Judgment, 19 December 1978, ICJ Reports 1978, p. 3.

Second, while subscription to the Statute's optional clause has not increased [167] and has suffered defections by those permanent members of the Security Council who had been subscribers,[168] a number of important conventions have adopted compulsory jurisdiction clauses [169]. To be sure, none of these examples constitutes a jurisdictional *carte blanche*; exceptions have been carefully carved out.

Third, some tribunals are staking claims to jurisdiction in areas which States parties have *explicitly* excluded. In the *Southern Blue Fin Tuna* case, a major arbitral award illuminating the jurisdictional scheme of the United Nations Convention on the Law of the Sea (UNCLOS), the Tribunal, while finding itself without jurisdiction, stated:

> "The Tribunal does not exclude the possibility that there might be instances in which the conduct of a State Party to UNCLOS and to a fisheries treaty implementing it would be so egregious, and risk consequences of such gravity, that a Tribunal might find that the obligations of UNCLOS provide a basis for jurisdiction, having particular regard to the provisions of article 300 of UNCLOS. While Australia and New Zealand in the proceedings before ITLOS [International Tribunal for the Law of the Sea] invoked article 300, in the proceedings before this Tribunal they made clear that they do not hold Japan to any independent breach of an obligation to act in good faith." [170]

The good faith provision to which the Tribunal referred, Article 300 of UNCLOS, provides:

---

167. ICJ, "Declarations Recognizing the Jurisdiction of the Court as Compulsory", https://www.icj-cij.org/en/declarations.

168. France denounced its optional declaration after *Nuclear Tests*, and the United States denounced the Truman Declaration in the midst of the *Nicaragua* case. *Nuclear Tests (Austl.* v. *Fr.)*, Judgment, 20 December 1974, ICJ Reports 1974, p. 253; *Nuclear Tests (New Zealand* v. *Fr.)*, Judgment, 20 December 1974, ICJ Reports 1974, p. 457 (hereafter *Nuclear Tests*); *Nicaragua*, *supra* footnote 110. The United Kingdom has further amputated its Declaration in response to the prospect of adverse judgments. Sir Alan Duncan, Amendments to the UK's Optional Clause Declaration to the International Court of Justice, United Kingdom Foreign and Commonwealth Office, 23 February 2017, https://questions-statements.parliament.uk/written-statements/detail/2017-02-23/HCWS489.

169. See e.g. Convention for the Protection of the Marine Environment of the North-East Atlantic, 22 September 1992, 32 ILM 1069 (hereafter OSPAR Convention), https://www.ospar.org/site/assets/files/1290/ospar_convention_e_updated_text_in_2007_no_revs.pdf; United Nations Convention on the Law of the Sea, 10 December 1982, 1833 UNTS 3 (hereafter UNCLOS), Part XV.

170. *Southern Bluefin Tuna Case (Austl. & NZ* v. *Japan)*, Award on Jurisdiction and Admissibility, Arbitral Tribunal constituted under Annex VII UNCLOS, 4 August 2000, 39 ILM 1359.

> "States Parties shall fulfill in good faith the obligations assumed under this Convention and shall exercise the rights, jurisdiction and freedoms recognized in this Convention in a manner which would not constitute an abuse of right." [171]

This seems a rather slender basis upon which to build such a sweeping revision of international jurisdiction. Under the old paradigm, objecting to jurisdiction could not have been "abusive", as there was no default obligation to resort to third-party dispute resolution. But the passage in *Southern Blue Fin Tuna* provides a fascinating insight into how seasoned international judges may be beginning to think that urgent international needs can trump the absence of consent and, in its place, serve as a basis for jurisdiction over States whose consent seemed dubious. Whether a non-consenting State will comply with the assertion of jurisdiction is another matter.

So much for Judge Moore's theory of jurisdiction based on consent!

The breath-taking dictum in *Southern Blue Fin Tuna* may be contrasted with the ICJ's statement in the *Genocide Convention* case:

> "The Court . . . has no power to rule on alleged breaches of other obligations under international law, not amounting to genocide, particularly those protecting human rights in armed conflict. That is so even if the alleged breaches are of obligations under peremptory norms, or of obligations which protect essential humanitarian values, and which may be owed *erga omnes*." [172]

Yet the Court has itself engaged in a compulsorisation of jurisdiction through other means, which will be considered in a moment.

The fourth indication of compulsorisation is to be found in the practice of international tribunals of issuing thoroughly reasoned *substantive* decisions while disclaiming jurisdiction. The two most dramatic examples of this phenomenon are the *Oil Platforms* case before the ICJ and the *Loewen* case before a North American Free Trade Agreement (NAFTA) Tribunal. In both instances, the Tribunal in question effectively found itself without jurisdiction but proceeded to deliver an elaborate decision on the merits, ostensibly as an *obiter dictum* [173].

---

171. UNCLOS, *supra* footnote 169, Article 300.

172. *Application of the Convention on the Prevention and Punishment of the Crime of Genocide (Bosn. & Herz.* v. *Serb. and Montenegro)*, Judgment, 26 February 2007, ICJ Reports 2007, p. 47 (hereafter *Bosnian Genocide case*), at para. 55.

173. *Oil Platforms (Iran* v. *US)*, Judgment, 12 December 1996, ICJ Reports 1996, p. 803; *Loewen Group, Inc. and Raymond L. Loewen* v. *United States*, Award, 26 June 2003, ICSID Case No. ARB (AF)/98/3.

Now, to appreciate the significance of *obiter dicta* in international law, it is necessary to put this curious judicial practice in its international context. Disputes in international investment law are about money, but in major inter-State cases in public international law the applicant rarely seeks or secures a money judgment; even if there is a money judgment, it is rarely what these cases are principally about. They usually seek an authoritative condemnation or vindication at the political level. If there is a money judgment, *Chorzów Factory* notwithstanding, money damages are more often than not symbolic rather than truly reparative and virtually never erase the harm. So, from this angle, these "jurisdictionless" *dicta* on the merits may be, in effect, meaningful decisions in cases in which the tribunal acknowledges that one of the parties has not consented to jurisdiction.

The fifth indication of compulsorisation of jurisdiction is to be found in the transformation of advisory opinions into decisions that are supposed to be reserved for the ICJ's contentious jurisdiction. The doctrine enunciated by the Permanent Court of International Justice (PCIJ) in the *Eastern Carelia* opinion is, for all intents and purposes, dead [174]. *Namibia* [175], *Western Sahara* [176], *Legality of Nuclear Weapons* [177] and, most dramatically, the *Wall* [178] were all grounded in active disputes, decided not only without consent but in two instances over the strong protest of the State parties in interest. The *Wall* opinion actually issued an order to a party in interest which had objected to jurisdiction [179]!

Is this a positive constitutive development?

The consent requirement for international adjudication has often been criticised as atavistic and an obstacle to the evolution of international law. But, in the context of an international political system which lacks a sheriff, one of the contributions of the consent requirement has been that, though it limits the number of cases going to adjudication, it obviates enforcement and virtually ensures compliance; each compliance with an international judgment helps to reinforce the law in dispute and, at the constitutive level, the effectiveness and legitimacy

174. *Status of Eastern Carelia*, Advisory Opinion, 23 July 1923, PCIJ (Ser. B), No. 5.

175. *Legal Consequences for States of the Continued Presence of South Africa in Namibia (South West Africa) notwithstanding Security Council Resolution 276*, Advisory Opinion, 21 June 1971, ICJ Reports 1971, p. 16 (hereafter *Namibia*).

176. *Western Sahara*, Advisory Opinion, 16 October 1975, ICJ Reports 1975, p. 12 (hereafter *Western Sahara*).

177. *Legality of Nuclear Weapons*, *supra* footnote 113, at para. 66.

178. *The Wall*, *supra* footnote 160.

179. *Id.*, at para. 163 (3) (B)-(C).

of international decision. States would not consent to binding third-party decision of specific disputes unless they had gauged the upside and downside of a probable judgment and calculated that, even if they were to lose and suffer the downside, they would still be net better off losing and eliminating the dispute as an irritant in bilateral relations than they would be continuing without a festering dispute, with all the political and economic costs it entails. With each litigant entertaining these types of strategic calculations, as long as the court or tribunal to which they repaired or which they specially created respected their qualified consent and did not exceed the common upside/downside risk spread, whoever proved to be the loser could be counted on to comply with the decision.

As the consent requirement for the exercise of jurisdiction withers, however, enforcement or implementation becomes an increasing challenge. This is part of a larger shift in international law over the past century from a system in which effectiveness translates to rights into a system in which rights are created without regard to effectiveness and are then expected to be somehow *made* effective [180]. But the evolution of jurisdiction without consent and the production of decisions without enforcement becomes part of an even more complex political reality.

More cases may be brought by international norm entrepreneurs as strategic components of their long-term political programmes; the entrepreneurs will not expect that a specific judgment or opinion will resolve a dispute or remedy a pathological situation but instead hope that a favourable judgment will enhance the authority of their political programme, contribute, in the long term, to its installation as effective law and, not least, burnish their professional reputations. Consider in this regard, *Namibia* [181], the *Wall* case [182], *Nicaragua* [183], *Nuclear Tests* [184], *Legality of Nuclear Weapons* [185], *South China Sea* and the three capital punishment cases lodged against the United States on the basis of the Optional Protocol to the Vienna Convention on Consular Relations [186].

180. See *infra* Chapter VIII.
181. *Namibia*, *supra* footnote 175.
182. *The Wall*, *supra* footnote 160.
183. *Nicaragua*, *supra* footnote 110.
184. *Nuclear Tests*, *supra* footnote 168.
185. *Legality of Nuclear Weapons*, *supra* footnote 113.
186. *Avena and Other Mexican Nationals (Mex.* v. *US)*, Judgment, 31 March 2004, ICJ Reports 2004, p. 12; *LaGrand (Ger.* v. *US)*, Judgment, 27 June 2001, ICJ Reports 2001, p. 466; *Vienna Convention on Consular Relations (Para.* v. *US)*, Order, 10 November 1998, ICJ Reports 1998, p. 426.

This trend has consequences both for States and for public international tribunals. For States, it means that alongside the traditional elective arbitration in which two States agree to submit a dispute to third-party decision with the expectation that the loser can and will comply, a new form of application has been added. States in the twenty-first century are likely to find themselves as respondents in cases in which they have *not* made the *a priori* calculation that acquiescing to jurisdiction is strategically sound because, win or lose, they will be net better off if the dispute is resolved. In addition, as we saw in the preceding chapter, more courts and tribunals apply the contextual-policy-based mode rather than the textual-rule-based mode. This bodes to exacerbate the enforcement or implementation phase [187].

International lawyers in the twenty-first century may anticipate this problem by building *a priori* enforcement solutions which obviate *post hoc* compliance. Consider, in this regard, the Iran-United States Algiers Accord; it established and funded a pay-out mechanism even before the Claims Tribunal had commenced its operations and had rendered a single award [188]. In a different arena, Article 52 *ad hoc* committees under the International Centre for Settlement of Investment Disputes (ICSID) Convention have required a performance bond before commencing their review.

This development also presents quandaries to the international lawyers who compose courts and tribunals. When States or NGOs judicialise political conflicts or press internationally popular political issues before international courts and tribunals without the consent of the respondent, those institutions find themselves impaled on the horns of a dilemma. If they apply strictly what they believe to be the law and decline jurisdiction or decide against the party trying to judicialise a popular political issue, they are likely to be roundly criticised by the political bodies that appoint their members and fund their budgets. Recall, in this regard, the withering criticism which the General Assembly directed at the judges of the ICJ after the 1966 judgment in the *South West Africa* case and the Court's *volte face* in the *Namibia*

187. *Land and Maritime Boundary between Cameroon and Nigeria (Cameroon* v. *Nigeria)*, Judgment, 10 October 2002, ICJ Reports 2002, p. 303; *Jus ad Bellum – Ethiopia's Claims 1-8*, Partial Award of the Eritrea-Ethiopia Claims Comm'n, Decision of 19 December 2006, 45 ILM 430; *Abyei Arbitration (Gov't of Sudan* v. *Sudan Peoples' Liberation Movement/Army)*, Final Award, 22 July 2009, PCA Case No. 2008-07.

188. See *Iran-United States: Settlement of the Hostage Crisis*, 18-20 January 1981, 20 ILM 223.

opinion in 1971 [189]. If, however, the Court anticipates this reaction and makes a manifestly political decision, as many believe it did in the *Wall* opinion, then it presents itself as an unreliable forum for States that seek a classic neutral forum to apply their choice of law to the resolution of a dispute they contemplate submitting.

One of the responses to this quandary has been the development of a "signalling" function by the ICJ. In the *Interhandel* case, the Court declined, implausibly, to find that after almost two decades of pursuit of justice in the American legal system, the Swiss corporation Interhandel had still failed to exhaust domestic remedies [190]. But by pointedly affirming its confidence in the US justice system, the Court signalled to the respondent its own expectation. Shortly after the Court's decision on admissibility, the United States settled the case.

In the *Nuclear Tests* cases between Australia and New Zealand on the one hand, and France on the other, the Court, after rather impetuously finding sufficient jurisdiction to issue a mild interim measure, managed to evade the embarrassment of an open defiance of its decision by exchanging subtle signals with France that enabled France to acquiesce to the substance of the treaty in issue while allowing the Court to find the dispute moot [191].

These changes have led to a number of corresponding changes in the application function. Rendering decisions in complex and volatile political contexts increasingly draws international courts and tribunals into the political process. They may actually apply the contextual-policy-based mode rather than the textual-rule-based mode but redact their judgments and opinions as if they were decided by rule application. In many instances, these judgments and awards are not likely to be enforced in a strict sense.

---

189. *South West Africa (Liberia* v. *South Africa)*, Judgment, 18 July 1966, ICJ Reports 1966, p. 6; *Namibia, supra* footnote 175; also John Dugard, *The South West Africa/Namibia Dispute: Documents and Scholarly Writings on the Controversy between South Africa and the United Nations*, 1973, at pp. 484-489 (analysing international responses to the *Namibia* opinion); Leo Gross, "Conclusions", in *id.*, *The Future of the International Court of Justice*, Vol. 2, 1976, p. 727 *et seq.*, at 747 (describing the ICJ's *volte face* between the *South West Africa* and *Namibia* cases as the "nadir" of the ICJ's fortunes); Richard A. Falk, "The South West Africa Cases: An Appraisal", *Int'l Org.*, Vol. 21 (1967), p. 1 *et seq.*, at 18-21 (discussing the unpopularity of the 1966 decision).

190. *Interhandel (Switz.* v. *US)*, Judgment, 21 March 1959, ICJ Reports 1959, p. 6.

191. *Nuclear Tests (Austl.* v. *Fr.)*, Order, 22 June 1973, ICJ Reports 1973, p. 98; *Nuclear Tests, supra* footnote 168.

Section 6. Appliers as prescribers

The remarkable trends and projections of the democratisation of international lawmaking which we reviewed in Chapter V raises the question of whether international courts and tribunals, the quintessential law-appliers in international law's principal island, should join the trend and, when seised of disputes, become opportunistic lawmaking institutions. Sir Robert Jennings, who served as President of the ICJ, wrote:

> "*Ad hoc* tribunals can settle particular disputes; but the function of the established 'principal judicial organ of the United Nations' must include not only the settlement of disputes but also the scientific development of general international law . . . there is therefore nothing strange in the ICJ fulfilling a similar function for the international community." [192]

Apparently, this broad self-assignment is not to be confined to the ICJ. In speaking of international maritime boundary law, Judge Rüdiger Wolfrum declared:

> "It is the feature of this law not to be static but to be open for a progressive development by the international courts and tribunals concerned. It is the responsibility of these international courts and tribunals not only to decide delimitation cases while remaining within the framework of such *acquis judiciares* but also to prove for the progressive development of the latter." [193]

Now, obviously, a decision institution that reasons its awards and then publishes them will ineluctably affect expectations. When the PCIJ was being designed, Arthur Balfour, surely thinking of a court far more restrained than one afire with a mission of "scientific development of general international law", still observed that "the decision of the Permanent Court cannot but have the effect of gradually moulding and modifying international law" [194]. And he added cryptically, "This may be good or bad".

---

192. *East Timor (Port.* v. *Austl.)*, Judgment, 30 June 1995, ICJ Reports 1995, p. 90 (hereafter *East Timor*), at 133-134 (Separate Opinion of Judge Ranjeva) (citing Sir Robert Jennings, *The Role of the International Court of Justice in the Development of International Environmental Protection Law*, 1992).

193. *Dispute concerning Delimitation of the Maritime Boundary between Bangladesh and Myanmar in the Bay of Bengal (Bangl./Myan.)*, Judgment, 14 March 2012, ITLOS Reports, p. 4, at para. 137 (Declaration of Judge Wolfrum).

194. *Continental Shelf (Tunis./Libya)*, Judgment, 21 April 1981, ICJ Reports 1981, p. 3, 29 (Separate Opinion of Judge Oda) (citing PCIJ Documents Concerning the

The response to Balfour's doubt must be that it is a good thing for courts, along with scholars and civil society in general, *to contribute* to the ongoing process of formation of international law through the persuasiveness of their proposals. Judges Jennings and Wolfrum, by contrast, were speaking of a self-conscious vocation of international tribunals to make new law or to legislate. Is there a Charter-based or, for that matter, customary international law mandate for the ICJ to engage in the "scientific development of general international law"? That would be quite different from Balfour's anticipation of a role "gradually moulding and modifying international law" and could have unintended consequences with respect to the role of international tribunals. In a consensual system, will States, who are not compelled to submit to jurisdiction, beat a path to the doors of appliers who hold themselves out as competent to make and retroactively apply new law to the disputes before them?

The contemporary international lawmaking process is, as we have seen, a far richer, coaxial process of communication in which messages of content, authority and control intention are modulated among all politically relevant actors, who, in the aggregate, are continuously making assessments of whether prescriptions have been established, are being maintained or have been terminated. This is a dialectical process of wide participation and myriad patterns of give and take. Should international judges, who certainly have a superior understanding of some aspects of international law, also consider themselves active participants in this lawmaking process by using the cases which come before them as opportunities for international lawmaking?

For a court or tribunal of specific powers – especially one that has been endowed with a choice-of-law clause, such as Article 38 of the Statute – and one whose docket depends on the consent of the parties who appear before it, the self-assignment of a new power of using resolution of disputes submitted for law-application as an opportunity for changing (and retroactively applying) the law contradicts the idea of specific powers to decide a case by reference to law rather than equity. Unless, that is, part of the function of international courts and tribunals is to engage in the "progressive development of international law".

It is difficult to see where the judges might find such an authorisation. The Court does not engage in the give and take of the contemporary

---

Action Taken by the Council of the League of Nations under Article 14 of the Covenant).

lawmaking process. For the Court, moreover, unlike the International Law Commission, there is no entity that serves (as does the General Assembly for the ILC) as an *ad referendum* principal which can review proposed prescriptions before they become law. The Court's decisions are final and unappealable. Nor is the Court endowed with an explicit or implied authority to make law. The Charter does not authorise the Court to engage in this function. Article 38 of the Statute of the Court – the choice-of-law clause of that Tribunal – states that its "function is to decide in accordance with international law". If Article 38 stopped there, one might argue that "international law" has come, by operation of customary law, to include some sort of general "progressive development" competence. But Article 38 proceeds to designate the material to which the Court is to have reference. It makes no mention of progressive development.

Any international arbitral body is ordinarily expected to resolve a routine dispute by reference to the governing law which the parties expect, using the textual-rule-based mode. Should the ICJ be any different? To be sure, litigants may explicitly authorise the Court and similar entities to look beyond *lex lata*, as occurred in the *Tunisia/Libya Continental Shelf* case, and the parties may also authorise the Court to ignore the law and to decide *ex aequo et bono* [195]. And, implicitly, parties may authorise a court or other implementing agency to elaborate and supplement when the assignment is the application of an instrument of general provisions (for example, certain human rights instruments or an investment treaty containing a broad concept such as "fair and equitable treatment") to a wide range of factual situations, not all of whose contingencies can be anticipated [196].

Parties, whether in international or national law, referring disputes to a tribunal, and not one of the other modalities of dispute resolution, presumably want a legal answer. If existing prescriptions or the compromissory formulations do not allow for an answer, some judicial creativity is appropriate, or the alternative would be a judgment of *non liquet* [197]. But, properly understood, *non liquet* is an extremely rare occurrence because no formal legal system and no code prescribes for

195. *Continental Shelf (Tunis./Libya)*, Judgment, 24 February 1982, ICJ Reports 1982, p. 18, at 23 (Article I of Compromise).

196. See Reisman, "Canute Confronts the Tide", *supra* footnote 129, at p. 634.

197. See *Boundary Dispute Concerning the Taba Area*, Award of the Egypt-Isr. Arb. Tribunal, 29 September 1988, 27 ILM 1421. See W. Michael Reisman, *Fraudulent Evidence Before Public International Tribunals: The Dirty Stories of International Law*, 2014.

every eventuality. The law is full of "holes" which decision-makers, applying the textual-rule-based mode, are constantly and routinely plugging by analogy, teleology, the application of more general community policies and all the other modes of generative logic that constitute the juridical method in this mode of decision. But do those *ad hoc* improvisations, while binding the parties, become law for everyone else?

Only when it becomes clear that no accepted community policy exists and that the community has decided to leave certain matters or sectors unregulated or in a "civic order" [198], and the legal system does not instruct the court to act as a legislator in these circumstances [199], does the question of rendering a judgment of *non liquet* arise.

There may be circumstances in which: (1) the relevant community has not arrived at a decision regarding regulation of a certain problem or sector; (2) the community is prepared *faute de mieux* to live with the resulting costs and consequences; and (3) politically significant groups are unwilling to acquiesce in the imposition of a legal regime on the as yet unregulated issue. For these circumstances, *non liquet* shares a place with discretionary judicial self-limitations such as the political question doctrine, non-justiciability, findings of the absence of a dispute and the doctrine of inherent limitations of the judicial function, as developed by the ICJ in the *Northern Cameroons* case [200].

Does an international court, notwithstanding this general practice, have an implied licence to legislate or "progressively develop" international law in the cases that come before it? Since the ICJ requires an explicit authorisation to engage in decision *ex aequo et bono*, it seems clear that the Statute was not intended to bestow a general power of equitable decision. As Professor Tomuschat has put it,

> "although international law evolves in a creeping process similar to the growth of common law, where judges take new directions and open up new horizons, they are invariably required to act *lege*

198. Myres S. McDougal, Harold D. Lasswell and Lung-chu Chen, "Nationality and Human Rights: The Protection of the Individual in External Arenas", *Yale LJ*, Vol. 83 (1974), p. 900 *et seq.*

199. As does Switzerland: "A défaut d'une disposition légale applicable, le juge prononce selon le droit coutumier et à défaut d'une coutume, selon les règles qu'il etablirait s'il avait à faire acte de législateur". Constitution fédérale, RO 101, Article 1 (Switzerland). But, significantly, the last paragraph of Article 1 obliges the judge performing this role to be guided by appointed legal doctrine and case law, suggesting that a more limited supplementation rather than an extensive revision is contemplated.

200. *Northern Cameroons (Cameroon* v. *UK)*, Judgment, 2 December 1963, ICJ Reports 1963, p. 15.

> *artis* in the (sometimes erroneous) belief that the rule applied was developed in a constructive effort to synthesize elements in force as component parts of the legal order. Judges are not called upon to act with the explicit intention to create new law. If they do so, they fail in their professional duties" [201].

The proper international judicial role, it is submitted, is neither a general lawmaking role under the rubric of "progressive development" nor the caricature of blind application of "rules", legislation or agreements. It is, rather, a conception of a judicial role, restricted like any other, with limitations that are accepted and honoured by the role player. Within this role, the textual-rule-based mode is employed. Substantive rules are seen as communications carrying relevant and authoritative policy information that must be shaped to the idiosyncratic texture of each controversy, to provide a decision that best approximates the minimum order and larger policy objectives of the community. This is no easy task, not the least because of the constant possibility of infiltration, whether in determining the facts or specifying the law, of personal political preferences and prejudices, some operating at levels of consciousness so deep that the judge may be unaware of them. Hence the need for techniques of self-scrutiny for all who participate in decision-making [202]. For jurists and the systems they serve, biographical and autobiographical methods of self-analysis are not, in this perspective, mere vanity entertainments or luxuries. They are indispensable judicial skills, directly related to the protection of public order.

Section 7. National judges

When a national court is seised of a case that involves international issues, it becomes a functional international applier, with some advantages and disadvantages over its international counterparts. In terms of advantages, the national court enjoys a *compulsory* jurisdiction over those matters assigned to it, coextensive with the territory and control in which it operates; if judgment enforcement should prove

---

201. Christian Tomuschat, "The International Law of State Immunity and Its Development by National Institutions", *Vanderbilt J. of Transnat'l L.*, Vol. 44 (2011), p. 1105 *et seq.*, at 1137.

202. See *supra* Chapter IV; see also Lasswell and McDougal, *supra* footnote 69, at p. 591 *ff.*; Reisman, "Tormented Conscience", *supra* footnote 105; Reisman, "1995 Siebenthaler Lecture", *supra* footnote 11.

necessary, mechanisms are in place. But not all national judiciaries are of high quality. Some may be corrupt or lack independence. Even judges within national judiciaries that meet an international best practices standard may be influenced, at some level of consciousness, by national interests. Most important, the national judge, the critical actor in the national court when it operates as a functional international tribunal, must mediate conflicting obligations: the constitutional obligations of the State which he or she serves as judge and international obligations incumbent on international decision-makers [203].

At the beginning of the twenty-first century, we observe contradictory trends with respect to the role of national courts as international appliers. As a function of globalisation, more and more apparently domestic cases on national dockets contain significant international law issues. In addition, NGOs in their quest for an effective forum increasingly seek to bring international human rights issues to national courts. A number of national courts have assumed extensive extraterritorial international criminal jurisdiction for matters that concern their own nationals. NGOs have pressed for national courts in some jurisdictions to assume a vigorous universal jurisdiction over international crimes. By contrast, the Statute of the ICC represented a collective decision by the Member States of the United Nations *against* a universal jurisdiction for national courts, reposing contingent criminal jurisdiction in an international institution.

Section 8. International arbitrators

Various forms of international arbitration have become important supports for private transnational economic exchanges. Unless authorised to act as an *amiable compositeur*, the international commercial arbitrator is obliged to apply law in the textual-rule-based mode, but it is the law of that national legal system – its authorised political objectives and the means for their achievement – which the parties have selected or to which the arbitrators are directed by principles of conflict of laws. This certainly involves engaging in an enquiry into policy in the sense in which it must be consulted in the contextual-policy-based mode, but it is the policy of the legal system which governs the dispute and not an artefacted policy derived by the arbitrators for that particular case. The international commercial arbitrator is not tasked with making

203. See *infra* Chapter XVI for further discussion.

new policy; that is, creating new political goals and new instruments for achieving those goals. That is a province assigned to others in the national community whose law is being applied. To be sure, some civil codes explicitly authorise and require judges confronted by a *lacuna* to act as if they were the legislator rather than return a judgment of *non liquet*. An arbitrator applying that choice of law of the parties would similarly have a derivative competence to "legislate" *pro hac vice* but without legislative effects beyond that case.

Some legal systems – one thinks of the United States in certain historical periods – are more generally comfortable with the vocation of "judge-made" law or judicial legislation; the ostensible mode of decision is rule-based and textual, but the actual mode is policy-based and contextual. There, the legislature is the designated lawmaker, but judges are deemed to have a contingent case-by-case lawmaking role whose effects are amplified by *stare decisis*. Whatever one's view of that legal convention, it is *not* part of the province and vocation of the international commercial arbitrator, other than in those circumstances in which the applicable law explicitly authorises an applier to act as the legislator where there is a real *lacuna*.

Arbitrators execute the mandate of the parties, whose common consent is the source of their jurisdiction. If parties expressly authorise arbitrators to decide *ex aequo et bono*, the latter may depart from law otherwise applicable and the terms of otherwise applicable contracts and decide according to their individual sense of justice. National courts, which play an indispensable role in international commercial arbitration, should have no hesitation in lending the powers of the State they serve to the enforcement of such an *ex aequo et bono* award. After all, the parties had effectively authorised the arbitrators to rewrite their contract, so the action of doing so is within the boundaries of their contractual consent. And of course, the State has already decided that if the parties consent to waive their right to adjudication and elect, instead, to privatise the resolution of their dispute, the State apparatus will implement that agreement.

The situation is entirely different when there has been no such authorisation by the parties. In that situation, the arbitrator purporting to decide *ex aequo et bono* or an arbitral system that purports to endorse such excursions can hardly expect the apparatus of the State to ignore both its own commercial and constitutional policies as well as the fact that its own citizen has not agreed to waive them yet still to enforce the idiosyncratic visions of the arbitrators.

Section 9. Parallel proceedings

The scope of multiple parallel procedures can be defined narrowly and exclusively or broadly and inclusively. For many scholars, procedures are considered to be parallel if they are both (or all) judicial or, at least, judicial and arbitral. This is the legal focus in municipal contexts where it is generally confined to parallel and contemporaneous judicial procedures, in some instances, parallel arbitral procedures and, in instances in which the New York [204] or Panama Convention [205] is in force, simultaneous judicial and arbitral procedures.

In municipal law, because of a plethora of courts and tribunals of varying types, endowed with *compulsory* jurisdiction and distributed horizontally and vertically, there are many occasions in which disputes may fulfil the jurisdictional and admissibility requisites of two or more forums. Because of variations in procedural and substantive law, some of these forums may seem more favourable to one of the litigants. That possibility can provoke a dash to different court houses, sometimes even by the same litigant. Domestic principles of institutional economy and procedural justice are offended by substantially the same case being pursued simultaneously in two different but effective forums. Doctrines of *lis alibi pendens* and *forum non conveniens* arrest the multiplication *in limine litis* and in a predictable and orderly way [206].

International law's political structure differs in profound ways from domestic legal arrangements. To comprehend the phenomenon of parallel proceedings in the international applicative function, the focus of enquiry may have to be wider and more inclusive. For one thing, the degree of organisation and effectiveness of international law varies more widely than it does in advanced domestic legal systems.

---

204. Convention on the Recognition and Enforcement of Foreign Arbitral Awards, 1958 ("New York Convention"), https://www.newyorkconvention.org/new+york+convention+texts.

205. Inter-American Convention on International Commercial Arbitration, concluded at Panama City on 30 January 1975, http://www.oas.org/en/sla/dil/inter_american_treaties_B-35_international_commercial_arbitration.asp.

206. Sometimes, parties to international disputes intentionally design parallel procedures. Consider the *Taba* case, *supra* footnote 197. Article VII (2) of the Egypt/Israel Peace Treaty stated that disputes "shall be resolved by conciliation or submitted to arbitration". When a boundary dispute arose in the course of implementing the treaty, Israel pressed for conciliation, while Egypt insisted on arbitration. The Parties, in negotiating their *compromise*, allowed for both positions: the arbitration would commence and then suspend, while the two party-appointed arbitrators on the tribunal proceeded to conduct a conciliation procedure. If the conciliation proved unsuccessful, the arbitration would proceed. In fact, the conciliation effort failed, and the arbitration resumed and produced a final award.

Normatively, as noted at the outset of these lectures, international law asserts that its writ and general principles run to the furthest reaches of its planetary and near-space realms. But when its domain is viewed in terms of degree of organisation and predictable remedial effectiveness, international law takes on an archipelagic character in which "islands" of organised and effectively applied law operate alongside "offshore zones" in which the expected effectiveness is considerably lower and, in still others, in which the law simply yields to unilateral political decision. Indeed, no less an authority than Hugo Grotius, in his *De Jure Belli ac Pacis*, conceded that, even with respect to a just war, international law's *ultima ratio* in his theory, "it can scarcely be known by external indications, in a just war, what is the proper limit of self-defense, or recovery of property, or of exaction of punishment; so that it is by all means better to leave this to the conscience of the belligerents than to appeal to extraneous decision" [207].

In international law, the level of actual integration of various legal programmes is low. Treaties nibble at only one part of a problem. Moreover, the processes of lawmaking and law-application – where the rubber is supposed to hit the road – are neither unified nor even coordinated. Omnibus treaties, which undertake to prescribe for all the facets of a phenomenon and also to create mechanisms for interpreting and applying their law to disputes arising under them, such as the 1982 UNCLOS, are rare. Although often envisaged as *part* of a larger political, social or environmental programme, individual treaties tend to be narrower in scope, treating only "targets of opportunity", those aspects of a general problem on which political agreement can be reached at that point in time. Thus, an environmental treaty may address only that part of a current problem that is politically ripe for agreement and will incorporate a dispute-resolving procedure confined to that specific problem. Short of even that agreement, the treaty-making may confine itself to "standard-setting" and simply ignore an application procedure. This is not to minimise these efforts. In the longer term, they may be significant achievements.

In the aggregate, this piecemeal approach to treaty-making produces treaties with dispute-resolving mechanisms that are only competent for that part of the general problem the treaty engages. So it is sometimes necessary, in order to fashion a meaningful remedy in a particular

207. Grotius, *De Jure Belli ac Pacis*, LIB.II, Cap. II, Vol. I, at pp. 249-250.

instance, to invoke several different treaties, each with its own provision for the application of its substantive rights.

Take environmental issues: an environmental problem does not always fall neatly within the boundaries of a single treaty. As a consequence, the international lawyer charged with finding a remedy is often compelled to try to shape a bespoke integrated strategy, straddling a number of different treaties and their respective dispute resolution arrangements. To carry this off, she must either press one of the relevant tribunals to expand its *ratione materiae* jurisdiction on the basis of a theory of "ancillary jurisdiction" *or* she must initiate proceedings in several forums simultaneously. Both tactics incur systemic costs.

An expansive theory of ancillary jurisdiction introduces uncertainty about just what is being committed in treaties which were accepted on the expectation that they were confined to one part of a problem or, even short of that, were only standard-setting exercises for which the States parties were unprepared or unwilling to submit to judicially supervised implementation. Overall, an expansive theory of ancillary jurisdiction may solve the lawyer's problem for a specific case, but it reduces the future willingness of States to accept a jurisdiction which they thought was confined to one treaty. The knock-on effects for the legitimacy of the international judicial function, for the willingness of States to refer disputes to adjudication and for the general willingness to participate in the creation of "soft law" arrangements are systemically costly. By contrast, these problems do not arise in national courts of general jurisdiction; unlike their international counterparts, they can provide "one-stop" forums for the application of the law which has been prescribed by "one-stop" legislatures.

If we shift our attention to the large "offshore" areas in which international law simply expresses normative preferences without providing mechanisms for their implementation, we will encounter another reason for a broader focus for the systemic toleration of multiple simultaneous proceedings. Law, to be meaningful, must be authoritative and controlling. A puzzling feature of international law is that some of the most important norms, for all their authority, are not reliably controlling. To the extent that they become effective, it is due to *ad hoc* arrangements, "coalitions of the willing", informal alliances of governmental and non-governmental actors, operating simultaneously in different arenas with a common goal. The effectiveness of these arrangements depends, in the end, on their operation in multiple proceedings.

To illustrate these points, consider two cases, one for conservation, the other for the environment: the *Southern Bluefin Tuna* and the *Ireland-UK MOX Plant*.

In his General Course at The Hague Academy, which he revised and issued under the perennially apt title of "The Perplexities of Modern International Law", Shabtai Rosenne illustrated the challenges presented by the multiplicity of treaties and international forums in the *Southern Bluefin Tuna* cases. In that dispute, Rosenne wrote, "each party invoked a different treaty, each of which has its own dispute settlement provisions not mutually compatible" [208]. He went on to summarise what transpired.

> "The applicants instituted arbitration proceedings under Annex VII of the Law of the Sea Convention alleging breaches of the Convention, and immediately also requested ITLOS to prescribe provisional measures. In the *Southern Bluefin Tuna* (Provisional Measures) cases, ITLOS rejected a challenge to its jurisdiction to prescribe compulsory provisional measures under its residual jurisdiction, on the basis of its interpretation of its Statute. That was not decisive, since ITLOS only needed to establish that the arbitral tribunal to be constituted might prima facie have jurisdiction over the merits, for it to be in a position to prescribe provisional measures. The Arbitral Tribunal, after full written and oral argument, held that it was without jurisdiction to rule on the merits of the case. Following the practice of the ICJ, that Tribunal defined for itself the dispute that was before it and determined which of the two incompatible treaties was applicable. The Tribunal held that it would be 'artificial' to find that there were two distinct disputes (para. 54), and accordingly went on to determine for itself which was the governing Convention in the circumstances of the case." [209]

The *MOX Plant* cases proved to be even more complex.

In 1947, the UK opened the Sellafield nuclear site, on the western coast of England, directly across the Irish Sea from the Republic of Ireland [210]. The site included two nuclear reactors and a reprocessing

208. Shabtai Rosenne, *The Perplexities of Modern International Law*, 2004, at p. 104 (footnotes omitted).

209. *Id.*, at pp. 104-105.

210. *MOX Plant* (*Ir.* v. *UK*), Request for Provisional Measures and Statement of Case Submitted on Behalf of Ireland, ITLOS, 3 December 2001 (hereafter ITLOS Request for Provisional Measures), at para. 7, https://www.itlos.org/fileadmin/itlos/documents/

plant to produce plutonium fuel for atomic bombs [211]. The UK, through the State-owned company British Nuclear Fuels Limited (BNFL), continued to expand Sellafield's facilities through 1994, at which point it opened a new reprocessing plant on the site, known as "Thorp" [212] designed to ingest spent oxide fuel, a type of nuclear waste, until then being discarded by the UK and other countries, and to reprocess up to 97 per cent of it [213] into reusable nuclear fuel [214]. In 1996, BNFL completed construction of another on-site facility, the "MOX Plant" [215]. It was designed to transform Thorp's output into a type of nuclear fuel not used by the UK – mixed-oxide fuel, or MOX. According to the business plan, the MOX would be sold and transported by sea for use by other countries [216].

On environmental grounds, Ireland opposed the MOX Plant throughout its construction and appealed unsuccessfully multiple times to the United Kingdom Environment Agency (UKEA) to have the project shut down [217]. Finally, shortly before the plant was due to be commissioned, Ireland filed the first of what would become four parallel international judicial and arbitral proceedings. In these proceedings, Ireland maintained that, from the time of its construction in the 1950s, the Sellafield site had continually emitted nuclear radiation into the surrounding environment and that, as a result, the Irish Sea had become "among the most radioactively polluted seas in the world" [218]. Ireland further alleged that the MOX Plant would "requir[e] the transportation of unknown – and potentially very large – quantities of . . . hazardous radioactive materials [including plutonium] in close proximity to the

---

cases/case_no_10/request_ireland_e.pdf; Emma Law, "What Is Sellafield?", Gov.uk, 7 September 2018, https://nda.blog.gov.uk/2018/09/07/what-is-sellafield/.

211. Law, *supra* footnote 210.

212. BBC News, "Sellafield Thorp Site to Close in 2018", 7 June 2012, https://www.bbc.com/news/uk-england-cumbria-18353122; see also Law, *supra* footnote 210.

213. Martin Leafe, "End in Sight for Reprocessing Nuclear Fuel at Sellafield", Gov.uk, 24 January 2017, https://nda.blog.gov.uk/2017/01/24/end-in-sight-for-reprocessing-nuclear-fuel-at-sellafield/.

214. Law, *supra* footnote 210.

215. Access to Info. Under Article 9 of the OSPAR Convention *(Ir.* v. *UK)*, PCA Case Repository No. 2001-03, Memorial of Ireland of 7 March 2002 (hereafter OSPAR Memorial of Ireland), at para. 7, https://pcacases.com/web/sendAttach/609.

216. *Id.*; Charles de Saillan, "Disposal of Spent Nuclear Fuel in the United States and Europe: A Persistent Environmental Problem", *Harv. Envtl. L. Rev.*, Vol. 34 (2010), p. 461 *et seq.*, at 485.

217. Access to Info. Under Article 9 of the OSPAR Convention *(Ir.* v. *UK)*, PCA Case Repository No. 2001-03, Final Award of 2 July 2003, 23 RIAA 59 (hereafter OSPAR Award), at paras. 23, 27, 29-30, 32, 34, 36, https://pcacases.com/web/sendAttach/121.

218. ITLOS Request for Provisional Measures, at paras. 9-10; see also OSPAR Memorial of Ireland, at paras. 5-7.

territory of Ireland" and would result in "radioactive wastes [being] discharged directly into the Irish Sea" [219].

In 2001, while the UKEA was still considering whether to approve the opening of the MOX Plant for operation, Ireland initiated arbitral proceedings against the UK, at the Permanent Court of Arbitration (PCA) under the OSPAR Convention [220, 221]. Four months later, just after the UKEA approved the MOX Plant [222], Ireland initiated another proceeding, this time under (Article 287 and Annex VII) of UNCLOS, before an *ad hoc* tribunal at the PCA. Two weeks later, Ireland, as part of the UNCLOS Annex VII arbitration but before its *ad hoc* tribunal had been constituted, initiated a third proceeding in ITLOS. The purpose of this proceeding was to request provisional measures to suspend the MOX Plant's imminent opening to avert what Ireland claimed would be irreversible environmental injury.

ITLOS accepted the UK's commitment that it would not transport radioactive materials through the Irish Sea until October 2002 at the earliest [223] and concluded that "the urgency of the situation [did not] require . . . the provisional measures requested by Ireland, in the short period before the constitution of the Annex VII arbitral tribunal" [224].

Ireland's second proceeding had been brought under the Convention for the Protection of the Marine Environment of the North-East Atlantic. Popularly known as the "OSPAR Convention" [225], it held the promise for providing a remedy for a different aspect of the dispute. OSPAR Article 9 requires a State party to provide, upon request of any other party, "any available information in written, visual, aural or database form on the state of the maritime area, on activities or measures adversely affecting or likely to affect it and on activities or measures introduced in accordance with the Convention" [226]. But the OSPAR

219. OSPAR Memorial of Ireland, *supra* footnote 215, at paras. 7, 9. See also ITLOS Request for Provisional Measures, at para. 27; Maki Tanaka, "Lessons from the Protracted MOX Plant Dispute: A Proposed Protocol on Marine Environmental Impact Assessment to the United Nations Convention on the Law of the Sea", *Mich. J. Int'l L.*, Vol. 25 (2004), p. 337 *et seq.*, at 340.

220. *Ireland* v. *United Kingdom*, OSPAR Arbitration, PCA, https://pca-cpa.org/en/cases/34/.

221. OSPAR Memorial of Ireland, *supra* footnote 215, at paras. 51-54.

222. *Id.*, at para. 54.

223. *Id.*, at paras. 78-80.

224. *Id.*, at para. 81.

225. OSPAR Convention, *supra* footnote 169.

226. *Id.*, at Article 9 (2).

Tribunal concluded that Ireland had no colourable claims under the Convention [227], and dismissed the case [228].

Ireland's Annex VII dispute alleged that the UK had violated UNCLOS by "failing to take the necessary measures to prevent, reduce and control pollution of the marine environment of the Irish Sea". In 2001, the European Commission, in view of the then pending UNCLOS and OSPAR proceedings, filed a dispute at the European Court of Justice (ECJ), charging that in bringing claims against the UK under UNCLOS, Ireland had encroached on the ECJ's exclusive jurisdiction [229]. The ECJ held in 2006 that by filing under UNCLOS Annex VII claims that fell under European Community law, including claims expressly arising under the EC Treaty and Euratom Treaty Directives, Ireland had intruded on the ECJ's exclusive jurisdiction.

In the course of multiple rounds of briefing and two weeks of hearings of the Annex VII proceeding, the Annex VII Tribunal became aware of the European Community's investigation into whether Ireland had violated European Community law by bringing claims under UNCLOS Annex VII. At Ireland's request, the Tribunal issued an order suspending the UNCLOS arbitration pending judgment by the ECJ. When the ECJ found Ireland in violation of European Community law, Ireland withdrew its UNCLOS Annex VII dispute [230].

Southern Bluefin Tuna and especially *MOX Plant* illustrate one of the reasons we encounter parallel procedures in contemporary international law: the lawyer's search for a competent forum and an adequate remedy for which there is no single treaty and no single jurisdictional arrangement.

Although we international lawyers study them with devotion, judicial and arbitral decisions are exceptional in the international legal process. The great majority of decisions are shaped in international law's political institutions and by bilateral and unilateral action. Multiple parallel procedures occur at the highest level of those political institutions.

In the area of international security, the UN Charter's approach to parallel proceedings is expressed in overlapping jurisdictions and is spelled out in Charter Articles 10 to 12.

Article 11 (2) provides, in the relevant part:

227. *Id.*, at para. 185 *(v)*.
228. *Id.*, at para. 59; *Ireland* v. *United Kingdom*, *supra* footnote 220.
229. *Comm'n* v. *Ireland*, Case C-459/03, 2006 ECR I-04635 [2006], http://curia.europa.eu/juris/celex.jsf?celex=62003CJ0459&lang1=en&type=TXT&ancre=.
230. *MOX Plant Case (Ir.* v. *UK)*, Order No. 6 of 6 June 2008, PCA Case Repository No. 2002-01, https://pcacases.com/web/sendAttach/870.

> "The General Assembly may discuss any questions relating to the maintenance of international peace and security brought before it by any Member of the United Nations, or by the Security Council, . . . except as provided in Article 12, may make recommendations with regard to any such questions to the state or states concerned or to the Security Council or to both. Any such question on which action is necessary shall be referred to the Security Council by the General Assembly either before or after discussion."

Article 12 (1) decrees:

> "While the Security Council is exercising in respect of any dispute or situation the functions assigned to it in the present Charter, the General Assembly shall not make any recommendation with regard to that dispute or situation unless the Security Council so requests."

According to their text, when the Security Council is seised of a "dispute" or a "situation", the drafters of the Charter did not want the UN Organization to be speaking in multiple voices. Then only the Security Council was to speak.

Or so it would have seemed.

The ICJ's applications of these Charter provisions have found ways and contingencies in which the Assembly's – and the Court's own – role could be expanded parallel to the Council's primary responsibility.

In the *Certain Expenses* opinion, the Court effectively ratified the General Assembly's "Uniting for Peace" Resolution, expanding the role of the General Assembly in case of the paralysis of the Security Council. In the *Wall* opinion, the Court held that "[a] request for an advisory opinion is not in itself a 'recommendation' by the General Assembly 'with regard to [a] dispute or situation'" [231]. On the basis of this fine distinction, the Court continued, "while Article 12 may limit the *scope* of the action which the General Assembly may take *subsequent* to its receipt of the Court's Opinion . . . it does not in itself limit the authorization to request an advisory opinion" [232].

---

231. *The Wall*, *supra* footnote 160, at p. 148, para. 25.

232. *Accordance with International Law of the Unilateral Declaration of Independence in Respect to Kosovo*, Advisory Opinion, 22 July 2010, ICJ Reports 2010, p. 414, at para. 24.

At the same time, the Court expanded its own role by distinguishing the "legal question" from the "political aspects" of a question[233], allowing itself, at its discretion, to open yet another parallel procedure. Thus, in the *Wall* opinion, the Court issued clear dispositives to a non-consenting State with respect to a situation of which the Security Council was seised. The implication of the Court's jurisprudence on this matter seems to be one in which the application of Charter Article 12 (1)'s instruction on procedures being pursued in parallel by the two – or three – principal UN organs is one of case-by-case discretion, arguably as a function of the perceived gravity and urgency of the matter at bar.

The Court explicitly ratified these innovations in its *Kosovo* opinion when it noted, with seeming equanimity, that

> "there has been an increasing tendency over time for the General Assembly and the Security Council to deal in parallel with the same matter concerning the maintenance of international peace and security . . . it is often the case that, while the Security Council has tended to focus on the aspects of such matters related to international peace and security, the General Assembly has taken a broader view, considering also their humanitarian, social and economic aspects"[234].

In this instance, the elevation of the Assembly to a potential parallel proceeding role in security matters was one more step in the demand of the Assembly from the earliest days of the UN Organization for a more meaningful role than the one assigned it by the Charter. With all due respect, to suggest that the Assembly has been confining itself in these initiatives to "their humanitarian, social and economic aspects" is a small part of the story. Parallel proceedings here are a technique of power-sharing.

233. *Id.*, at para. 27.
234. *Id.*, at para. 41.

CHAPTER VIII

PARTICIPATION ARRANGEMENTS FOR STATES: THE TRANSFORMATION OF SELF-DETERMINATION

> "In writings on political institutions there is a good deal of discussion about the nature and the origin of the State, which is usually represented as being an entity over and above the human individuals who make up a society, having a one of its attributes something called 'sovereignty,' and sometimes spoken of as having a will (law being often defined as the will of the State) or as issuing commands. The State, in this sense, does not exist in the phenomenal world; it is a fiction of the philosophers. What does exist is an organization, i.e., a collection of individual human beings connected by a complex system of relations. Within that organization different individuals have different roles, and some are in possession of special power or authority, as chiefs or elders capable of giving commands which will be obeyed, as legislators or judges, and so on. There is no such thing as the power of the State; there are only, in reality, powers of individuals – kings, prime ministers, magistrates, policemen, party bosses, and voters."
>
> Alfred R. Radcliffe-Brown [235]

The introduction of the concept of self-determination into the vocabulary of international law along with its qualifier – "of peoples" – has had an immense effect on the arrangements governing the establishment, transformation and termination of territorial communities. The campaign of decolonisation, which is associated with and is sometimes treated as if it were interchangeable with self-determination, is winding down; once the last remaining colony has been liberated, the era of decolonisation will have ended. In contrast, self-determination, the claim of groups of people to establish a political community as a means of achieving their common goals, never ceases. In a world of many groups inhabiting the same spaces, the self-determination of any particular group inevitably conflicts with other groups and, no less important, with other individuals.

Section 1. The process of consociation and the demand for self-determination

Aristotle's observation that man is a social animal answers the "what" but not the "why" question; it is the answer to the "why" which

235. Alfred R. Radcliffe-Brown, preface to Meyer Fortes and Edwin E. Evans-Pritchard (eds.), *African Political Systems*, 1940, at p. xxiii.

is necessary to explain the ongoing dynamic of what Max Weber called "consociation" [236]. The men and women of our species do things they believe, rightly or wrongly, will benefit them. Nowhere is this more apparent than in their efforts to create, join and maintain groups. Individuals marry and establish families, extended families, tribes, clans, States and other territorially based organisations and alliances or confederations of them. They join religious sects, clubs, fraternities, sororities, organisations of all types, cartels, gangs, terrorist cells – every type of association. They do this because they expect to enhance their chances of survival and security, to win greater opportunities for accumulating wealth, for learning, for sharing affection, for experiencing a sense of virtue and meaning and, where it is part of the bargain, for collecting on it by redeeming the promise of rewards in an afterlife.

That is not to say that every group with which individuals affiliate is voluntary and that every membership is based on prior and informed consent. Every person is born into some groups whose values are inculcated from the tenderest age; in this sense, the German *Bildung* and French *formation* better capture the actual experience than does the English noun "education". Some people come to feel imprisoned in one or more of their groups and may try to liberate themselves. Conversely, leaders everywhere try, with varying degrees of coercion, to prevent withdrawal or defection from their respective groups. A key responsibility of every group leader is to generate, sustain and enforce loyalties, for it is on the basis of such loyalties that leaders may demand periodic contributions of wealth and other forms of support, even sacrifice of life itself. Disloyalty, whether characterised as treason or apostasy, is subjected to severe penalties.

For groups which are based on real or fancied consanguinity, membership is acquired by birth. For other groups, induction rituals may range from innocuous hazings to circumcision, ritual scarring or mutilation, to hideous rites such as ritual murders, *Bluttkit* or "bones". Once inside groups, people are taught to display various identification symbols which may range from a proudly worn lapel pin, to a secret handshake, saluting a flag or belting out a national anthem, tribal chant or company song.

No matter how groups are composed or structured and whether or not they are territorially based, the defining characteristic of each group

---

236. Max Weber, *Economy and Society: An Outline of Interpretive Sociology* (New York: Bedminster Press 1968), at p. 652.

– the essential feature that makes it a group – is the distinction between members and non-members. Members are entitled to benefits. Non-members are outsiders and, as such, are not so entitled; sometimes, non-members or outsiders are even denied recognition as human beings [237].

A truth which the elites of groups sometimes forget is that people join and remain in groups precisely because they expect to derive certain benefits, whatever they may be. However strenuous and even coercive the efforts of leaders to maintain loyalty, failure to provide the most basic of the expected reciprocals of any particular group membership – personal security, economic and other life opportunities and, no less important, emotional meaningfulness – will ultimately and inevitably alienate at least some of the individuals from one group and tug them to other existing or nascent groups. In international politics and especially in war, leaders try to undermine competing groups and their leaders by depreciating these reciprocals while exaggerating the supposed advantages of association with their own group.

Because the very notion of a group imports peripheral social boundaries within which members are to enjoy advantages that will be denied outsiders, every group must have what we may call "participation arrangements". Whether they are articulated, or implicit, such arrangements relate to accession and exclusion, participation, internal rights, duties and expulsion. As the benefits accruing to members increase and, especially in crises, the rules about acquisition of membership and the degree of compulsion of the rules about responsible behaviour within the group become more demanding.

One way of understanding how participation arrangements work in the international legal system is to think of them in terms of an inclusive group with ever smaller and smaller groups, each nesting within the next larger one. Each group and subgroup, as such, has its own membership and participation arrangements, modes of creating and applying entry rituals and policing loyalty and internal standards of behaviour. Common to all of these various rules is that they are designed to maintain a boundary between members and outsiders. Many individuals are simultaneously members of different groups; their loyalties to those groups are not always reciprocally compatible.

The most prominent members of the international law group have been effectively organised and territorially based States. Although

237. See generally Hans Kohn, *The Idea of Nationalism: A Study in its Origins and Background*, 1944.

we speak of States as units, for example, when we say, "France and Italy have concluded an agreement", or "China and the United States conferred at the United Nations today", each of these members of the most inclusive international law group is itself akin to a club, each with its own internal participation arrangements, rituals and standards of behaviour. But in sharp contrast to the previous era, these latter participation arrangements – each State's laws of nationality – are increasingly subjected to efforts at regulation by international legal arrangements [238]. Parallel to this, many liberal States have undertaken to regulate within their own national spaces the terms of subgroup formation, their induction and exclusion arrangements and the degree of severity of their application.

Section 2. The international membership criteria: from membership by power to membership by right

A century ago, the rules and rituals for acquiring membership in the international legal system were relatively simple, self-enforcing and brutal: prospective members who aspired to be territorially organised had to be demonstrably capable of defending their space against others. If not, those others were not precluded from trying to seize and appropriate it. Would-be leaders of a territorial community who gained and maintained control also had to be able to fulfil the minimum *external* obligations of international membership. Although some theologians purported to derive certain membership principles from what they deemed to be natural law, State elites acknowledged no international legal responsibility with respect to the welfare of their own nationals. Even at this early stage, however, elites were obliged to provide specific protections for the nationals of other members when they operated in their midst and were entitled to demand reciprocal treatment for their own nationals when they ventured abroad [239].

Inter-State membership rituals were expressed in the practices of "recognition", the formal acknowledgement by one State that another territorial community was accepted as a member with all the rights and privileges of that status. Recognition was sometimes simply declaratory of factual situations, acknowledging, in Jellinek's memorable phrase, the "normative force of the factual" [240]; sometimes it was (and continues

238. See *infra* Chapter XI.
239. *Island of Palmas (or Miangas) (Neth.* v. *US)*, Award, 4 April 1928, PCA Case No. 1925-01.
240. Georg Jellinek, *Allgemeine Staatslehre*, 1905, at p. 330.

to be) tacit. In some contexts, however, the act of recognition by others was itself a decisive ingredient in constituting or creating factual situations. But the essential prerequisite for membership as a State was not a collective decision by others. It was the exercise of effective control of the territory concerned. Other members of the international system might detest a candidate and its elite, indeed oppose it by direct or surrogate military intervention, as the United States and other European States did when they sent expeditionary forces to fight the Red Army after the Russian Revolution. But if the candidate proved itself capable of gaining and maintaining effective control of its territory and population, it could claim the benefits of membership and they could not long be denied.

For the most part, as will be recalled from the review of the historical dimension in Chapter II, Section 3, formal membership in the international legal system was largely confined to a number of world empires and other principalities, initially based in Europe and then in North and South America. Indeed, international law was early styled the "Public Law of Europe" [241]. (But even when the term was in vogue, it betrayed parochialism, excluding, as it did, the Ottoman, Persian and Chinese Empires as well as a few smaller non-European States which had managed to preserve their independence.) All of the empires were comprised of amalgams of territories and peoples with varying international legal statuses [242]. "In the inter-war years . . . direct rule by aliens and sheer exploitation gave way to alternatives such as indirect rule, collaborative arrangements with local elites, self-government, quasi-independence, and other means to secure imperialist interests." [243] Nomenclature aside, the internal territories shared in common their effective subordination to a particular imperial centre.

In the nineteenth century, the emergence to independence of the Spanish Empire's possessions in Central and South America introduced more members into the international club. The elites of these sometimes shaky new States were, for the most part, of European extraction, ruling within their respective territories the more numerous indigenous peoples. Because the territories claimed by the new States were still fair game for the remaining European empires, the newcomers tried to amend

241. Julius Goebel, Jr., *Struggle for the Falkland Islands: A Study in Legal and Diplomatic History*, 1927, at p. 120.

242. See Sir Mark Frank Lindley, *The Acquisition of Backward Territory in International Law: Being a Treatise on the law and Practice Relating to Colonial Expansion*, 1926; see also *supra* Chapter II.

243. Prasenjit Duara, *Sovereignty and Authenticity*, 2003, at p. 247.

the international participation arrangements based on effectiveness by inverting the Roman praetorian edict of *uti possidetis* [244]. Members of the region came to venerate their juridical creation, but their own continued independence and membership in an international system which was still largely based on effective power owed at least as much to the shelter afforded by the Monroe Doctrine, issued by the United States in 1823, as it did to their doctrine of *uti possidetis*.

Historians believe that the greatest formative influence on the constitutive scaffolding of contemporary international law was the Peace of Westphalia. In fact, the Versailles Conference, which produced the network of Peace Treaties concluding World War I, has had a far greater influence on the contemporary constitutive structure and content of modern participation arrangements [245]. Versailles was the first diplomatic conference to systematically and formally permit significant numbers of individuals and groups, who lacked the power necessary to become States, to petition the then elites of the international community to have the territories which they purported to represent recognised as and transformed into independent States. Some of these various groups were precursors of "would-be States" or "proto-States"; others were entities we would now recognize as NGOs [246].

Even more important than Versailles's bestowal of this limited procedural franchise was the substantive law secreted in its interstices. Versailles validated the demand that peoples who were not yet organised as States, in some cases scarcely imaginable as such, might nonetheless be entitled to become independent under international protection. The basis of their claim was not their current or even prospective effectiveness (a test which their prayerful presence at Versailles demonstrated they had failed). Quite the contrary. Their claim was based on an essentially moral principle: "self-determination".

The "self" in the principle of "self-determination" was a misnomer, for the groups which had to invoke it were precisely those that had been unable to create and mobilise a sufficiently strong and motivated base of loyalists and, thus, could not *self*-determine in a system whose

244. Ironically, *uti possidetis*, has come to have a potentially negative effect on self-determination claims. See *infra* Section 3 of this chapter.

245. Margaret MacMillan, *Paris 1919: Six Months That Changed the World*, 2002. See also Oleg I. Tiunov, "Concepts and Features of International Law: Its Relation to Norms of the National Law of the State", *St. Louis LJ*, Vol. 38 (1994), p. 915 *et seq.*, at 920 (arguing that rather than the Peace of Westphalia, the Treaty of Versailles and other more recent developments have shaped the modern state system).

246. See *infra* Chapter X, Section 3, for discussion of NGOs.

participation arrangements turned on power. Even the high moral tone associated with self-determination was inapt. At its inception, self-determination was designed and used, quite selectively, as an imperial technique for divesting vanquished or declining empires of their territories which would henceforth benefit from the "protection" of the victorious empires. It did not occur to victors, acting under the banner of self-determination, to apply the principle to their own imperial possessions. But, in a new context, they would soon find themselves ensnared in the rhetorical web they had spun.

Versailles laid the basis for a constitutive arrangement that persisted through the rest of the twentieth century and which, in modified form, may continue to exercise some influence on membership decisions in the twenty-first century. The new arrangement consisted of three planks:

- *first*, the general principle of self-determination imported a *prima facie* entitlement of distinct peoples living within existing States to demand their own political communities and to be recognised as fully fledged members of the international legal system, even if they could not win that status by their own efforts;
- *second*, the principle was to be effected through collective decision, by means of the competence of the organs of the international community to decide whether and in what form these communities should be formed; and,
- *third*, a corollary, which became more and more explicit, imported a collective international responsibility to protect the territorial integrity and political independence or "sovereignty" of those communities, many of which could not have done so on the basis of their own efforts.

By 1945, an additional corollary stated that conquest was no longer a means for acquiring title. It was not retroactive, though it has not proved immune to the exercise of naked power as well as the justicial anachronism dynamic discussed in Chapter III, Section 5, Paragraph 3.

Thus, this new constitutive arrangement purported to abrogate the prerequisite of effectiveness, which had been the basis of the claim to membership under the prior constitutive arrangement.

The Peace Conferences were not the first time that some participants in the international process purported to view events in terms of a morality, divine or secular. Some of the early writings of international law were essentially moral tracts whose authority was often derived from or justified by assembling references to religious texts and natural law. Even now, as we saw in Chapter III, moral judgements, based on neither treaties nor State practice, intertwine with authoritative symbols and in some circumstances can influence international decision-making. But the distinctive and transforming event at Versailles, which was carried further by the United Nations Conference in San Francisco, was the official inversion of international law's old membership paradigm. The old arrangement had proceeded from effectiveness to rights. The new one was to proceed from legislated rights to effectiveness. The old constitutive arrangement was, by its nature, self-enforcing; the new paradigm required measures of implementation by others.

Under the new constitutive arrangement, an elite unable to establish or maintain control over a territory might still hope to secure full rights to membership based not on its own effective power but on a novel principle of international law. Under the old arrangement, an elite which proved unable, for want of internal or external resources, to establish and maintain effective control over a territory could not win international legal membership. Under the new constitutive arrangement, an elite which, relying on its own resources, was unable to establish or maintain control over a territory might still secure full rights to membership based on a new principle of international law. But now the *right* to membership was somehow supposed to *transform* into *effectiveness*.

The introduction of an essentially rights-based approach in this period was not unique to international law. Analogous developments were taking place in many domestic legal systems, thanks to a combination of shifting social tectonics and newly dominant political philosophies as well as a need to deflect potentially revolutionary forces. But in contrast to the more loosely organised international system, effective centralised governance in many of these States enabled actual implementation of programmes of internal value redistribution. (In other States, the programmes were financed by deficit and the day of reckoning was simply put off.)

The second plank of the new constitutive arrangement was to be collective decision in international organisations. Thanks to the procedural rules of many of these organisations, political influence within the organisation did not always correspond to actual political and economic power. Under the old arrangement, the status of statehood and its international legal perquisites derived from the effective control of the elite that was aspiring to manage a territory or of an outside power that had resolved, for its own political, economic or ideological reasons, to support that aspiring elite and even supplement with its own resources what the aspiring elite lacked. "Constitutive recognition" by collective decision was not necessary under the old arrangement. But the second plank of the new constitutive arrangement held that collective decision was to be taken by the membership of the international organisations. At Versailles, membership decisions for components of the vanquished empires had been made by the small group of elderly white men who governed the victorious empires in World War I. After World War II, they were replaced by new international organisations of more heterogeneous membership.

Over time, those who benefited by gaining membership through the new collective decision process were able to reinforce and even expand its key postulates, thanks to a type of "network" or "bandwagon" effect. More and more new States whose putative elites lacked sufficient power to create, or, in some cases, once created, even to maintain them against internal or external adversaries, were being brought into existence on the basis of the novel international principle. By 1960, a much more diverse group of men and women in the UN General Assembly were making key parts of membership decisions; more and more of the Assembly's Member States were themselves beneficiaries of the new membership arrangement.

The third plank of this revised constitutive arrangement was the generation of a new corollary: the continuing collective international responsibility for maintaining the independence and effectiveness of the new States. Declaring that a candidate is henceforth to be deemed a Member State is a verbal act; as such, it is virtually costless. The *maintenance* of the new member, which had lacked the power and other resources to self-determine itself into existence, requires more than words; over time, moreover, it could prove to be onerously expensive. The implications of this new international responsibility were only gradually appreciated.

The point bears emphasis. "Rights", whether political or economic, can be legislated merely by issuing the appropriate words and symbols through an authoritative channel. But neither power nor wealth can be created in this fashion. Dressing policy preferences in the agreed symbols of law may count for something [247], but the actual creation of power and wealth requires the ongoing mobilisation of people, skills and resources, often against competitors who believe that a proposed

247. See *supra* Chapter III, Section 2.

adjustment in existing arrangements will work to their detriment and who, consequently, can be expected to mount a resistance whose intensity will be proportional to what the competitors believe they have at stake.

Thus, the international system would shortly find that its innovation carried a coordinate responsibility: to supply the resources that would make the new States effective. The old arrangement had been based on a rough and often nasty but self-enforcing mechanism; the new one required an ongoing investment of some of the organised international community's limited resources in order to maintain the new States. The shakier the new States were, the more external resources were required. As explained in Chapter II, the competition for those resources, amid many other international goals and constituencies, has become even more intense, while the maintenance costs *erga omnes* of failing, *faux* or weak States have increased.

One of the unintended consequences of the installation of the principle of self-determination in contemporary international law has been the ongoing encouragement of a fissiparous process. Since the establishment of the United Nations, the formal institutions and informal arrangements of international law have affirmed a right of peoples to establish their own political communities and have assumed an obligation to assist in the process of establishment. Article 1 (1) of the UN Charter installed, as a major purpose of the new organisation, the development of friendly relations among nations based, among other good things, on "self-determination of peoples". Article 55 repeated it, and Article 56 enlisted all Members of the United Nations to joint and separate action for its achievement. The drafters of the Charter made some effort to confine self-determination to the components of other States. Article 73 did not quite extend a right of self-determination to non-self-governing territories; they were entitled to "self-government", but the provision did prescribe mandatory standards for their governance and development. Trust territories, in contrast, in Article 76, were to advance towards independence, depending on their circumstances and the wishes of their inhabitants.

In spite of the deliberate and measured restraint of Article 73, an accelerated process of decolonisation commenced shortly after the establishment of the United Nations. In a very brief period, independent Governments led by indigenous leaderships emerged in most of what had been the territories and colonies of the European empires. By 1960, the UN General Assembly, which had expanded from an original fifty to ninety-nine States, produced a Declaration on the Granting of Independence to Colonial Countries and Peoples, which "solemnly proclaim[ed] the necessity of bringing to a speedy and unconditional end colonialism in all its forms and manifestations" [248]. In 1971, the ICJ, in its advisory mode, said that

> "[t]he subsequent development of international law in regard to non-self-governing territories, as enshrined in the Charter of the United Nations, made the principle of self-determination applicable to all of them" [249].

The nineteenth-century legal arrangement with respect to membership, in its unorganised yet self-enforcing form, was almost an international legal analogue of social Darwinism. It generally produced Governments that were effective within their territories, if not necessarily popular or ruling in a manner consistent with what were then deemed to be enlightened standards of governance. If the would-be Governments were themselves ineffective or unsupported by outside power, others, who were, could be expected to try to fill the vacuum. In any event, the comparatively primitive state of transnational communications meant that ungovernable territories existing at the margins could be ignored.

The arrangement ushered in by the United Nations midwifed States not on the basis of objective criteria of effectiveness, but on the basis of a right. In 1945, awarding that right was still disciplined by the Charter's qualifying language of "the particular circumstances of each territory and its peoples and their varying stages of advancement" [250]. By 1960, self-determination had been liberated from any such discipline. The Declaration on the Granting of Independence to Colonial Countries and Peoples stated unequivocally that "[i]nadequacy of political, economic, social or educational preparedness should never serve as a pretext for delaying independence" [251]. And, indeed, such conditions did not delay independence for a number of new States whose political, economic, social or educational preparedness was marginal.

After 1960, some territories were being recognised as States and given membership in the United Nations even though they did not meet the effectiveness criteria of prior international arrangements: the Governments of some of these States did not control all of their own territories; indeed some of them controlled only a few *arrondissements*

248. GA Res. 1514 (XV), 14 December 1960.
249. *Namibia*, *supra* footnote 175.
250. UN Charter, *supra* footnote 108, Article 73 *(b)*.
251. GA Res. 1514 (XV), *supra* footnote 248, at para. 3.

of their capital cities. (Some others were effectively controlled, but by the invisible hands of their former metropolitans.) In some of these territories, human services declined; they were supplied, if at all, by networks of NGOs which had emerged as important international actors [252].

By the turn of the twenty-first century, an authoritative vocabulary had been codified to describe this type of State: "least developed States", "*faux* States", "failed States", "imploded States" and "weak States". Ironically, coincident with this downward trend, international legal demands with respect to standards of domestic governance became more explicit, ambitious and authoritative, crystallising into a code associated with the protection of human rights [253].

Some of the alarming trends, reviewed in Chapter II, relate to failed, *faux* and weak States. Programmes to alleviate the conditions of the populations within failed or failing States have been discussed at the international level; goals were declared, and some were implemented by international aid agencies, other Governments and NGOs. Periodically, agencies of the United Nations or regional organisations functioned as the *de facto* Governments of some territories whose internal politics precluded effective self-government. After the terrorist attacks on the US in 2001, these theretofore episodic efforts were increased as Governments which felt threatened by militant Salafism were forced to the realisation that *faux*, failing and weak States could serve as cradles, crucibles and launching pads for transnational terrorism, narco-traffic, piracy and other forms of transnational crime, uncontrolled migration and as petri dishes for the types of communicable diseases that can leap across national boundaries. Whether sufficient international resources to address these challenges are going to be made available as the twenty-first century advances is an important challenge. The formal organs of international law were slow to accept that the proliferation of failing or failed States and the dangers associated with them were, in part, an unintended consequence of the new membership arrangements and especially the broad application of the right to self-determination. Yet, even then, the UN General Assembly continued to issue resolutions affirming the right of self-determination, as have virtually all the architectonic human rights instruments. In 1974, the ICJ, citing the provisions of the Charter, the Declaration on the

252. See *infra* Chapter X, Section 3.
253. See *infra* Chapter XII.

Granting of Independence to Colonial Countries and Peoples, and other General Assembly resolutions, reaffirmed the right to speedy decolonisation but seemed to give priority to self-determination over decolonisation [254]. That was a significant policy choice, for decolonisation, as noted, is a finite historical process, which will conclude when the results of the Western colonial era have been unwound; self-determination, by contrast, is an unending process. If self-determination continues to be decoupled from effectiveness, the burdens on the resources of the international community could increase even more.

More recent decisions reflect belated appreciation of the problems that a broad and undiscriminating application of the principle of self-determination can produce. In the *East Timor* case, the ICJ found itself without jurisdiction but issued a rather non-committal declaration to the effect that the parties in the case before it agree that "East Timor remains a non-self-governing territory and its people has the right to self-determination" [255]. The Court neither endorsed nor associated itself with what it recorded [256].

The extended violent death throes of the Yugoslav Federation, whose impending dissolution into separate ethnic republics was initially greeted as a vindication of the right of self-determination, soon forced a reappraisal. In her lectures at The Hague, then Professor Higgins observed of former Yugoslavia that "[t]he situation can only be described as legally confused", an observation whose prescience was borne out by later decisions of the ICJ [257]. There was belated recognition of the dark underside of self-determination in ethnically heterogenous territories in which inclusive, transethnic national identifications were weak or non-existent. In such settings, all that each act of self-determination was accomplishing was enabling one ethnic or religious group within a territory – one "people" – to assert or "determine" itself, seize political power and monopolise its perquisites, while "undetermining" other groups within the same territorial space. Self-determination for Jews in Israel undetermined Palestinians; self-determination for Croats

254. *Western Sahara*, *supra* footnote 176.

255. *East Timor*, *supra* footnote 192, at p. 90, para. 31.

256. Three years later, the then President of Indonesia offered the people of East Timor independence if they wished it. They did and overwhelmingly expressed their wish in a referendum. In what was becoming a pattern, a UN Transitional Administration was established for East Timor, after which the tiny territory emerged to a full, if unsteady, independence.

257. Rosalyn Higgins, *Problems and Process: International Law and How We Use It*, 1994, at pp. 40-41.

undetermined Serbs in the Kraijna; self-determination for Kosovars undetermined Serbs in Kosovo, and so on.

Nor has self-determination always proven to be a peaceful process. Precisely because self-determination in these situations upends existing relationships, it will be resisted by those about to suffer undetermination. Nor is the process of self-determination always confined to a particular territory, especially when ethnic distribution is not congruent with political boundaries. Application of the principle of self-determination, which in Woodrow Wilson's romantic vision seemed entirely irenic and internal to a territory, was generating nasty violent conflicts, sometimes yielding inefficient or even failing States, auguring further fragmentation and posing threats to regional and international peace.

As UN Secretaries-General were usually the ones tasked with managing the detritus of unsuccessful self-determinations, they were among the first to sound the alarm. Because self-determination, by contrast to decolonisation, often imported secession with its attendant disruptions, Secretary-General U Thant stated as early as 1970:

> "So, as far as the question of secession of a particular section of a Member State is concerned, the United Nations' attitude is unequivocal. As an international organization, the United Nations has never accepted and does not accept and I do not believe that it will ever accept the principle of secession of a part of its Member State." [258]

Secretary-General Boutros Boutros-Ghali took an even more forceful position. His "Agenda for Peace", prepared in 1992 at the request of the Security Council, stated that

> "[f]ierce new assertions of nationalism and sovereignty spring up, and the cohesion of States is threatened by brutal ethnic, religious, social, cultural or linguistic strife. Social peace is challenged on the one hand by new assertions of discrimination and exclusion and, on the other, by acts of terrorism seeking to undermine evolution and change through democratic means . . . if every ethnic, religious or linguistic group claimed statehood, there would be no limit to fragmentation, and peace, security and economic well-being for all would become ever more difficult to achieve" [259].

258. U. Thant, "Press Conference held in Dakar, Senegal", *UN Monthly Chronicle*, Vol. 7 (4 January 1970), at p. 36.

259. UN Secretary-General, An Agenda for Peace-Preventive Diplomacy, Peace-making and Peace-Keeping: Report of the Secretary General, 17 June 1992, UN Doc. A/47/277-S/24111, at para. 17.

The wars in former Yugoslavia provided painful examples of what self-determination in ethnically and religiously mixed States can actually mean. The conflicts proved resistant to diplomatic solutions; even the prospect of international war crimes trials failed to deter the alarmingly widespread commission of atrocities. In retrospect, investing the international effort to stabilise and sustain ethnically heterogeneous States, for all of their internal tensions, seemed, on balance, a more plausible solution – if an effective oversight role for international human rights institutions could be designed and put in place.

Consider the Balkans: for almost forty-five years in the latter half of the twentieth century, the Yugoslav Federation had succeeded in containing many of the exclusive identifications of that corner of the Balkans and bringing to the forefront a composite secular, transethnic "Yugoslav" identity. It had failed to achieve a high human rights quotient in some key sectors, but it had maintained minimum order and permitted the members of the different groups to live together, intermarry and move about the territory in search of more attractive life opportunities. The reality and expectation that Yugoslavia would continue to be a transethnic community minimised if they did not eliminate the strategic importance of who people were and where they lived. The historian Margaret MacMillan has written:

> "The peoples of Yugoslavia lived together peacefully, if not always happily under Tito's firm rule because, as a Croat put it, 'every hundred yards we had a policeman to make sure we loved each other very much'. When Tito died and his Communist Party fell to pieces, the different ethnicities in Yugoslavia, urged on by unscrupulous demagogues turned on each other." [260]

The critical implication of the break-up of Yugoslavia was not only territorial but psycho-political. As the plausibility of the "Yugoslav" identity decayed, older identities inevitably revived. More and more erstwhile "Yugoslavs" began, not irrationally, to reidentify themselves and others as Serbs, Croats, Bosniacs, Roman Catholics, Orthodox Christians or Muslims. Those who tried to resist in favour of retaining a transethnic secular identity found it less and less plausible, for the predicate of that identity had been the Yugoslav Federation; but it was being dismantled and soon no longer existed. In this new situation, the spatial intermingling of peoples that had been a beneficent consequence

---

260. Margaret MacMillan, *War: How Conflict Shaped Us*, 2020, at p. 15.

of the Yugoslav Federation began to take on a new and fearful meaning. As parts of the Federation seceded in the name of ethnic nationalism, non-ethnics suddenly found themselves redefined, *in situ*, as minorities or, worse, as *irridenta*, facing, in the case of one of the new ethnic States, a majority Government that revived and adopted the symbols of an earlier regime searingly remembered for the intense racial and ethnic violence it practised.

In this rapidly emerging new reality, group security for ethnic and language groups, a concern that had been in the process of becoming progressively irrelevant in a federated entity, acquired urgent new importance. Territorial contiguity for each group became the obsession of its security specialists. If forced population transfers were resisted, they were accomplished by pogroms, gross atrocities and massacres. Atrocities were committed by all sides but, according to reliable reports, were most attributable to Serbian regular and irregular forces [261]. None of this should have come as a surprise, for this was not the first occurrence in the United Nations era of the violence that attends the dissolution of a multi-ethnic State: recall the massive violence that accompanied the self-determination of Pakistan from India and, later, Bangladesh from Pakistan.

Secretary-General Boutros-Ghali was not the only one to draw attention to the acute human rights problems latent in acts of self-determination. Other views reflecting the dark undersides of self-determination began to appear. In 1995, the General Assembly issued a Declaration on the occasion of its fiftieth anniversary in which it retreated from its unqualified endorsements of self-determination. The Member States will, the General Assembly said,

> "[c]ontinue to reaffirm the right of self-determination of all peoples, taking into account the particular situation of peoples under colonial or other forms of alien domination or foreign occupation, and recognize the right of peoples to take legitimate action in accordance with the Charter of the United Nations to realize their inalienable right of self-determination. This shall not

261. *Bosnian Genocide case*, *supra* footnote 172; *Prosecutor* v. *Radislav Krstic*, Judgment of the Int'l Crim. Trib. for the Former Yugoslavia, 19 April 2004, Case No. IT-98-33-A, at paras. 2-3 ("The depravity, brutality and cruelty with which the Bosnian Serb army ('VRS') treated the innocent inhabitants of the safe area are now well known and documented. Bosnian women, children and elderly were removed from the enclave, and between 7,000–8,000 Bosnian Muslim men were systematically murdered" (internal footnotes omitted)).

be construed as authorizing or encouraging any action that would dismember or impair, totally or in part, the territorial integrity or political unity of sovereign and independent States conducting themselves in compliance with the principle of equal rights and self-determination of peoples and thus possessed of a Government representing the whole people belonging to the territory without distinction of any kind" [262].

That narrowed the ambit within which self-determination could operate. The principle of self-determination was too sacred a cow simply to be dispatched to the abattoir of international law, but the Assembly was trying to put it out to pasture.

In 1998, the Supreme Court of Canada, a judicial body that had demonstrated on many occasions an admirable commitment to international human rights and, in particular, to the rights of indigenous peoples, issued its opinion on the lawfulness of the possible secession of the province of Quebec [263]. After reviewing trends of decision on self-determination, the Court concluded that "[t]he international law principle of self-determination has evolved within a framework of respect for the territorial integrity of existing states". That was quite a restriction, but the Court allowed that what it called "external" self-determination was still available in international law with respect to three categories of aspirants: those under colonial rule; those under foreign occupation; and, with somewhat less certainty, a people whose effort "to exercise its right to self-determination internally is somehow being totally frustrated". But the Court acknowledged that, even with its own more restrictive approach to the principle of self-determination, a claim to political independence based upon effective power would still result in the establishment of a new State:

> "No one doubts that legal consequences may flow from political facts, and that 'sovereignty is a political fact for which no purely legal authority can be constituted . . .', . . . Secession of a province from Canada, if successful in the streets, might well lead to the creation of a new state." [264]

The Court's "legal consequences from political facts" hearkened back to the pre-Charter constitutive arrangement in which the establishment

262. GA Res. 50/6, 9 November 1995.
263. *Reference re: Secession of Quebec*, [1998] 2 SCR 217 (Can.).
264. *Id.*, at para. 142.

of new States was based on effective power. The scope for self-determination that remained was being more narrowly and contingently defined and the criterion of effectiveness was being cautiously and reluctantly readmitted to the lexicon of constitutive participation arrangements in international law.

The principle of self-determination was a major human advance over the pre-existing legal arrangement. It was installed in international law at a time when there was no vocabulary for human rights, and it served perforce as the essential conception of human rights. As a substitute for human rights, however, it was insufficient, inasmuch as indigenous no less than alien elites could abuse the human rights of those subject to them; moreover, in heterogeneous populations the self-determination of one group involved the subordination of other groups. If self-determination solved one human rights problem, it failed to solve others and aggravated or even created new problems, which, if not addressed, could frustrate the humanitarian impulse which had animated the principle of self-determination in the first place.

One need not recite, once again, the evils and iniquities of European *and* non-European colonialism (vestiges of the latter still persisting and too often overlooked) and imperial control and their inevitable moral hazard, nor should one ignore their survival in various regions: the exploitation of one group by another was a defining legal practice of the previous epoch and its persistence is noxious. The principle of self-determination inspired the decolonisation movement and became the basis and vocabulary for challenging the morality of the existing order; it has an honoured place in the history of international law. But the international community has learned from bitter experience that self-determination is not always a human rights panacea nor is it a necessary precondition for such a panacea. The problem in the case-by-case application of the principle of self-determination has been the failure to integrate self-determination in particular cases with the other relevant policies of international law in ways sensitive to the unique context of each case so as to achieve the best possible approximation of all of the policies concerned [265].

One should note, first, a certain anachronism in the current application of the principle. When self-determination entered international law's lexicon, there was, as noted earlier, no authoritative vocabulary for

265. See *infra* Chapter XIV, Section 2, Paragraph 4, for discussion of the procedural Principle of Contextual Integration.

human rights. In retrospect, it is clear that self-determination was being pressed into service as an omnibus and highly general term for what is now the elaborated and still evolving codex of human rights in international law. Proponents of self-determination then simply assumed that human dignity would be achieved if a "people" were governed by an indigenous leadership in its own territorial space rather than by an ethnically or racially distinct elite from a distant land. Experience has shown, sadly, that the assumption is simplistic.

In the twenty-first century, there will be fewer and fewer "pure" tribal States or even tribal areas within States. An increasing number of different ethnicities and different clans, tribes and subtribes, language and dialect groups, and socio-economic classes perforce live, cheek by jowl, in the same politically organised spaces. In this situation, the solution to group conflict can no longer simply be the superordination of group after group in an endless division and subdivision based on the automatic application of an absolute right to self-determination. Rather, the solution must be found in the effective application of internationally prescribed human rights. The international legal process now has more efficient means for accomplishing minimum order and human dignity.

Even the so-called "remedial self-determination" may have to be used sparingly. Although its justification is the occurrence of massive human rights deprivations, application of the remedy of self-determination in specific cases must still promise to establish a tolerable public order system and not to lay the basis for deprivations on other internal groups whose un-self-determination will then lead them to agitate for their own self-determination. Other solutions may be found in the effective application of internationally prescribed human rights, if necessary, through forms of interim or contingent international governance. The point of emphasis is that the international legal process now has more varied and effective means of accomplishing minimum order and human dignity within territories than the automatic application of a one-size-fits-all principle of self-determination, with its own pathogenic potentials.

Section 3. The ironic role of uti possidetis

If the ambit of the operation of the principle of self-determination has been narrowed in recent practice, an important contingent role for it remains in circumstances in which the only feasible remedy for gross and persistent violations of the human rights of a population is secession and the establishment of an independent State. In this regard, recall the doctrine of *uti possidetis*, which had been adapted from Roman law by the new republics in Central and South America as a way of protecting the independence which they had just wrested from their colonial master. As a device to protect self-determination, *uti possidetis* has, ironically, been transformed into a doctrine which will often have the effect of restraining self-determination in situations of decolonisation. In Cairo, in 1964, the Conference of African Heads of State and Government of the Organization of African Unity declared that all of the Member States "solemnly . . . pledge themselves to respect the frontiers existing on their achievement of national independence" [266].

The purpose of the Cairo Declaration was explained as "respect for the principle of the intangibility of frontiers inherited from colonization" [267]. Given the fact that European States had created the boundaries in Africa without regard to the tribes and clans which were henceforth divided by these boundaries, the future implications of the Cairo Declaration for self-determination were uncertain. In the case concerning the *Frontier Dispute* between Burkina Faso and Mali [268], Judge Abi-Saab, in a thoughtful separate opinion, noted the irony:

> "At first sight, it may indeed seem paradoxical that peoples that have struggled for their independence should set so much store by their 'colonial heritage'. At the beginning, however, at the time when the Latin American countries were achieving independence, the principle of *uti possidetis* was formulated to serve a dual purpose: first, a defensive purpose towards the rest of the world, in the form of an outright denial that there was any land without a sovereign (or *terra nullius*) in the decolonized territories, even in unexplored areas or those beyond the control of the colonizers; secondly, a preventive purpose: to avoid or at least to minimize conflict occurring in a relationships among the successors, by freezing the carved-up territory in the format it exhibited at the moment of independence." [269]

Professor Steven Ratner has observed that

266. OAU AGH/Res. 16 (I), July 1964.
267. *Id.*
268. *Frontier Dispute (Burk. Faso* v. *Malawi)*, Judgment, 22 December 1986, ICJ Reports 1986, p. 554.
269. *Id.* at pp. 661-662 (Separate Opinion of Judge Abi-Saab).

> "the easy embrace by governments of *uti possidetis* and the suggestion that it is now a general rule of international law to govern the breakup of states lead to two distinct, yet opposite, spillover effects that endanger global order at this time of ethnic conflict" [270].

The second danger to which Professor Ratner draws attention goes to the frustration of self-determination:

> "[T]he extension of *uti possidetis* to modern breakups leads to genuine injustices and instability by leaving significant populations both unsatisfied with their status in new states and uncertain of political participation there. By hiding behind inflated notions of *uti possidetis*, state leaders avoid engaging the issue of territorial adjustments – even minor ones – which is central to the process of self-determination." [271]

Professor Ratner proceeds to propose four guidelines, largely influenced by territorial and prior boundary considerations. But when the international community finds that it must resort to self-determination as the only plausible remedy for severe human rights deprivations, should the issue be prior territorial boundaries or the creation of future coherent territorial communities?

Section 4. Recognition

As long as the principle of effectiveness controlled membership arrangements and the principle of self-determination did not reign, it was entirely proper for Governments in their own membership decisions to do whatever served their strategic interests. The modality by which such decisions were taken was generally called "recognition"; the term referred broadly to the ways that one State elite determined its attitude and adjusted its actions with respect to an aspirant for membership. When an existing State or coalition of States was so powerful that its attitude and resultant actions could determine whether an aspirant to membership would in fact prove to be effective, recognition could properly be characterised as "constitutive" of that new State. When the internal effectiveness and external context of the aspirant ensured

270. Steven R. Ratner, "Drawing a Better Line: *Uti Possidetis* and the Borders of New States", *Am. J. Int'l L.*, Vol. 90 (1996), p. 590 *et seq.*, at 591.
271. *Id.*

its survival with or without the approval and support of other States (if not in the face of their military opposition), the act of recognition could be no more than "declaratory" of the attitude and course of action which the recognising State would henceforth practise with respect to the new State. Securing the recognition by other States may have been convenient for the aspirant, but it was not existential.

In 1950, before the ramifications of the principle of self-determination were fully appreciated, a United Nations study observed the absence of international legal obligations with respect to recognition:

> "The recognition of a new State, or of a new government of an existing State, is a unilateral act which the recognizing government can grant or withhold. It is true that some legal writers have argued forcibly that when a new government, which comes into power through revolutionary means, enjoys, with a reasonable prospect of permanency, the habitual obedience of the bulk of the population, other States are under a legal duty to recognize it. However, while States may regard it as desirable to follow certain legal principles in according or withholding recognition, the practice of States shows that the act of recognition is still regarded as essentially a political decision, which each State decides in accordance with its own free appreciation of the situation." [272]

If self-determination and the autonomy of territorial communities have, indeed, become cardinal principles of contemporary international law, should not other States be precluded from using any other grounds with respect to a new candidate for international membership?

In 1992, the European Community issued Guidelines on the prerequisites for recognition, which were more in keeping with a progressive constitutive arrangement based on fundamental human rights principles:

- respect for the provisions of the Charter of the United Nations and commitments subscribed to in the final act of Helsinki and in the Charter of Paris, especially with regard to the rule of law, democracy and human rights;
- guarantees for the rights of ethnic and national groups and minorities in accordance with the commitments subscribed to in the framework of the Commission on Security and Cooperation in Europe (CSCE);

272. UN Secretary General, Memorandum on the Legal aspects of the Problem of Representation in the United Nations, 8 March 1950, UN Doc. S/1466.

- respect for the inviolability of all frontiers which can only be changed by peaceful means and by common agreement;
- acceptance of all relevant commitments with regard to disarmament and nuclear non-proliferation as well as to security and regional stability; and
- commitment to settle by agreement, including where appropriate by recourse to arbitration, all questions concerning State succession and regional disputes.
- The Community and its Member States will not recognise entities which are the result of aggression. They would take account of the effects of recognition on neighbouring States [273].

The United States made similar statements [274].

For a brief period, it seemed as if the international legal system might be advancing towards adoption of the sort of internationally prescribed recognition arrangement that Sir Hersch Lauterpacht had proposed in 1947 [275]. However, the principle of effectiveness (not to speak of political convenience) continues to be the lodestar of most State recognition practice. When efforts at collective constitutive recognition fail, actors accommodate to an unyielding reality. Recall the doctrine of the Canadian Supreme Court in *In Re Quebec*. Conversely, when an aspirant meets the exacting standards of statehood and is effective within its territory yet is forcefully opposed by another powerful actor, legal fictions are put in place to deny formal membership while granting many of its incidents. These entities have been nicely styled "phantom States" [276].

The international reluctance to recognise the Government of Somaliland is inconsistent with the European Community policy, for that territorial community amply fulfils the criteria of effective statehood and self-determination. Indeed, Somaliland exists in a region in which some States that enjoy *de jure* recognition do not fulfil all of these criteria. Similarly, the reluctance to *formally* acknowledge the status of Taiwan is manifestly driven by concerns about offending a major

273. EC Declaration on the "Guidelines on the Recognition of New States in Eastern Europe and in the Soviet Union", 16 December 1991.

274. Civil Strife in Yugoslavia: The United States Response: Hearing Before the Subcomm. on European Affairs of the S. Comm. On Foreign Relations, 102nd Cong. 1-3 (1991) (Statement of Senator Joe Biden, Chairman of the Senate Foreign Relations Comm.).

275. Sir Hersch Lauterpacht, *Recognition in International Law*, 1947, at p. 6.

276. Daniel L. Byman and Charles King, "The Phantom Menace", *New York Times*, 16 August 2011, at p. 21.

power which continues to claim that territory. Different considerations have impeded the formal recognition of Palestine. In situations such as these, quasi-diplomatic relations are often established [277].

Thus, much of the recognition arrangement is often more myth system than operational code: many States may acknowledge the existence and relevance of international standards, but they continue to demand a unilateral right to recognise or withhold recognition of States without international review of their decisions. That may be changing. In recent years, the United Nations has begun to play a distinctly more active role in the establishment and transformation of participants. In contested elections in Zimbabwe, Kenya and Ivory Coast, the United Nations took an active role, even though all of them were plainly matters within domestic jurisdiction.

It is tempting to view admission to a universal international organisation, such as the United Nations, as a form of collective international, if not necessarily constitutive, recognition. But the actual dynamics of admission underline the largely unilateral character of the arrangement. It is only upon recommendation by the Security Council that the General Assembly admits a new member, so any permanent member may block admission. Admission to United Nations membership may indicate support for a new member of the international system and, by providing access to that arena, enhance its effectiveness. But refusal to admit does not necessarily deprive a territorial community of other membership rights in other international community processes; the scope of those rights will depend upon the strength and political adroitness of the State concerned.

In the future, one would hope that the process of recognition will increasingly be inclusive and collective and that enlightened international standards, like many of the European Guidelines, will be applied. Enlightened decisions would also take account of the minimum order consequences, at the local as well as global level, of the admission to membership of a new State.

---

277. As, for example, in the Taiwan Relations Act, 22 USC, para. 3301-3316 (1979); see also David Rowe, *Informal "Diplomatic Relations": The Case of Japan and the Republic of China*, 1975, at p. 14 (characterising the relations that developed in the 1970s between Japan and the Republic of China as a "system for conducting their business . . . in the absence of normal inter-governmental agencies and instrumentalities for doing so").

CHAPTER IX

SOVEREIGNTY AND HUMAN RIGHTS: CHANGING THE INTERNAL ARRANGEMENTS OF STATES BY EXTERNAL MEANS

> "To those for whom the greatest threat to the future of international order is the use of force in the absence of a Security Council mandate, one might ask – not in the context of Kosovo – but in the context of Rwanda: If, in those dark days and hours leading up to the genocide, a coalition of States had been prepared to act in defence of the Tutsi population, but did not receive prompt Council authorization, should such a coalition have stood aside and allowed the horror to unfold?"
>
> Kofi Annan[278]

One of the key prizes of membership in international law's club of States is sovereignty. Floods of ink have washed over the term and congealed into an almost theo-legal carapace. Stripped of its mysticism, sovereignty is simply the demand of each territorial community, however small and weak with respect to other States and however it has organised itself internally, to be permitted to govern itself without interference from other, larger or more powerful States and, at least until 1945, without interference by any of the agencies of the organised international community. Everyone demands respect for the sovereignty of their own State – except when it is inconvenient. On a human rights mission to a country then suffering under a prolonged and violent military dictatorship, a clergyman, known for his courageous and outspoken liberalism, leaned towards me and whispered, "We need an intervention!"

Insulation from interference by international organisations was an assurance which State elites sought before joining them. The Covenant of the League of Nations had established as a cardinal principle that matters "solely" within the domestic jurisdiction of a State were not to be subjected to the competence of the League. That insulation became more porous in the Charter of the United Nations. Its Article 2 (7) confirmed part of this principle but added that it "shall not prejudice the application of enforcement measures under Chapter VII". This

278. UN, "Secretary-General Presents His Annual Report to General Assembly", Press Release, 20 September 1999, SG/SM/7136, GA/9596.

effectively subordinated national sovereignty to the requirements of world order.

Article 2 (7) neatly captures the tension between two fundamental policies of contemporary international law. The international legal system is unimaginable without some concept of sovereignty, for States are the indispensable means for local order and the provision and protection of human rights. But the contemporary international legal system is also inconceivable as a system without an international prerogative to interfere with sovereignty, at the very least when the maintenance of minimum world order requires it.

The ink was scarcely dry on the Charter before the notion of a sovereign *domain reservé* came under further assault. Factors such as decolonisation, guilt over the irresolute response to the atrocities committed during World War II, official abhorrence of racial discrimination and, more generally, the installation of a progressively more ambitious code of human rights all worked to install an evolving set of standards of international minimum requirements for governance *within* States.

Effective restrictions on sovereignty have come in many forms. International media-made law, as described in Chapter V, Section 3, has elaborated an implicit but even more inflected, though inconsistently applied, code of good governance. Even the infrastructural arrangements of national economies have become subject to international regulation. For several decades, international financial institutions relied on the technique of "conditionality" to compel changes in the internal arrangements of States before financial benefits would be proffered. In IMF practice, so-called "structural adjustments" were ostensibly designed to create internal economic structures conducive to national development [279]. The technique was abandoned, in large part, in the 1990s but has recurred in the twenty-first century.

During the period in which the technique of conditionality was used, it was not extended to policing human rights matters. In contrast, the European Union, as we saw in the preceding chapter, has used various forms of political conditionality with respect to compliance with international human rights prescriptions as a condition for extending recognition or allowing membership in the European system. Pre-accession requirements were put in place and domestic practices were

279. IMF, Policy Development and Review Department, Conditionality and Fund-Supported Programs – Overview, 20 February 2001, https://www.imf.org/external/np/pdr/cond/2001/eng/overview/.

assessed in their terms. How strictly these various programmes have been applied after admission and how consistent has been the insistence on meaningful, continuing compliance is another matter.

International investment arbitration, which emerged later in the century, has evolved into an additional form of international supervision over national governance and has come to play a more particularised role in supervising the internal arrangements within States parties to them. Bilateral investment treaties (BITs), of which there are now almost 3,000, seek to establish an orderly framework for investment by creating, in the language of a typical United Kingdom BIT, "favourable conditions for greater investment by nationals and companies of one state in the territory of the other state". "Favourable conditions" consist not only of natural phenomena like climate, ecology, geography and human resources but include, critically, an effective legal system, including impartial courts, an efficient and legally disciplined bureaucracy, and that measure of transparency in decision-making which is now recognised by the international standard of governance as a necessary control mechanism over Governments' decision-making.

Thus, BITs, like a number of other contemporary international arrangements, have raised international law's standard for scrutiny over the ways States conduct their internal affairs. And, unlike many other soft arrangements, BITs have bite, for they generally allow a qualifying investor, with neither the intercession nor leave of its own State, to invoke an international tribunal to review State action, in terms of whether it constituted "fair and equitable" treatment. When foreign investment is a significant part of a national economy, as it sometimes is in developing countries, internal governmental regulatory activity thus finds itself increasingly subject to formal international supervision by a network of international tribunals and institutions. This development is far-reaching, but it pales in comparison to the much more radical demand by some within the international community to intervene forcibly in a State to change a regime which is grossly violating the internationally prescribed human rights of its own citizens.

Section 1. Human rights and regime change

From its very origins, the international human rights movement danced around the antinomy between national sovereignty and the international protection of human rights. The great human rights instruments affirm fealty to both the sovereignty of States *and* the human rights of their citizens. The Helsinki Accords of 1975, for example, included, as co-equal principles, the familiar affirmations of sovereign equality, the inviolability of frontiers and non-intervention in internal affairs *along with* respect for human rights and fundamental freedoms, a term which included freedom of thought, conscience and religion, and self-determination. Ultimately, however, the international protection of human rights rests on the necessary postulate that, if it comes to a competition between the State and the protection of human beings, human beings should prevail. Former UN Secretary-General Kofi Annan, as the quondam protector of both State sovereignty and internationally guaranteed human rights, said it best: "State sovereignty, in its most basic sense, is being redefined . . . . States are now widely understood to be instruments at the service of their peoples, and not vice versa" [280].

The implications of the incipient constitutive change to which Kofi Annan referred cannot be overstated. In its most dynamic sense, modern international human rights law's central concern is how to transform regimes whose essential means of governance are repressive terror and torture into Governments whose methods of operation better approximate internationally prescribed governance standards.

A major purpose of the ICC is to indict culpable *sitting* Heads of State, and that purpose necessarily (and not coincidentally) imports a regime change. The indictment by the Special Court for Sierra Leone of Charles Taylor, then the elected President of Liberia, was a clear example of purposive international regime change [281], as was the indictment of Slobodan Milosevic by the International Criminal Tribunal for the former Yugoslavia and the indictments of President Al-Bashir and the initiation of enquiry of Col. Muammar Qaddafi by the ICC [282].

If the internal organisation and modes of governance of each State are now expected to meet certain prescribed international standards, a tension comes into play between the classical legal principles of State sovereignty and autonomy on the one hand, and internationally protected human rights on the other. In specific cases, that tension can become a clear contradiction. There is no theoretical agreement, but in

280. Kofi A. Annan, "Two Concepts of Sovereignty", *The Economist*, 18 September 1999, at p. 49.

281. *Prosecutor* v. *Taylor*, Indictment of the Special Ct. for Sierra Leone, 7 March 2003, No. SCSL-2003-01-I.

282. *Prosecutor* v. *Milošević*, Indictment of the Int'l Crim. Trib. for the Former Yugoslavia, 22 May 1999, No. IT-99-37.

practice modern international law has tried to resolve this contradiction in the following way: State sovereignty prevails in all but the most egregious instances of widespread human rights violations, in which case multilateral or, in extreme situations, unilateral action may be taken to secure an immediate remedy or even to change a regime. The resolution of the contradiction is imperfect, however, and controversy often arises in specific cases.

Contradictory principles can never produce a tidy jurisprudence, but these particular principles have allowed decision-makers to distinguish between lawful and unlawful regime changes. Consider a few examples from recent memory. In 1968, the Security Council applied Chapter VII of the Charter against the white minority Government of Rhodesia on the ground that it was a threat to the peace [283]. Internally, the regime of Ian Smith may well have been pathological, but it was hardly pathogenic, in the sense of threatening other States.

Similarly, with the blessing of the United Nations and the Organization of American States (OAS), the United States invaded Haiti to oust the military dictatorship and to reinstate the elected Government of Jean-Bertrand Aristide. The Security Council characterised the regime of General Raoul Cedras as a threat to the peace; though it was brutal internally, it posed no external threat [284]. In contrast, the Taliban Government, which provided the platform for Al-Qaida's aggressive acts, was characterised as a threat by the Security Council because its internal regime breached and also continued to threaten external peace [285].

Unilateral actions to change a regime, which were undertaken without UN authorisation, have not always been deemed unlawful. Consider the case of Nicaragua. In the 1970s, the United States had begun to withdraw its support from the Government of General Anastasio Somoza Debayle and to shift it to what appeared to be a broad-based and democratically inspired Sandinista National Liberation Front (Frente Sandinista de Liberación Nacional, FSLN). In 1977, the United States terminated military assistance and pressed other States, notably Israel and Guatemala, to stop supplying armaments to the Somoza Government. The United States went still further, initiating a resolution by the OAS calling for "the immediate and definitive replacement of

283. SC Res. 253, 29 May 1968, at p. 5.
284. SC Res. 940, 31 July 1994.
285. SC Res. 1378, 14 November 2001. But note that the resolution did not authorise, in terms, unilateral military intervention in Afghanistan.

the Somoza regime" [286]. The resolution, which was passed by OAS, was conditioned on securing a commitment from the Sandinistas to support a democratic, pluralist and non-aligned Government. The FSLN cabled its agreement on 12 July 1979. But the creation of a Marxist State by the Sandinistas, in violation of that commitment, led the United States to support the eponymous Contras in the long war that followed – a war that was terminated only when the Sandinistas, under international pressure, permitted an internationally supervised election to be conducted and were voted out of office.

Some ten years later, the United States again participated in a regime change when the OAS ministers condemned the usurpation of an election in Panama by General Manuel Antonio Noriega. Although the OAS General Assembly had urged "all the states to refrain from taking unilateral actions" [287], the George H. W. Bush Administration invaded Panama, put the recently elected Government in place and captured, tried and convicted Noriega in a US court.

During the same period, many other entirely unilateral and internationally unauthorised regime changes took place. The year 1979 alone witnessed four of them. Tanzania invaded Uganda and replaced the Idi Amin dictatorship with a Government led by a former elected president whereupon it withdrew. France invaded what was then known as the Central African Empire, imprisoned the self-styled emperor Jean Bedel Bokassa and put in power a former president of the country, David Dacko; France then withdrew. Vietnam invaded Cambodia, expelled the Khmer Rouge Government from Phnom Penh and put Hun Sen in power; it, too, withdrew. The Soviet Union invaded Afghanistan, overthrew and killed President Hafizullah Amin, installing Babrak Karmal as President, then subsequently replacing him with another puppet, Dr Najibullah [288].

None of these forcible regime changes in 1979 received any prior international or even regional authorisation. With the exception of the Soviet invasion of Afghanistan, however, all the other regime changes met with the general, if not unanimous, approval of the international community [289]. France and Vietnam installed friendly Governments in

286. Inter-American Comm'n on Human Rights, Report on the Situation of Human Rights in the Republic of Nicaragua, 30 June 1981, OEA/Ser.L/V/II.53, Doc. 25 (citing the Declaration adopted at the Seventeenth Meeting of Consultation of Ministers of Foreign Affairs on 23 June 1979).

287. OAS GA Res. 900, 18 November 1989, at para. 4.

288. See Anthony Arnold, *Afghanistan: The Soviet Invasion in Perspective*, 1985.

289. See GA Res. ES-6/2, 14 January 1980.

place of the regimes which they had ousted, but of the four only the USSR's military forces remained substantially present in the country it had invaded. In the Security Council, the United States objected to the Hun Sen Government in Phnom Penh. Reviewing the conflicting principles in the Charter, the US Permanent Representative, with, apparently, no sense of irony, said:

> "[W]e must look at one essential, contemporary fact. The troops of one country are now occupying the territory of another and have imposed a new government upon it by force of arms. That fact leads us to the conclusion that the solution to the problem we are discussing is clear: Viet Nam must immediately withdraw its armed forces from Kampuchea." [290]

Thereafter, the United States supported the Khmer Rouge Government as the properly credentialled representative of Cambodia in the United Nations [291]. Most of the rest of the world seemed to think that whatever may have been Hanoi's motives in changing the regime in Phnom Penh, putting an end to the Khmer Rouge nightmare was praiseworthy.

In 1982, Israel invaded Lebanon and tried to put Bashir Gemayel in power. Within days, Gemayel was assassinated in a massive bombing and the Israeli plan collapsed. Although there was no indication that Israel planned a long-term occupation of Beirut, it seemed that Israel believed that a Gemayel Government would be friendly and might prove to be dependent on Israel. The Israeli attempt at regime change was almost universally condemned [292].

Unilateral and unauthorised regime changes, however noble their motives may be, have a great potential for abuse; many of them certainly realised that potential. Consider the Kennedy Administration's abortive invasion of Cuba in 1961, in which it sought to replace the Castro Government with one it found more congenial; or the Johnson Administration's invasion of the Dominican Republic to reverse a popular coup and install a Government led by its then perennial President, Joaquin Balaguer; or the Reagan Administration's invasion of Grenada to suppress a coup; or the Soviet Union's various regime

290. UNSCOR, 34th Session, 2110th meeting, 13 January 1979, UN Doc. S/PV.2110, at p. 7.

291. See generally *United Nations Yearbook (1979)*, UN Sales No. E.82.I.1, at pp. 271-295.

292. *United Nations Yearbook (1982)*, UN Sales No. E.85.I.1, at pp. 428-432.

changes in Central Europe; or China's annexation of Tibet, which was accompanied by some regime change rhetoric.

Yet, in terms of human rights, some unilateral regime changes were beneficial for the people of the country concerned. The United States, for example, facilitated the comparatively peaceful expulsion of Philippine President Ferdinand Marcos and the ascendance to power of Corazon Aquino by a timely scramble of US fighter planes over Manila.

The ostensible justification of unilaterally policing international governance standards in other States is often a disguise for interventions driven by entirely different motivations. In some regime changes, efforts were taken – with varying degrees of conviction and success – to develop an international legal justification. In others, the States involved cultivated a refractory disregard for the law. In 1919, for example, as the Allied powers sought to change the Bolshevik regime in Russia, Winston Churchill observed sarcastically:

> "Were they at war with Soviet Russia? Certainly not; but they shot Soviet Russians at sight. They stood as invaders on Russian soil. They armed the enemies of the Soviet Government. They blockaded its ports, and sunk its battleships. They earnestly desired and schemed its downfall. But war – shocking! Interference – shame!" [293]

In earlier regime changes, the actors seemed to be following the lapidary advice of Philander Knox, Attorney General in President Theodore Roosevelt's Cabinet. When Roosevelt mused as to whether a legal argument should be framed to justify the US manipulation of the secession of Panama from Colombia (a major and internationally controversial regime change of the time) and the Canal Treaty that was promptly concluded as part of the package, Knox responded, "Oh, Mr. President, . . . do not let so great an achievement suffer from any taint of legality" [294].

The United States' action in Iraq in 2003 and the vicissitudes it entailed for all concerned provoked a short-term reconsideration of the international trend. The justifications that were invoked for that intervention ranged from non-compliance with UN Chapter VII resolutions, to pre-emptive self-defence against existing weapons of mass destruction (and when that phantom arsenal evaporated, pre-

293. Winston S. Churchill, *The Aftermath*, 1929, at p. 243.

294. Tyler Dennett and John Hay, *From Poetry to Politics*, 1933, at p. 381 (quoting Lyman Abbott, *Reminiscences*, 1915, at pp. 139-140).

emptive self-defence against the intention and ability to assemble and use them), to alleged Iraqi cooperation with Al-Qaida, to part of the "War on Terror" and, belatedly, to relieve the Iraqi people of vast and continuing human rights violations. Controversies about this dizzying kaleidoscope of rationalisations were momentarily eclipsed by the exigencies of implementing the regime change itself. On 23 September 2003, then UN Secretary-General Annan, whose lack of sympathy for the American initiative had been manifest, said to the General Assembly:

> "Whatever view each of us may take of the events of recent months, it is vital to all of us that the outcome is a stable and democratic Iraq – at peace with itself and with its neighbours, and contributing to stability in the region." [295]

In a grudging way, it was an acknowledgement of the irrevocability of even the most ill-conceived unilaterally initiated regime change and, prospectively, an argument against such initiatives. Yet the tension between violent repression and national sovereignty would not disappear.

The Responsibility to Protect, written concisely, if inelegantly, as R2P, is an international legal initiative that purports to require the Security Council to take "timely and decisive" action to protect civilian populations when a State "manifestly fails" to protect its population from genocide, war crimes, crimes against humanity and ethnic cleansing [296]. Any affirmation that gross violations of human rights within a State are matters of international concern is always welcome, but R2P retreats by lodging the international responsibility to act to protect, when the State fails to do so, exclusively in the Security Council. That may have reassured those elites threatened by international human rights, for the Council is often likely to be blocked by the veto of one of its permanent members. Yet UN actions in the early twenty-first century in Libya, Côte d'Ivoire, Kenya and Zimbabwe, implicating externally induced regime change in response to periods of instability and violence in weak States, suggest that R2P may be evolving in ways beyond what its creators intended.

---

295. UN Secretary-General, Secretary-General's Address to the General Assembly, 23 September 2003, https://www.un.org/sg/en/content/sg/statement/2003-09-23/secretary-generals-address-general-assembly.

296. UN Secretary-General, Implementing the Responsibility to Protect, 12 January 2009, UN Doc. A/63/677, at paras. 9 and 26.

Even when the conditions for the application of R2P are present, the selection of the means of implementation appears to be based on the opportunities the specific situation presents. In Côte d'Ivoire, Kenya and Zimbabwe, various United Nations organs attempted to broker deals between feuding political factions to protect civilians caught in election violence. In Kenya and Zimbabwe, the United Nations was successful in its negotiation efforts. By contrast, in Libya and Côte d'Ivoire, the Security Council was willing to authorise military force to protect civilians *against the wishes of a functioning Government*.

These few examples show that, theories of sovereignty notwithstanding, one persistent and controversial strain of modern international law's membership arrangements is about effecting adjustments in policies, personnel and political structures of presumptively "sovereign" States, through a variety of strategic modes, initiated from outside the State and not excluding military intervention. Some of the unilaterally induced changes were viewed contemporaneously or retrospectively as lawful; some were not. (We will undertake to identify – and appraise – the criteria of lawfulness of the operational code for this matter in Chap. XIII.) The question for international law in the twenty-first century is when, if at all, should externally induced regime change take place and how should it be accomplished?

Criteria for appraisal are available: international human rights instruments provide an authoritative template for domestic governance. The standard is not achieved in many States; civil society groups and the media routinely report human rights violations in timely and graphic fashion. But if civil society groups are now performing the invoking function in these matters, it is not clear as to who should perform the application function: who should enforce the human rights domestic governance framework in specific instances and how should it be done?

Even in systems of the most egregious human indignity, human rights transformations are best accomplished autochthonously, without external interference and especially without unilateral military intervention. Nevertheless, if there must be intervention from the outside, surely it is better for all if it is persuasive rather than coercive, indirect rather than direct, and inclusively authorised and accomplished rather than exclusively and unilaterally effected.

The problem with the implementation of these apparently self-evident propositions is to be found in the constitutive structures of the international system, which we reviewed in Chapter IV. In the first part of the twenty-first century, we find ourselves in the third type of constitutive process, partially effective. Recall that in 1995, in the Supplement to the Agenda for Peace, then Secretary-General Boutros-Ghali observed of "preventive diplomacy and peacemaking; peacekeeping; peace-building; disarmament; sanctions; and peace enforcement" that

> "[t]he United Nations does not have or claim a monopoly of any of these instruments. All can be, and most of them have been, employed by regional organizations, by ad hoc groups of States or by individual States" [297].

In the best of all worlds, the optimal way of using the military instrument in defence of the values of world order is through authorisation by the Security Council, acting in conformity with the procedures of the UN Charter and with broad political support in the General Assembly. The Agenda for Peace was crafted at a moment of international optimism about the possibilities of collective international action. It seemed that international law was moving from the third to the fourth type of constitutive process, from partially effective to effective.

But events have confirmed that the political dynamics which determine the structure of the constitutive process are not likely to allow for evolution to the fourth type of constitutive process. The values of international law and of the Charter itself cannot always be achieved by the Security Council operating through the Charter's procedures. Thus, Annan, in the context of NATO's internationally unauthorised bombardment of Serbia for purposes declared to be based on concerns for human rights within the then province of Kosovo, had to acknowledge that it was "tragic . . . but there are times when the use of force may be legitimate in the pursuit of peace" [298]. Bear in mind that the use of force to which he referred was an unauthorised unilateral one which was especially destructive: the extended aerial bombardment of the infrastructure of a Member of the United Nations [299]. In the Secretary-General's statement about intervention in Rwanda, which is quoted in the epigraph to this chapter, the issue was not the lawfulness of regime change as such but whether it could ever be accomplished

297. *Id.*, at paras. 23-24.

298. UN, "Secretary-General's Deeply Regrets Yugoslav Rejection of Political Settlement; Says Security Council Should Be Involved in Any Decision to Use Force", Press Release, 24 March 1999, SG/SM/6938.

299. UN, "Secretary-General Presents His Annual Report to General Assembly", Press Release, 20 September 1999, SG/SM/7136, GA/9596.

by unauthorised unilateral and violent means. The Secretary-General apparently then thought that in some extreme situations it could.

Ironically, just as international law had uneasily begun to accommodate itself to regime change as an exceptional lawful remedy, human rights-driven regime changes effected by military instrument, whether nationally or internationally initiated and supervised, have come to seem less and less feasible. The reasons for this development relate to fundamental and reciprocally stimulating changes in the technology of weapons, their proliferation, the asymmetry of adversaries and the decay of much of the conventional law of armed conflict.

In environments as different as Peru, during the Shining Path insurrection, Sri Lanka, during the insurrection of Tamil Eelam, in Afghanistan under Russian and then under United Nations authorised NATO action, Iraq under its occupation, and in NATO's humanitarian but later expanded mission in Libya in 2011, it has become painfully clear that a relatively small but highly organised and disciplined force is capable of controlling or paralysing a very large country. Shining Path never numbered more than 12,000 people in a country of more than 25 million; Tamil Eelam counted less than 20,000 members in a country of 19 million. The forces of Al-Qaida and Islamic State, like the earlier insurrections, were mounted by forces considerably smaller than the militaries of the States they confronted. In both cases, a coherent counter-ideology, intense discipline, the availability of lethal and highly mobile and innovative weapons used in a new form of warfare, ruthlessness in the selection of targets and the execution of operations, and the inculcation within insurgent ranks of an ethos of self-sacrifice were sufficient to counter the forces of a much larger body politic.

Faced with an adversary using this type of *modus operandi*, the targeted Government or its foreign or international organisational allies may often find a forceful response counterproductive, precisely because it can drive more of the general population to the other side. A more discriminating response, which, in the circumstances of these types of internal conflicts, cannot avert collateral damage, is sure to be decried by those parts of the international human rights community and the media that have become the primary invokers for human rights deprivations. Shining Path was neutralised, at least temporarily, by the fortuitous apprehension of its leader, Abimael Guzmán. Tamil Eelam was ultimately defeated by military methods which were themselves of dubious lawfulness. In determining candidates for human rights-driven regime change, determining who is responsible for the deterioration of human rights is becoming ever more difficult.

Regime change requires regime changers. The uncertainty as to who is the principal human rights violator and as to whether intervention will improve the situation is only one deterrent to action. Insofar as the world constitutive process continues to approximate the third model, the changers must be recruited on an *ad hoc* basis as coalitions of the willing, for which service fewer and fewer may volunteer. Diplomatic, economic and ideological strategies may be deployed, sometimes with success. But no matter how hideous a regime may be in terms of the governance of its population, direct external military action *on the ground* to change it now seems likely to be the exception. Ironically, the installation of international human rights has been challenged by the principle of effectiveness, in this instance, by the gruelling task of making human rights effective in States whose governance is notable for their absence.

In one possible future, external participation in regime change will be authorised by the Security Council. In another, it will be pursued selectively with general approval but without specific authorisation through diplomatic and economic instruments and by covert actions. A future in which the developments which have been described here are reversed entirely seems unlikely.

Section 2. Governments-in-exile

Finally, a consideration of techniques of externally induced regime change would be incomplete without a brief note on the so-called "Governments-in-exile" which enjoy a shadowy lawfulness in contemporary international law. On occasion, a group of individuals may try to influence from abroad the internal politics of their particular State by lobbying foreign Governments or international organisations, organising fellow exiles, providing information or even arms to cohorts at home, planning or executing invasions to overthrow what we might call "the Government-*in-situ*", and so on.

While these activities by nationals seem to be entirely internal political matters, they all must be conducted from the territory of another State and that State must decide, as a matter of its own policy, whether or not to permit – and beyond that to assist – them. The other State may try to use this agitation as a means of influencing the Government-*in-situ*. In some circumstances, the State from which the exiles are operating may permit the formation on its territory of a Government-in-exile. In effect, the State that allows its territory or resources to be so used is engaged in an effort at regime change.

The Government-in-exile is not a Government at all but a political and legal technique whose purpose is to influence, undermine or replace a particular Government-*in-situ* by trying to challenge and deprive it of its authority and, through that strategy, to undermine its control. The technique is available to exiled nationals or those abroad who identify with a real or mythic community associated with the territory controlled by the Government-*in-situ*.

The important international legal point is that the Government-in-exile technique cannot be deployed without the support or, at least, tolerance of other Governments. From the perspective of the host or haven-granting State and of all other States which must react in some fashion to a Government-in-exile's pretensions and claims, decisions about whether to provide money and access to individuals or to encourage them to form a Government-in-exile, to allow that Government-in-exile to operate or to allow it to enjoy any of the perquisites of statehood are part of the complex practice of promoting regime change.

The Government-in-exile technique flourishes in eras in which key actors seek not only to be members of the international political system but to transform it radically. Thus, the periods after the French Revolution, the Russian Revolution and the movement of decolonisation and anti-imperialism witnessed the formation of many Governments-in-exile. Many of these entities were given observer status within the UN General Assembly, where many Member States sympathised with their aspirations. That status enhanced their capacity to influence relevant decisions within those organisations.

The Government-in-exile technique is susceptible to abuse but it can also be a major instrument for inducing change within authoritarian systems in which power is so concentrated that internal resistance is all but impossible. We may expect it to be used in the twenty-first century. Its lawfulness is likely to turn on a case-by-case basis, on the human rights deficits of the Government-*in-situ*, the impossibility of indigenous transformation despite popular demand for it, the comparative human rights potential of the Government-in-exile and the extent of indigenous support for it.

CHAPTER X

THE ACTORS THEORY TRIES TO IGNORE

"What the cameras don't see, don't exist."

Harry Bartel [300]

Neither Henry Kissinger's proclamation that "History is the memory of states" [301] nor Thomas Carlyle's equally grandiloquent "The History of the World . . . was the biography of Great Men" [302] is distinguished for its empiricism: each adopts an arbitrary focus and then simply chooses to ignore all the other actors and their respective memories. But those others are there, and contemporary international law and its practitioners can no longer afford to ignore them, for they are not simply what international law is attached to; as Judge Higgins has put it, they must now all be reckoned as "participants" in the international legal process [303]. Certainly, many of the types of assignments international lawyers will encounter which we hypothesised in the first chapter require a broader conception of the range of actual *dramatis personae* of international law. Moreover, to understand the operation of many of the decision functions, you will need to identify all the effective participants. The question is not, as some scholars ask, whether they *should* be allowed to participate. They *are* participating, and since the loyalties of people, the ultimate actors in all social process, are increasingly transitive or transferable and the same individuals may operate, at different times, through many different composite actors, it is all the more urgent to identify the range of key actors who have become competitors and collaborators of States and the various transformations and hybridisations which these actors often undergo in practice.

Section 1. Intergovernmental organisations

Modern international law has witnessed the creation of a large number of international organisations, with permanent secretariats of

300. Deborah Shai, "Opera Buffa", in *id.*, *American Spectacles and Other Cultivated Illusions*, 1993, at p. 144.
301. Henry Kissinger, *A World Restored: Metternich, Castlereagh and the Problems of Peace, 1812-22*, 1964, at p. 331.
302. Thomas Carlyle, *On Heroes, Hero-Worship, and the Heroic in History*, Houghton Mifflin ed., 1907 (orig. 1840), at p. 18.
303. Higgins, *supra* footnote 257, at p. 39.

varying types and varying internal decision-making arrangements. The United Nations is viewed as the premier organisation, charged, as it is, with the maintenance of international peace and security. But international organisations cover the gamut of contemporary human enterprise.

By the final decades of the twentieth century, international organisations had become indispensable legal techniques for transnational challenges that require collective action for their resolution. They are sometimes romanticised as harbingers of world Government, but it is important to remember that they are created by Governments and other actors as techniques. We tend to personalise international organisations, and we speak of "the United Nations", "the IMF", and so forth, but, in analytical terms, they are simply a means for implementing a programme embodied in a treaty. Instead of the usual performance of the treaty by the respective States parties, however, some parts of performance are assigned to a group of individuals, known as a "secretariat" who operate in accordance with an explicit legal arrangement. The secretariat's assignment may involve performance of any of the functions of decision: intelligence or gathering information about the parties' performance; the formulation and promotion of new arrangements; their prescription as organisational policy; provisional characterisation of non-performance or violation of Member State obligations; applications; terminations of arrangements; and appraisals of the aggregate performance of the international organisation in question.

Much has been made of the so-called "separate legal personality" of international organisations as a signal achievement of contemporary international law, and while it certainly qualifies as a new variable in action, legal theory cannot triumph over reality; believing that these entities have untrammelled freedom of action will usually lead to disappointment. For the whole cannot be greater than the sum of its parts, and an international organisation is, in the final analysis, the sum of the States which created it and a tool created by States which have not renounced their claim of sovereignty.

However restricted the intentions of the designers of international organisations may have been, the creation of a secretariat as a means of performance brings about a qualitative change in a treaty. Individuals who are committed to the treaty and whose livelihoods depend on it become active participants. While their role is legally defined and confined, their contribution becomes a new variable in the implementation of the treaty.

Each State that elects to participate in a multilateral institution realises a different constellation of costs and benefits, but there are some common denominators. Each State sacrifices a measure (varying from State to State) of freedom of action in the area of regulation in return for a package of benefits that is expected to include comparable restraints on the actions of others. Each State expects to gain some amplification of national power in the pursuit of specific objectives when the multilateral institution which it joins becomes the vehicle for action that might otherwise have been undertaken (if at all) unilaterally.

Once established, international organisations are themselves both participants and arenas in which other participants interact. But in the world constitutive process, they always remain policy instruments of States. For small and very small States, multilateral institutions may become their major avenues for diplomacy, far outstripping bilateral relations and offering the most prized diplomatic posts. The small States' votes in these institutions may become their most formidable and possibly their only base of power; at critical moments their representatives may find themselves strategically placed, actively courted and acquiring a degree of influence and material assistance far beyond what they might expect as ambassadors in a traditional bilateral relationship [304]. By contrast, the larger the State and the greater its power, the more bilateral will be preferred over multilateral diplomacy, and the more measured the attitude towards international organisations.

But no State can afford to be oblivious to international organisations: as described in Chapter II, worldwide communications and the movement of persons, goods and services have created interdependencies to the point where the resources of even the most effective States can no longer adequately and economically achieve their objectives without the authority and material support available only through stable external alignments.

All that said, international organisations are odd political creations. Within each – despite the constant celebration of its supposedly pre-eminent *institutional* authority – the actual assignment of each State's representative is to pursue that State's particular objectives and to reinforce the powers of the organisation only insofar as it contributes to that end. From the standpoint of national Government officials charged with the conduct of their country's external affairs,

304. Ilyana Kuziemko and Eric Werker, "How Much Is a Seat on the Security Council Worth? Foreign Aid and Bribery at the United Nations", *J. Pol. Econ.*, Vol. 114 (2006), p. 905 *et seq.*

an international organisation is an instrument of policy to be wielded, like other instruments, in the pursuit of national interest, only some of which are common. Though some of these Government personnel may harbour secret loyalties to the larger international community, their public commitments, supported by oath and often reinforced by threats of severe criminal sanctions and promises of material and symbolic rewards, continue to be to their own States. Within some States, there may be official programmes – in schools, churches and the media – extolling an organisation like the United Nations, but it is only insofar as it serves the national interest. Primary loyalty to the State continues to be demanded and policed [305].

Notwithstanding their soaring rhetoric at ceremonial moments, few national officials are romantic about international organisations, for they know that the organisations' structure and powers have been hammered out in tough negotiations with their counterparts. They know that the highest-level personnel in the organisations have been selected and vetted by high-ranking Government representatives and, in effect, serve at their pleasure. They know and jealously insist on the power to select the managerial level of the organisations and, as in most selection processes, seek to replicate their own values in the persons they select. They have ensured that the organisations do not become financially independent so that the monetary resources of such institutions will depend upon continuing contributions by Governments. Above all, they are careful to ensure that the capacities of these institutions to engage in some specific form of coercive action depend upon provision of the necessary resources by member Governments.

As in all groups, legal arrangements are created *within* political processes and, not surprisingly, incorporate the values and demands of the most politically relevant actors. It should come as no surprise, therefore, that in their constitutions and prescribed procedures, critical international organisations reflect the relative power positions of the States that formed them at the time of the institution's creation. After all, politics is, at its most elemental, the pursuit of values by means of power; those who have more power are hardly likely to create institutions that minimise or neutralise that power and can then be used by their competitors to discriminate against their own interests. But the constitution of each organisation must still incorporate the divergent interests of many States, so the life of every arrangement and political

305. See *infra* Chapter XVI for further discussion of the personal dilemmas.

institution, as we saw in Chapter III, is marked by a constant testing and stressing of legal and other power arrangements, by those who feel themselves short-changed by them and who agitate for changes they believe will benefit them.

In a power arena, power is the coin of exchange and actors quite naturally seek to preserve or expand these "monetary reserves". International organisations, for all their internal legal character, continue to be arenas of the larger power process. All members of international organisations struggle to hold on to the power they have gained in their arrangements or to acquire more. In the United Nations, where organisational power is essentially assigned to the Security Council in which five States have permanent membership with a veto right over decisions they oppose, there is a constant struggle between small and mid-sized powers, on the one hand, who seek to change or "reinterpret" the Charter system, and, on the other, the permanent members who seek to preserve their status and "acquired rights". While the struggle often pits emotive symbols such as "democracy" and "equality" against equally emotive symbols such as "fidelity to law", it is essentially a struggle for power and influence. The same State that insists on "democracy" in one context is likely to insist on its "sovereign rights" *vis-à-vis* a smaller State in yet another and, of course, to indignantly denounce as an unlawful interference in its domestic jurisdiction any examination of the absence of democracy in its own internal processes.

One of the techniques of international institutional diplomacy is to clothe claims of special interest in the signs and symbols of common interest [306]. Happily, the very multiplicity of actors with diverse interests operates, in the aggregate, as some restraint on the pursuit of special interest, while the constant reiteration by all (whatever the degree of sincerity) of the symbols of common interest helps to reinforce the authority that undergirds the organisation.

Once an organisation is established, however, its internal power process may become quite different from the surrounding power arena. To some extent, institutions may acquire lives of their own – engaging employees who devote their careers and sometimes even their lives to them. Organisations can generate affirmative attitudes and loyalties. And although every organisation is created by and reflects a political power process, once an organisation is established, the formulation of its procedures in the language of the law brings the lawyers into

306. See *supra* Chapter III, Section 2.

play, introducing a complex calculus of distinctive legal values that henceforth becomes one of the factors influencing how the organisation will operate. Elements such as these are, in their own way, bases of power which introduce new factors into the international political process.

Consider from among the diversity of appliers which we surveyed in Chapter VII, the United Nations. The Charter has created other organs besides the Security Council. In many of them, power is distributed differently than it is in the Security Council. The permanent members of the Council represent most of the population, wealth and power of the world community; almost all of the power in the world community is represented in the Council itself. From time to time, the other organs of the United Nations may be mobilised by coalitions of smaller opposing States attempting to change the allocation of power within the institution. When this happens, the more powerful and organisationally endowed States react in ways that try to preserve their power. Thus, the ICJ has a broadly defined competence. Its Statute provides that "[t]he jurisdiction of the Court comprises all cases which the parties refer to it and all matters specially provided for in the Charter of the United Nations or in treaties and conventions in force" [307]. None of its fifteen members, a collegium whose membership selection arrangements were designed to include the nominees of the permanent members of the Security Council, has a veto. So one can envision initiatives to change the UN structure, which would surely be vetoed in the Security Council, producing a different and veto-proof outcome in the Court [308]. Although implementation of such a judgment will ultimately depend on the discretion of the Security Council, the mere authority of a judgment, or even an advisory opinion as to what the law is, may, in some contexts, have a significant political valence.

The most avid proponents of multilateralism hold to the belief that international organisational paralysis results from transient problems: the Cold War, the North-South division, the Palestine problem, the United States' invasion of Iraq and Afghanistan, the stand-off between China and the US, and so on. Solve the relevant transient problem, the multilateralist believes, and the organisations will finally be able

307. Statute of the International Court of Justice, 26 June 1945, 33 UNTS 933 (hereafter ICJ Statute), Article 36, para. 1.

308. See e.g. *Certain Expenses of the United Nations*, Advisory Opinion, 20 July 1962, ICJ Reports 1962, p. 151; *The Wall*, *supra* footnote 160. For an examination of this, see W. Michael Reisman, "The Constitutional Crisis in the United Nations", *Am. J. Int'l L.*, Vol. 87 (1993), p. 83 *et seq*.

to function as planned. Yet when the transient problem is resolved (or simply recedes because it has ceased to be important to key actors), the organisations still prove unable to act effectively just when they are most needed.

The reason for the paralysis is hardly recondite. Despite a degree of homogenisation of global culture in certain strata of the world's population, the elites (and many of the rank and file) of these States continue, as we noted earlier, to operate with identifications, demands and matter-of-fact assumptions about past and future that are significantly different from those held by their counterparts in other States. As a result, they perceive events and assess outcomes differently, a fact which becomes painfully apparent when organisations have to make fundamental decisions about world order.

As they are currently structured, the organisations often prove unable to act effectively, whether because of a veto right or a requirement of consensus. But the procedures that prove unable to avoid institutional paralysis are not accidental. They reflect interests and power distributions. Moreover, an adjustment of procedures is not likely to resolve the problem, for the obstacles to action are reflections of the international political process itself. So the alternatives for a State that is able to act are to proceed unilaterally or to do nothing, understanding that unilateral action might be deemed inconsistent with the law. Recall, in this regard, our discussion in Chapter IV of the four different constitutive processes and the latent perils, as explained in Chapter III, Section 6, to which one is exposed when acting according to the operational code.

To be sure, some coalitions of organisations and some regional organisations are sometimes more effective. But there is a paradoxical inverse relationship between the effectiveness of international organisations and popular attitudes within democracies towards them. In democratic societies, in which popular opinion may be mobilised and become a critical political variable, effective international organisations may provoke complex and inconsistent reactions in sectors of the public. The *raison d'être* of the modern State is to provide security and the conditions for welfare, while remaining responsive to individual demands. The more that international organisations attract loyalty and operate effectively, the more they are likely to generate anxieties and contradictory reactions in both the leadership and rank and file of precisely those States that are meaningfully democratic – a reaction demonstrated by the often ambivalent popular responses to the European Union and the bizarre animus against the United Nations by certain fringe groups in the United States [309].

Feelings such as these are likely to be further aggravated by the perception of loss of power which membership in each organisation engenders: citizens in stronger States will always feel that they have not received a measure commensurate with the responsibilities and costs that their power in the larger arena actually imposes on them; citizens of weaker States, insisting on the international norm of "sovereign equality", will always bemoan the asymmetrical distribution of power in the institution concerned [310].

Yet, despite all these trends and counter-trends and mixed record of achievements, international organisations remain indispensable for transnational matters that require collective action.

Section 2. Transnational corporations or MNES

The flowering in the nineteenth century of the modern corporate structure proved to be a critical stimulus for the development of world capitalism and what has become a continuously self-transforming global civilisation of science and technology. Corporations, the ICJ observed, have a "very important and extensive role in the international field" [311]. The technique of the corporate legal personality permits individuals and teams to assemble and focus capital, labour and enterprise in innovative productive ventures, to take calculated but defined risks by means of the technique of limited liability and, for transnational corporations, to distribute the components of economic activity among different national jurisdictions so as to secure the most advantageous economic, regulatory and tax regimes.

In earlier eras, the profiles of castles, palaces, cathedrals and mosques formed the characteristic skyline of the cities of the world. By the late twentieth century, the MNE had emerged as the era's distinctive form of national and transnational social organisation; in the twenty-first century, corporate skyscrapers form the craggy skyline that identifies the world's major cities. MNEs, disposing of enormous amounts of capital, labour and technology, commanding large numbers of people

309. Dahl, *supra* footnote 66, at p. 319.
310. UN Charter, *supra* footnote 108, Article 2, para. 1.
311. *Case concerning Barcelona Traction, Light and Power Company, Limited (Belg.* v. *Spain)*, Judgment, 5 February 1970, ICJ Reports 1970, p. 3 (hereafter *Barcelona Traction*), at 33.

and often providing them with the welfare benefits rivalling those associated with the State, now even exceed in size and influence many Governments. In some instances, MNEs have exercised virtual control over sovereign Governments, as in the so-called "banana republics" of an earlier era.

In liberal capitalist systems, as we saw in Chapter II, Section 4, the elites of MNEs may play a role in the formulation of foreign policies and international legal positions of the States within which they operate, trying to shape national policies that will facilitate realisation of their own economic objectives. In the United States, lobbies of corporations with critical foreign interests – for example, mineral extractive companies, which by their nature must operate transnationally – try to influence not only national legislation but also specific planks of national foreign policy. By the latter half of the twentieth century, MNEs were acting on the international plane without governmental intermediation, dealing directly with international financial and trade agencies, international environmental initiatives and international development programmes, in all of which their active participation had become critical.

No international legal arrangement or legal standard governs the creation of corporations; incorporation remains a national prerogative. If national laws are lax or loosely enforced, as they are in some jurisdictions, corporate entities may be created and used for criminal purposes and in ways violative of international law [312]. Once created, corporations are deemed nationals of the States within which they are registered, a curious and perhaps anachronistic transposition of the law with respect to persons [313]. Only the States in which the corporations are registered may espouse their claims before the ICJ, although States whose nationals are equity holders in a corporation registered in another State may engage in diplomatic protection of their nationals' equity. Thanks to many BITs, equity holders may pursue remedies on their own behalf before *ad hoc* international tribunals.

---

312. See Michael A. Becker, "The Shifting Public Order of the Oceans: Freedom of Navigation and the Interdiction of Ships at Sea", *Harv. Int'l LJ*, Vol. 46 (2005), p. 131 *et seq.*, at 132-133 (noting that "flags of convenience" – certain countries' open registration system for ships – are undertaken for economic and sometimes criminal purposes); Jeremy Firestone and James Corbett, "Maritime Transportation: A Third Way for Port and Environmental Security", *Wid. L. Symp. J.*, Vol. 9 (2003), p. 405 *et seq.*, at 406 (noting the criminal purpose underlying registration under a flag of convenience).

313. See *infra* Chapter XI, Section 1, Paragraph 1, for an analysis and a critique.

Although the international legal system has not installed arrangements regulating the creation of MNEs, it has tried to prescribe standards for their behaviour when they operate transnationally. Various attempts have been made by international organisations, Governments, NGOs, members of the public and even MNEs themselves to prescribe standards for corporate behaviour in the areas of human and labour rights, in particular, non-discrimination, environmental protection, product safety, good governance, bribery and corruption. The network of private regulatory entities in the global financial system is vast and complex, whether for the setting of the LIBOR (London Inter-Bank Offered Rate) or SIBOR (Sterling Overnight Interbank Average Rate) rate or the determination of whether an "event" has triggered credit default swaps.

Professor Peter Muchlinski has usefully identified six modes of regulation of MNEs: self-regulation; regulation by NGOs; national regulation; bilateral regulation; regional regulation; and multilateral regulation [314]. Some of these regulatory initiatives may prove particularly important in the future.

In 1974, the UN Economic and Social Council (ECOSOC) adopted resolutions establishing a UN intergovernmental commission and a Centre on Transnational Corporations to develop a code of conduct for MNEs [315]. The Commission on Transnational Corporations prepared various drafts of a Code of Conduct for Transnational Corporations [316]. Before the end of apartheid in South Africa, corporations were specifically prohibited from operations that would support the apartheid regime [317]. In the area of governance, corporations were to pledge to observe domestic laws, respect the national sovereignty and economic and development goals of their host countries [318] and to refrain from interfering in the internal affairs or intergovernmental relations of the host country [319]. Corporations were to abstain from corrupt practices,

314. Peter T. Muchlinski, *Multinational Enterprises and the Law*, 2nd ed., 2007.

315. ESC Res. 1908 (LVII), 2 August 1974; ESC Res. 1913 (LVII), 5 December 1974.

316. Report of the Intergovernmental Working Group on a Code of Conduct on its Fifteenth, Sixteenth, and Seventeenth Sessions, 5 June 1982, UN Doc. E/C.10/1982/6.

317. Development and International Economic Co-operation: Transnational Corporations, 12 June 1990, UN Doc. E/1990/94 (hereafter Draft Code of Conduct on Transnational Corporations), at para. 15 (the proposed text of the draft Code is contained in the annex).

318. *Id.*, at paras. 7-11.

319. *Id.*, at paras. 16-19.

such as giving or receiving bribes [320]. In their business practices, corporations were to abide by the principles set out in the International Labour Organization's (ILO) Tripartite Declaration governing conditions of work [321], and they were to "make every effort" to operate in a manner that would "enable them to contribute to the economic and social development of the countries in which they operate" [322], including by "strengthening . . . the scientific and technological capacities of developing countries" [323]. Corporations were also required to institute consumer protection standards and environmental protection regulations [324]. The second section of the draft Code established the United Nations Commission on Transnational Corporations as the "international institutional machinery for the implementation of the Code" [325]. But the draft Code proved controversial and failed to win the support of a majority of States and other stakeholders [326]. Some of the resistance to the draft Codes may have derived from their provenance. Originating in the UN system, they reflected the perspectives then held by developing countries and manifested hostility to MNEs. Although the Code was never finalised or adopted, it had some prescriptive effect through incorporation in part into later codes [327].

While the first version of the UN Code was still under discussion, the OECD, an organisation of capitalist and capital-exporting States, adopted a Declaration on International Investment and Multinational Enterprises, including a set of Guidelines for Multinational Enterprises [328]. The Guidelines call on companies to refrain from accepting or offering

320. *Id.*, at para. 20.

321. *Id.*, at para. 25. In 1977, the ILO adopted a Tripartite Declaration (Government, Employer, Worker) calling on MNEs to promote equal opportunity and collective bargaining in employment and to obey international agreements such as the Universal Declaration of Human Rights, the International Covenant on Civil and Political Rights, the International Covenant on Economic, Social and Cultural Rights, and others. The Declaration was not legally binding. For a summary, see Sean D. Murphy, "Taking Multinational Corporate Codes of Conduct to the Next Level", *Colum. J. Transnat'l L.*, Vol. 43 (2005), p. 389 *et seq.*, at 405-408; ILO, Tripartite Declaration Concerning Multinational Enterprises and Social Policy, 16 November 1977, 17 ILM 422 (1978).

322. Draft Code of Conduct on Transnational Corporations, *supra* footnote 317, at paras. 21-24.

323. *Id.*, at para. 36.

324. *Id.*, at paras. 37-43.

325. *Id.*, at paras. 66-70.

326. See Statement of Miguel Marin-Bosch, Chairman, Reconvened Special Session of the Commission of Transnational Corporations, UN Doc. E/1990/94/Add.1 (1990).

327. The Commission on Transnational Corporations was downgraded in 1994 with integration into the UN Conference on Trade and Development. See ESC Res. 1994/1, 14 July 1994; Murphy, *supra* footnote 321, at p. 405.

328. OECD, Guidelines for Multinational Enterprises, 15 ILM 969 (1976).

bribes [329]; to take account of the social and economic development goals of their host country [330]; to disclose important information about their business [331]; and to refrain from anti-competitive practices [332]. The Guidelines also direct enterprises to recognise the rights of employees to bargain collectively and form labour unions [333]. Enterprises are encouraged to diffuse science and technology into the host countries [334].

The OECD Guidelines, which were revised in 2000, call on enterprises to respect the human rights of those affected by their businesses and to work towards building local capacity and human capital [335]. New regulations also call on enterprises to contribute to the elimination of child, forced and slave labour and to refrain from discriminating among their employees "on such grounds as race, colour, sex, religion, political opinion, national extraction or social origin", unless in pursuit of an affirmative action policy [336]. An additional section was added stating that enterprises "should . . . take due account of the need to protect the environment, public health and safety, and generally to conduct their activities in a manner contributing to the wider goal of sustainable development" [337]. The new Guidelines expanded the section on corruption to include a prohibition on offering or receiving bribes and added a section on consumer protection [338].

In the international realm, NGOs have also promulgated voluntary codes of conduct for corporations. The Sullivan Principles, which were formulated by Reverend Leon H. Sullivan in 1977, were aimed at regulating the behaviour of MNEs operating in apartheid South Africa. Eventually over one hundred MNEs pledged not to allow racial segregation in their businesses. The Sullivan Principles generated a broader covenant for corporate responsibility when the Global Sullivan Principles of Social Responsibility were extended in 1999 to include principles such as employees' freedom of association, protection of the environment and promotion of sustainable development [339].

329. *Id.*, at p. 972.
330. *Id.*, at p. 972.
331. *Id.*, at p. 972-973.
332. *Id.*, at p. 974.
333. *Id.*, at p. 975.
334. *Id.*, at pp. 976-977.
335. OECD, Guidelines for Multinational Enterprises, 40 ILM 237 (2001), at 240.
336. *Id.*, at p. 241-242.
337. *Id.*, at p. 243.
338. *Id.*, at pp. 244-245.
339. Global Sullivan Principles of Social Responsibility, 1999.

Some MNEs are subject to transnational restraints that have been imposed by their own Governments. US companies, for example, are subject to the Foreign Corrupt Practices Act of 1977 (FCPA) which prohibits any "domestic concern"[340] from using the mails or other means of inter-State commerce "corruptly in furtherance of an offer, payment, promise to pay, or authorisation of the payment of any money, or offer, gift, promise to give, or authorisation of the giving of anything of value to" a foreign official, political party or political candidate for the purpose of:

> "(A) *(i)* influencing any act or decision of such foreign official in his official capacity, *(ii)* inducing such foreign official to do or omit to do any act in violation of the lawful duty of such official, or *(iii)* securing any improper advantage; or
>
> (B) inducing such foreign official to use his influence with a foreign government or instrumentality thereof to affect or influence any act or decision of such government or instrumentality,
>
> in order to assist such domestic concern in obtaining or retaining business for or with, or directing business to, any person."[341]

The FCPA exempts "facilitating or expediting" payments, "the purpose of which is to expedite or to secure the performance of a routine governmental action by a foreign official, political party, or party official"[342].

Cognate legislation has been adopted in other countries. But State regulations controlling the overseas activities of their corporations have moved only cautiously beyond the area of corruption. Several European States have instituted mandatory social and environmental reporting requirements[343]. For example, France's 2001 Nouvelles Régulations Economiques (NRE) and subsequent implementing legislation require publicly traded French companies to disclose information about a range of social issues such as human resources, labour standards and community interests, including the company's impact on development

---

340. 15 USC, para. 78dd-2 (2018).
341. 15 USCS, para. 78dd-2*(a)*(1) (2018).
342. 15 USCS, para. 78dd-2*(b)* (2018). For a critique of this broad exception and the FCPA more generally, see Reisman, *Folded Lies*, *supra* footnote 83, at pp. 160-164.
343. See Global Reporting Initiative, Government Initiatives to Promote Corporate Sustainability Reporting Roundtable, 2001, http://www.uneptie.org/outreach/reporting/docs/GrI_govtmeeting.pdf, at pp. 3-10.

of the territory surrounding its business [344]. The NRE also require disclosure of the company's environmental impact and efforts at management and protection [345].

In a number of countries, corporations have been held to account by private citizens and NGOs who have filed lawsuits under national law. In the United States, the Alien Tort Claims Act (ATCA) served as a vehicle for aliens who are the victims of a tort "committed in violation of the law of nations or a treaty of the United States" to sue the perpetrators of the tort [346]. Some US federal courts have allowed suits to proceed against corporate defendants under the ATCA for discrimination, crimes against humanity, war crimes, environmental devastation and torture, but the Supreme Court has now effectively closed the possibility [347]. The susceptibility of corporations to suit in US courts for violations of customary international law remains uncertain.

To an extent, lawsuits and the threat of lawsuits which are brought by individuals may act as controls on MNEs insofar as they may compel them to pay compensation for wrongs committed, whether in anticipation of the suits or as a result of them and, over the longer term, by inducing them to change their practices. Such suits may also act as indirect controls by generating negative publicity for the targeted companies, which may suffer decreased sales and even consumer boycotts. Indeed, the greater cost for companies may be less the direct pay-out from jury awards in the lawsuits and more from the prospect of declining revenue as a result of public discontent with their policies and the increasing costs of raising capital.

NGO campaigns to publicise corporate conduct violative of human rights and widely accepted labour practices sometimes are able to

344. Lucien J. Dhooge, "Beyond Voluntarism: Social Disclosure and France's Nouvelles Régulations Economiques", *Ariz. J. Int'l & Comp. L.*, Vol. 21 (2004), p. 441 *et seq.*, at 450.

345. *Id.*, at p. 451.

346. 28 USC, para. 1350 (2018).

347. See e.g. *Sarei* v. *Rio Tinto*, PLC, 456 F. 3d 1069 (9th Cir. 2006) (reversing lower court judgment dismissal on political question and comity grounds of mine workers' claims against mining company for racial discrimination, environmental devastation, war crimes and crimes against humanity); *Aldana* v. *Del Monte Fresh Produce*, NA, Inc., 416 F. 3d 1242 (11th Cir. 2005) (vacating dismissal of plaintiff national trade union officers' claims against produce company for mental torture); *Wiwa* v. *Royal Dutch Petroleum Co.*, 226 F. 3d 88 (2nd Cir. 2000) (reversing dismissal on grounds of *forum non conveniens* of Nigerian plaintiffs' claims to have suffered human rights abuses at the hands of oil company colluding with the Nigerian Government); *Kiobel* v. *Royal Dutch Petroleum Co.*, 133 S. Ct. 1659, 1669 (2013) (alleged violations must "touch and concern" the US); *Jesner* v. *Arab Bank*, PLC, 138 S. Ct. 1386, 1390 (2018) (foreign corporations may not be sued under the ATCA).

transform a respect deprivation or "shaming" sanction into a monetary deprivation when a company's customers react, in organised or spontaneous consumer boycotts. Because this is not yet a global phenomenon, corporations from States in which such informal controls do not operate often take the place of corporations that have been forced to leave. In a cruel irony, the successors may continue the offensive practices which were the real target of the sanctions but which, thanks to the reduction in competition, may now be conducted even more profitably.

In response to negative publicity regarding their business practices or in the shadow of threatened negative publicity, many MNEs have developed their own codes of conduct or signed onto voluntary codes developed by NGOs or intergovernmental organisations [348]. Though the codes have been praised for raising standards in some instances, they have also been criticised "as largely or potentially MNC [multinational corporation] public relations ploys" [349]. Be that as it may, these codes demonstrate the complex operation of the prescription and application functions of contemporary international law and the potential for more effective applications with respect to MNEs in the future.

Section 3. Non-governmental organisations

The number of NGOs operating on the local, national and international levels has increased dramatically since the end of the Cold War, but NGOs have been influential actors in many of the decision functions of the international political system for far longer. NGOs focusing on specific issues, for example opposition to the slave trade, emerged in the late eighteenth century [350]. Other issues which spurred NGO formation in the nineteenth century included pursuit of peace, worker solidarity,

348. See Lance Compa and Tashia Hinchliffe-Darricarrere, "Enforcing International Labor Rights through Corporate Codes of Conduct", *Colum. J. Transnat'l L.*, Vol. 33 (1995), p. 663 *et seq.*, at 675-683 (describing Levi Strauss's and Reebok's codes of conduct). Although Japanese companies are not widely susceptible to liability in Japan for the actions of contract factories abroad, many have issued corporate codes of conduct for their overseas suppliers, though the codes are more abstract than international codes and only generally reference labour and human rights. Koji Ishikawa, "The Rise of the Code of Conduct in Japan: Legal Analysis and Prospect", *Loy. L.A. Int'l & Comp. L. Rev.*, Vol. 27 (2005), p. 101 *et seq.*

349. Murphy, *supra* footnote 321, at p. 421.

350. The Pennsylvania Society for Promoting the Abolition of Slavery was founded in 1775, followed in 1787 in Britain by the Society for Effecting the Abolition of Slave Trade and in 1788 by the Société des Amis des Noirs in France. Steve Charnovitz, "Two Centuries of Participation: NGOs and International Governance", *Mich. J. Int'l L.*, Vol. 18 (1997), p. 183 *et seq.*, at 191-192.

free trade and the development of international law [351]. By the end of the nineteenth century and especially following World War I, NGOs were often functioning as pressure groups for ethnic groups seeking protection or independence. At the 1919 Paris Peace Conference, Jewish groups made presentations to the Governments in attendance and proposed peace treaty language [352]. Many other ethnic groups aspiring to statehood appeared at the conferences [353].

The effectiveness of NGOs in influencing policymaking ebbed and flowed from their early beginnings until the end of the Cold War, surging in periods of peace immediately following the world wars and rising dramatically after the end of the Cold War [354]. While it is difficult to find precise statistics on NGOs, primarily because there are so many of them and they emerge and transform so quickly, estimates suggest there are between 25,000 and 30,000 international NGOs in operation – a number all the more impressive if taken with the numerous domestic NGOs [355]. Two million NGOs are estimated in the United States alone. In Russia, where virtually none existed during the Cold War, there were 65,000 in 2000 [356], though the Government's tolerance of them has declined markedly [357]. Illustrating a different measure of NGO political significance, Jessica Mathews has written that NGOs "deliver more official development assistance than the entire UN system (excluding the World Bank and the IMF)" [358].

Various explanations have been offered for the proliferation of NGOs. Chief among them is the refinement and increased availability

351. *Id.*, at pp. 192-195.
352. *Id.*, at p. 214.
353. See MacMillan, *Paris 1919*, *supra* footnote 245.
354. See generally Charnovitz, *supra* footnote 350.
355. In 1995, a UN global governance report estimated that nearly 29,000 international NGOs were operating. Another more conservative estimate in 1999 put the number of international NGOs at 26,000 – an increase of 20,000 from 1990. "The Non-Governmental Order", *The Economist*, 9 December 1999 (hereafter "Order", *The Economist*) (citing the *Yearbook of International Organizations*). The 2006-2007 edition of the *Yearbook of International Organizations* counts 26,700 international NGOs, which does not include those that are apparently or currently inactive (an additional 26,063 NGOs). *Yearbook of International Organizations* (2006), at p. 3024, appendix 3, table 1a.
356. "Sins of the Secular Missionaries", *The Economist*, 27 January 2000 (hereafter "Sins", *The Economist*).
357. Amnesty International, "Russia: New 'Foreign Agents' Bill Further Erodes Freedom of Expression and Association", 19 November 2020, https://www.amnesty.org/en/latest/news/2020/11/russia-new-foreign-agents-bill-further-erodes-freedom-of-expression-and-association/.
358. Jessica T. Mathews, "Power Shift: The Rise of Civil Society", *Foreign Affairs*, January-February 1997, at p. 51.

of communications technologies, which we considered in Chapter II, and which allow low-cost communication and coordination of group activities worldwide. NGOs can reach a vaster audience and at a far lower price, via a website or email distribution than they could with a printed and "snail-mailed" newsletter. Ease of communication has also heightened public awareness about many of the problems that NGOs champion. Access to technology in developing countries, though more limited than elsewhere, has allowed citizens from formerly sequestered societies to publicise and transnationalise the problems and challenges they face, fostering greater global interest and invocations of international decision in those causes.

Another, less celebrated explanation for the NGO explosion is the increased provision of Government funding to NGOs. Many Governments have come to use NGOs, along with corporations, to privatise aid distribution formerly carried out directly by Governments [359]. As the number of NGOs has increased, NGOs have had to compete for Government and private funding. This has led some to become skilled at self-presentation in the media, even turning to professional marketing campaigns to increase their visibility [360].

NGOs may be distinguished according to their objectives and sources of funding. On the spectrum of objectives, there are political or "campaigning" NGOs that focus on highlighting a particular problem with the goal of encouraging or influencing governmental action and performing promotive or invocative functions [361]. Examples of political NGOs include Amnesty International, which works to free political prisoners, and Greenpeace, which focuses on environmental issues.

In contrast to political NGOs, there are service or "aid" NGOs, which concentrate on distribution of goods and provision of services in the developing world or in conflict/post-conflict areas. Prominent examples of service NGOs include Médecins Sans Frontières and CARE [362]. Some NGOs, such as Oxfam, mix political and service objectives [363].

---

359. See Charnovitz, *supra* footnote 350, at 284; "Sins", *The Economist*, *supra* footnote 356.

360. "Sins", *The Economist*, *supra* footnote 356.

361. *Id.*

362. Though service NGOs focus primarily on the provision of aid, they also engage in some campaigning to raise awareness of the plight of those that they serve.

363. Oxfam defines its mission as "fight[ing] inequality to end poverty and injustice". Oxfam, "What We Believe", http://www.oxfam.org/en/about/what/.

"Technical" NGOs are composed of specialists in fields relevant to international issues or agreements [364]. Steve Charnovitz has traced participation of technical NGOs to the mid-nineteenth century when scientists attended the international conferences on sanitation, statistics, metrics and penitentiaries [365]. Today technical NGOs have been instrumental in developing and enforcing scientific treaties, such as the Chemical Weapons Convention whose verification system was designed by chemical-manufacturing associations [366]. NGOs have also proved important actors in the area of debt reduction for poor countries. Under the auspices of the WTO, NGO lawyers have trained representatives from poor countries in trade law [367].

Two other types of NGOs have mixed objectives which are determined by their sources of funding and support. Government NGOs, formerly called "front organisations" and now known by their slightly derisory acronym, GONGOs, are often held out as ostensibly independent NGOs, but they are funded solely or almost exclusively by a Government and are used as instruments of national policy [368].

In the United States, the National Endowment for Democracy (NED) was founded and is funded by the Federal Government and makes grants to democracy-promoting organisations around the world [369]. Much of the NED's funds are distributed through the National Democratic Institute and its counterpart the International Republican Institute (IRI), the latter describing itself as a "nonprofit, nonpartisan organization committed to advancing freedom and democracy worldwide by developing political

364. See Sylvia Ostry, "The WTO and International Governance", in Klaus Gunter Deutsch and Bernhard Speyer (eds.), *The World Trade Organization Millennium Round: Freer Trade in the Twenty-First Century*, 2001, p. 285 *et seq.*, at 288-289 (describing technical NGO networks devoted to increasing NGO participation in policy decisions by providing better information and NGO networks devoted to providing trade policy information to developing countries).

365. Charnovitz, *supra* footnote 350, at 198-199.

366. "Order", *The Economist*, *supra* footnote 355.

367. *Id.*

368. During the Cold War, the United States alleged that numerous organisations were Soviet front organisations. A notorious example which reached the courts was the World Peace Council (WPC), which advocated unilateral nuclear disarmament by the West. See e.g. *De Allende* v. *Baker*, 891 F. 2d 7, 9 (1st Cir. 1989); *Abourezk* v. *Reagan*, 785 F. 2d 1043, 1048 (DC Cir. 1986). In court cases challenging the denial of visas for WPC members, the US Government relied on the opinion of the Department of State that the WPC was controlled by the Soviet Government.

369. David Lowe, "History", National Endowment for Democracy, https://www.ned.org/about/history/.

parties, civic institutions, open elections, good governance and the rule of law" [370].

Other GONGOs are less forthcoming about their purpose or funding, which sometimes belies their names. For example, the Sudan Human Rights Association replaced an authentic non-governmental association of the same name after the National Congress Party came to power in a 1989 coup. The members of the original organisation fled into exile, but the "Sudan Human Rights Organization" remained, with a new mission of"protecting the reputation of the Sudan, fending off attacks on the Sudanese government and way of life by the western media and western organizations, and refuting unfounded allegations concerning the Sudan" [371].

Another category of NGOs includes missionising, values-based or religious groups (RINGOs), which are often funded by religious organisations or private donors and proselytise and promote particular religious values. Examples of such organisations include World Vision, Catholic Relief Services and the Salvation Army. Precise information on the extent and scope of activities of Islamic RINGOs is not readily available [372].

From the time of the Paris Peace Conference of the First World War, NGOs have performed the decision function of promotion in international parliamentary diplomatic arenas. NGO participation in international organisations has been formalised in the post-World War II period. Five NGOs hold UN observer status: the International Committee of the Red Cross, the International Federation of the Red Cross and Red Crescent Societies, the International Olympic Committee, the Inter-Parliamentary Union and the Sovereign Order of Malta [373]. Other organisations have been granted consultative status pursuant to Charter Article 71, according to which the ECOSOC"may

370. IRI, "FAQs", https://www.iri.org/who-we-are/faqs. While disclaiming affiliation with the Republican Party, IRI states that its funding comes from US tax dollars. See also National Democratic Institute, "Frequently Asked Questions", https://www.ndi.org/faqs.

371. Ann Elizabeth Mayer, "Universal Versus Islamic Human Rights: A Clash of Cultures or a Clash with a Construct?", *Mich. J. Int'l L.*, Vol. 15 (1994), p. 307 *et seq.*, at 370, n. 290 (citing Africa Watch, "Sudan: Sudanese Human Rights Organizations", *News from Africa Watch*, 4 November 1991, at p. 6).

372. Scholarly articles on Islamic non-governmental organisations almost all study Islamic RINGOs in certain country contexts. See e.g. Quintan Wiktorowicz and Suha Taji Farouki, "Islamic NGOs and Muslim Politics: A Case from Jordan", *Third World Q.*, Vol. 21 (2000), p. 685 *et seq.*

373. UN, "Intergovernmental and Other Organizations", https://www.un.org/en/sections/member-states/intergovernmental-and-other-organizations/index.html.

make suitable arrangements for consultation with non-governmental organizations which are concerned with matters within its competence. Such arrangements may be made with international organizations and, where appropriate, with national organizations after consultation with the Members of the United Nations concerned" [374].

With the increasing potential for NGO influence on promotion and prescription, granting or withholding consultative status has become intensely political.

In implementing Article 71, three levels of "consultative status" may be granted to NGOs: general, special and roster, depending on the breadth of the group's interest in ECOSOC's activities [375]. NGOs with general consultative status have the greatest participation rights and may submit items for the ECOSOC agenda, attend meetings as observers and request the right to speak [376]. Other UN organs, including the United Nations Educational, Scientific and Cultural Organization (UNESCO) and the World Health Organization (WHO), have granted NGOs consultative rights similar to those employed by ECOSOC [377]. Even if an NGO does not have formal consultative status, it may still work informally with various UN organs, collaborating on projects, offering suggestions, promoting policies or requesting assistance [378].

NGOs also work at the national and subnational level with national and local Governments and directly with civil society at the local level. They act as pressure groups, lobbying national Governments for domestic policies favourable to their aims and for State action in international organisations. NGOs sometimes maintain complex relations with national Governments; for some activities, Governments are a major source of NGO funding. "[M]any 'non- governmental' groups are becoming contractors for Governments. Governments prefer to pass aid through NGOs because it is cheaper, more efficient – and more at arm's length – than direct official aid." [379] As NGOs become

374. UN Charter, *supra* footnote 108, Article 71.
375. Consultative status for ECOSOC is governed by ESC Res. 1996/31, 24 July 1996. See also UN Department of Economic and Social Affairs, "NGO Branch", http://www.un.org/esa/coordination/ngo/.
376. Charnovitz, *supra* footnote 350, at p. 267.
377. See UNESCO, Directives Governing UNESCO's relations with Non-Governmental Organizations, http://portal.unesco.org/en/ev.php-URL_ID=48884&URL_DO=DO_TOPIC&URL_SECTION=201.html; WHO, Principles Governing relations with Nongovernmental Organizations, https://www.who.int/governance/civilsociety/principles/en/.
378. See e.g. WHO, Principles, *supra* footnote 377 (detailing "working relations" as informal, rather than formal relations).
379. "Sins", *The Economist*, *supra* footnote 356.

more powerful, with bigger budgets to spend, they may present a challenge to the authority of local government in the areas in which they operate. In working with local governments to deliver aid and services, NGOs, merely by being effective, may even undermine the authority of Governments that are unable to deliver comparable aid.

Increased power should be matched by increased responsibility under international standards. NGOs have gained a heightened status and are undertaking some activities formerly performed by States, yet they have not become subject to the international human rights instruments designed to apply to States when they perform those activities. If this trend persists, will privatisation of government functions through NGOs (and MNEs) decrease the applicability and enforcement of human rights in the newly privatised sector[380]? The increased recognition of non-State actors in international law, Professor Andrew Clapham persuasively argues, should cause them to be bound by at least the customary international law of human rights[381]. Sir Henry Maine famously tracked progressive social trends from "status" to "contract"[382]: in parallel fashion, international law in the twenty-first century would do well to focus on whoever performs a particular function rather than only focus on the insignias of the State apparatus.

The long-term effect on world order of the current spurt of NGO growth is uncertain. One possible future could witness the continued proliferation and strengthening of NGOs to the point where their direct assistance to people would become the basis of popular loyalty, displacing loyalty to Governments. Another possible future would see NGOs' provision of direct assistance to citizens leading to a greater role in policy formation. A diversion of loyalty from Governments to groups which designate themselves as the authentic representatives of civil society could also decrease Governments' command over international negotiation.

The proliferation of NGOs may, however, portend negative consequences. Democratic government allows for the formation of common policy and its effective implementation. The proliferation of NGO voices, asserting different interests, could lead to a fragmentation of policy if Governments are forced to spend great amounts of their time responding to and accommodating narrowly focused but effective

---

380. See Andrew Clapham, *Human Rights Obligations of Non-State Actors*, 2006, at p. 12, 44.

381. *Id.*, at pp. 82-83.

382. Sir Henry Maine, *Ancient Law*, 1861.

NGOs rather than fashioning arrangements that reflect the national common interest. Thus, Jessica Mathews has warned that "[m]ore and more groups promoting worthy but narrow causes could ultimately threaten democratic government" [383]. Much will depend on the internal governance and degree of inclusive representativeness of NGOs. If the dominant NGOs are not representative, then, in a cruel irony, "civil society" will come to manifest the very democratic centralism that compelled the appearance of civil society. Professor Siegfried Wiessner observes:

> "With the exception of Amnesty International and few others, democracy within an NGO is limited to voting with the pocketbook: if members disagree with a decision from the top, they will not try to dislodge the leaders, but simply stop paying their dues. Dissent is remedied by exiting from the organization. Some organizations aren't even membership-based such as a foundation or a trust." [384]

The proliferation of effective voices from civil society may also induce greater governmental accountability as information is transmitted around the world more efficiently, enabling diverse groups to coordinate plans of action and more efficiently demand compliance with international law. Thus, a projected future of increased NGO power could lead Governments to become more responsive to demands that they comply, for example, with human rights or environmental standards.

A future of robust NGO activity is by no means assured. One way of controlling NGOs would be to restrain the technology that has done so much to foster their proliferation: the Internet.

Section 4. Terrorists and terrorist groups

Terrorism is a political-military method involving the intentional destruction of a median target in order to deliver a political message to a different target. Many Governments resort to the technique of publicised small-scale demonstrations of internal force to communicate a political commitment to a larger internal audience: "to show them that we mean business"! Terrorist attacks are different in that they

383. Mathews, *supra* footnote 358.
384. Siegfried Wiessner, "Legitimacy and Accountability of NGOs: A Policy-Oriented Perspective", in W. Michael Reisman *et al.* (eds.), *International Law in Contemporary Perspective*, 2004, at p. 307, 309.

act against internationally impermissible targets with the immediate effect of killing civilians or destroying property, an intermediate effect of intimidating the publics of which they are part and an ultimate intended effect of demonstrating that the Government is incapable of maintaining order. Terrorists use these methods, whether as one part of their repertory or as their essential *modus operandi*[385].

In the context of international participation arrangements, the designation "terrorist" has been used to deny those designated terrorists participatory privileges. Government leaders are wont to insist that they "never negotiate with terrorists". But they have, indicating that in many instances terrorism has not been an end in itself but a means to an end. Political agreements have been concluded with terrorists with the expectation that they would abandon those methods. The term "terrorist" has also been applied to groups and individuals operating transnationally who practise a type of sacramental terror: violence for its own sake or violence for such vague and ill-defined objectives that it amounts to terrorism for its own sake. With these groups, political solutions are not possible. In internal conflicts, Governments frequently characterise all terrorists as engaged in terror for its own sake.

For much of the twentieth century, major groups deemed terrorist, such as the Stern Gang, the Palestinian Liberation Organization (PLO), Hamas, the African National Congress, the Mau Mau, the Irish Republican Army, the Tamil Tigers, the Kurdish PKK (Kurdistan Workers' Party), Shining Path, FARC (Revolutionary Armed Forces of Colombia), ELA (Revolutionary People's Struggle), Abu Sayyaf, ETA (Basque Homeland and Liberty), and so forth, had nationalist or separatist aspirations: securing independence and State status for a territory or special rights or supremacy for a particular ethnic or religious group within a territory. Many of these conflicts were internal civil wars in which the side using terror was viewed in many Western countries as criminal. Members of the Non-Aligned Movement, the beneficiaries of the great era of decolonisation, often viewed these groups (if they were fighting in other countries) sympathetically as "freedom fighters" or "national liberation" guerrillas struggling against the vestiges of Western colonialism, and some have defended the lawfulness of their methods as the only means available for securing internationally lawful goals. In some cases, the characterisations were inverted.

385. See W. Michael Reisman, "International Legal Responses to Terrorism", *Hous. J. Int'l L.*, Vol. 22 (1999), p. 3 *et seq.*, at 6-7.

These conflicting views prevented agreement on a comprehensive definition of "terrorist" and obstructed the adoption of a UN anti-terrorism convention. But a number of conventions were developed that criminalised specific terrorist acts that threatened international public order: the Diplomats and Internationally Protected Persons Convention (1973)[386], the Hostage Convention (1979)[387], the Protection of Nuclear Materials Convention (1980)[388], the Protocol to the Montreal Convention (1988)[389], the Navigation Security Convention (1988)[390], the Protocol on Platforms on the Continental Shelf[391] and the Terrorist Explosives Convention (1997)[392].

The schools and clinics of terrorism have had some distinguished graduates who have undergone a political *legitimatio* and become major and respected actors on the world stage. Menachem Begin helped to orchestrate the bombing of the King David Hotel in Jerusalem in 1946, protesting British policy in Palestine; three decades later, as Israeli Prime Minister, he shared the 1978 Nobel Peace Prize with Anwar Sadat, his Egyptian counterpart. Sadat had dark moments in his own past; during World War II, he had negotiated with the Nazis on behalf of the Young Officers. PLO leader Yasser Arafat won the 1994 Nobel Peace Prize. Nelson Mandela's African National Congress employed terrorist violence in its struggle against apartheid in South Africa; Mandela was classified as an international terrorist by the US Department of State even after his release from prison in 1990[393]. Mandela, too, was awarded the Nobel Peace Prize in 1993, and in 1994 he became the President

386. Convention on the Prevention and Punishment of Crimes against Internationally Protected Persons, Including Diplomatic Agents, 14 December 1973, 1035 UNTS 167.

387. International Convention against the Taking of Hostages, 17 December 1979, 1316 UNTS 205 (hereafter Hostages Convention).

388. UN Secretary-General, Measures to Eliminate International Terrorism, 5 August 1993, UN Doc. A/48/267 (citing Convention on the Physical Protection of Nuclear Material, 3 March 1980, 1458 UNTS 125).

389. Protocol for the Suppression of Unlawful Acts of Violence at Airports Serving International Civil Aviation, Supplementary to the Convention for the Suppression of Unlawful Acts against the Safety of Civil Aviation, 24 February 1988, 27 ILM 628 (1988).

390. See Measures to Eliminate International Terrorism, *supra* footnote 388 (citing Convention for the Suppression of Unlawful Acts Against the Safety of Maritime Navigation, 10 March 1988).

391. See *id.* (citing Protocol for the Suppression of Unlawful Acts against the Safety of Fixed Platforms Located on the Continental Shelf, 10 March 1988, 1678 UNTS 29004).

392. International Convention for the Suppression of Terrorist Bombings, 15 December 1997, 2149 UNTS 284.

393. See Beverly Allen, "Talking 'Terrorism': Ideologies and Paradigms in a Post-modern World", *Syracuse J. Int'l L. & Com.*, Vol. 22 (1996), p. 7 *et seq.*, at 8.

of South Africa. Thus, conventions and protocols notwithstanding, neither participation in terrorist acts nor membership in terrorist groups has proved a bar to ascension to political power and international honour.

The goals of these examples of successful use of terrorism were national liberation; once achieved, terrorist techniques were abandoned. The twenty-first century has been marked by the growth of religious-based, non-territorial terrorist groups, conducting so-called Fourth Generation War. A transitional example, which was still localised, was Aum Shinrikyo, which carried out a deadly sarin gas attack on the Tokyo subway system in 1995. The most prominent current examples are Islamic State and Al-Qaida and their various allied militant Salafist groups. Because they are not tied to a struggle for the liberation of a specific piece of land, they have developed a global reach, in some instances securing the services of international gangs. At the same time, the adroit use of the globalisation of media outlets has allowed them to magnify the effects of their terrorist acts. The 9/11 attacks had an enormous immediate effect: the deaths of almost 3,000 people. Their intermediate effects, displayed worldwide by media images of the destruction of the World Trade Towers, stirred great fear in the United States and other States and provoked the US to thrash out militarily. In other quarters, it stirred admiration for Al-Qaida and its leader.

The deadliness and audacity of the attacks, as well as the fear they caused, provoked an unprecedented response by the US Government. Earlier Al-Qaida attacks on US targets, such as the bombings of the US Embassies in Kenya and Tanzania and of the *USS Cole*, were met with one-off missile strikes on training camps and suspected weapons facilities and various covert actions. After the 9/11 attacks, by contrast, the US Government launched an invasion of Afghanistan to destroy Al-Qaida and the Taliban Government that had afforded it safe haven and an operational platform. The aggregate effects of the 9/11 attack are still evolving. Al-Qaida-linked or inspired groups and the Islamic State have conducted major attacks on transit systems in Europe, Africa and Asia.

Before 9/11, the dominant international judicial view held that an "armed attack" for the purposes of application of Article 51 of the UN Charter could only be carried out by the armed forces of a State or by armed groups sent or sponsored by a State. In its 1986 *Nicaragua* decision, the ICJ wrote that an armed attack could include

> "the sending by or on behalf of a State of armed bands, groups, irregulars, or mercenaries, which carry out attacks of armed force against another State of such gravity as to amount to *(inter alia)* an actual armed attack conducted by regular forces" [394].

Apparently, it was inconceivable that a non-State-sponsored terrorist group could carry out an attack of a gravity sufficient to be considered an armed attack giving rise to a right of self-defence. Even after 9/11, in its 2004 *Wall* advisory opinion, the ICJ rejected Israel's claim to be acting in self-defence against terrorist attacks because, among other reasons, Israel did not claim that the attacks against it were State-sponsored [395]. The gravity and destructiveness of a terrorist act was not the decisive factor.

International political responses to 9/11 changed that. Al-Qaida's actions were viewed as an armed attack, giving rise to the right of self-defence. The day after the attacks, the UN Security Council adopted Resolution 1368, specifically condemning the 9/11 attacks and calling them a "threat to international peace and security". Resolution 1368 also reaffirmed the "inherent right" of self-defence in accordance with the UN Charter [396]. Two weeks later, the Security Council in Resolution 1373 "*[r]eaffirm[ed]* the inherent right of individual or collective self-defence as recognized by the Charter of the United Nations as reiterated in resolution 1368 (2001)" [397]. NATO reacted similarly by invoking Article V of the North Atlantic Treaty, which addresses the occurrence of an armed attack and States' subsequent right to individual and collective self-defence under the UN Charter [398].

Non-military efforts to control and disrupt terrorism continue. Though an international anti-terrorism convention has yet to be agreed, the Inter-American Convention against Terrorism entered into force

394. *Nicaragua*, *supra* footnote 110, at p. 103.

395. *The Wall*, *supra* footnote 160, at p. 194 ("Article 51 of the Charter thus recognizes the existence of an inherent right of self-defence in the case of armed attack by one State against another State. However, Israel does not claim that the attacks against it are imputable to a foreign State").

396. SC Res. 1368, 12 September 2001.

397. SC Res. 1373, 28 September 2001.

398. Article 5 states: "The Parties agree that an armed attack against one or more of them in Europe or North America shall be considered an attack against them all and consequently they agree that, if such an armed attack occurs, each of them, in exercise of the right of individual or collective self-defence recognised by Article 51 of the Charter of the United Nations, will assist the Party or Parties so attacked." North Atlantic Treaty, 4 April 1949, 34 UNTS 243.

on 10 July 2003[399]. The United Nations, in addition to individual States, has made great efforts to restrict the flow of terrorist financing. Under the auspices of the 1267 Sanctions Committee – named for UN Security Council Resolution 1267 (1999), which imposed travel and finance restrictions on the Taliban[400] – the Security Council has created a monitoring regime for numerous Security Council resolutions mandating travel bans, asset freezes and prohibitions on support to Al-Qaida and the Taliban[401].

It requires a leap of imagination to conceive of terrorists, as they now operate, as beneficiaries of participation arrangements in international law. But the very effectiveness of these groups and the apparent inability to achieve their long-term neutralisation by military means may ultimately portend some sort of political adjustment. That can only be accomplished by making their leadership beneficiaries, if only *pro tempore*, of international legal participation arrangements. Witness Afghanistan where the Taliban, after years of castigation as a terrorist group, has evolved into an indispensable negotiating partner to end a conflict that does not admit of a military solution.

Section 5. Gangs

NGOs seek to influence international decisions or provide services to States. MNEs seek to maximise wealth. Both participate in the international legal system, depending upon it and, like others, trying to secure adjustments favourable to their activities. Groups that agitate to seize control of Governments or to expel a foreign elite may resort to terrorist methods, but they have political programmes and upon achieving power acquire an interest in international legal order as soon as it promises to benefit them. Gangs, in stark contrast to these other types of actors, have neither political programmes nor constituencies. They seek to serve themselves and operate parasitically and, if necessary, violently, on global social processes and on the apparatus of the States in which they operate.

The extent to which gangs now affect the governance of States cannot be overstated. One US official wrote in 1997:

399. OAS, Inter-American Convention against Terrorism, 3 June 2002, 42 ILM 19 (2003).

400. SC Res. 1267, 15 October 1999.

401. See UN Security Council, Security Council Committee pursuant to Resolutions 1267 (1999), 1989 (2011) and 2253 (2015) concerning Islamic State in Iraq and the Levant (Da'esh), Al-Qaida and associated individuals, groups, undertakings and entities, https://www.un.org/securitycouncil/sanctions/1267.

> "Mexico, Russia and most of the countries of the Caribbean and Latin America have described criminal organizations as a major, if not the major, threat to their national security. Italy is struggling to maintain the integrity of its political institutions in the face of direct criminal challenge. Some Chinese officials acknowledge privately that south China is virtually beyond their control because of the operations of criminal gangs. Many other countries, such as Nigeria, Taiwan or the Seychelles, have simply reached accommodations with criminal groups, either turning a blind eye to their activities or providing them with cover of national sovereignty." [402]

In contemporary perspective, these examples seem almost quaint. Moisés Naím has written:

> "Throughout the twentieth century . . . investigators around the world took the model of the American and Sicilian Mafia as their blueprint. Propelled by this mind-set, the search for traffickers – almost always in drugs – led to what investigators thought could be only corporate-like organizations: structured disciplined hierarchical . . . . Only recently has this mind-set begin to shift. Thanks to al Qaeda the world now knows what a network of highly motivated individuals owing allegiance to no nation and empowered by globalization can do." [403]

Transnational organised crime engages in cybercrime, smuggling of migrants, maritime piracy, trafficking in persons for sexual exploitation and trafficking in heroin and cocaine, armaments, wildlife, timber and counterfeit products.

Globalisation has already generated new legal arrangements – national and international – to address its various goals. These arrangements, like all laws, create opportunities for those who are willing and able to circumvent them. Thus, "[i]n 2001, the European Commission claimed: ' . . . traditional hierarchical structures are being replaced by loose networks of criminals'" [404].

---

402. William J. Olson, "International Organized Crime: The Silent Threat to Sovereignty", *Fletcher F. World Aff.*, Vol. 21 (1997), p. 65 *et seq.*, at 67.

403. Moisés Naím, *Illicit: How Smugglers and Traffickers and Copycats are Hijacking the World Economy*, 2005, at pp. 5-6.

404. United Nations Office on Drugs and Crime, The Globalization of Crime: A Transnational Organized Crime Threat Assessment, 2010, at p. 27, n. 7 (citing Commission of the European Communities, Towards a European Strategy for Preventing Organized Crime: Joint Report from Commission Services and Europol, at p. 8).

Gangs are opportunistic, and it is no surprise that they operate transnationally when it serves their objectives. John Robb has observed:

> "Third-generation gangs have ridden the rapid growth of the transnational criminal economy, which already has a UN-estimated gross world product of $2.5 trillion a year (this criminal economy grows in parallel with globalization). They are heavily involved in drugs, kidnapping, protection rackets, and smuggling of all types. To protect their activities, these gangs target governments with bribery and intimidation. Given that most of their activities are beyond the reach of any one government to influence, they have become very effective at subverting states through elimination of the state's monopoly on violence and the distortion of legitimate market activity." [405]

A US official has proposed that

> "the international community must develop timely and effective responses to protect the integrity of government itself and to prevent the criminalization of much of the world's financial processes and the subversion of many of its members" [406].

But it is far from certain that the international community, as currently organised, will be able to address this challenge effectively. Interpol was founded in 1923 and had a marred history before falling into disuse. It was reorganised in 1956. The Convention against Transnational Organized Crime entered into force in 2003. But these international efforts have been challenged by the magnitude of transnational crime. Nor are there procedures for dealing with States whose own apparatus has been so compromised by gangs that, in effect, it is itself part of the criminal organisation. The role of gangs in collaboration with terrorists has also emerged as a major challenge for the twenty-first century.

Section 6. The constellation of members of the international legal system in the future: interdependencies and hybridisations

Worldwide communications and movements of persons, goods and services, and the resultant economic links, have created new interdependencies and new collaborations.

405. John Robb, *Brave New War: The Next Stage of Terrorism and the End of Globalization*, 2007, at p. 92.
406. Olson, *supra* footnote 402.

> "As the global information economy grows and develops, we will see unique roles ascribed to the primary players of the former geopolitics model. We may see nation states become more 'corporation-like' and TNCs [transnational corporations] become more 'state-like', but, realistically, the information economy of the future will allow for many new kinds of geopolitical interaction. New players will undoubtedly enter the information geopolitics scene, and new roles will be concomitant with the evolution of new forms of power." [407]

States create corporations as instruments of governmental policy and then invest in private corporations in other States. Sovereign wealth funds straddle the line dividing States and MNEs. Governments "outsource" governmental functions – including some deemed the essence of sovereignty – to corporations and NGOs in myriad public-private partnerships. Some State elites and corporate leaders collaborate with gangs. Gangs may come to control certain Governments. Some national intelligence agencies are believed to create or support terrorist groups while terrorist groups may secure political control of territorial communities and even assume their places in international organisations. Hybrid arrangements like these are likely to become more common as the twenty-first century advances and may make it more difficult to apply the diverse policies animating participation arrangements effectively.

All the forms of membership and participation which we have considered are legal artefacts through which individuals, whether they are part of the elite or the rank and file, interact in order to secure their respective objectives.

There are occasions when the legal systems which have recognised and given standing and other perquisites to these various forms of association disregard them and look, instead, to the reality behind them. Thus, in circumstances in which the corporate form is being used fraudulently or its recognition would defeat other values, developed legal systems instruct their decision-makers to "pierce the corporate veil". Given the phenomenon of hybridisation, one of the continuing challenges of international law will be to identify the circumstances in which a participatory arrangement should be pierced and the ways in which the consequences of piercing should be dealt with.

---

407. Thomas M. Edwards, "Information Geopolitics: Blurring the Lines of Sovereignty", in Heather N. Nicol and Ian Townsend Gault (eds.), *Holding the Line: Borders in a Global World*, 2005, at p. 26.

In cases such as *Nottebohm*[408], *Flegenheimer*[409] and *Mergé*[410], international decision-makers pierced the "veil" of nationality ostensibly to determine the real linkage between the individual concerned and the State purporting to extend its nationality. In 2001, the Security Council, for the first time, pierced the veil of statehood with respect to Afghanistan and found that it was a State controlled by a terrorist organisation. It authorised coercive action to change the regime, commencing a civilian-military campaign which continued for decades with scant success. International investment arbitration tribunals have been importuned to pierce corporate veils of MNEs either to extend or deny jurisdiction to a claimant.

A major challenge for international lawyers is the development of a theory and praxis for this sort of piercing of the veil. The problem may arise in international organisations with respect to accreditation, in diplomatic recognition, in recognition of nationality ascriptions and in international investment arbitration. We will consider some of these in the following chapter.

408. *Nottebohm (Liech.* v. *Guat.)*, Judgment, 6 April 1955, ICJ Reports 1955, p. 4.
409. *Flegenheimer Claim (US* v. *Italy)*, 1958, 25 ILR 91, 150.
410. *Mergé Case (US* v. *Italy)*, 1955, 14 RIAA 236.

CHAPTER XI

THE EVOLUTION OF INDIVIDUALISM: REGULATING NATIONAL CONTROL OF PERSONS

> "As civilization has progressed individualism has increased; and so has the right of the individual citizen to decide upon the ties between himself and his native country. There was a time when governments and not individuals decided if a man was allowed to change his nationality or residence."
>
> Van Vollenhoven [411]

Section 1. The globalisation of diasporas and its international legal implications

In any organisation, a would-be leader must have followers; people are the ultimate and indispensable political resource. Without people and the capacity to motivate and mobilise them, neither the elites of States nor of any other collectivity can operate. No surprise, then, that the international law which had largely been created and maintained by European territorial elites was just as concerned about arrangements for who controls people as about who controls the territories people inhabit. People were generally associated with those lands and identified by reference to them. By contrast, international law is increasingly faced with people on the move and, in a radical shift, is concerned with protecting them from their own Governments.

However rudimentary the means of travelling, people have always moved, whether for economic, climatic or military reasons and whether voluntarily or involuntarily; human history is, in one dimension, a chronicle of elective and survival migration. The twentieth century was witness to massive migrations, some coerced, some elective. Many of them did not lead to assimilation in the new countries. Part of this was due to the ease of communication and travel between old and new countries [412], part to the reasons for migration, part to national doctrines in the new homes resisting the incorporation of outsiders rather than

---

411. *North American Dredging Company of Texas (US)* v. *United Mexican States*, Gen. Claims Comm'n, 1926, 4 RIAA 26.

412. Michael Fullilove, *World Wide Webs: Diasporas and the International System*, 2008, at p. 8.

extolling diversity. Yet twentieth-century migrations, as large as many were, pale against the sheer scale of movement in the early decades of the twenty-first century:

> "Today people are moving as they have never moved before. In 2004 the world counted 175 million documented international migrants, 3 percent of humanity. Perhaps half as many again were undocumented . . . . Another 20 million refugees and displaced persons rounded out the picture . . . . The 2000 US census found more than 30 million foreign-born residents, or 11.1 percent of the population. Of these, 13.3 million, or 44 percent had arrived in the 1990s. In Western Europe, close to 30 million, are foreign born. In other destinations of choice immigrants appear to make up the bulk of the labor force, as is the case in the Gulf. A full 58 percent of Kuwaiti residents are in fact not Kuwaiti. The population of the United Arab Emirates is 74 percent foreign." [413]

Thanks to the ease and economy of returning to one's home of origin, a proportion of migrants do not move in order to settle and become part of a new homeland. They move in order to earn enough to return home.

Many immigration magnet States, for their part, have been receptive to the contronymic "guest workers", migrants who were neither expected, encouraged nor sometimes allowed to assimilate. Other host States either acquiesced or encouraged non-assimilation of those who remained.

Diaspora is the continuing identification by successive generations of migrants and their descendants with an often idealised foreign homeland without, however, any intention of returning and resettling there. By the late twentieth century, diaspora had become a widely shared and often defining experience for many ethnicities. Its political utility as a mobilisable resource was not lost on elites who learned to cultivate their own diasporants for political and economic purposes. Such practices are facilitated by electronic communication and the ease and economy of travel between "home" and "homeland". It may have impacts on elite management of their populations, on international security and, perforce, on the international legal arrangements with respect to nationality [414].

---

413. Naím, *supra* footnote 403, at p. 89.
414. Fullilove, *supra* footnote 412, at pp. 101-104.

The diaspora experience and its coordinate bifurcation of perspectives of the individual diasporant present special challenges to liberal States, those States which have had the greatest influence on shaping international human rights arrangements and whose internal dynamics press them to comply with those arrangements.

An early test of these complex developments is to be found in the still fascinating American case concerning Tomoya Kawakita, a natural-born American of Japanese descent. Kawakita's parents had settled in the United States, but discriminatory American immigration laws of the time precluded them, as Japanese, from acquiring American nationality. Their son Tomoya, then a teenager, had been sent by his parents to Japan to live for a period with relatives. By chance, young Kawakita arrived shortly before Japan attacked Pearl Harbor and the war between Japan and the United States commenced. Meanwhile in the United States, Kawakita's parents, along with the other Japanese on the West Coast, were interned.

In Japan, young Kawakita was not interned as an enemy alien because the Imperial Japanese Government deemed him Japanese *jure sanguinis* and not American. As part of the general mobilisation, he was assigned work as an interpreter in a prisoner-of-war facility. After Japan's defeat, Kawakita returned to his family in the United States where he was apprehended and tried for treason, a capital crime, convicted and sentenced to death. He was found to have harangued and taunted American POWs, but the worst of his actions would seem to have fallen short of what international law now considers torture or war crimes. The verdict was confirmed by the Supreme Court [415].

I have tried to understand the psychology of a dual national such as young Kawakita, especially in the situation in which he found himself. Kenzaburo Oë, the brilliant Japanese novelist, who became a sort of spokesman for the so-called "post-war generation", Japanese who came of age during the war, described the atmosphere in Japan and the effects of the powerful system of inculcation:

> "Throughout the war, a part of each day in every school was devoted to a terrible litany. The Ethics teacher would call the boys to the front of the class and demand of them one by one what they would do if the Emperor commanded them to die. Shaking with fright, the child would answer: 'I would die, Sir! I would rip open my belly and die.' Students passed the Imperial portrait with their

415. *Kawakita* v. *United States*, 343 US 717, 72 S. Ct. 950, 96 L. Ed. 1249 (1952).

eyes to the ground, afraid their eye-balls would explode if they looked his Imperial Majesty in the face." [416]

How many young Japanese would have been able to withstand this brainwashing?

The post-judicial sequel to the Kawakita case is instructive: President Eisenhower commuted his sentence to life imprisonment and, ten years later, President Kennedy released and expelled him from the United States and barred him from returning. Thus, the national demand for primary loyalty, especially in times of crisis, was affirmed by the highest level of the American judiciary, but the impossible dilemma of the multiple national was, in effect, acknowledged and tempered by a measure of Executive clemency.

Given the factor of increasing demographic mobility, will the Kawakita phenomenon become a recurring phenomenon for liberal Governments in the twenty-first century? How will it be played out in manifestly ethnic or tribal States? It has already reared its head in conflicts involving Al-Qaida, Islamic State and their offshoots which actively recruit diasporant co-religionists in other States [417].

Para. 1. The globalisation of corporate nationals

International regulation over national control of persons has also been rendered more complex by the emergence and evolution of the MNEs. The technique of creating an artificial legal personality in a corporate form has enabled people to mobilise vast amounts of capital and technology while limiting financial risk to a pre-set but publicly notified level and has facilitated the intergenerational transmission of investments. The technique has proved to be a critical factor in the growth of wealth and has become a central instrument of the global economy. As we noted in Chapter X, Section 2, international law has assimilated corporate entities to the category of real persons; by analogy to ascription of nationality to persons on the basis of the place of birth or *jus soli*, international law ascribes corporate nationality to the place of incorporation. Not surprisingly, business managers have learned the advantages of multiplying corporate identities as investment vehicles

416. Kenzaburo Oë, *A Personal Matter*, trans. John Nathan, 1968 (orig. 1964), at p. viii.

417. See Neil A. Lewis, "A Nation Challenged: Legal Issues; US Ponders How to Handle Seized American", *New York Times*, 4 December 2001.

through a sort of legal parthenogenesis. MNEs have come to be composed of bouquets of diverse "national" corporate entities arranged in intricate levels of parentela.

The international legal arrangement has enabled corporate managers (and, inevitably, some criminal enterprises) to use corporate nationalities adroitly and flexibly in ways that maximise their freedom to pursue their interests; by taking advantage of different treaty arrangements, they are able to invoke the most indulgent international protections while opting for national regulatory efforts which are most congenial to (or least intrusive or effective for) specific investments. In theory, forum shopping may be a race to the top as well as a race to the bottom, but those given the option of choosing their own regulator are more likely to head downward [418]. The net result has been increasing difficulty in regulating MNEs; some of the international efforts have been reviewed in the preceding chapter.

Para. 2. Nationality goals for the twenty-first century

The classical inter-elite arrangement treated people as appurtenances or fixtures on the land, essentially assimilated to its flora and fauna and conveyed to the new sovereign with each transfer of title. As such, people were the property of each sovereign who could dispose of them as it wished, to the point of even determining the content of their inner lives and their religious codes: *cuius regio eius religio*.

The trend from that classical position to contemporary goals and practices has seen an effort to limit absolute national control of people with respect to almost all of the values of the contemporary human rights code. The international human rights programme seeks to supervise and enforce internationally prescribed standards for national exercise of control over people. But "the squeaky wheel", the folk saying goes, "gets the grease". The finite attention and finite resources of the intergovernmental and non-governmental human rights institutions focus on the issues for which specific interest groups agitate most intensely. Consequently, some egregious violations may get less attention. Moreover, insufficient attention has been directed to the precursors of massive human rights violations: national processes of civic and religious enculturation, which generate intense identifications

418. Jens Dammann and Henry Hansmann, "Globalizing Commercial Litigation", *Cornell L. Rev.*, Vol. 94 (2008), p. 1 *et seq.*

and disidentifications. A by-product of this process has often been to create vivid negative depictions of "the other" and to foment or validate hatreds [419].

Section 2. International regulation of the competence to ascribe nationality

In the struggle for control of people, States traditionally insisted on the exclusive competence to ascribe their nationality to specific persons. Thus, in an early twentieth-century treaty relating to the conflict of nationality laws [420], the States' parties agreed that

> "[i]t is for each State to determine under its own law who are its nationals. This law shall be recognized by other States in so far as it is consistent with international conventions, international custom, and the principles of law generally recognized with regard to nationality" [421].

The limitations on national competence to which the Convention vaguely referred have proved elusive [422]. The Harvard Research proposed some extreme examples:

> "If State A should attempt, for instance, to naturalize persons who have never had any connection with State A, who have never been within its territory, who have never acted in its territory, who have no relation whatever to any persons who have been its nationals, and who are nationals of other states, it would seem that State A should clearly have gone beyond the limits set by international law. Thus, if State A should attempt to naturalize all persons living outside its territory but within 500 miles of its frontier, it would clearly have passed those limits; or similarly if State A should attempt to naturalize all persons in the world holding a particular political or religious faith or belonging to a particular race." [423]

---

419. David and Beatrix Hamburger, *Learning to Live Together: Preventing Hatred and Violence in Child and Adolescent Development*, 2004. See also Raul Hilberg, *The Destruction of European Jews*, 1961.

420. Convention on Certain Questions Relating to the Conflict of Nationality Laws, 12 April 1930, 179 LNTS 89.

421. *Id.*, Article 1.

422. "The Law of Nationality", Special Supplement to *Am. J. Int'l L.*, Vol. 23 (1929), p. 26 *et seq.*

423. *Id.*

If these plainly egregious examples are uncontroversial, more common seriatim ascriptions of nationality on the basis of descent *(jure sanguinis)* are not.

Early in the twentieth century, the accumulation of movements of people and the resulting overlapping ascriptions of nationality to the same persons began to produce conflicts. In an early case before the PCIJ, *Nationality Decrees*, Britain and France clashed over the claim of Britain to ascribe its nationality to people resident in French protectorates and possessions in North Africa and asked the Court whether the ascription of their nationality by States was a matter "solely within the domestic jurisdiction" and unregulated by international law. The Court explained that

> "[t]the words 'solely within the domestic jurisdiction' seem rather to contemplate certain matters which, though they may very closely concern the interests of more than one State, are not, in principle, regulated by international law. As regards such matters, each State is sole judge" [424].

The Court concluded that ascription of nationality, at *that* moment, was solely a matter of national prerogative.

> "The question whether a certain matter is or is not solely within the jurisdiction of a State is an essentially relative question; it depends upon the development of international relations. Thus, in the present state of international law, questions of nationality are, in the opinion of the Court, in principle within this reserved domain." [425]

Yet, the Court found that

> "it may well happen that, in a matter which, like that of nationality, is not, in principle, regulated by international law, the right of a State to use its discretion is nevertheless restricted by obligations which it may have undertaken towards other States" [426].

And, indeed, in *Nationality Decrees*, the Court found that treaties between the United Kingdom and France concerning certain nationality matters had "internationalised" a matter that would otherwise have

424. *Nationality Decrees Issued in Tunis and Morocco*, Advisory Opinion, 7 February 1923, PCIJ (Ser. B) No. 4, at pp. 23-24.
425. *Id.*, at p. 24.
426. *Id.*

fallen "solely within the domestic jurisdiction" of one of the States concerned.

In making the questions of international competence to ascribe nationality a function of the present state of international relations, the Court left the way open for the possibility of future international review of ascriptions of nationality, a development which could have enabled international restraint on abusive exercises of that power by States. But this promising trend was taken in quite a different direction by the ICJ. In the *Nottebohm* case [427], the Court determined that an ascription of nationality would not be recognised for purposes of allowing espousal by that State of the claim of its "national" before the Court, unless that State could establish that there was a "genuine link" between it and its national [428]. The result in this case was that the claimant, whose only nationality was that of Liechtenstein, the State espousing his claim, was effectively deprived, for meaningful international procedural purposes, of *all* nationality and all access to international justice.

The innovation of the ICJ in *Nottebohm* was faithfully followed by an Italian-United States Mixed Claims Commission in the *Flegenheimer* case [429]. The Commission refused to recognise a United States ascription of nationality to the claimant because of the absence of a genuine link with the United States. The same commission denied standing to the American wife of an Italian national because"the family did not have its habitual residence in the United States and the interests and the permanent professional life of the head of the family were not established there. In fact, Mrs Mergé has not lived in the United States since her marriage, she used an Italian passport in traveling to Japan from Italy in 1937, she stayed in Japan from 1937 until 1946 with her husband, an official of the Italian Embassy in Tokyo, and it does not appear that she was ever interned as a national of a country enemy to Japan" [430].

The consequence of each of these cases was that a claimant, with a *prima facie* cognisable and remediable grievance supported by a State attesting that the claimant had its nationality, was denied a day in court.

427. *Nottebohm, supra* footnote 408, at p. 23.

428. Judge Reed observed in dissent that the Court was transferring "criteria designed for cases of double nationality to an essentially different type of relationship". *Id.*, at p. 42 (Dissenting Opinion of Judge Read).

429. *Flegenheimer Case (US* v. *Italy)*, Decision of the Italian-US Conciliation Comm'n, 20 September 1958, 14 RIAA 327.

430. *Mergé Case (US* v. *Italy)*, Italian-US Conciliation Comm'n, 1955, 14 RIAA 236, 248.

By contrast, the Iran-United States Claims Tribunal bent the genuine link doctrine in a more permissive way to assign standing to nationals of both Iran and the United States:

> "[T]he Tribunal holds that it has jurisdiction over claims against Iran by dual Iran-United States nationals when the dominant and effective nationality of the claimant during the relevant period from the date of the claim arose until 19 January 1981 was that of the United States. In determining the dominant and effective nationality, the Tribunal will consider all relevant factors, including habitual residence, center of interests, family ties, participation in public life and other evidence of attachment." [431]

The ILC seems to have concluded that this latter line of decision has become customary international law. Article 7 of its draft Articles on Diplomatic Protection provides:

> "A State of nationality may not exercise diplomatic protection in respect of a person against a State of which that person is also a national unless the nationality of the former State is predominant, both at the time of the injury and at the date of the official presentation of the claim." [432]

While this deals efficiently with the problem of the dual national who is endowed with two effective (but not equally effective) nationalities, it does not address the problem of the individual caught on the horns of Mr Nottebohm's dilemma; the claimant who has, in an international procedure, only one nationality which the defendant State contends, as a jurisdictional defence, does not meet the international test of genuineness.

The result of these trends is curious. Except for the sorts of egregious abuses which were inventoried in the Harvard Research, international law still does not impose limitations on national ascriptions of nationality. Yet international tribunals may deny standing to a claimant or a State acting on its behalf if that claimant's nationality is not based upon what the tribunal seised of the case believes to be a "genuine" or effective link.

In an ironic twist, the seemingly progressive initiative begun by the PCIJ in 1923 has proved to be regressive insofar as it relates to

431. *Islamic Republic of Iran* v. *US*, 5 Iran-US Cl. Trib. Rep. 251 (1984).

432. ILC, Report of the International Law Commission: Fifty-Sixth Session, 3 May-4 June and 5 July-6 August 2004, UN Doc. A/59/10, at p. 19.

the protection of human rights. And it is increasingly anomalous: the liberal approach of international law with respect to MNEs and other corporate claimants, who may select and operate through procedurally advantageous nationalities without regard to a genuine link, now contrasts with a stringently restrictive approach to individual claimants. At times, the contrasting treatments border on the absurd. In the *Soufraki* arbitration [433], the Tribunal, in finding itself without jurisdiction on the basis of the nationality of the claimant, observed *obiter dictum* that had the claimant chosen to organise himself as a corporation, which he could have done, jurisdiction over the deprivation which he claimed had violated his international rights might have been well founded.

The legal situation will be particularly cruel for the increasing number of people who move or are constrained to move about the planet for business or family or any other quotidian reason. If, at the moment of claim, they have only one acquired nationality, will they be able to demonstrate that it is sufficiently "genuine" and "effective" to enable them to thread their way through the ever-tinier needle's eye of international justice? Neither the *Nottebohm* holding nor the ILC's efforts at mitigation can remedy this problem. One solution would be to discard the genuine link test in circumstances of a single nationality, perhaps on the theory that the denial of important *incidents* of nationality in such a case would be impermissible because, in effect, by denying them the opportunity to secure the protection of international rights, it would render them to that extent stateless. Such an adjustment of the law would equalise the treatment of individuals with corporate entities, which are not subject under customary international law to a genuine link test.

The anomaly caused by this disparity of treatment has been exacerbated by the contrasting treatment available under the common regime created by the proliferating bilateral and multilateral investment treaties. Most BITs enable nationals to pursue specified remedies from international tribunals for the investments which qualify under the BITs. They may seek these remedies on their own initiative and without the intermediation of their Government. The ability of individuals who have arranged to conduct their transactions through a corporate form to migrate from jurisdiction to jurisdiction with no requirement more onerous than registration contrasts with the treatment accorded

433. *Hussein Nuaman Soufraki* v. *The United Arab Emirates*, Award, 7 July 2004, ICSID Case No. ARB/02/7.

individuals who cannot take that step. One would hope in the future to see a greater degree of flexibility with respect to this aspect of ascription of nationality. After all, if corporations, which are no more than individual human beings using the corporate fiction, are permitted to shop for the best international protection for their investments, why should individuals, who do not use the corporate fiction, be prohibited from racing to the top, by shopping for the best human rights protection or any human rights protection?

Section 3. International regulation of withdrawal or termination of nationality

Without a nationality, the individual is stateless and cannot legally cross borders, has no rights of residence within a territory and lacks the right to practise a profession, or, in many places, even to attend public schools. Statelessness is a veritable *mort civil*. Yet, *with* a nationality, individuals may find themselves subject not simply to an encompassing legal (and tax) jurisdiction but also to potentially intense claims for loyalty and sacrifice; failures to fulfil some of those claims may be subject to capital punishment. Nationality, as the legal expression of a nexus to a territorial community and its Government, entails burdens and benefits.

In the context of enhanced possibilities for personal mobility, an international law concerned with protecting individual human dignity is confronted by a double challenge. It must develop appropriate arrangements for stringently regulating a Government's capacity to withdraw nationality and, by expatriating individuals, rendering them stateless; yet it must also preserve the individual's right to voluntarily sever the national link and to abjure a nationality.

When a Government expels a person from his or her country, language group, culture, family and friends, it is imposing a fearful punishment. No wonder the great Socrates elected death over expulsion from his city-State to a comfortable retirement in the sun. Indeed, the capacity of a Government to withdraw nationality is so powerful a sanction that its mere availability may act to chill the exercise of many other civil liberties. Efforts by proponents of international human rights to introduce some restraints on the exercise of this awesome power in the hands of State elites have enjoyed only limited success. Article 15 (2) of the Universal Declaration of Human Rights provides that "No one shall be arbitrarily deprived of his nationality nor denied the right to change his nationality" [434]. The American Convention on Human Rights provides in Article 20 (3) that "no one shall be arbitrarily deprived of his nationality" [435]. Some adverbs reverse the apparent meaning of the sentences they modify. The adverb "arbitrarily" in each of these human rights provisions transforms the purport of each to mean that States *may* denationalise as long as they do not do it in an arbitrary fashion. The European Convention on Nationality gives even broader rights to States parties to withdraw nationality [436].

At least one international court has provided some insulation from the abuse of this power by establishing a restrictive standard and making it subject to international scrutiny. In *Ivcher Bronstein* [437], the Inter-American Court of Human Rights held that Peru's putative withdrawal of the claimant's nationality violated his right to nationality prescribed in the Inter-American Convention. In contrast to that encouraging regional decision, the US Supreme Court, after constitutionally limiting the power of involuntary denationalisation in a series of decisions, has reversed course and has steadily enlarged the Federal Government's power to withdraw nationality. Currently, it allows its withdrawal from naturalised citizens, while, for the moment, prohibiting withdrawal from those who are native born [438].

In an important decision, which we considered earlier, the Iran-United States Claims Tribunal used the genuine link doctrine as a permissive device [439]. The obstacles to voluntary expatriation which one of these States imposed on its nationals appeared to be a significant factor in its decision. In his concurring opinion in that case, Judge Mosk observed that:

> "Iranian law imposes Iranian nationality on a broad spectrum of people, makes it very difficult to renounce that nationality and drastically penalizes persons who succeed in doing so.
>
> Thus, some United States citizens have not been able to renounce their Iranian nationality or have not been willing to do so because of their reluctance to give up their properties and forsake their right to visit family in Iran." [440]

434. Universal Declaration of Human Rights, *supra* footnote 115.
435. American Convention on Human Rights, 22 November 1969, 1144 UNTS 123.
436. European Convention on Nationality, 6 November 1997, 37 ILM 44.
437. *Ivcher-Bronstein v. Peru*, Judgment, 6 February 2001, Inter-Am. Ct. H.R. (Ser. C), No. 74.
438. *Rogers* v. *Bellei*, 401 US 815, 91 S. Ct. 1060, 28 L. Ed. 2d 499 (1971).
439. *Islamic Republic of Iran* v. *US*, *supra* footnote 431.
440. *Id.*, at p. 272 (Concurring Opinion by Judge Mosk).

In a footnote, Judge Mosk further noted:

> "Iranian citizens cannot abandon their nationality until, *inter alia*, they reach the 'full age' of 25, they have the approval of the Council of Ministers and they make arrangements to transfer to Iranian nationals all rights in real property in Iran (including that which they 'may acquire by inheritance'). Those who renounce their Iranian nationality must leave Iran or be expelled, and such persons can only thereafter visit Iran once, and then, only with 'special permission' from the Council of Ministers . . . The following are examples of those who are deemed Iranian nationals: a woman who marries an Iranian national; children of Iranian father; and those who have a father of foreign nationality, and who are born in Iran and who continue to reside in Iran for one year immediately after reaching the full age of 18." [441]

When Governments perceive themselves to be enduring severe national crises, they may respond by suspending or narrowing the right of the individual to effect voluntary renunciations of nationality. In periods of low crisis, the importance and urgency of this form of control recedes and fewer limitations are imposed on voluntary expatriations. In the twenty-first century, recurring crises and the prevalence of the diaspora phenomenon may exacerbate this cycle. Unfortunately, international law has not provided a clear standard which might serve as a compass for review. The drafters of Article 15 of the Universal Declaration of Human Rights failed to clarify whether that pesky adverb, "arbitrarily", is confined to deprivation of nationality or whether it was also intended to modify the second half of the sentence: denial of the individual's right to change nationality. By contrast, the European Convention on Nationality provides in Article 8 (1) that "each State Party shall permit the renunciation of its nationality provided the persons concerned do not thereby become stateless". The Covenant on Civil and Political Rights does not address this issue.

In 1926, Judge Van Vollenhoven, whose *obiter dictum* is the epigraph of this chapter, reflected on the increasing freedom of individuals to expatriate themselves and contrasted it with earlier periods when no such freedom existed [442]. But Van Vollenhoven's optimism may have been too hasty; these earlier periods have not yet passed. They should.

441. *Id.* at p. 268, n. 1.
442. *North American Dredging Company*, *supra* footnote 411.

Because freedom of association is so critical to human dignity, the European Convention would appear to provide the best model for emulation in the twenty-first century.

Section 4. The transnationalisation of identities

As discussed in Chapter II, the new century is already witnessing the increasing transnationalisation of complex identities. Policy about the voluntary renunciation of nationality by operation of law will occur with respect to individuals who identify with foreign Governments or non-territorial movements which are ranged against States (or elite formations within them) who claim those individuals as nationals. Adherents and sympathisers of Al-Qaida or other Salafist groups who are nationals of States which militant Islam deems hostile are increasingly being subjected to criminal sanctions for disloyalty or treason. Moreover, co-religionists who are not affiliated with them are coming under greater suspicion [443]. The law has been applied unevenly in the United States [444].

In this regard, the old and troubling decision of the House of Lords in the case of *Joyce* v. *Director of Public Prosecutions* has reacquired relevance [445]. Joyce, a Naziphile and supporter of Irish independence, was a natural-born US citizen, long resident in the United Kingdom. During World War II, he removed to Germany where he delivered English-language pro-Nazi radio broadcasts to the United Kingdom. After the war, he was tried, sentenced and hung for treason, even though the grounds for finding him to be a British national, an obvious prerequisite for treason against the British Government, were, at best, tenuous.

Joyce was an unappealing character, but the political dilemma he faced was hardly unique during World War II. Many people in colonial or subordinated situations threw their lot in with the Axis powers simply because they thought the alignment could advance their own national aspirations. While enemy leaders and rank and file would, quite properly, be tried for war crimes or crimes against humanity

443. As the first edition of this book was going to press, the United States witnessed Representative Michelle Bachman's public insinuation that a Muslim civil servant assisting the Secretary of State was a security threat because of alleged and unsubstantiated ties to the Muslim Brotherhood.

444. See discussion following.

445. *Joyce* v. *Director of Public Prosecutions*, House of Lords, 1 February 1946 [1946] AC 347, 365.

after the war, was it appropriate to try nationalist and anti-colonialist leaders for treason against a State to which they neither felt nor affected allegiance? The question will recur in the twenty-first century. Indeed, John Walker Lindh was treated comparatively leniently [446], even though he actually bore arms for the Taliban against the United States, while others, such as Messrs Padilla and Hamdan [447], were prosecuted more severely.

Multiple nationality is sometimes no more than a matter of multiple documents. But sometimes, as in the case of Tomoya Kawakita, it is virtually genetic. From a human rights perspective, I would propose that two types of punishment of a multiple national be distinguished: punishment for commission of violations of the law of war or crimes against humanity *jure gentium* should be vigorously prosecuted no matter what the nationality of the perpetrator. Punishment for manifesting what proves to have been the "wrong" loyalties without having committed international law violations should be eschewed. That said, the recommendation is unlikely to be adopted and the direct relation between national crisis and demands for full loyalty will weigh heavily on dual or multiple nationals in the twenty-first century. They may continue to find that, whatever they do, they will come under suspicion in times of crisis and can expect severe punishment if they prove to have chosen the losing side.

Section 5. Nationality as the basis for protection in external areas

One of the legal powers of States (and, when exercised, a benefit for persons having their nationality) is the espousal of the claims of their nationals for injuries by other States or in circumstances in which other States are deemed responsible. The ILC has proposed extending to States the additional competence to exercise diplomatic protection for stateless persons and refugees who are lawful and habitual residents of their territory [448]. Given the greater mobility of people in the twenty-first century, this is a progressive proposal. A State may also represent its nationals insofar as they are shareholders in a foreign corporation if the injury in question was caused directly to them.

---

446. Adam Liptak, "John Walker Lindh's Buyer's Remorse", *New York Times*, 23 April 2007, at A12.

447. *Rumsfeld* v. *Padilla*, 542 US 426, 124 S. Ct. 2711, 159 L. Ed. 2d 513 (2004); *Hamdan* v. *Rumsfeld*, 548 US 557, 126 S. Ct. 2749, 165 L. Ed. 2d 723 (2006).

448. Report of the ILC, *supra* footnote 432, at p. 19.

National rights to espouse and protect corporations continue to be conceived as if legal entities such as corporations were the same as natural persons. In reality, of course, the corporation or other legal entity, unlike the person, is neither a person nor is it like a person; it is merely an artefact, a technique by which capital and other intellectual property can be concentrated and applied to particular investments through publicly supervised methods of limitation of risk. In *Barcelona Traction*[449], the ICJ decided that Belgium, the State whose nationals then held more than 80 per cent of the equity in Barcelona Traction, could not represent the Belgian shareholders of a Canadian corporation in the ICJ, even though Canada, the State of registration, was no longer disposed to represent the corporation as a whole. The Court indicated that in circumstances in which a corporation was "reduced to a position of impotence such that it could not have approached its national State, Canada, to ask for its diplomatic protection", the shareholders could revert to their own States which would then be deemed to have standing.

Paradoxically, the acknowledgement of the essential purpose of this arrangement – a day in court for those who claimed their international rights had been infringed – was not adapted to benefit Belgium on behalf of shareholders of its nationality, despite the fact that Canada was no longer exercising diplomatic protection.

In 2007, the Court had occasion to revisit the issue in *Diallo*[450]. Diallo, a Guinean national long resident in Congo, had created a closely held corporation under Congolese law. He alleged that his corporation had been injured by actions of the Congolese Government. The Court concluded that, with respect to injuries allegedly suffered by the Congolese corporation, Diallo could not be represented by Guinea under a theory of "substitution". The Court averred that it had "carefully examined State practice and decisions of international courts and tribunals in respect of diplomatic protection of *associés* and shareholders"[451], but, according to the Court, the material failed to demonstrate an exception in customary international law allowing for protection by substitution. Alas, the Court gave no indication as to what material it had examined and how it reached that critical conclusion.

It would seem that, in this matter, the ICJ continues to elevate form over substance, following the fiction of the corporation as a "national"

449. *Barcelona Traction*, *supra* footnote 311, at p. 31.
450. *Ahmadou Sadio Diallo (Guinea* v. *Dem. Rep. Congo)*, Judgment, 24 May 2007, ICJ Reports 2007, p. 582 (hereafter *Diallo*).
451. *Id.*, at pp. 615-616.

rather than as a technique. In terms of the human rights goals of international law, the result is anomalous, for MNEs will be able to secure international protection by forum shopping in the global BIT mall, while individual aliens of lesser means who operate only through local companies will be confined to the shop around the corner.

Espousal has been viewed by Governments as well as by the ICJ as a discretionary matter; the State of nationality is not obliged to extend diplomatic or judicial or arbitral protection. That arrangement seems ill-adapted to the reality of the twenty-first century. As more and more nationals of States move about the planet in productive enterprise that benefits the common interest, national obligations to provide human rights protections will cease to be meaningful if they are not extended through the form of diplomatic protection wherever those nationals are found. One would hope that what has been accepted until now as the discretionary character of diplomatic protection will be challenged by human rights bodies and then adjusted accordingly in national legislation.

Section 6. The function of the exhaustion rule

Any discussion of the espousal by a State in the twenty-first century of claims for injuries which its own national has suffered at the hands of another State or, where direct action is permissible, by the injured national, must consider the "exhaustion rule".

> "The principle of exhaustion of local remedies restricts the applicability of diplomatic protection by precluding resort to dispute settlement on the international level until the injured person has exhausted the legal remedies – judicial or administrative proceedings – available in the state allegedly responsible for the injury." [452]

To those who view diplomatic protection of nationals as a euphemism for stronger State intervention in the affairs of relatively weaker States, the exhaustion rule seems like a thin but nonetheless useful line of defence. By contrast, the rule will seem atavistic to those who believe that international dispute resolution, by its nature, is always superior to its national analogues. Whatever its historical origin, there are

452. Nsongurua J. Udombana, "So Far, So Fair: The Local Remedies Rule in the Jurisprudence of the African Commission on Human and Peoples' Rights", *Am. J. Int'l L.*, Vol. 97 (2003), p. 1 *et seq.*

compelling reasons, related to the structure of the world constitutive process, for retaining the rule in the twenty-first century.

One reason is economy: there are relatively few international dispute resolution processes as compared to the many such institutional arrangements available at the domestic level. Moreover, international decision is not renowned for its celerity. And a simple local dispute can become more complex and venomous thanks to the political factors which spring into play whenever such a dispute is raised to the international level. In addition, internationalising it often exacerbates diplomatic relations between the States concerned; factors unrelated to the actual dispute, such as national prestige or the implications for the political prospects of internal actors, raise the stakes and impede resolution. In sum, the international political system is better off if a dispute between a State and a foreign national can be expeditiously resolved in the local context in which it first occurred.

There are, however, some exceptions. In *Interhandel*, Switzerland contended that "[w]hen an international decision has not been executed, there are no local remedies to exhaust" [453]. This seems sensible. Why should a claimant that had exhausted whatever domestic remedies may have been required before repairing to and winning in an international tribunal be obliged to return to the defendant State's court and to start the process all over again?

Other widely accepted exceptions to the exhaustion rule are less persuasive when analysed in policy terms. For example, it is said there is no need to exhaust local justice when there is no local justice to exhaust. Intuitively that is appealing and may redound to the benefit of international policies concerned with improving national governance procedures. But in diverting attention to another goal, it may actually undermine the essential policy purpose of the exhaustion rule. A distressing number of States have poor internal governance. Some have corrupt governance. Whether or not local processes meet an international standard, the exhaustion rule affords the putative defendant Government an opportunity to rectify a violation of international rights at the local level.

How much effort should injured aliens be required to invest at the local level before their States may proceed to act on their behalf internationally? At what point does exhaustion, legally, if not literally, set in? The ILC inferred that it did not set in as long as there remained

453. *Interhandel*, *supra* footnote 190.

"any available and effective local remedy". The Tribunal in the *Finnish Shipowners* case held:

> "If what the parties in these respects contend is right – and the Arbitrator is of the opinion that it is so – then it appears that the *raison d'être* of the local remedies rule, in a case of an alleged initial breach of international law, can be solely that all the contentions of fact and propositions of law which are brought forward by the claimant Government in the international procedure as relevant to their contention that the respondent Government have committed a breach of international law by the act complained of, must have been investigated and adjudicated upon by the municipal Courts up to the last competent instance, thereby also giving the respondent Government a possibility of doing justice in their own, ordinary way." [454]

That is a very high threshold.

The ICJ, for its part, has tried to apply the exhaustion rule with more contextual sensitivity. In *Interhandel*, the Court held that:

> "The rule that local remedies must be exhausted before international proceedings may be instituted is a well-established rule of customary international law; the rule has been generally observed in cases in which a State has adopted the cause of its national whose rights are claimed to have been disregarded in another State in violation of international law. Before resort may be had to an international court in such a situation, it has been considered necessary that the State where the violation occurred should have an opportunity to redress it by its own means, within the framework of its own domestic legal system. *A fortiori* the rule must be observed when domestic proceedings are pending, as in the case of Interhandel, and when the two actions, that of the Swiss company in the United States courts and that of the Swiss Government in this Court, in its principal Submission, are designed to obtain the same result: the restitution of the assets of Interhandel vested in the United States." [455]

In that case, the claimant, a Swiss national, had pursued remedies through the hierarchy of US courts for more than fifteen years before

454. *Finland Shipowners Arbitration (Fin.* v. *UK)*, 3 RIAA 1479 (1934).
455. *Interhandel*, *supra* footnote 190, at p. 27.

the Swiss Government finally applied to the ICJ on its national's behalf. Shortly thereafter the US Supreme Court remanded the case, and the prospects were that it would start once again to wend its way through the levels of the federal judiciary. The ICJ, apparently undaunted by that prospect, found that the dispute was not yet ripe for international resolution because adequate remedies still existed in United States law. As suggested in Chapter VII, Section 5, this may have involved the ICJ's signalling function. If so, the signal seems to have worked, as the United States settled the case shortly after the admissibility judgment.

By contrast, in its advisory opinion in the *PLO* case, the Court decided that a dispute should go directly to international arbitration even though no domestic remedies had yet been exhausted; at that moment, the issue was pending in a court of first instance in the United States where it was, in fact, satisfactorily resolved [456]. In the *ELSI* case [457], a Chamber of the ICJ dealt with a similar situation in which considerable efforts had been expended in Italian courts. The Chamber conceded that "[i]t is never easy to decide, in a case where there has in fact been much resort to the municipal courts, whether local remedies have truly been 'exhausted'" [458]. The Chamber held that "it is sufficient if the essence of the claim has been brought before the competent tribunals" [459] and concluded that, in that instance as a practical matter, there were no further remedies.

Earlier in the *Ambatielos* award, an arbitral tribunal limited the scope of the exhaustion rule. Local remedies, it said,

> "[i]nclude not only reference to the courts and tribunals, but also the use of the procedural facilities which municipal law makes available to litigants before such courts and tribunals. It is the whole system of legal protection, as provided by municipal law, which must have been put to the test before a State, as the protector of its nationals, can prosecute the claim on the international plane . . .
>
> It is clear, however, that [this statement] cannot be strained too far. Taken literally, it would imply that the fact of having

456. *Applicability of the Obligation to Arbitrate under Section 21 of the United Nations Headquarters Agreement of June 26, 1947*, Advisory Opinion, 26 April 1988, ICJ Reports 1988, p. 12.

457. *Elettronica Sicula SpA (ELSI) (US* v. *Italy)*, Judgment, 20 July 1989, ICJ Reports 1989, p. 15.

458. *Id.*, at para. 63.

459. *Id.*, at para. 59.

neglected to make use of some means of procedure, even one which is not important to the defense of the action, would suffice to allow a defendant State to claim that local remedies have not been exhausted and that therefore, an international action cannot be brought. This would confer on the rule of the prior exhaustion of local remedies a scope which is unacceptable.

In the view of the Commission the non-utilisation of certain means of procedure can be accepted as constituting a gap in the exhaustion of local remedies only if the use of these means of procedure were essential to establish the claimant's case before the municipal courts." [460]

In an important multilateral initiative, a package deal struck between developing and capital-exporting countries combined a number of reciprocal concessions: a waiver of the exhaustion requirement for the claimant; a commitment by the respondent State to agree to go to an effective institutional decision-maker; and a commitment by the claimant's State not to engage in what is euphemistically called "diplomatic protection of nationals". This package of swaps is central to the Washington Convention, and it has become a core feature in the genre of BITs [461].

In acknowledgement of the place of BITs, the ICJ has recently described the "role of diplomatic protection [as] somewhat faded, as in practice recourse is only made to it in rare cases where treaty regimes do not exist or have proved inoperative" [462]. Yet even in investment settings, in which the exhaustion rule has been waived, it seems to stubbornly re-emerge in other forms. In *Loewen* v. *United States* [463], a case arising under a treaty without an exhaustion requirement, the Tribunal found itself without jurisdiction because, in effect, there had been no exhaustion of domestic remedies. The Tribunal held that where the agency of an alleged violation of a right is a court, a claimant must at least pursue remedies within the judicial hierarchy before invoking an international jurisdiction, even when the arbitral regime waives the exhaustion requirement. This judicial adjustment is consistent

460. *The Ambatielos Claim (Greece* v. *UK)*, 12 RIAA 83, 120 (1956).

461. Convention on the Settlement of Investment Disputes between States and Nationals of Other States, 18 March 1965, 575 UNTS 159 (1965). See also W. Michael Reisman, "The Past and Future of the Great Compact: White & Case International Arbitration Lecture", *ICSID Rev. – Foreign Inv. LJ*, Vol. 33 (2018), p. 56 *et seq*.

462. *Diallo*, *supra* footnote 450.

463. *Loewen Group, Inc. and Raymond L. Loewen* v. *US*, Award, 19 July 2002, ICSID Case No. ARB (AF)/98/3.

with the policy of the exhaustion rule; the real question becomes how much "exhaustion" is required, whether domestic effort to allow the respondent State a reasonable opportunity to provide a remedy is enough, or whether the claimant must pursue exhaustion to the point of exhaustion. The *Loewen* decision has been criticised on a variety of grounds but its holding that where a lower court is the agency of the alleged violation of an international right, higher courts, to which a statutory right of appeal obtains, should be exhausted seems sound.

A variant of the exhaustion rule has re-emerged as a precondition for invoking international investment arbitration. In an award in 2003, a tribunal held:

> "The fact that an investment has become worthless obviously does not mean that there was an act of expropriation; investment always entails risk. Nor is it sufficient for the disappointed investor to point to some governmental initiative, or inaction, which might have contributed to his ill fortune. Yet again, it is not enough for an investor to seize upon an act of maladministration, no matter how low the level of the relevant governmental authority; to abandon his investment without any effort at overturning the administrative fault; and thus to claim an international delict on the theory that there had been an uncompensated virtual expropriation. In such instances, an international tribunal may deem that the failure to seek redress from national authorities disqualifies the international claim, not because there is a requirement of *exhaustion* of local remedies but because the very reality of conduct tantamount to expropriation is doubtful in the absence of a *reasonable* – not necessarily exhaustive – effort by the investor to obtain correction." [464]

If the foreign claimant first resorts to a national court, the defendant State enjoys an informal exhaustion opportunity; it can always obviate international jurisdiction by using that opportunity to resolve the matter at the local level. Paradoxically, the "fork-in-the-road" rule, as elaborated by some investment tribunals, effectively eliminated this possibility by precluding the party which had sought a remedy at the national level from repairing thereafter to international arbitration. The consequence of this interpretation of the "fork-in-the-road" rule

464. *Generation Ukraine, Inc.* v. *Ukraine*, Award, 16 September 2003, ICSID Case No. ARB/00/9, at para. 20.30.

was that entities which had an international arbitral option and would jeopardise it by seeking to resolve the dispute at the national level went directly to international decision.

Section 7. The calvo doctrine and the exhaustion rule

Governments sometimes insist that foreign nationals agree, as a condition of operating in their territories, to commit themselves to repair only to local institutions, which will apply national rather than international law to their disputes. The so-called "Calvo Clause", the technique which Governments use to accomplish this objective, is an *exclusive* choice-of-forum and choice-of-law clause [465]. But, in contrast to the exhaustion rule, which functions as a *precondition* to resorting to international processes, a Calvo Clause is designed to preclude *any* resort to international processes.

In strictly contractual terms, the Calvo Clause is quite straightforward: if a foreign investor is willing to sign such a clause and to waive resort to international processes, its proponents ask, why treat such a waiver differently from any other arms-length contractual commitment that has been freely negotiated and voluntarily entered into? The foreign national has simply signed a choice-of-law and a choice-of-forum clause, both of which happen to specify the national legal processes of the host State. Moreover, the foreign investor may well have secured some benefit as a consideration for waiving its international law rights.

Until now, international tribunals have rejected Calvo Clause claims on the ground that the State bringing the national claim is actually bringing its own claim: the national, the argument goes, cannot waive the *State's* claim. In the leading case of *North American Dredging Co.*

465. In *North American Dredging Co.* v. *Mexico*, the Calvo Clause at issue was quite explicit on the exclusion of recourse to international law:

> "The contractor and all persons, who, as employees or in any other capacity, may be engaged in the execution of the work under this contract either directly or indirectly, shall be considered as Mexicans in all matters, within the republic of Mexico, concerning the execution of such work and the fulfillment of this contract. They shall not claim, nor shall they have, with regard to the interests and the business connected with this contract, any other rights or means to enforce the same than those granted by the laws of the republic to Mexicans, nor shall they enjoy any other rights than those established in favor of Mexicans. They are consequently deprived of any rights as aliens, and under no conditions shall the intervention of foreign diplomatic agents be permitted, in any matter related to this contract."

North American Dredging Company, *supra* footnote 411, at paras. 26-27.

v. *Mexico*, the Tribunal undertook to explain why, in effect, the clause would be reduced to nothing more than an exhaustion rule:

> "Under the rules of international law may an alien lawfully make such a promise? The Commission holds that he may, but at the same time holds that he can not deprive the government of his nation of its undoubted right of applying international remedies to violations of international law committed to his damage. Such government frequently has a larger interest in maintaining the principles of international law than in recovering damage for one of its citizens in a particular case, and manifestly such citizen can not by contract tie in this respect the hands of his government . . . . The obvious purpose of such a contract is to prevent abuses of the right to protection, not to destroy the right itself–abuses which are intolerable to any self-respecting nation and are prolific breeders of international friction." [466]

This reasoning is based on several venerable fictions, which have become even more artificial in BIT regimes, for there the private claimant is endowed with the power to initiate arbitration without the intermediation or espousal of its own State; whatever damages it can prove relate to its own injury and not to the injury of its State.

All of the various protections of nationals are essentially human rights protections. Nationality vests individuals with the "right to have rights", a notion Hannah Arendt memorably put forward to articulate the insight that membership in a political community is the precondition for the enjoyment of all other rights. The protections afforded by the State, the modern political community, are based on and restricted to individuals who qualify as nationals [467]. At its conceptual core, however, the international human rights programme has no such restrictions and should not try to emulate them.

---

466. *Id.*, at para. 11.
467. Hannah Arendt, *The Origins of Totalitarianism*, 1973, at p. 296.

CHAPTER XII

THE PRESCRIPTION AND APPLICATION OF INTERNATIONAL HUMAN RIGHTS PROTECTIONS

"Had the world learned, there would have been no Cambodia and no Rwanda and no Darfur and no Bosnia."

Elie Wiesel [468]

Section 1. The individual in international human rights law

International human rights programmes import negative restraints and affirmative privileges. In their negative sense, they establish limits on the actions which Governments may take against those subject to their jurisdiction and control. In this respect, they function as criteria for appraising and, where necessary, for adjusting controls over people when they prove inconsistent with international arrangements. In their affirmative sense, the prescriptions of the international human rights programmes compel Governments to enhance opportunities for individuation, self-fulfilment and the exercise of personal autonomy. Recall Judge Van Vollenhoven's words quoted in the preceding chapter: "as civilization has progressed individualism has increased" [469].

A person who is a realised individual is endowed with a core sense of self-worth, able to clarify their own interests and to appraise and to act on those interests. But individuals are not islands. Individualism also imports equipping the individual with the competence to activate positive identifications with other individuals and groups and, equally important, to be able to assess those identifications and, if desired, to change them. Thus, the programme for the protection of human rights cannot focus exclusively on the promotion of desirable *individual* traits but must also concern itself with shaping a social and economic context which encourages and sustains individuation. Fostering individual human rights perforce involves creating a public order of human dignity.

Throughout the history of our species, the potentiality for the development and cultivation of individuality was the monopoly of an elite,

468. Elie Wiesel, Speech at Buchenwald Concentration Camp, 4 June 2009, https://www.americanrhetoric.com/speeches/eliewieselbuchenwaldspeech.htm.

469. *North American Dredging Company*, *supra* footnote 411.

usually men and usually in urban centres in economies producing a surplus beyond survival needs, which could be appropriated for elite consumption. Individuality, as we now conceive it, was not deemed a general human trait or even potential but was taken to be an attribute of nobility or high caste. The very idea that it was a general human potential and that its cultivation might be widely disseminated and encouraged would have been viewed as biologically ludicrous and politically seditious. As for *human* dignity, the concept was almost blasphemous; in many traditions, only God had dignity.

The formal installation of capitalism as a secular creed, coexisting with but reshaping parts of the Judeo-Christian tradition, is closely associated with Adam Smith's *Wealth of Nations*, a book which was more a treatise on morals than on economics. The idea that self-interest is a virtue, that its pursuit, oblivious to common interests, will somehow work out for the better for everyone, required first and foremost a radical reshaping of inherited morality. In the United States, one finds this doctrine of ruthless individualism in the works of the social Darwinists and in William Graham Sumner and Andrew Carnegie; their efforts to divert morality into this sterile channel were not completely successful. Older doctrines of altruism, self-sacrifice and the conscious clarification and implementation of community interest continued, tempering the potentiality for a savage anarchism latent in the unbridled individualism of nineteenth-century capitalism. The various doctrines of individualism were refined in the twentieth century by the liberal establishments of Western countries whence they were poured, thanks to the efforts of a number of great internationalists, into the contemporary international human rights documents. These rest on profound assumptions about individualism.

Consider a few examples. The Preamble to the UN Charter "reaffirm(s) faith in fundamental human rights, in the dignity and worth of the human person, in the equal rights of men and women" [470]. This commitment is confirmed as a purpose of the UN Organization in Article 1 of the Charter. The Universal Declaration of Human Rights recognises the "inherent dignity and . . . unalienable rights of all members of the human family" and in Article 1 states "all human beings are born free and equal in dignity and rights. They are endowed with reason and conscience and should act towards one another in a

470. UN Charter, *supra* footnote 108, Preamble.

spirit of brotherhood"[471]. Indeed, the provision of the minimum rights affirmed in the Declaration is prerequisite to the international legal capacity of a State to demand the loyalty of its citizens. Article 29 (1) of the Declaration, perhaps its most radical provision, states: "Everyone has duties to the community in which the free and full development of his personality is possible."[472] The negative implication, whether or not intended by the drafters, is that individuals denied the possibility of the free and full development of their personalities do not owe duties to the community in question and may agitate against it.

The social conditions, which had provided the context for the growth of individualism, have created a concept and a focus rather than a fixed definition. A good deal of liberal and socialist theory argued, for more than a hundred years, not about the value of individualism as a goal but rather about the relation between individualism and the public order system within which it is nurtured. The debate continues about the appropriate personality traits and the environing public order system for individualism and human dignity. Even in contexts where material abundance and tradition enhance the possibilities of individualism, the appropriate content of the term and the political strategies for achieving and maintaining it are not conclusively determined. Many have deplored the consequences of the suppression of individualism, while others have lamented the dangers of excesses of individualism.

Trends towards individualism and trends towards totalitarian democracy and collectivism may coexist in an uneasy balance. Individualism became a major trend and motif in the West because of a conjunction of historical factors and the intense political agitation of certain groups and individuals. In retrospect, it seems (and is often presented as) an ineluctable organic development from postulates deeply rooted in Western culture. But the value of individualism as a political goal was not inevitable nor is its continuity assured. Even now, it coexists, in many cultures and strata, with equally authentic cultural demands that are incompatible with it.

Since 1945, at the initiative of leading Western modernising States, passionate members of NGOs and charismatic leaders have tried to establish a set of ground rules of political and other social organisation based upon what are taken to be universally valid and self-evident principles. It is the Universal Declaration of Human Rights, adopted by

471. *Id.*, Preamble, Article 1.
472. *Id.*, Article 29 (1).

the UN General Assembly in 1948, which proponents presented as the universal "standard of achievement". With minor variations, regional human rights treaties in Europe, the Americas and Africa have adopted the principles and even the language of the Universal Declaration. Since 1948, a network of institutions of varying degrees of compulsoriness and effectiveness have worked to implement them. Consider some representative provisions of the Universal Declaration:

> "*Article 2*
>
> Everyone is entitled to all the rights and freedom set forth in this Declaration, without distinction of any kind, such as race, colour, sex, language, religion, political or other opinion, national or social origin, property, birth or other status.
>
> *Article 5*
>
> No one shall be subjected to torture or to cruel, inhuman or degrading treatment or punishment.
>
> *Article 16 (1)*
>
> Men and women of full age, without any limitation due to race, nationality or religion, have the right to marry and to found a family. They are entitled to equal rights as to marriage, during marriage and at its dissolution.
>
> *Article 16 (2)*
>
> Marriage shall be entered into only with the free and full consent of the intending spouses.
>
> *Article 18*
>
> Everyone has the right to freedom of thought, conscience and religion; this right includes freedom to change his religion or belief, and freedom, either alone or in community with others and in public or private, to manifest his religion or belief in teaching, practice, worship and observance.
>
> *Article 19*
>
> Everyone has the right to freedom of opinion and expression; this right includes freedom to hold opinions without interference and to seek, receive and impart information and ideas through any media and regardless of frontiers.
>
> *Article 21 (3)*
>
> The will of the people shall be the basis of the authority of government; this will shall be expressed in periodic and genuine

elections which shall be by universal and equal suffrage and shall be held by secret vote or by equivalent free voting procedures.

Article 26 (2)

Education shall be directed to the full development of the human personality and to the strengthening of respect for human rights and fundamental freedoms. It shall promote understanding, tolerance and friendship among all nations, racial or religious groups, and shall further the activities of the United Nations for the maintenance of peace.

Article 30

Nothing in this Declaration may be interpreted as implying for any State, group or person any right to engage in any activity or to perform any act aimed at the destruction of any of the rights and freedoms set forth herein."

These legal formulations of rights and duties are manifestations of a larger worldview, reflecting key value goals of Western civilisation that evolved and spread over the rest of the world over the course of centuries. The late Professor Onuma Yasuaki, my friend and colleague at The Hague Academy, wrote:

> "This human-rightization constitutes part of the globalization that began in the late twentieth century, which itself constitutes part of the development of the West-centric ordering of the world that emerged from the late fifteenth to early sixteenth centuries . . . . Although this West-centric ordering of the world was strongly resisted by non-Western people, it gradually came to be accepted by them. One reason for this acceptance is the attractiveness of modern Western ideas and cultures. Democracy, human rights, modern medical science, modern European literature and art and 'American' pop culture are some of the examples." [473]

In applying them transcivilisationally, to use Professor Onuma's term, to societies rooted in other traditions, five of these human rights values are critical: power, respect, enlightenment, affection and rectitude or religion:

– As for *power*, the insistence is on democratic and representative forms of governance, effective equality and equal access to power

473. Onuma Yasuaki, *International Law in a Transcivilizational World*, 2017, at p. 415.

for men and women and the freedom of expression without prior restraint, even in matters that are of great sensitivity to others.

- As for *respect*, the insistence is on the inherent dignity of all people without regard to race, religion, colour, sex, sexual orientation and the entitlement of all to equal respect.
- As for *enlightenment*, the insistence is on the freedom of enquiry which may and, indeed, must go into anything of interest to the enquirer; there is no forbidden knowledge.
- As for *affection*, the insistence is, as a matter of *legal* right, on the freedom of the individual to cultivate agapeic and erotic relations, whether homosexual or heterosexual. Technologies have been developed that can separate sexual activity from procreation, allowing sexual pleasure to be cultivated for its own sake. The right of a woman to control her own fertility is viewed as a corollary of her autonomy and independence.
- As for the development of personal codes of *rectitude*, the insistence is on the freedom of *all* religions; the obligation to respect them; the separation of the State from religion and the prohibition on the State from supporting any particular and all religions; and the right of religions to seek to proselytise and convert members of other religions. The act of voluntary conversion is not viewed as apostasy but as an important exercise of an individual's self-determination.

These values, which the formal instruments of international law designate as "universal" are, indeed, "universalisable", in contrast to ethnically or religiously restrictive values which limit their reach and confine their benefits to members of a particular group. But "universalisable" values are not necessarily universally held. Nor are they "natural". Lest one forget, many of these values are the result of momentous conflicts in Western civilisation. It was the Reformation, an event attended by great violence, that laid the basis for the idea, not self-evident, then or now, to true believers of any faith or value system, that different religions are equally legitimate and can flourish side by side within a public order system that is committed to maintaining freedom of confession and its expression. Civilisations that have not undergone something comparable to the Reformation have difficulty even understanding the notion of freedom of religion.

Indeed, in some settings, freedom of *religions*, in the plural, is viewed as a contradiction in terms: allowing other faiths to proselytise your co-religionists is viewed as complicity in apostasy. As for sexual equality and sexual freedom, now so central to individual self-expression in Western civilisation, these values are viewed in some civilisations and religious systems as the official installation of a policy of promiscuity, a particularly pernicious form of evil, corrupt and corrupting.

It is not simply that Western civilisation makes its commitment to and practice of these values manifest and that their often extravagantly enlarged images are aggressively exported as part of the global commoditisation of its goods and services. Nor is it only that a globalising entertainment industry, under the constant imperative of efficiency, must try to operate in every possible market and, with its products, inevitably transmits many of these values. These are, after all, private efforts. The critical factor is that many of these values are defended and sometimes aggressively pressed by Western Governments, NGOs and the international institutions they have established as the international legal standard.

Having "universalised" the values of Western civilisation through the human rights treaties, those committed to them try to enforce them upon other States through the international and national institutions that have become the infrastructure of the international human rights system: those parts of the planet in which these values are not being implemented are, by definition, deviant and backward and are targeted for development and social change and, at its most comprehensive and grandiose, "nation-building". While the words "development and social change" have a positive resonance for the citizens of those doing the changing who imagine that they augur a greater and greater approximation of "universal" (read "our universal") standards, what they mean to many of those who are being targeted for "development" is a coercive dismantling of their own cultural system, self-amputations of their own being, to use Marshall McLuhan's vivid expression [474].

Thus, that part of international law dedicated to prescribing applying international human rights law is not exempt from the dialectical process inherent in all law, discussed in Chapter III, Section 5, Paragraph 2. In the twenty-first century, it may prove to be violent, but it is inescapable as it is at the very core of a public order of human dignity.

474. Marshall McLuhan and Quentin Fiore, *War and Peace in the Global Village*, 1968, at p. 5.

Section 2. Modern human rights applications

In earlier periods, as explained in the preceding chapter, the protection of the individual in international law was essentially restricted to ensuring that the "minimum international standard" was afforded to one's own nationals while they were in other States; their own States could pursue claims on their behalf through diplomatic espousal. The contemporary prescription of human rights is a radical departure as it involves prescriptions that undertake to limit rather than enhance the power of the elites of States with respect to the treatment of their *own* nationals in their own territories. Moreover, it has established institutions to implement them.

Many of the major human rights prescriptions of the current era emerged from traumatic international experiences which excited a popular demand for adjustments in international law to prevent a recurrence of the horrors that had just been experienced. The origins of the Universal Declaration of Human Rights can be found in meetings of international law specialists during World War II who, from diverse viewpoints, shared the diagnosis that aggressive war was a symptom of totalitarian regimes and that a world composed of systems of national public order which respected basic human rights was a prerequisite for a future peaceful world.

A number of important treaties have been negotiated and have achieved wide subscription. Many of them are standard-setting instruments which do not require parties to accept a compulsory system of implementation. As a consequence, the day-to-day practice of international human rights law involves a search for a forum which disposes of the jurisdiction and control necessary to effect a meaningful remedy. Thus, claimants have often repaired to national courts asking them to find that the conventional human rights standards in question have become customary international law and, as such, they fall within their competence.

The usual test for the emergence of customary international law is wide State practice by relevant actors accompanied by certain subjective expectations of authority: the so-called *opinio juris sive necessitas*. This is not an easy test to meet; but when it is met, its advantage is that it will enjoy wide support which will also extend to its implementation. Some scholars, playing advocative roles seeking to extend the reach of human rights, hasten to conclude that their preferred norm has emerged as custom. Other scholars and some courts have tried to devise new theories of customary international law that obviate demonstrations of practice and *opinio juris* or authority and control. These techniques affirm the myth system but fail to transform normative formulations into effective prescriptions of international law. The more the function of promotion is conducted in the guise of prescription, the greater the need for – and the greater the challenge of securing – "implementation".

Of the institutions created to implement them, only certain regional courts may be said to have a compulsory jurisdiction. Significantly, the European Court of Human Rights, the most effective of these institutions, long exercised a jurisdiction confined to a relatively limited number of States, all of whom were more or less democratic, shared key sociocultural values and had effective internal administrations.

Even with these common characteristics, the pace of the adoption of enforceable human rights obligations occurred in carefully measured and fully considered stages; none of the sequential Protocols to the European Convention on Human Rights was far ahead of domestic arrangements in the States concerned. Outside the European region, where democracy, common values and effective administrations were less often found, States have shown little willingness to accept compulsory modes of implementation.

This experience suggests that a "top-down" strategy of human rights lawmaking is unlikely to produce, by itself, effective law [475]. It has, however, had some significant benefits. The legitimacy which human rights treaties lacking international implementation mechanisms have given to NGOs in civil society in their efforts to promote and invoke law in domestic arenas has proved to be an unanticipated but important benefit [476].

Many of the major international, regional and national human rights programmes have emerged from complex international lawmaking processes best understood in terms of the processes described in Chapter V: a process of communication in which authority and control signals attend certain normative formulations and render them meaningful prescriptions for the community concerned. A genealogy of many of the major human rights instruments shows that they often commenced with a small group of individuals who clarified their own objective, then used the resources of modern communications

475. Oona Hathaway, "Do Human Rights Treaties Make a Difference?", *Yale LJ*, Vol. 111 (2000), p. 1935 *et seq.*

476. See Beth Simmons, *Mobilizing Human Rights: International Law in Domestic Politics*, 2009.

to mobilise other non-governmental groups, which in turn influenced key national Governments to espouse a particular programme. Once the programme was initially drafted, the same process increased the pressure on more reluctant members of the international community, such that an international legal instrument might ultimately emerge. If the instrument contained provision for a standing secretariat, a group of individuals, in collaboration with friendly officials in State parties, could press for further development.

The initial human rights instruments were issued as declarations rather than treaties, precisely because the States concerned were, at the time, ill-disposed to lock themselves into a network of binding obligations. Notwithstanding that resistance, the same complex process of lawmaking has been able to transform many of these declarations into customary international law or even, as some scholars characterise it, *jus cogens*. Non-State actors have contributed greatly to the development and formulation of human rights law. Individuals such as H. G. Wells, Quincy Wright and Hersch Lauterpacht played a large role in the genesis of the Universal Declaration of Human Rights [477]. Raphael Lemkin, while lecturing at the Yale Law School, coined the term "genocide" and fought tirelessly for the formulation and adoption of the convention outlawing it. A coalition of more than 1,000 NGOs campaigned successfully for the establishment of the ICC [478]. Jody Williams led the campaign to ban landmines, with the support of the International Red Cross and Diana, Princess of Wales.

Section 3. Human rights protections in the twenty-first century

If one applies the decision function analysis elaborated in Chapter VI to the current international human rights programme, it is apparent that most of the activity is taking place in promotion and invocation, largely originating in civil society. The application function has proved to be the least effective. The focus of activity taking place in this critical area of law is shifting from formal international arenas to national courts, which are activated on the initiative of NGOs or the plaintiffs' bar. The application of human rights protection may well continue to shift increasingly to civil society initiatives, if international institutions,

---

477. W. Michael Reisman, "Private International Declaration Initiatives", in Commission nationale consultative des droits de l'homme (eds.), *La Déclaration universelle des droits de l'homme 1948-98*, 1999, p. 79 *et seq.*

478. See William R. Pace and Mark Thieroff, "Participation of Non-Governmental Organizations", in Roy S. Lee (ed.), *The International Criminal Court: The Making of the Rome Statute, Issues, Negotiations, Results*, 2011, p. 391 *et seq.*

whose guiding personnel are selected by States, prove less enthusiastic about the implementation of these protections.

Certainly, sensitivity to human rights has become a critical dimension of international politics and it may be contrasted with the virtual absence of such a dimension in earlier periods. Yet, meaningful application in the cases of even the most egregious violations continues to be sporadic and opportunistic. In a cruel inversion, more attention often seems to be lavished on less vicious violations, while the most vicious are neither prevented nor effectively punished. Moreover, apparent victories are often drained of meaning when the practice in question resurfaces in a different form. Consider the transnational slavery trade: supposedly abolished in the nineteenth century, it reappears in the twenty-first in the widespread practice of trafficking.

In the future, it will be important for those committed to the values of human dignity to insist upon effectiveness, to candidly acknowledge the failure to achieve it and to avoid retreating into a *Begriffshimmel*, in which a grim reality is replaced by a universe of luminous concepts which can be recited and analysed *ad infinitum*. Progress will then be registered in terms of "clarifications" of norms, scholarly disputations about whether certain norms should be elevated to *jus cogens*, or fixations on the refinement of internal procedural arrangements, all of which, from the hapless perspective of the victims, might just as well have never been prescribed. The myth system will be ever lovelier, the operational code ever grimmer.

This has already occurred with respect to genocide, a hideous crime which has been prohibited in multiple legal instruments but which, in instance after instance, has not been prevented, even when it is notoriously underway. James Traub, in his excellent study of Kofi Annan's tenure as Secretary-General, quotes Nancy Soderberg on the Rwandan genocide. Soderberg, then a high-ranking official in President Clinton's National Security Council, said that"even if the tragedy in Somalia had never occurred, it is unlikely President Clinton would have ordered US troops to deploy to Rwanda or supported a United Nations-authorized force to enter the country to try to stop the killing once it occurred . . . . The ugly truth is that at the root of the failure to act is a belief . . . that the United States has little responsibility to protect the lives of the victims of an ongoing genocide" [479].

479. James Traub, *The Best Intentions: Kofi Annan and the UN in the Era of American World Power*, 2006, at p. 59.

To which Traub added bitterly, "in this the United States was little different from its fellow members of the so-called international community"[480].

Instead of meaningful action to arrest genocides, there is a tendency for the custodians of the world community to hasten to establish more courts or tribunals *after* the fact. Then a few score people are tried and punished, and the international human rights community celebrates the event and congratulates itself that the law has been vindicated. If the victims could speak from their graves, they would testify that it has not.

If this distressing pattern is allowed to persist and the programme of the international protection of human rights, so promising at its inception, focuses only on the lesser problems, while the grossest violations are not arrested, the twenty-first century will bode ominously to surpass its predecessor in horrors.

480. *Id.*

CHAPTER XIII

CONTINGENCIES FOR THE USE OF FORCE: MYTH SYSTEM AND OPERATIONAL CODE

> "There will be times when nations – acting individually or in concert – will find the use of force not only necessary but morally justified."
>
> Barack Obama [481]

Within efficiently organised States, the use of violence is supposed to be the monopoly of the governmental apparatus and is expected to be employed solely for the defence of the realm, the maintenance of community order and the implementation of its law. Much of national constitutional law is dedicated to setting and monitoring procedures for initiating and supervising the modes of – and constraints on – the State's use of its monopoly.

Since the second decade of the twentieth century, major programmes have sought to create and assign a similar monopoly to international organisations and, in certain *ad hoc* arrangements, to various collectivities of States. These initiatives have been accompanied by efforts to prescribe restraints on and punishments for the unlawful use of violence both within and between States. Some scholars view these initiatives as the major enterprise and test of the meaningfulness of modern international law [482]. If the formal legal prescriptions on these matters have not proved to be particularly effective in practice, that has not prevented them from becoming a major girder of the myth system, one which has proved virtually impervious to erosion by practice, no matter how dramatically it diverges.

The Preamble to the UN Charter opens with the words:

> "We the Peoples of the United Nations determined to save succeeding generations from the scourge of war, which twice in

481. Remarks by the President at the Acceptance of the Nobel Peace Prize, Obama White House Archives, 10 December 2009, https://obamawhitehouse.archives.gov/the-press-office/remarks-president-acceptance-nobel-peace-prize.

482. See e.g. Thomas Franck, "The Power of Legitimacy and the Legitimacy of Power: International Law in an Age of Power Disequilibrium", *Am. J. Int'l L.*, Vol. 100 (2006), p. 88 *et seq.*; Oona A. Hathaway and Shapiro J. Shapiro, *The Internationalists: How a Radical Plan to Outlaw War Remade the World*, 2017.

our lifetime has brought untold sorrow to mankind . . . do hereby establish an international organization to be known as the United Nations." [483]

The introduction of the words "the Peoples" rather than "the Governments", the usual formulation in treaties, seemed to underline that the objective of avoiding war was universally accepted [484].

If the Preamble failed to banish war from international politics, it did succeed in banishing it from the rest of the Charter. The word "war" does not recur in the Charter, replaced by "force". Article 2 sets out Principles with which Members "shall act in accordance". Article 2 (4) refers to the "threat or use of force against the territorial integrity or political independence of any state or in any other manner inconsistent with the Purposes of the United Nations". By contrast, the Charter's Preamble seems to contemplate that the use of force might be a more frequent occurrence: "armed force shall not be used, save in the common interest". Chapters VI and VII, which deal, in effect, with the outbreak of war, scrupulously avoid that term. [485] Rather, Article 2 (6) utilises terms such as the "maintenance of international peace and security" and Article 39 speaks of "threat to the peace, breach of the peace, or act of aggression" [486]. Subsequent authoritative illuminations of the broadly phrased prohibition in Article 2 (4) have also preferred the term "force" or "military force". Thus, the Declaration on Friendly Relations, which was adopted by the General Assembly in 1970 as a codification of general principles of international law [487], deals with military force. Similarly, the General Assembly's Definition of Aggression, adopted of 1974, states, in Article 1: "Aggression is the use of armed force by a State against the sovereignty, territorial integrity or political independence of another State, or in any other manner inconsistent with the Charter of the United Nations." [488] The term "law of war" has similarly been replaced by "humanitarian law". "War crimes" continue in legal usage.

If only adjustments in words translated into adjustments in behaviour!

---

483. UN Charter, *supra* footnote 108, Preamble.

484. See *Documents of the United Nations Conference on International Organization*, Vol. 6, 1945, at p. 359.

485. See UN Charter, *supra* footnote 108, Article 2, para. 4.

486. *Id.*, Article 33, para. 1, Article 39.

487. See GA Res. 2625 (XXV), 24 October 1970; Report of the Special Committee on Principles of International Law Concerning Friendly Relations and Co-operation among States, 1970, UN Doc. 1/8018.

488. Article 1 of GA Res. 3314 (XXIX), 14 December 1974; Report of the Special Committee on the Question of Defining Aggression, 1974, UN Doc. A/9619.

For complex reasons which we considered in some of the preceding chapters, the various initiatives to control the use of force have not proved brilliant successes. The threat and use of military force have become fundamental to sustaining minimum order. The failure of international institutional arrangements to monopolise the legitimate use of violence and effectively maintain it has meant that States have felt compelled to invest in arsenals and much of the maintenance of minimum world order continues to be an offshore zone of the international legal system, where it is sustained by the war system described in Chapter II, Section 5.

Vilfredo Pareto observed that where the State's monopoly of violence is ineffective, other formations fill the vacuum. In grudging acknowledgement of the cogency of Pareto's insight and of its own limitations and failures, the world constitutive process has also undertaken to prescribe and supervise the contingencies and permissible modes and intensities by which States and other actors, using the various strategic instruments, may try to influence each other. Given the myth system's commitment to a monopoly by formal institutions of the lawful use of force, the contingent allowance for unilateral applications of coercive strategies to stop particularly egregious actions remains controversial [489]. This should occasion no surprise. Operational codes can be expressed normatively but, given their discrepancies from the myth system, assessments of the lawfulness of their applications in specific cases will always lack the seeming certainty of "black-letter" applications by the textual-rule-based mode of decision.

Contemporary principles setting the conditions under which States may resort to military force, the *jus ad bellum*, began to take shape in the early part of the twentieth century and were largely codified in the UN Charter. The unilateral and discretionary threat or use of proactive military force, until then lawful, was henceforth prohibited; reactive military force was to be limited to self-defence against a significant armed attack and, even then, only insofar as, and until, the international community could come to the assistance of a victim of unlawful military force. As we will see in the next chapter, when force was used, it was to be necessary, proportional and discriminating. Thus, the Charter arrangement essentially closed off the *jus ad bellum* by prohibiting all proactive exercises of force. All that remained of the *jus ad bellum* was reactive military action for purposes of self-defence and that was

489. Vilfredo Pareto, *The Mind and Society*, Vol. 4, p. 1519 (1935).

permitted only on the occasion of having suffered an armed attack and, even then, only until the Security Council could respond.

Each of these formal arrangements has undergone substantial adjustment, such that the operational code now diverges considerably from the comparative clarity of the text of the Charter. But the acceptance of the lawfulness of the operational code is far from universal, causing crises in international law on each occasion in which States or coalitions of States claim to exercise what they deem to be a lawful *jus ad bellum*.

If the Charter purported to close down the *jus ad bellum* by prohibiting unilateral and discretionary uses of military force, a number of exceptions came to be tolerated, in some organised and unorganised arenas, though their scope and authority have remained, as we will see, controversial. Let us consider the proactive and reactive arrangements, as they have actually developed.

Section 1. A proactive jus ad bellum

Para. 1. Decolonisation wars

As part of the process of decolonisation, which we considered in Chapter II, proactive uses of military force not specifically authorised by the Security Council for purposes of decolonisation were tolerated by international institutions and coalitions of States. Indonesia expelled the Dutch colonial administration from West Irian without suffering significant sanction. India expelled Portugal from enclaves in the subcontinent. North Vietnam conducted a long war, with covert as well as overt phases, to "liberate" South Vietnam. Indonesia seized the Portuguese territory of East Timor and the United Nations essentially accommodated itself to the seizure. The ICJ, when presented with an opportunity to hold the action unlawful, found itself without jurisdiction. Examples such as Armenia's seizure of Nagorno Karabakh from Azerbaijan have proved more controversial, perhaps because the situation was not conventionally "colonial", as the term was understood.

All of these actions involved a State using military force proactively across State boundaries. Some were resisted unilaterally, but none was made the subject of an effective international sanction. Moreover, a number of authoritative documents purporting to be constitutive arrangements have affirmed that other States are legally obliged to assist entities struggling for their decolonisation or self-determination. Thus, the Declaration on Principles of International Law Concerning Friendly Relations (1970) provides in a pertinent part:

"By virtue of the principle of equal rights and self-determination of peoples enshrined in the Charter of the United Nations, all peoples have the right freely to determine, without external interference, their political status and to pursue their economic, social and cultural development, and every State has the duty to respect this right in accordance with the provisions of the Charter." [490]

The operational implications of this right are quite remarkable:

"Every State has the duty to refrain from any forcible action which deprives peoples . . . of their right to self-determination and freedom and independence . . . . In their actions against, and resistance to, such forcible action in pursuit of the exercise of their right to self-determination, such peoples are entitled to seek and to receive support in accordance with the purposes and principles of the Charter." [491]

Note here that "peoples" have the right to "resist" when a State forcibly impedes their right to "self-determination" and "freedom and independence". The State against which peoples are struggling must refrain from any action that impedes the struggle. Third States are obliged to help the struggling peoples and, by implication, cannot be held legally responsible by the targeted State for helping the peoples struggling against them. This "inversion" is not limited to a few historical atavisms. While decolonisation may have had a historically specific reference for some drafters and may have been limited to South Africa, Portuguese overseas territories and Israel, terms such as "self-determination" and "freedom and independence" are open-ended and could be applied to any group that a majority of the General Assembly might wish to indulge.

The Convention against the Taking of Hostages of 1979 is even more explicit in setting out the implication of the inversion. Article 1 (1) defines the offence prohibited by the Convention as follows:

"Any person who seizes or detains and threatens to kill, to injure or to continue to detain another person (hereinafter referred to as the 'hostage') in order to compel a third party, namely, a State, an international intergovernmental organization, a natural

490. GA Res. 2625 (XXV), *supra* footnote 487; Special Committee Report on Friendly Relations, *supra* footnote 487.

491. See GA Res. 2625 (XXV), *supra* footnote 487.

> or juridical person, or a group of persons, to do or abstain from doing any act as an explicit or implicit condition for the release of the hostage commits the offence of taking of hostages ('hostage taking') within the meaning of this Convention." [492]

But Article 12 of the same Convention provides in a pertinent part:

> "[T]he present Convention shall not apply to an act of hostage-taking committed in the course of armed conflicts as defined in the Geneva Conventions of 1949 and the Protocols thereto, including armed conflicts mentioned in Article 1, Paragraph 4, of Additional Protocol I of 1977, in which peoples are fighting against colonial domination and alien occupation and against racist regimes in the exercise of their right of self-determination, as enshrined in the Charter of the United Nations and the Declaration on Principles of International Law concerning Friendly Relations and Co-operation among States in accordance with the Charter of the United Nations." [493]

Treaties such as these indicate that the groundwork for a conception of international law as it relates to the use of military instrument was diverging from the formal institutions. The legitimisation in international instruments of decolonisation and self-determination, even amid the general prohibition on uses of force, was laying the basis for a modern version of a just war [494].

Para. 2. Wars of national liberation

Once the symbols of self-determination and decolonisation acquired authority, as was explained in Chapter VIII, many actors characterised their military actions under this rubric. In 1965, for example, the white minority in Rhodesia purported to declare its independence on the basis of the principle of self-determination; the Smith Government's "Unilateral Declaration of Independence" quoted liberally from the American Declaration of Independence [495]. For all of these rhetorical efforts, the white Rhodesian Government was viewed as unlawful

492. Hostages Convention, *supra* footnote 387.

493. *Id.*, Article 12.

494. A parallel development can be found with regard to the way just wars are to be fought: the *jus in bello*. See *infra* Chapter XIV.

495. Details of the Unilateral Declaration of Independence (Southern Rhodesia), 11 November 1965, can be found in David Armitage, *The Declaration of Independence: A Global History*, 2007, p. 243 *et seq.*

and condemned by the Security Council. In wars designed to replace indigenous Governments with purportedly Socialist or Communist variants, by contrast, the invocation of symbols of decolonisation and self-determination proved more successful. The "war of national liberation" was, of course, simply a war, but the uplifting rubric helped evade a general insistence on the application of the Charter prohibition.

Para. 3. Assistance in internal wars

A major form of military action in the early United Nations period involved the provision of matériel and military guidance to forces fighting in internal wars. In the *Nicaragua* case, the ICJ held that what was, in many ways, a proxy participation did not violate the *jus ad bellum*. Moreover, the supplying State did not incur responsibility for violations of international law committed by the forces to whom matériel was supplied, as long as the forces were not under the control of the supplying State. The Court

> "does not believe that the concept of "armed attack" includes . . . assistance to rebels in the form of the provision of weapons or logistical or other support. Such assistance may be regarded as a threat or use of force, or amount to intervention in the internal or external affairs of other states" [496].

Thus, neither the US support for the Nicaraguan Contras nor the Nicaraguan Sandinista's support for rebels in neighbouring States was found to have violated the *jus ad bellum*, though both violated the principle of non-intervention. In the course of the military campaign in Iraq, accounts linked Iran to weapons used by militant groups in Iraq [497]. Though the United States protested against Iranian involvement, there was no suggestion that Iran's provision of arms constitutes an armed attack or a violation of the *jus ad bellum*.

Para. 4. Humanitarian intervention

In a number of instances, States have conducted proactive cross-border military action ostensibly to arrest an ongoing humanitarian crisis. During the Cold War, several military interventions were justified

496. *Nicaragua*, *supra* footnote 110, at p. 104.

497. Sheryl Gay Stoberg and Marc Santora, "Bush Declares Iran's Arms Role in Iraq is Certain", *New York Times*, 15 February 2007, at A1.

on multiple grounds, including humanitarian concerns [498]. When India intervened in East Pakistan amid gross human rights abuses and violence in 1971, it claimed not only to be protecting the Bengali population but also to be acting in self-defence against Pakistani attacks on refugees and villages on the Indian side of the border [499].

In December 1978, Vietnam invaded Cambodia, removing the barbarous Khmer Rouge regime that had caused the deaths of more than 2 million people in its three years in power. Though Vietnam claimed to be exercising its right of self-defence in response to repeated border incidents, the Vietnamese action had the effect of a humanitarian intervention by removing the Khmer Rouge [500]. Analogously, when Tanzania invaded Uganda in 1979, the Tanzanian Government initially claimed that it was acting in self-defence; only later were humanitarian concerns about Idi Amin's regime put forward as a justification for the intervention [501].

Although we are here in one of international law's offshore zones in which grave violations of human rights were occurring, many international lawyers applied the textual-ruled-based mode of decision and characterised such interventions as violations of the Charter. But no sanctions were imposed. In a number of instances, subsequent appraisals characterised the actions as unlawful but were accompanied by statements of satisfaction that the right thing had been done.

In the case of NATO's intervention in Kosovo, presented by its architects as a pure humanitarian intervention, no sanctions were applied to States that took military action for the protection of fundamental human rights within another State. Though institutional review and academic commentary on the legality of the NATO action have been mixed, many hold that intervention was the correct moral response to the crisis. The Security Council sent a UN humanitarian mission and a peacekeeping force to Kosovo [502].

---

498. Examples of this pattern include the interventions of India in East Pakistan in 1971, Vietnam in Cambodia in 1978 and Tanzania in Uganda in 1979. See Natalino Ronzitti, *Rescuing Nationals Abroad through Military Coercion and Intervention on Grounds of Humanity*, 1985, at pp. 95-106.

499. *Id.*, at pp. 95-96.

500. *Id.*, at pp. 98-99.

501. *Id.*, at pp. 102-105.

502. SC Res. 1239, 14 May 1999 ("Noting with interest the intention of the Secretary-General to send a humanitarian needs assessment mission to Kosovo"); SC Res. 1244, 10 June 1999 (authorising establishment of international security and civil presences in Kosovo).

Para. 5. Protections of nationals abroad

A number of powerful States have claimed the right to use military force in other States in order to protect their own nationals. Some scholars argue that Charter Article 2 (4)'s prohibition on the use of force outlaws this. Others contend that State practice since the framing of the Charter shows acceptance of the right to defend nationals abroad.

The paradigm case of a use of force to defend nationals abroad was the Israeli action to free its citizens on a flight which Palestinian skyjackers diverted to Entebbe, Uganda. When the Ugandan Government offered no assistance in resolving the hostage stand-off, Israel landed an elite military unit at the Entebbe airport, freed the hostages and killed the hijackers. At the Security Council, Israel justified its action on a theory of self-defence, extending to protection of its nationals who were in mortal danger [503]. Some western States were supportive of the Israeli claim, while the then Communist bloc denounced the intervention on the ground that peaceful means should have been used but, interestingly, not on the ground that a right to protect nationals did not exist. The Security Council did not sanction Israel for its actions at Entebbe [504].

Claims of a right to defend nationals in incidents such as the US invasions of Grenada and Panama have been condemned largely on the grounds that defence of nationals was a pretext and was actually being used to change the Government in each country. But since the end of the Cold War, many uses of force for the protection of nationals abroad have largely gone unchallenged [505], suggesting that the right has received widespread acceptance in circumstances in which that was its purpose.

Para. 6. Military exercises as a form of threat

In strategic terms, threats are a credible communication by an actor, whether it be a community or an individual participant, conveying interest, capacity and contingent intention if the interest is not respected.

---

503. Eleanor C. McDowell, "Introductory Note", in United Nations: Security Council Debate and Draft Resolutions Concerning the Operation to Rescue Hijacked Hostages at the Entebbe Airport, 15 ILM 1224-1225 (1976).

504. *Id.*

505. Examples include the United States in Liberia (1990), France and Belgium in Rwanda (1990, 1993, 1994) and the United States in Sierra Leone (1997). For these and further examples, see Tarcisio Gazzini, *The Changing Rules on the Use of Force in International Law*, 2005, at pp. 170-171, n. 311.

Threats put another actor on notice that if it does not desist from or adjust certain behaviour, coercive measures will be taken.

The term "threat" suffers from a pejorative connotation in ordinary usage and threats are prohibited, along with the use of force by Article 2 (4) of the Charter. But threats are a critical, indeed indispensable, part of politics and, in particular, lawmaking; when used skilfully and in support of public order, threats actually obviate violence. Threats are beneficial in the maintenance of minimum public order, precisely because they facilitate political adjustments without resort to overt conflict.

States with the capacity to do so routinely use military exercises or fleet movements as a form of threat. Though military exercises have not historically been understood to be governed by a *jus ad bellum*, the States that conduct them and the States that are subjected to another State conducting the military exercise near their territory understand such manoeuvres as threats. They are designed to communicate intent and capacity to apply the military instrument on the occurrence of certain contingencies.

Despite the general understanding of their threatening nature, military exercises have never been authoritatively characterised as unlawful. For example, although diplomatically and politically protested, repeated Chinese military exercises near Taiwan have not been condemned as unlawful [506]. Iran has carried out war games presumably intended to demonstrate strength to the United States and Western European Governments displeased with its nuclear developments.

In February 2007, in response to a US naval build-up in the region, itself a threatening communication, the Iranian military announced that it had successfully test-fired new missiles capable of hitting and sinking warships in the Persian Gulf and northern Indian Ocean [507]. Such military manoeuvres have been generally regarded as a form of symbol-driven threat communication between the countries involved, rather than unlawful shows of force. Such military manoeuvres do not appear to be viewed as unlawful.

Like any strategic instrument, threats can be abused, but when abuse occurs, it arises not from the nature of threats *per se* but from the political

506. See e.g. Mary Kwang, "China Expands Scale of War Games near Taiwan", *Straits Times*, 26 June 2001, at A2; Steve Mufson, "China Plans to Resume War Games: Military Exercises to Be Held 11 Miles from Taiwan Islands", *Washington Post*, 16 March 1996, at A01.

507. See e.g. Nazila Fathi, "Iran's Leader Warns the US About Carrying Out Any Attack", *New York Times*, 9 February 2007, at A10.

purpose of a particular threat. It is difficult to read Article 2 (4) of the Charter to mean an absolute prohibition of threats as such. Would a unilateral threat from a State or a regional alliance to deploy its military against a State which had massed its troops at its border in preparation for an aggressive action constitute a violation of international law?

The UN Charter prohibits threats against the territorial integrity or political independence of another State or threats against the purposes of the Charter. It is absurd to read it as prohibiting threats that support them.

Para. 7. Reprisals

A reprisal is a unilateral punishment exacted by military force for a violation of the law of armed conflict. In the first and second constitutive process structures [508], reprisals functioned as unilaterally applied systemically lawful sanctions in support of the law of war. Many scholars take the position that the effect of the UN Charter is the prohibition of military reprisals along with all other unilateral resorts to military force; their function, some suggest, is now performed by non-military countermeasures [509].

A number of instances of unilateral military actions which were characterised by the States undertaking them as lawful exercises of the right of self-defence appear to have, in fact, been reprisals. Some of these appear to have been deemed to be lawful exercises of force. Consider the 1993 US bombing of Iraqi intelligence headquarters in Baghdad in response to an Iraqi attempt to assassinate former President George Bush during his visit to Kuwait. *Lege artis*, the United States characterised the action as an act of self-defence, but factually the bombing is more realistically characterised as a reprisal. Regardless of the nomenclature, only China of the fifteen Security Council members questioned the legality of the raid and Western States and Russia supported its lawfulness [510]. US bombings of Sudan and Afghanistan in 1998 in response to attacks on the US Embassies in Kenya and Tanzania were similarly tolerated by the international community. The

508. See *supra* Chapter IV.

509. For discussion and citation of sources, see Matthias Ruffert, "Reprisals", in Rüdiger Wolfrum (ed.), *Max Planck Encyclopedia of Public International Law*, Vol. 8, 2012, at pp. 927-930.

510. For a fuller analysis of the US action against Iraq, see W. Michael Reisman, "The Raid on Baghdad: Some Reflections on Its Lawfulness and Implications", *Eur. J. Int'l L.*, Vol. 5 (1994), p. 120 *et seq.*

1986 US bombing of Libya, though characterised by the United States as self-defence, was surely a reprisal. Other examples include the US bombardment of Syrian military facilities after the Assad Government used chemical weapons in its civil war. The US assassination of Iranian General Soleimani in January 2020 provoked a limited missile attack by Iran on US military bases in Iraq. International reaction to many of these actions has been mixed. Interestingly, the US did not respond to the Iranian counteraction to the assassination of Soleimani, even though serious injuries had been suffered by US personnel [511].

Para. 8. Spheres of influence

During the Cold War, both the United States and the Soviet Union asserted the right to intervene in their respective spheres of influence or critical defence zones to prevent Governments from switching their international alignment. With the Monroe Doctrine, the United States had long asserted a right to intervene in the Western Hemisphere to prevent the reassertion of European power. In the division of the world at the end of World War II, the United States and the Soviet Union tacitly recognised each other's spheres of power [512]. Though the Eisenhower Administration entered office promoting the idea of "rollback", the United States did not act when the Soviet Union intervened in Hungary in 1956 to suppress a Hungarian revolt against Soviet control. The Soviet policy was formalised a decade later with the Brezhnev Doctrine, which proclaimed that the Soviet Union had acted in Czechoslovakia to prevent damage to the socialist commonwealth [513]. On the US side, President John F. Kennedy as early as December 1961 proclaimed:

> "[I]f the nations of this Hemisphere should fail to meet their commitments against outside Communist penetration – then I want it clearly understood that this Government will not hesitate in meeting its primary obligations, which are to the security of our Nation!" [514]

511. Dan Lamothe, "Bracing for a Possible Iranian-linked Attack in Iraq, US Officials Warn the 'The Threat Streams are Very Real' ", *Washington Post*, 30 December 2020.

512. Michael Dobbs, *Six Months in 1945: FDR, Stalin, Churchill, and Truman; From World War to Cold War*, 2012.

513. See Reisman, "Old Wine", *supra* footnote 42, at pp. 173-175.

514. Address by President John Kennedy, American Society of Newspaper Editors, 20 April 1961, reprinted in *Public Papers of the President of the United States, John F. Kennedy, 20 January to 31 December 1961*, 1962, at p. 304.

In 1965, President Lyndon B. Johnson used this rationale to justify the US intervention in the Dominican Republic [515]. In the twenty-first century, China has indicated "core interests" in land and maritime areas which bear a striking resemblance to the spheres of influence or critical defence zones of the twentieth century [516].

During the Cold War, neither superpower's claims were effectively sanctioned at the time, though specific uses of force by each were protested by the other and its allies. It is likely that more general protests against the doctrines' lawfulness were not lodged because all States had an interest in the stability of the balance of power between the superpowers. In any event, given that the doctrines were proclaimed by the superpowers of the time, forceful protest was not a plausible option. To be sure, absence of protest does not mean that all States viewed the doctrines as lawful, but the claims and interventions they justified were tolerated for decades. Whatever their perception of lawfulness, they may have helped to preserve world public order by creating stable expectations about when the superpowers would use force.

Para. 9. Regime change

I considered regime change earlier in these chapters. Though the most drastic example of regime change – the US invasion of Iraq and the toppling of Saddam Hussein's regime – has been almost universally condemned, not all instances of unilateral, militarily-induced regime change have been so derided. There was no regional opposition to internationally assisted regime change in Libya in 2011, and the resistance to such change in Syria in 2012 seemed more a result of the presumed impossibility of effective international action than concerns about its prospective lawfulness.

Earlier regime changes, considered in Chapter IX, Section 1 in the context of human rights and briefly in Paragraph 4 of this section on humanitarian intervention, which were unauthorised by the Security Council, were not widely condemned as unlawful. Examples include the Tanzanian invasion of Uganda, the French invasion of the Central African Republic and the Vietnamese invasion of Cambodia. Similarly,

515. Abraham F. Lowenthal, *The United States and the Dominican Republic to 1965: Background to Intervention*, 10 Caribbean Studies 30 (1970).

516. "Zeng, Jinghan *et al.*, "Securing China's Core Interests: The State of the Debate in China", *International Affairs* (Royal Institute of International Affairs 1944-), Vol. 91, No. 2, 2015, pp. 245-266, http://www.jstor.org/stable/24538911, accessed 4 May 2022.

the 2001 US invasion of Afghanistan, ostensibly an act of self-defence, received broad but not universal international support. In contrast, the 1979 Soviet invasion of Afghanistan was widely criticised. Several criteria differentiate military-induced regime changes that have been accepted as lawful from those that have been condemned. A regime change is likely to be regarded as lawful if: (1) the regime that was targeted was widely condemned as pathological; (2) the intervening State did not plan to use the intervention to increase its influence in the State or region permanently; (3) the change was feasible; (4) the change could be accomplished in a relatively short period of time; and (5) the internal stability of the target State was likely to improve over the long term after the regime change [517]. Regional support has also emerged as a factor in determining the lawfulness of the change, for example, the Arab League's condemnation of the Qaddafi Government. If these criteria, particularly the first three, are satisfied, then past decision suggests that a regime change may be regarded as lawful by a majority of States.

The record of externally induced regime changes succeeding in ameliorating the internal situation which provoked them is not encouraging.

Para. 10. Just war as a jus ad bellum

The outer boundaries of the *jus ad bellum* have been blurred by the reintroduction in scholarly discussion of just war theories. Jihad is only one example; President Obama's Nobel acceptance speech, which is quoted in the epigraph to this chapter, is another, notable as much for its content as for the occasion at which it was delivered: the awarding of the Nobel Prize for Peace.

Just war theories predated and, for those who adhere to the concept, continue to stand as a justification independent of the Charter framework for the use of force. Just war theories *per se* need not be incompatible with the Charter arrangement insofar as they are only applied to the question of whether *the Security Council*, acting in accordance with the Charter, should authorise or apply military force in particular cases. But just war theory challenges the Charter when its arguments are invoked to justify unilateral action unauthorised by the Council. Then,

---

517. For greater exposition of these criteria and regime change in general, see W. Michael Reisman, "Why Regime Change is (Almost Always) a Bad Idea", *Am. J. Int'l L.*, Vol. 98 (2004), p. 516 *et seq.*

the philosophical method of natural law is being treated not only as an independent source of international law but as one which can trump constitutive arrangements.

As we saw in our discussion of symbols of authority in Chapter III, Section 2, natural law is essentially a dialogue among members of one epistemic community which assumes its premises and intellectual procedures to be of universal validity. Carl Schmitt, in his characteristically provocative style, criticised the notion of just war for demonising adversaries and making conflicts more and more savage. Humanitarian intervention, it should be noted, is not necessarily a just war doctrine, insofar as it purports to base itself on specific instances of violations of internationally protected human rights deemed to be fundamental to the entire international community.

Section 2. Reactive, anticipatory and pre-emptive self-defence

Constitutive arrangements with respect to reactive *jus ad bellum*, the right of self-defence, have undergone developments no less complex and controversial than that of proactive *jus ad bellum*. The Charter, which established very narrow contingencies for self-defence, was unprecedented. Among the factors that made such a novel arrangement acceptable to those charged with the maintenance of national security within States was the undertaking by the major powers in the Security Council to cooperate to ensure the collective defence of victims of aggression. But even those who may have assumed that the Security Council would wield the power the Charter assigned it in each appropriate case did not imagine that it would act quickly. Still, reaction time was less critical then, given the character and potential of national arsenals, which consisted essentially of kinetic weapons of relatively limited range, often requiring significant time for mobilisation and pre-positioning before activation.

Prior to the expanded development and refinement of aerial warfare, weapons were usually limited in reach to the peripheries of the States that might come under attack. A surprise attack could thus be costly to its victim but was not likely to be decisive and certainly not existential. Most important, critical weapons were likely to be available in militarily significant quanta only to other States whose elites, however different their cultures and values might be, generally shared territoriality as a common base of power and a continuing interest in the maintenance of the State system, of which all were part. Each elite's own territorial base made it at once member, beneficiary and hostage to the system, susceptible to the ongoing dynamic of reciprocity and retaliation that sustains the key international law arrangements.

These factors shaped a common interest in a legal regime restricting the contingencies for self-defence to an actual armed attack. Indeed, the ICJ, in the watershed decision in the *Nicaragua* case, purported to limit the right of self-defence even further, to an armed attack *of significant scale*, thereby prohibiting unilateral acts of self-defence in response to what came to be called "protracted low-level warfare" [518]. One may question the wisdom of the Court's decision, but it clearly represented a considered policy choice consonant with the ideas underlying the Charter. At times when the Security Council was frozen by the Cold War, self-defence would become the only possible response to attack. As long as determining the contingency for resort to defensive violence was left to the discretion of a beleaguered State, the Court may have reasoned, international violence would be minimised if the legal threshold for resorting to self-defence were set at a higher level and that this restrictive threshold were rigorously enforced.

The development of weapons and their proliferation continued. Wholly apart from the doubts that had arisen about the Security Council's capacity for timely and effective action, the introduction of vastly more destructive and rapidly delivered weapons began to put the efficacy of the legal regime itself into question. The reason was simple: the opportunity for meaningful self-defence could be seriously set back, if not irretrievably lost, if an adversary, armed with much more destructive weapons and poised to attack, had to be allowed to initiate its attack (which could mean to win the war) before the right of self-defence was triggered into operation. This development prompted a claim to expand the right of reactive self-defence to "anticipatory self-defence" against imminent attacks.

Anticipatory self-defence is supposed to vouchsafe the security of the intended victim when the total military situation is such that whoever strikes first can cause a politically or militarily unacceptable measure of damage, if not win outright. But the move from reactive to anticipatory self-defence required replacing the objectively verifiable prerequisite of an "armed attack" with the subjective perception of a "threat" of an imminent attack that, in the sole judgement of the State believing itself

518. *Nicaragua*, *supra* footnote 110, at pp. 103-104.

about to become a target, was so palpable, imminent and prospectively destructive that the only defence was its prevention.

While all these considerations were redolent of the *Caroline* incident and could thus respond to the defensive needs of the putative victim, they did not fit easily into the Charter formula and presented serious systemic challenges [519]. Anticipatory self-defence was, and is, open to abuse by self-serving interpretations in ways that the older right of reactive self-defence was not. Hence, the authority of anticipatory self-defence remained cloudy, and much of formal legal doctrine rejected its lawfulness. Nevertheless, security planners could not afford to exclude the possibility of its eventuation.

In the meanwhile, the democratisation of international law, which we reviewed in Chapter V, was revealing a dark underside that was bringing to bear new stresses on the inherited arrangement. One of the factors that had made the inherited *jus ad bellum* effective was the concentration of weapons in the hands of territorial elites who were subject to the dynamic of reciprocity and retaliation that undergirds international law in this area. That dynamic does not operate for non-State actors, for they are neither beneficiaries of nor hostages to the territorial system. As long as non-State actors did not amass significant arsenals, their indifference or even hostility to world public order was inconsequential.

The proliferation of atomic, biological and chemical weapons, the so-called ABC weapons, and the prospect of their diffusion into the hands of non-State actors has changed that. Even if an anti-ballistic missile (ABM) system could screen the few nuclear weapons likely to be fired intercontinentally from the territory of an adversary, the United States, on the morning of 11 September 2001, awoke to a new reality which many other Governments immediately appreciated and which some were also to experience.

There are many other ways that the cluster of non-State groups referred to as Al-Qaida and Islamic State can deliver highly destructive weapons to what has since come to be called "the Homeland". Biological and chemical weapons, which are unlikely to be used by States but could be weapons of choice for certain types of terrorist groups, cannot be screened by an ABM system. Nor can an effective ABM system, if such exists, prevent the infiltration and detonation of a

---

519. See Jennings, "Caroline and McLeod", *supra* footnote 104. Craig Forcese, *Destroying the Caroline: The Frontier Raid that Reshaped the Frontier*, 2018.

"dirty bomb". Deterrence cannot operate without an address to deter. As President George W. Bush, perhaps belatedly, confessed: "Deterrence – the promise of massive retaliation against nations – means nothing against shadowy terrorist networks with no nations or citizens to defend." [520] These developments have given new impetus to a claim of *pre-emptive*, by contrast to anticipatory, self-defence.

The self-determined contingency for pre-emptive self-defence is broader than the contingency for anticipatory self-defence. The claim to engage in pre-emptive self-defence is a claim to entitlement to use high levels of violence unilaterally, without prior international authorisation, to arrest an incipient development that is not yet operational or directly threatening, but that, if permitted to mature, could be seen by the potential pre-emptor as susceptible to neutralisation only at a higher and possibly unacceptable cost [521]. Although different definitions have been proffered, pre-emptive self-defence is essentially a "nip in the bud" strategy, in which the party pre-empting unilaterally determines (1) that there is a bud to nip and (2) the circumstances and quanta of military force to be used in nipping it.

Pre-emptive self-defence differs from anticipatory self-defence in that those contemplating the latter can point to a palpable and imminent threat. Thus, anticipatory self-defence (which was not in the contemplation of the drafters of the Charter, though claimed by many to have been grafted thereon by subsequent practice [522]) is at least akin to the armed attack requirement of Article 51 of the Charter; there may be palpable evidence of an imminent attack and objective third parties may be able to verify it. A claim for pre-emptive self-defence can point only to a possibility among a range of other possibilities, a contingency. As one moves from an actual armed attack as the requisite threshold of reactive self-defence, to the palpable and imminent threat of attack, which is the threshold of anticipatory self-defence, and from there to the conjectural and contingent threat of the mere possibility of an attack at some future time, which is the threshold of pre-emptive self-defence, the self-assigned interpretive latitude of the would-be unilateralist becomes wider. Yet the nature and quantum of evidence that can satisfy the burden of proof resting on the unilateralist becomes less and less

---

520. George W. Bush, Commencement Address at the United States Military Academy in West Point, 1 June 2002.

521. W. Michael Reisman and Andrea Armstrong, "The Past and Future of the Claim of Preemptive Self-Defense", *Am. J. Int'l L.*, Vol. 100 (2006), p. 525 *et seq.*

522. Derek W. Bowett, *Self-Defence in International Law*, 1958, at p. 183.

defined and is, by the very nature of the exercise, extrapolative and speculative. Moreover, the evidence, such as it is, need not persuade an international jury of its peers but only the would-be pre-emptor. This creates a classic *quis custodiet* problem.

The evolution of weapons systems that are ever more rapid and destructive and that may be initiated without warning or with very narrow warning windows has been invoked as a justification for pre-emption. But ultimately the central issue is assessment by the risk-averse security specialists of one international actor of the intentions of another actor who has or may acquire certain weapons. In an international system marked by radically different cultures, values and, as a consequence, assessments of tolerable risk, factual perceptions, their extrapolations into imagined scenarios, and then their strategic assessments, an act of pre-emptive self-defence, based upon one actor's self-perceived good faith conviction, will often appear to some actors to be serious, even hysterical misjudgement or paranoia and to still others cynical, naked aggression.

Imitation is said to be the highest compliment. And in this instance, the United States has developed some unlikely – and from its perspective, undesired – admirers. North Korea and Iran quickly adopted the US claim in defence of their own international positions [523]. North Korea has justified its further development of nuclear weapons as essential to its self-defence against US claims of a right to pre-emptive self-defence [524]. Russia, too, jumped on board. "Whether we like it or not", Russian Defence Minister Ivanov said, "the pre-emptive use of force in the modern world is a reality. While this principle exists, we are not going to relinquish it voluntarily" [525]. Such legal mimesis may accelerate the drift away from the binary formulation of Article 51 (which presents its own problems) towards a vaguer, and possibly less stable, definition of the right to use force [526].

523. President George W. Bush, The President's State of the Union Address, The White House, 29 January 2002, https://georgewbush-whitehouse.archives.gov/news/releases/2002/01/20020129-11.html (noting that Iraq, North Korea and Iran constituted an "axis of evil").

524. Foreign Ministry of North Korea, Memorandum of DPRK Foreign Ministry, 3 March 2005 (stating: "Therefore, it is quite natural that the DPRK has manufactured nukes for self-defence and continues to do so to cope with the policy of the Bush Administration aimed at mounting a pre-emptive nuclear attack on it").

525. "Russia Not Planning to Give up right of Pre-emptive Strikes – Defence Minister", BBC, 20 October 2003.

526. Reisman and Armstrong, *supra* footnote 521, at pp. 549-550.

In their inferences with respect to evolving custom, international law scholars are supposed to take account of the policies and practices of all nations. Although the US pre-emptive policy has now retreated to a more qualified and limited claim, other States may reactively adopt exaggerated pre-emption policies with respect to their own latent adversaries, thus skewing assessments of international consensus and practice back towards a position that ironically may no longer be claimed by those major powers that had initially brought the claim to the fore. Hence, what appears to be a growing adoption of claims to pre-emptive self-defence in limited circumstances may mistake political posturing for international consensus, with grave consequences for both the expectation and eventuation of violence.

Even if claims to pre-emptive self-defence are henceforth limited to military actions in protracted low-level conflicts and not permitted for "Pearl Harbor-type" initiations of inter-State war, all such claims are clearly incompatible with conceptions of the legal use of force in self-defence as understood by the ICJ in its recent decisions.

A discrepancy between practice and formal law – between myth system and operational code [527] – is hardly unique to the international legal system. But uncertainty about precisely what the law prohibits is always an invitation to adventurism, and adventurism with highly destructive and non-discriminating weapons is a particularly frightening prospect. In any event, if one were to hazard a prediction in this fluid situation, it would be that a conception of lawful self-defence incorporating only the *Caroline* doctrine will continue for most matters; beyond that, the right of self-defence will have been relaxed only for the so-called "War on Terror". Even when a pre-emptive self-defence action is undertaken, its lawfulness, if it can claim any, should turn, in significant part, on the extent to which the use of force is confined to the threat posed and the proportionality of the measures taken.

Thus, the *jus ad bellum* in contemporary international law has proved to be considerably more complex than the extraordinary clarity of its articulation in the myth system.

527. See *supra* Chapter III, Section 6.

CHAPTER XIV

THE USE AND ABUSE OF MILITARY FORCE: *JUS IN BELLO*

> "[T]he only legitimate object which States should endeavour to accomplish during war is to weaken the military forces of the enemy."
>
> St Petersburg Declaration, 1868 [528]

All strategic instruments are directed towards reducing the ambit of their target's choice by compelling it to adopt policies or positions it would not otherwise take. The military instrument is supposed to force the target to adjust its behaviour by application of force. (In earlier periods, the military instrument was used to annihilate the target or every person in the field capable of wielding a weapon. The St Petersburg Declaration, a humanitarian milestone in the law of armed conflict, immediately after the quotation in this chapter's epigraph, added "that for this purpose it is sufficient to disable the greatest possible number of men".) Other strategic instruments paint from a more varied palette. Indulgent techniques seek to secure the target's compliance by promising "rewards" which are openly granted and willingly received or by covertly tendering "bribes".

When the strategic instruments are used by or on the authority of international organisations, they are properly referred to as "sanctions". When they are applied unilaterally, the State or States applying them may characterise them as "sanctions", thereby implying an international legal authority for their deployment, but they are more accurately referred to in their more coercive forms as warfare (or economic warfare, as the case may be) and in their milder forms as "retorsions".

Whether or not they are explicitly violent, all deprivatory techniques seek to secure compliance by taking something of value or withholding opportunities. The consequence of the application of an indulgent strategy is still the attenuation of the target's ambit of choice; the target is constrained to relinquish advantages or opportunities it had otherwise expected and would have wished. But neither the target nor the people or things on its periphery suffer *manifest* damage when

528. Declaration Renouncing the Use, in Time of War, of Explosive Projectiles Under 400 Grammes Weight, 29 November-11 December 1868, reprinted in *Am. J. Int'l L.*, Vol. 1 (1907), p. 95 *et seq.*

indulgent strategies are used. Deprivatory techniques, in contrast, secure compliance by sequestering or destroying diverse power bases or instruments of influence of the target. In their application, strategies may have collateral consequences for third parties and their property.

The sociologist Georg Simmel observed that the "emancipation" of the German serfs was a misnomer. There was no liberation, only the replacement of one form of social control with another [529]. Similarly, short of an individual's withdrawal into hermit-like isolation, there is no collective escape, at any level of social organisation, from using and being the target of the various modes of influence. However, three factors may work to alleviate this dismal prospect. The first arises from the fact that the actual application of force is often not needed; the second arises from the complexity, volatility and reciprocally manipulatable relationship which the "strong-weak" dichotomy actually conceals, as we saw in Chapter III, Section 7, in our discussion of power; and the third arises from the authoritative restraints that the international legal process has prescribed and is sometimes able to compel on the coercive uses of the various instruments of strategy.

Section 1. The "MNPD principles"

Until now, the foundational principles of the international law of armed conflict have been based upon the sharp distinction between combatants and non-combatants and the imperative that any use of force be demonstrably necessary, proportional to that necessity and as capable as possible of differentiating between combatants and non-combatants. These MNPD principles (military necessity, proportionality, differentiation) require that military strategies be planned, applied and appraised in terms of these criteria. Rules of engagement must be crafted to apply these principles in the anticipated context for which they have been designed. Major military campaigns are supposed to be subjected to critical post-mortems to determine the extent to which the MNPD principles were met such that the actual application of coercion in that case was internationally lawful.

An analysis of what is involved in strategic action is important because one of the MNPD elements in determining the lawfulness of the initiation of the use of a coercive instrument is the quotient of its proportionality to its necessity for achieving a licit objective and the

529. Georg Simmel, "Superiority and Subordination as Subject-Matter of Sociology", *Am. J. Soc.*, Vol. 2 (1896), p. 167 *et seq.*

extent to which the instrument being applied is capable of differentiating between those who are proper targets of coercion and those who are not. In this regard, two additional but related concepts require some discussion: collateral damage and permissible and impermissible targets.

The purpose driving the requirement of the parsimonious use of coercion is to ensure to the extent possible that people who are *not* responsible for the targeted behaviour will not be hurt by the use of strategic instruments designed to change that behaviour. Unfortunately, once one goes beyond clubs and knives applied at closest range, no modern weapon regularly delivers its punch with the "surgical precision" claimed by its manufacturers and operators [530]. Some unintended damage to persons or things peripheral to the target is a virtually inescapable feature of destructive strategies. The injury and destruction of helpless people and objects on the periphery of a target is called, euphemistically, "collateral damage", a term whose clinical neutrality may anesthetise the moral imperatives of those deploying purposive violence. Modern techniques developed by Mao Zedong and Võ Nguyên Giáp and now referred to as "third" and "fourth generation war" largely ignore the legal issue of collateral damage, transforming it, like terrorism, into an instrument of purposive violence.

For a century, customary international law has tried to define lawful primary targets and to establish boundaries of tolerance for collateral damage; a number of its more recent codifications have missed their target [531]. Some efforts have focused on prohibiting certain weapons. But relatively few weapons – or, more generally, instruments of strategy – have been deemed to be *per se* lawful or unlawful [532]. In order to be used lawfully, they must be selected for particular contexts and missions, taking account of their properties and, in particular, their capacities to differentiate between combatants and non-combatants in real time.

Until now, the critical notions of damage and collateral damage have been conceived for and applied to applications of the military instrument,

---

530. Even these "precise weapons" which successfully injure or kill only their intended targets still collaterally damage those who love and depend upon the intended victims; in this sense, collateral damage is inevitable and may extend through time, even generations.

531. W. Michael Reisman, "Holding the Center of the Law of Armed Conflict", 100:4 AJIL 852 (October 2006).

532. *Ibid.* On the categorisation of weapons into Parts A and B of the *jus in bello*, see *infra* Section 3 of this chapter.

apparently on the assumption that the other strategic instruments do not cause collateral damage. But only look at the "what-it's-attached-to", and it is readily apparent that none of the four instruments of policy is inherently non-destructive. Each may be and often is used in ways that produce significant destruction, and it is often visited on those peripheral to the target rather than on the target itself.

Kinetic weapons are highly destructive and the destructiveness in many contexts increases in direct proportion to their explosive force [533]. The inevitability of collateral damage is less obvious for some of the other instruments. The ideologic or propagandic instrument – the purposive modulation of signs and symbols by one side to a conflict towards the rank and file of the adversary – was used prior to, during, and after Desert Storm in 1991 to encourage the Shi'a in the south of Iraq and the Kurds in the north to rise against the Ba'athist and largely Sunni regime. In both cases, it could be anticipated that the propaganda, if it were successful, would ignite a chain of events ultimately causing substantial collateral damage in the insurrection and the brutal suppression that would follow it, especially if the US-led coalition that had encouraged the insurrection did not come to its assistance. In fact, the coalition did not, and the foreseeable consequences ensued in the southern sector; some of its delayed consequences will be felt for generations.

Two points must be emphasised. First, damage – in an empirically referential sense – is not caused exclusively by uses of the *military* instrument. Other instruments may have destructive consequences. In fact, the military instrument, as we have seen, in its communicative or threat stage, is used in non-destructive and essentially communicative ways. The sequence is quite simple. Threats and coordinate demonstrations of power are perceived by the intended target. Like Dr Johnson's hapless "man about to be hung", they concentrate the target's mind in a way that words alone do not, stimulating careful assessments of relative power positions correlated with the degree of importance of the issues at stake. Where the assessments indicate probabilities of net losses, they lead to appropriate non-belligerent adjustments. The military instrument is more likely than the other instruments to be effective in this stage precisely because "wait and see" is a risky response when faced with a military threat.

---

533. See Reisman, "Raid on Baghdad", *supra* footnote 510.

Second, damage is not caused exclusively by the application of material assets, by the arsenal's "sticks and stones". Words can cause direct and collateral damage as well. One of the common methods of propaganda – "psychwar" (psychological warfare) – seeks to exacerbate latent conflicts between different ethnic, religious and tribal groups within the adversary in order to undermine elite control or to require the elite to divert resources to suppress internal resistance. Propaganda of this sort is hardly without collateral damage: tensions between ethnic groups may produce violent incidents or even widespread pogroms. Even if they do not produce the desired effect immediately, long after the particular conflict has ended, the residue of hatred that has been endorsed and made more acute will lurk in peoples' consciousness, like a time bomb or a quiescent virus to be transmitted from one generation to the next until it bursts forth seemingly spontaneously or is detonated by some other event. Unlike explosive ordinance, propaganda cannot be set to self-destruct. Thus, ironically, the immediate and temporally extended collateral damage caused by non-military instruments, such as the economic and propagandic, may be greater than that of the military instrument. During a period of "wait and see", collateral damage can cumulate. In contexts in which "wait and see" is irrational in the face of a credible threat to use the military instrument, the communication phase of that modality may actually cause less collateral damage than non-military instruments.

Curiously, the MNPD analysis is not transposed, *mutatis mutandis*, to assessments of the lawfulness of the planning, application and retrospective assessment of applications of the other instruments. The apparent reason for this is the mistaken assumption that only the military instrument can be highly destructive; non-military strategies are assumed to be inherently non-destructive or non-lethal. While rigorous application of human rights instruments to military applications is now demanded if not necessarily carried out, it has not been demanded with anything approaching that intensity to the other strategic instruments. The consequences of this practice can be very grave. State-sponsored propaganda, for example, is often used to exacerbate hatred between different groups, which contravenes a fundamental policy of international law (articulated, for example, in the Convention on the Elimination of Racial Discrimination[534]) to limit the propaga-

534. International Convention on the Elimination of All Forms of Racial Discrimination, 7 March 1966, 660 UNTS 195.

tion of racial hatred and the crimes against humanity it brings in its wake.

Non-military instruments should be tested just as rigorously against the MNPD principles *before* a decision is made to initiate or to continue to apply them. Were non-military instruments so tested, they could, in some cases, be found to fail and to require adjustment or abandonment. The economic and propagandic instruments are problematic mainly because of their comparative incapacity to discriminate between licit and illicit targets and because of their enduring collateral consequences.

Since GATT and WTO prescriptions may be expected to increasingly limit *unilateral* uses of economic deprivations, intensive uses of economic sanctions in the twenty-first century, if they are to be lawful, could well be effected through international organisations. In such applications, compliance with international law and, particularly with the MNPD criteria, should be mandatory. Some movement towards this is to be found in the attempt by UN organs to use so-called "smart sanctions" when they deploy the economic instrument.

Section 2. Absolute and relative prohibitions of the jus in bello

The *jus in bello* is comprised of two parts: what we may call "Part A" consists of principles to be applied in determining the proper use and quantum of force in specific cases, and "Part B", which contains a set of absolute prohibitions. The application of Part A uses perforce the contextual-policy-based mode of decision; applications of Part B use the textual-rule-based mode. Part A is quite indulgent to the specialists in violence in international conflict, for it permits them to apply violence to adversaries as long as it is occasioned and justified by military necessity; is proportional to that necessity; and is as discriminating with respect to combatants and non-combatants as the context allows. In the application of the MNPD principles, the warrior is allowed a significant margin of appreciation, for this part of the law recognises and takes account of the complexity and variability of battle situations. As long as the warrior's applications remain within the margin of appreciation delimited by the MNPD principles, unintended deaths and injuries caused to non-combatants are characterised as "collateral damage" rather than war crimes and incur neither criminal nor civil liability [535].

535. W. Michael Reisman, "Compensating Collateral Damage in Elective International Conflict", *Intercultural Hum. Rts. L. Rev.*, Vol. 8 (2013), pp. 1-18.

In Part B, in contrast, the crafters of international law impose *absolute* limits on the use of certain instruments and modes of violence. The limits may not be suspended on the ground that those instruments or modes might be militarily necessary and proportional to that necessity in a particular situation. Practices as diverse as perfidy, poisoning of wells, the use of poison gas or dumdum bullets, the initiation of aggressive war and the intentional killing of non-combatants could plausibly promise significant, even decisive, advantages to the tactician or strategist in some situations. But even then, resort to Part B's prohibited modes and instruments is supposed to be impermissible – and to remain so even if the adversary resorts to them.

Some Part B limitations, for example those which are designed to ensure protection of the environment, may recommend themselves because they promise to be beneficial to both victor and vanquished in a temporal-extensive sense; a victory achieved at the expense of a liveable habitat would be pyrrhic. Other limitations are humanitarian and entirely altruistic; though they deprive a party of military advantage, they may not be suspended even in the absence of reciprocation.

In the period after World War II, Part B enjoyed a dramatic expansion, signalled by the installation in the legal lexicon of the rather Orwellian term "International Humanitarian Law" in place of the erstwhile grimly designative titles of "Law of War" or "Law of Armed Conflict". To track the expansion, one need only compare the limited codex of crimes which the London Charter set out for the Nuremberg Tribunal with the far more elaborate itemisation of crimes in Articles 7 and 8 of the Statute of the ICC or the recent jurisprudence of the ICJ applying human rights law to various parts of the *jus in bello* [536].

Section 3. The decay of absolute prohibitions

Human rights proponents have celebrated the new prohibitions in Part B yet largely ignored the retreat of some the most fundamental

536. Compare: Agreement by the Government of the United Kingdom of Great Britain and Northern Ireland, the Government of the United States of America, the Provisional Government of the French Republic and the Government of the Union of Soviet Socialist Republics for the Prosecution and Punishment of the Major War Criminals of the European Axis, 8 August 1945, 82 UNTS 280; with: ICC Statute, *supra* footnote 134. See *Armed Activities on the Territory of the Congo (Congo* v. *Rwanda)*, Judgment, 3 February 2006, ICJ Reports 2006, p. 6; *Armed Activities on the Territory of the Congo (Congo* v. *Uganda)*, Judgment, 19 December 2005, ICJ Reports 2005, p. 168; *The Wall*, *supra* footnote 160. See also Jean-Marie Henchaerts and Louise Doswald-Beck (eds.), *Customary International Humanitarian Law*, 2005.

prohibitions from Part B to Part A. This retro-shifting goes far in undermining the protections of non-combatants in the law of armed conflict. Consider three examples.

At the very heart of the law of armed conflict is the effort to protect non-combatants by insisting on maintaining the distinction between them and combatants. The venerable requirement that lawful combatants wear uniforms and bear arms openly is an indispensable and easily implemented and policed means for protecting non-combatants. Thanks to these distinguishing insignias, belligerents can distinguish adversaries from civilians. The requirement is not without cost to belligerents, for in many situations feigning to be a civilian provides a degree of protection and offers an element of surprise. The traditional mechanism for enforcing this requirement was the denial of the protections of the law of war to those violating it. "The customary punishment for unprivileged participation in hostilities has been death." [537]

Certain changes in the law of armed conflict have eroded this historic rule. Article 37 (1) of the first Additional Protocol to the Geneva Conventions of 1949 [538], which is entitled "Prohibition of perfidy", provides:

> "1. It is prohibited to kill, injure or capture an adversary by resort to perfidy. Acts inviting the confidence of an adversary to lead him to believe that he is entitled to, or is obliged to accord, protection under the rules of international law applicable in armed conflict, with intent to betray that confidence, shall constitute perfidy. The following acts are examples of perfidy:
>
> . . .
>
> *(c)* The feigning of civilian, non-combatant status.
>
> Article 44 of the first Protocol, entitled 'Combatants and prisoners of war', provides:
>
> 1. Any combatant, as defined in Article 43, who falls into the power of an adverse Party shall be a prisoner of war.
>
> 2. While all combatants are obliged to comply with the rules of international law applicable in armed conflict, violations of these rules shall not deprive a combatant of his right to be a combatant

537. Michael Bothe, Karl J. Partsch and Waldemar A. Solf, *New Rules for Victims of Armed Conflicts*, 2013, at p. 244.

538. Protocol Additional to the Geneva Conventions of 12 August 1949, 8 June 1977, 1125 UNTS 3, Article 37, para. 1.

or, if he falls into the power of an adverse Party, of his right to be a prisoner of war, except as provided in Paragraphs 3 and 4.

3. In order to promote the protection of the civilian population from the effects of hostilities, combatants are obliged to distinguish themselves from the civilian population while they are engaged in an attack or in a military operation preparatory to an attack. Recognizing, however, that there are situations in armed conflicts where, owing to the nature of the hostilities an armed combatant cannot so distinguish himself, he shall retain his status as a combatant, provided that, in such situations, he carries his arms openly:

(a) During each military engagement, and

(b) During such time as he is visible to the adversary while he is engaged in a military deployment preceding the launching of an attack in which he is to participate.

Acts which comply with the requirements of this Paragraph shall not be considered as perfidious within the meaning of Article 37, Paragraph 1 *(c)*.

4. A combatant who falls into the power of an adverse Party while failing to meet the requirements set forth in the second sentence of paragraph 3 shall forfeit his right to be a prisoner of war, but he shall, nevertheless, be given protections equivalent in all respects to those accorded to prisoners of war by the Third Convention and by this Protocol. This protection includes protections equivalent to those accorded to prisoners of war by the Third Convention in the case where such a person is tried and punished for any offences he has committed.

5. Any combatant who falls into the power of an adverse Party while not engaged in an attack or in a military operation preparatory to an attack shall not forfeit his rights to be a combatant and a prisoner of war by virtue of his prior activities.

6. This Article is without prejudice to the right of any person to be a prisoner of war pursuant to Article 4 of the Third Convention.

7. This Article is not intended to change the generally accepted practice of States with respect to the wearing of the uniform by combatants assigned to the regular, uniformed armed units of a Party to the conflict."

Article 44 relaxes the historic requirement for at least one side to a conflict and abandons the sanction which enforced it.

This change was not inadvertent. Some who pressed for it simply wished to favour the so-called National Liberation combatants – to help them win – without regard for the consequences for non-combatants. Others rationalised the change with the hope that, in return for relaxing the uniform and open arms requirement, irregular forces would acquire an incentive to buy into and comply with other parts of the law of war. The rationalisation was of doubtful logic and even more doubtful morality. It was illogical because even if irregulars did henceforth comply, the fact that they and any future adversary could now – lawfully – fight without uniforms and without bearing arms openly meant that their adversaries would be unable to distinguish them as foes and as a result could not help but kill or injure *more* non-combatants. It was of doubtful morality because, even if the rationalisation proved correct and other parts of the law of war were henceforth respected by belligerents who theretofore had no incentive to respect it, that gain was being purchased with the lives of non-combatants. And, indeed, this is what happened!

At the end of the nineteenth century, the overwhelming percentage of those killed or wounded in war were military personnel. Towards the end of the twentieth century, the great majority of persons killed or injured in most international armed conflicts have been civilian non-combatants [539].

Nuclear weapons provide a second disturbing example. When it comes to kinetic weapons, the essential equation is that the bigger the bang, the less the discrimination between combatant and non-combatant and between licit military target and other parts of the environment. By their nature, the biggest bangs will cause the most extensive violations of the MNPD principles. It is sobering to recall that the single uranium bomb dropped on Hiroshima killed 78,000 human beings instantly or soon after. Another 37,000 inhabitants of the city simply disappeared. Compared to what contemporary arsenals can boast of, that bomb was a primitive device.

In 1996, the ICJ was presented with the opportunity of advising the UN General Assembly and the WHO on the legality of nuclear weapons [540]. Without regard to the question of the political imprudence of the initiative, the question itself is certainly not frivolous. It is clear that if nuclear weapons were now to be used, they would make a shamble of international law's effort to effectively discriminate between

539. George H. Aldrich, "The Hague Peace Conferences: The Laws of War on Land", *Am. J. Int'l L.*, Vol. 94 (2000), p. 42 *et seq.*, at 48.
540. *Legality of Nuclear Weapons*, *supra* footnote 113.

combatants and non-combatants, not to speak of the effort to preserve a liveable habitat for the survivors.

For all their contingent horror, nuclear weapons performed a useful, albeit hazardous function during the Cold War. But with the end of the Cold War, the strategic deterrent system – the contraposed, roughly equal nuclear arsenals which were insusceptible to be neutralised by a "first strike" and which, accordingly, guaranteed mutually assured destruction should the weapons ever be used – had become redundant. In the meanwhile, the demand for non-proliferation, nuclear reduction and ultimate nuclear disarmament had increased and no longer seemed unrealistic. Perhaps that was the reason the requests for the advisory opinions came when they did.

The Court could have seized the moment and recorded the spectacularly obvious fact that nuclear weapons, in addition to their other externalities, simply cannot discriminate between combatants and non-combatants. Instead, the Court held that

> "in view of the present state of international law viewed as a whole, as examined above by the Court, and of the elements of fact at its disposal, the Court is led to observe that it cannot reach a definitive conclusion as to the legality or illegality of the use of nuclear weapons by a State in an extreme circumstance of self-defence, in which its very survival would be at stake" [541].

The implications of this holding for the law of armed conflict are far-reaching. Under modern international law, all unilateral uses of force must be in self-defence. The predicate of self-defence is survival. What responsible Government does not try to prepare for its self-defence, *a fortiori* for every imaginable "extreme circumstance"? By waffling as it did, the Court invited States not simply to reverse the steady shift of nuclear weapons into Part B but to reverse the political gravity and move them firmly into Part A. The Court even minimised the potential restraint of the MNPD principles by sanctioning in advance the use of nuclear weapons on the basis of the user's own assessment that it was facing "an extreme circumstance of self-defence"!

Advisory opinions are *erga omnes*, and the ratio of this one sanctions proliferation! North Korea and Iran, as well as any other State elites who are pondering joining or are already trying to slip stealthily into the nuclear weapons queue, are as entitled to prepare themselves for self-

541. *Id.*, at p. 263, para. 97.

defence in "extreme circumstances", as is any other State. The more States acquiring nuclear weapons, the greater the likelihood of still further proliferation and the greater the probability of nuclear wars – and nuclear terrorist actions – with weapons incapable of discriminating between combatants and non-combatants [542].

Torture provides a third melancholy example. It has been planted in Part B, but in the so-called "War on Terror", its use – and the results obtained – have been allowed [543]. The presumed justification for the selective use of torture was and continues to be that Al-Qaida and Islamic State and the groups that operate in their penumbra, who routinely and intentionally flout the most basic restraints in the law of armed conflict, threaten great and unlawful destruction. Because these adversaries cannot be deterred, defence against them requires information. In some "real-time" circumstances, the argument goes, only interrogations employing torture can secure it.

From an international legal standpoint, what is involved here is more – and more serious – than episodic violations of the law. This is a claim to move an absolutely prohibited practice from Part B to Part A; that is, to apply the MNPD principles, on a case-by-case basis, to an activity which, until that time, had been made subject to an absolute prohibition. Nor have elements within the US Executive and Congress been the sole proponents of this shift. The House of Lords has called for a case-by-case approach to the question of the admissibility of evidence gained by torture [544]. Other apologists for torture have invoked various "ticking bomb" scenarios. In more elegant fashion, philosophical arguments

542. The ICJ had another opportunity to revisit the issue in the *Marshall Islands* case but found that there was no dispute. *Obligations Concerning Negotiations Relating to Cessation of the Nuclear Arms Race and to Nuclear Disarmament (Marshall Islands* v. *UK)*, Judgment, 5 October 2016, ICJ Reports 2016, p. 834.

543. See Articles 3 and 13 of the Geneva Convention Relative to the Treatment of Prisoners of War, 12 August 1949, 75 UNTS 135; Article 7 of the International Covenant on Civil and Political Rights, 16 December 1966, 999 UNTS 171; Convention against Torture and Other Cruel, Inhuman or Degrading Treatment or Punishment, 10 December 1984, 1465 UNTS 85.

544. *A and Others* v. *Sec'y of State for the Home Dep't*, [2005] UKHL 71. The House of Lords unanimously held evidence obtained from torture to be inadmissible in the courts of the United Kingdom. Yet, the Lords were divided four to three on the relevant test. The minority view, articulated by Lord Bingham, argued that courts must exclude evidence if there exists a "real risk" that the evidence may have been obtained by torture. *Id.*, at para. 56. But the majority agreed with Lord Hope's standard. *Id.*, at para. 145 ("When everything possible has been done, it may turn out that the matter is left in doubt and that, using their expertise, SIAC cannot be satisfied on the balance of probabilities that the statement in question has been obtained by torture. If so, in my view, SIAC can look at the statement but should bear its doubtful origins in mind when evaluating it"). See Cherie Booth, "Commentary", *Financial Times*, 2 March 2006.

have sought to justify in situations of extreme crisis – Churchill's "supreme emergency" – the opportunistic application of utilitarian analyses to erstwhile deontological prohibitions [545].

All of these voices are engaged in the same sort of attempted retro-shift of an absolutely prohibited activity in the law of war from Part B to Part A whereupon demonstration of the operation of some urgent contextual factors, theretofore inadmissible, could render it lawful. The new claim, whether explicit or implicit, is that henceforth torture *may* be used if it is plausibly militarily necessary, proportional and discriminating.

But experience shows that torture, once sanctioned and however contingently and restrictively the authorisation for its application might try to be, metastasises quickly, infecting the whole process of interrogation. In other words, if torture is moved back to Part A, even an intended case-by-case method is likely to decay in crisis. Then torture bodes to become routinised, applied more and more widely and ultimately by all.

Those who believe in natural law are inclined to assume that once a human right has been legislated, it will, *ipso facto*, persist forever: the law, ever expanding and infused with new prohibitions, will always hold. But no law made by human beings endures simply by virtue of its own authority. As we saw in Chapter III, Section 5, Paragraph 2, in the dynamic of law's dialectic, every prescription requires continuous political support. Principles of international law, like any prescription, are abrogated when their consumers and custodians decide, for better or worse, to change them, whether by explicit abrogation, purportedly based on rational self-interest, or by persistent tolerated and unremedied violations (the latter often oblivious to rational self-interest). Part B prohibitions of the *jus in bello* – part of the fragile barrier between violence and savagery which the *jus in bello* seeks to maintain – are no exception.

545. Michael Walzer, *Just and Unjust Wars: A Moral Argument with Historical Illustrations*, 1977; but see his reconsideration in Michael Walzer, *Arguing about War*, 2004.

CHAPTER XV

THE CITIZENSHIP ROLE OF THE INTERNATIONAL LAWYER: FASHIONING GOALS FOR A PUBLIC ORDER OF HUMAN DIGNITY

> "The lawyer's citizenship role is by no means so clear cut. It is in the penumbra of the professional role, so to speak. We may define it residually as *those behavior expectations pertaining to the lawyer in relation to his community and society which are not those of every citizen and which are not part of the technical function of the lawyer*."
>
> Wardwell and Wood [546]

International law is so often criticised and even pilloried that international lawyers come to feel an almost professional obligation to defend the entire enterprise. We see "major" advances in tiny and often ambiguous "baby" steps and hasten to endorse decisions taken by its formal institutions, no matter how disappointing or anodyne they actually are. A convention to prevent genocide which provides no real means for doing so and, in fact, has failed to do so, is hailed as a major success [547]. A "Responsibility to Protect" is celebrated, despite the fact that it does nothing new. Things are viewed through an infinitely patient "developmental" prism, whose metrics are so refined that almost anything can be presented as "progress".

As well-intentioned as this professional loyalty may be, it is the *system* of international law which is the loser. Sir Hersch Lauterpacht, certainly no "enemy" of international law, asked rhetorically:"Shall international law, by refusing to admit its present imperfections and by elevating them to the authority of legitimate and permanent manifestations of a 'specific' law, abdicate the task of raising itself above the level of a primitive law of a primitive community?" [548]

One of the consequences of a posture of respectful denial is that appraisal, evaluation and recommendations for improvement of international law's performance – tasks indispensable to ensuring that any

546. Walter I. Wardwell and Arthur L. Wood, "The Extra-Professional Role of the Lawyer", *Am. J. Soc.*, Vol. 61 (1956), p. 304 *et seq.*
547. Reisman, "Acting *Before* Victims Become Victims", *supra* footnote 85.
548. Lauterpacht, *Function of Law*, *supra* footnote 107, at p. 431.

purposive human activity is actually achieving its purpose – are left to detractors.

Some external evaluative concept is a *sine qua non* for the international jurist because it enables the jurist to step outside of specific or general legal arrangements and to *evaluate* them in terms of the extent to which they are achieving the various goals which the jurist has identified for the system. Insofar as the arrangements are failing to achieve those goals, the jurist may then proceed to invent and promote alternatives. External evaluative criteria thus generate a tension between demand and expectation, aspiration and achievement, a tension which impels scholar and lawyer to seek alternatives. Without external evaluative criteria, we are locked in the textual-rule-based mode, confined to examining each decision in terms of its consistency with prior decisions and with "process", the procedural values of decision-making. Efforts at appraisal, such as they are, degrade into Panglossian endorsement.

Some theorists eschew the utility, even the possibility, of explicit goal clarification, preferring to rely on a global horde of atomised and passionately libidinised individuals, each seeking only his or her own interest, to arrive at community-wide positive outcomes, thanks to a benevolent "Invisible Hand" or a timely intervention by some *deus ex machina* to sort things out for the best. But even assessing the performance of the Invisible Hand and the *deus ex machina* requires criteria for appraisal.

Sir Hersch's term, "imperfections", does import an external criterion for evaluation; his was the model of a developed national legal system. In Chapters I and II, I explained why that criterion is insufficient for international law given the "what-it's-attached-to". Still, the term "imperfections" shows that *any* set of goals, no matter how imprecise, will serve the function of appraisal as long as the goal is distinct from the flow of behaviour which it evaluates. But the less precise the goal and the less inclusive its scope, the less guidance it provides.

Consider examining a specific flow of behaviour in terms of the following questions: Is this "good" for me? Is this "good" for my family? Is this "good" for my client? Is this "good" for my tribe? Is this "good" for my company or my industry? For my religion, sect or cult? For my nation? All the questioner can conclude by reference to such criteria is whether particular decisions and decision processes are indulging one or another group or one of its individual members; the only alternatives one can propose will be strategic or tactical adjustments crafted to make future decisions more indulgent for that group or individual. Because, as we saw in Chapter III, such narrowly formulated goals and the arrangements to achieve them inevitably engender the resistance of those excluded from their benefits, they may fail to benefit even the exclusive group they were designed to favour. By contrast, arrangements accommodating the interests of many will enjoy their support and obviate their compulsion.

Goals differ from shorter-term objectives. For some types of law jobs, narrower criteria may be called for by the role being performed. For example, many advocates (by contrast to mediators) conceive of themselves as professionally and ethically obliged to bend their efforts to make a decision process produce outcomes that discriminate in favour of their clients [549]. As for the international judge or arbitrator, goals may be limited to testing the consistency of prospective alternative decisions with prior "higher" decisions; their mandate and mode of decision-making, as noted earlier, is so prescribed [550]. Systemic appraisal, by contrast, requires a system-wide lens and the deployment of the contextual-policy-based mode of decision. For those discharging this role, other intellectual tools are required. As one shifts from the logical exercises of the textual-rule-based mode to a contextual-policy-based mode involving making and appraising choices, the importance of the "self" of the person conducting that activity increases. As the ultimate instrument of perception and evaluation, "calibration" of the self is a preliminary and continuing task.

A second preliminary task is the clarification of one's observational standpoint. For any issue, there are many possible vantages or standpoints, each determining *what* is viewed and *how* it is viewed. Both the reference and content of the term "law" or "choice" will vary depending on whether the standpoint is that of a member of the system observed who has internalised its folklore and myth or that of an outsider. Perceptions of the same phenomenon may vary, depending on the culture, class, gender, age and, in particular, on the observer's crisis experience.

The varieties of standpoints increase when one moves to the international plane, given the varieties of actors and their identifications. While no single standpoint is more authentic than another, narrower "me-oriented" standpoints are ill-adapted for systematic appraisal of international legal arrangements. Jeremy Bentham cautioned that "[e]

549. See *infra* Chapter XVI for a consideration of the international dimension of these roles.
550. Reisman, " 'Case Specific Mandates' ", *supra* footnote 140.

very body of men is governed altogether by its conception of what is its interest, in the narrowest and most selfish sense of the word interest: never by any regard for the interest of the people" [551]. Narrow evaluative criteria, based exclusively on the interests of a single nation, group, class, tribe or belief system can certainly provide the standards for appraisal, but their exclusivity limits their utility for appraising a system in which many other actors participate. The concept of common interest imports that legal arrangements should be so crafted as to serve common interests and not merely the special interests of particular individuals, classes, groups or States.

No magical transubstantiation is brought about merely by intoning the words "common interest", while seeking narrow and selfish ones. Even ostensibly consensual agreements may not serve the "common interest" [552]. Even when the parties are in a situation of power parity and their specific agreements are deemed by each to be in their *own* shared interest, they need not be in the interests of all other members of an existing or latent community or even in the interests of the smaller circle of those directly affected by them. The arrangements may be injurious to the interests of many others or may have been secured by compromising other common interests, for example the preservation of the environment.

We are inclined to assume that legal arrangements concluded by representative deliberative bodies *ipso facto* express their community's common interests. But not all members of a formal lawmaking body – be it a legislature, an *ad hoc* committee or a standing international conference – enjoy equal influence. Nor is the *representative* quality of all the participants in a legislature or international conference necessarily equal. Even in non-authoritarian systems, elites may strike deals that serve their own or preferred constituents' interests but not the interests of their wider rank and file.

From the perspective of a disengaged observer committed to, say, a world public order of human dignity, the outcomes of particular collective procedures are not automatically in the common interest. In collectivities composed of members enjoying roughly equal influence, outcomes may represent compromises, parts or all of which may be

551. Jeremy Bentham, *The Works of Jeremy Bentham*, Vol. 9, ed. John Bowring, 1843, at p. 102.

552. Unequal treaties exist, a fact obliquely recognised by the ICJ when it stated that negotiated agreements establishing maritime boundaries between States which are coastally adjacent or opposite must still be equitable. *North Sea Continental Shelf (Ger. v. Den.)*, Judgment, 20 February 1969, ICJ Reports 1969, p. 3, para. 85.

so vapid, empty or anodyne that they fail to address the challenges for which the process was initiated. Arrangements arrived at democratically may increase the legitimacy of outcomes, but they do not ensure that those outcomes are in the common interest, as determined from the vantage point of a disengaged observer.

This is not to say that the integrity of process is unimportant. But procedural refinements, no matter how scrupulously followed, do not guarantee that their results will be in the common interest when assessed by an observer against a set of systemic goals. Even if everyone who is deemed to be part of the accepted understanding of the term "everyone" in that particular situation is consulted, there is no Invisible Hand that ensures sound results or, for that matter, that assures any meaningful result at all.

Section 1. Transcivilisationalism and goal clarification

Professor Onuma Yasuaki also identifies goal clarification as a central intellectual task for the contemporary international lawyer, for which he proposes a transcivilisational approach [553]. His theory merits close examination. Civilisations' philosophic heyday was in the work of Edmund Burke, Jean-Jacques Rousseau and, of course, Georg Wilhelm Friedrich Hegel, the latter of the view that "not all peoples are to be counted among the *welthistorische Volksgeister*" [554]. In a time when equitable class and gender representation in decision-making is demanded and, at the United Nations, diversity is measured in terms of regional representation, the focus on civilisations seems rather retro; the results have not been especially democratic when international law plays the game of selecting winners and losers among competing civilisations. Thus, Article 9 of the Statute of the ICJ admonishes electors in the Security Council and General Assembly to be mindful "that in the body as a whole the representation of the *main* forms of civilization and of the *principal* legal systems of the world should be assured" [555]. ICJ Statute Article 38 (1) *(c)* is more explicitly judgemental, confining membership in the class of contributors to the formation of "general principles" to "civilized nations" [556].

---

553. Yasuaki, *supra* footnote 473.
554. George H. Sabine, *A History of Political Theory*, 3rd ed., 1962, at p. 630.
555. ICJ Statute, *supra* footnote 307, Article 9 (emphasis added).
556. *Id.*, Article 38 (1) *(c)*.

That these particular prescriptions are now viewed uneasily as anachronisms does not negate the fact that not all civilisations nor all the practices of a given civilisation are now acceptable goals; other values are determinative. The point is that even deploying transcivilisationalism as a working method for goal clarification requires extracivilisational criteria. Without them, transcivilisationism becomes a meme for some sort of collective historicism, ransacking (at least in theory) ancient troves of cultures for answers to problems they never encountered and that require, for their solution, looking far ahead, all the while filtering out those hideous elements that have fortunately been acknowledged and repudiated.

Professor Onuma, in his emphasis on goals, is correct: criteria are required for appraising existing international legal arrangements and for constructing future arrangements. But it is insufficient to distil them from existing institutions and arrangements because they are imprinted with power relationships and interests and, in a deeper sense, with the idiosyncratic values of dominant actors and their elites. If we do not address this challenge, the new masters, waiting in the wings, will simply imprint their own values so that, as in George Orwell's *Animal Farm*, the only change will be in personnel and vocabulary. Distilling the essence of the new or old masters will simply replicate them. International law needs an external set of values to serve as a fulcrum. Common interests should be expressed in terms of the production and distribution of all scope values, and they should be posited, not derived from civilisations or religious texts.

Section 2. Clarifying the common interest: principles of content and procedure for action and appraisal

The international lawyer should participate in clarifying and formulating the common interest of the most comprehensive world community and then subjecting its inherited arrangements and prospective decisions to appraisal in terms of the degree of their contribution to that common interest: first, to the maintenance or restoration of minimum order and, then, within the social space which minimum order requirements allow, to securing the optimum order for the abundant production and wide distribution of the values which people seek.

The following principles are proposed for appraisal of current and projected international legal arrangements in their contexts. The principles are value-consequential rather than institutional; that is, arrangements are desirable for their consequences in terms of the production and distribution of values in context rather than in terms of an *a priori* preference for certain types of international institutional arrangements. They are expressed at a level of generality which enables them to be adapted to a wide range of situations, many of which will be in international law's offshore zones and, accordingly, manifest low degrees of organisation. Applied in ensemble, they are likely to produce arrangements sustaining minimum order. Insofar as they succeed in promoting the common interest in those arrangements, they will allow for an approximation of human dignity.

Ten principles are postulated rather than derived or deduced from "higher" principles which might claim a divine or natural law provenance. Demonstrations of logical derivations from trans-empirical or highly ambiguous premises may contribute to legitimising legal arrangements *within* specific communities whose members accept those premises. But the international community is composed of a plethora of communities, divinities and hagiographies, each with its own premises, deities and value systems; if the method for formulating principles and evaluative criteria were confined to derivation from higher sources, the result would be, at worst, Babel and conflict or, at best, vapid compromises or anodyne generalities to which all can agree but which say little. My experience has been that people subscribing to very different first principles and different styles in derivation, irrespective of the faiths or creeds which they employ for justification, find it easier to cooperate in fashioning common legal arrangements if the methodological focus is shifted from a debate about premises to one about specific arrangements for the production and distribution of the values in question in arrangements approximating the common interest.

Para. 1. The Principle of Minimum Order

The *sine qua non* for all other goals is the maintenance or restoration of minimum order: the achievement not simply of a low level of violence but a low *expectation* of violence [557]. The Principle of Minimum Order means that whatever coercion is threatened or used to sustain particular arrangements serves the maintenance and restoration of order and not for its disruption. The concept of "minimum *world* public order" enables the appraisal of past and prospective arrangements and prospective

557. See *supra* Chapter II, Section 5.

decisions concerning security, not in terms of the interests of a single participant or group of participants but in terms of *everyone's* security.

Establishing and maintaining minimum world public order creates the social space for minimally coercive politics and for the design and operation of legal arrangements for the achievement of other value goals. But if minimum order is the indispensable basis for other collaborative and productive activity, it cannot, by itself, supply a comprehensive evaluative criterion. People seek many things besides minimum public order. Moreover, at any moment, there are many possible constellations for the production and distribution of the things that can provide, if only momentarily, quotients of stability. Some of those constellations may enhance minimum public order, while others may have the opposite effect. Plainly, a broader, external evaluative criterion must be deployed alongside that of minimum public order. If minimum order is indispensable, it cannot be celebrated to the exclusion of everything else.

In the absence of an effective, centralised institution monopolising coercion, the international political system has had to rely on other mechanisms. The design and appraisal of longer-term arrangements as well as specific short-term actions in terms of their contribution to minimum order must adjust to particular contexts, using mapping techniques, such as those set out in earlier chapters. Some arrangements may be counterintuitive. Thus, in context, a national navy's access to large areas of the ocean may be indispensable to the maintenance of the minimum order of the oceans. In a specific context, a unilateral intervention, unauthorised by the Security Council, might be the only way of restoring order in a particular State or region. Given the varying contexts and the volatility of international law, designing arrangements to meet the Principle of Minimum Order can be a challenging task. It may sometimes require more personal responsibility than simply endorsing what a particular institution has done or simply condemning, in terms of a rule and without reference to context, what a State or group of States may have done, the feasible options actually available and the aggregate consequences of each of them in terms of all the relevant principles and goals.

Para. 2. The Principle of the Avoidance of Surplus Violence

Minimum order does not import the absence of coercion. Indeed, the elimination of all coercion is a quixotic goal, for no social arrangement is or can be free from coercion or its threat or implication; the availability and effective use of coercion in support of public order is a critical component and one distinctive indicator of law. A pertinent question in the design or appraisal of any arrangement is (1) whether the coercion that is being threatened or applied has been authorised by the international community or is consonant with its expectations of authority; (2) independent of authorisation, whether, in the context in which it operates, it is the only feasible means for restoring public order; and (3) whether it is used with the utmost parsimony sufficient to maintain or restore minimum order. The Principle of the Avoidance of Surplus Violence has an analogue in the law of war's principle of proportionality, which we considered in the previous chapter; it is also related to the principle of effectiveness which we will consider below, in Paragraph 5.

Para. 3. The Principle of Enhancing Life Opportunities: Development

A public order of human dignity is distinguished by the life opportunities it affords to all the members of its communities. This is a goal to which the contemporary international legal system has committed itself at almost every level. Indeed, whatever its official ideology and level of development, the legitimacy of every modern Government depends in no small measure upon its ability to grow its economy, increase the national wealth and, through some form of distribution, whether by the provision of opportunity or by entitlement or a mix of both, to expand the life opportunities of its citizens.

In international law, "development" has become the omnibus term for this goal. In 1986, the UN General Assembly resolved not only that "the right to development is an inalienable human right" but that "*states* have the duty to take steps individually and collectively, to formulate international development policies with a view to facilitating the full realization of the right to development" [558]. The achievement of many other international human rights depends upon the State's effective performance of this development duty; without a vigorous and productive economy, it is simply impossible to realise many of the "guaranteed" human rights.

Subject to the Principle of Contextual Integration, which is treated in the next paragraph, existing and prospective arrangements should be

558. GA Res. 41/128, 4 December 1986.

evaluated in terms of whether they entail institutional adjustments that lead to a greater production *and* wider distribution of the key values or desired events which human beings seek while maintaining minimum public order. This goal cannot be assessed only in terms of wealth accumulation but should be specified cumulatively in terms of each value category:

Power: We may speak of power developments when there are net increases in support for and the effectiveness of processes (of varying degrees of institutionalisation) specialised to making decisions, whether about the constitutive process or the community's production and allocation of all other values.

Wealth: The wealth of a community may be measured in terms of the volume of its products (in all value categories), the levels of income of all members of that community and the aggregate resource base. But from the perspective of the assessment of development, a wealth development is measured in the increased capacity of a community to produce and distribute wealth.

Enlightenment: The reference is to the level of general knowledge retrievable at feasible cost and applicable to procedures for designing and implementing purposive change. Developments in enlightenment occur within a community when participation in the production of its knowledge pool increases, as does the pool itself, processes specialised to gathering, processing or disseminating knowledge relevant to decision are extended, and decision-makers increasingly resort to available enlightenment for the purposes of decision.

Well-Being: Well-being increases when more people have an increased life expectancy, a robust capacity for action and a decreased expectation of the incidence of disease, including anxiety. A positive well-being development occurs when processes specialised to enhancing well-being are created or expanded.

Skill: Skills refer to learned and culturally transmitted sequences of behaviour aimed at purposive manipulation and change of the environment or some aspect of the self. A skill development occurs when there is an increase in the skill pool of a community, where the skills of concern are specialised to performing tasks leading to the realisation of developmental goals and when the community's capacity to forge and disseminate new skills is increased.

Affection: Affection refers to positive sentiments towards others and to loyalty to groups. Life opportunities with respect to the affection value increase within a community when the opportunities for acquiring and expressing agapeic and erotic positive sentiments increase without distinction to gender or sexual orientation and when loyalties towards more inclusive groups are increased or reinforced. A negative affection development occurs with parochialisation or contractions to more exclusive identifications with attitudes towards others becoming less amiable or even hostile.

Respect: Respect refers to ego development in individual community members, correlation of status within a community to the merit of the contribution which the status holder makes to the community and the minimisation of individual and collective discrimination. The expectation of meritocratic reward acts as an incentive for investment in the production of other values. Hence, a respect development occurs when group members perceive themselves increasingly as full participants who are able to make claims in their own names as well as to be subjected to claims by others in their own name, when status is increasingly a meritocratic function and when patterns of individual and group discrimination are reduced.

Rectitude: A rectitude development occurs within a community when opportunities for the individual's free cultivation of rectitude increase, and the internalised codes of individuals are not only compatible with human dignity but also tolerant of other such codes.

Within the constraints of maintaining minimum order, it is important to examine the actual aggregate consequences of different arrangements in terms of their production and distribution of the things that human beings seek.

Para. 4. The Principle of Contextual Integration

Practical politics is less the science of identifying what is the "good" or the right thing to do in context and more often the art of accommodating and prioritising as many competing "goods" or "right things" as possible and compatible with the maintenance of minimum order.

This procedural principle proposes that appraisals of the quality of any existing or prospective legal arrangement not focus exclusively on that arrangement but locate it in context so that its aggregate effects on other value arrangements and in terms of other principles and goals can be taken into account. Some of those other arrangements are accommodative, others competitive.

This is particularly important in international law, which is rife with antinomies. Consider, for example, the policy to eliminate impunity by rigorously prosecuting serious violations of human rights. In some circumstances, the Principle of Contextual Integration might require that it yield to the need for amnesties as a means of re-establishing minimum order [559]. The Principle of Contextual Integration is particularly important in appraising beforehand the design and construction of institutions, an issue which I will treat in a moment.

Para. 5. The Principle of Economy

International law was long based on effectiveness [560], essentially validating what had been achieved by the exercise of power. Effectiveness was transformed into legal rights, rather than *vice versa*. As a result, the collective implementation of legal decisions, whether by groups of States or by international institutions, was not a paramount problem. Contemporary international law often reverses the formula: legal rights are prescribed and then must be made effective. Ambitious social goals seek to change patterns which had been established by application of power and the incumbent beneficiaries may be expected to resist. As international law's prescriptive reach has gone further and further, ensuring its implementative grasp becomes a constant preoccupation; implementability is also a key consideration in determining the content of prescriptions and arrangements as well as in setting the timetables for their implementation.

The melancholy but now commonplace term "donor fatigue" draws attention to the fact that the resources of the international community are finite. Hence, realistic timetables for the achievement of particular goals must be adopted and the most economic use of resources for implementation must be planned. Not everything set as a goal is immediately achievable or enforceable. Yet allowing some flexibility in timing should not be allowed to become an avenue of retreat into a fantasy in which political energy is devoted to elaborating a myth system which always remains tantalisingly just beyond realisation. The prospect of implementation should be sufficiently real, lest particular arrangements simply embroider the myth system and undermine the expectation of the effectiveness of international law.

559. Protocol Additional to the Geneva Conventions of 12 August 1949, and Relating to the Protection of Victims of Non-International Armed Conflicts, Article 6 (5), 8 June 1977, 1125 UNTS 609.

560. See *supra* Chapter VIII, Sections 2 and 4.

Para. 6. The Principle of Second-Best Solutions

Related to the Principle of Economy and the Principle of Contextual Integration is the principle of accepting approximate implementations. “Le mieux”, Voltaire famously observed, “est l’ennemi du bien”. Where preferred solutions cannot be achieved, alternatives which are better than the existing situation should be pursued on the condition that they do not preclude subsequent improvements with the potential of leading to a closer approximation of a satisfactory arrangement.

Para. 7. The Principle of Environmental Conservation

It is characteristic of a science-based and technological civilisation to consume more resources than have prior civilisations or cultures. Intensity of exploitation is aggravated by the surge in demand caused by world population growth [561]. The Principle of Environmental Conservation is essentially a specification of the procedural Principle of Contextual Integration, which mandates that both assessments of problems and proposed solutions be put in context. It has become particularly important to consider projected solutions in terms of their cumulative environmental impacts.

Para. 8. The Principle of Sustainable Development

On a planet of inelastic resources but elastic and growing demand, innovative modes of value production and distribution should be designed to be self-sustaining and not resource-consumptive.

Para. 9. The Principle of Cultivation of Rationality

Immanuel Kant stated a profound but often misinterpreted truth when he said “rational beings . . . together require universal laws for their survival” [562]. The efforts of the doctors of international law have largely been directed to prescribing those “universal laws”, rather than to fostering their prerequisite: “rational beings” who can make and apply those laws, making the choices that they entail. A major challenge in the twenty-first century will be how to enhance opportunities for

561. See *supra* Chapter II, Section 1.
562. Immanuel Kant, “Perpetual Peace”, in Carl J. Friedrich (ed.), *The Philosophy of Kant*, 1949, p. 453 *et seq.*, at 459.

individuals to cultivate rationality, the prerequisite to and the quest for universal laws expressing the common interest. To this end, these lectures have proposed the cultivation of techniques of self-scrutiny, the clarification of observational standpoint and methods of enquiry appropriate for the contextual-policy-based mode of decision-making.

Para. 10. The Principle of Valid Legal Process

One of the functions of organised and institutionalised decision-making is to ensure that whatever the vagaries of individual participants, the collective decision process produces rational results. This can be accomplished procedurally by insisting that due deliberation precede action, thereby minimising tendencies to impulsiveness and arbitrariness and the operation of subliminal biases and predilections, to all of which decision-making by human beings is prone. The probability and extent of their influencing choice-making increases when choices must be made in crisis by a single person or by small, closed groups [563]. The demand for orderly processes of decision in accordance with prescribed procedures – often under the rubric of "due process" – is deemed so important that, in many systems, its denial requires setting aside a decision that might otherwise have been substantively correct.

Implementing this principle in the current constitutive process will be challenging. Our review in Chapter IV of the different types of constitutive processes drew attention to the persistence of the demand for unilateral decision in the offshore zones of international law and especially in the face of massive human rights violations. The demand among international lawyers for institutionalised decision is particularly intense with respect to unilateral actions that purport to remedy grave human rights violations. Due process is sought both as a value in itself as well as a prophylactic, lest even more harm be done in an effort intended to remedy injury.

563. Irving L. Janis, *GroupThink: Psychological Studies of Policy Decisions and Fiascoes*, 1982.

CHAPTER XVI

INTERNATIONAL LAW AS A PROFESSION: DILEMMAS OF IDENTITY AND COMMITMENT

> ". . . we retain great misgiving about the propriety of what is being done, which we can only justify on the principle 'my country . . . right or wrong, my country'".
>
> Sir Hartley Shawcross [564]

Section 1. The Shawcross dilemma

After World War II, Greece was ripped by a vicious civil conflict. The royalist Government, along with conservative and centrist factions, was ranged against forces on the Left, including the Greek People's Liberation Army (ELAS), which was backed by the Greek Communist Party [565]. Like many of the so-called "internal wars" of the Cold War era, this particular war had major international involvements. The United Kingdom and later the United States supported the Government, while the Communist States of Eastern and Central Europe supported ELAS. At the time, Albania was still part of the Soviet bloc and, as a State contiguous to Greece, was a valuable asset for the insurgents.

One part of the conflict, the Corfu Channel incident, reached the docket of the ICJ by the time the civil war had largely been resolved. The case arose from an incident in the Straits of Corfu in 1946. A squadron of British warships, composed of two cruisers and two destroyers, had left the Greek port of Corfu whence it proceeded northward through a channel previously swept for mines in the North Corfu Strait. Outside the Bay of Saranda, one of the destroyers struck a mine and was heavily damaged. The other destroyer, which took her in tow, struck another mine. Despite itself suffering severe damage, the second destroyer succeeded in towing its sister ship back to Corfu. Three weeks later, British minesweepers swept the North Corfu Channel and cut and retrieved twenty-two moored mines [566].

564. Anthony Carty, "The Corfu Channel Case – and the Missing Admiralty Orders", *L. & Prac. Int'l Ct. & Tribunals*, Vol. 3 (2004), p. 1 *et seq.*, at 10 (quoting ADM 1/22504, Hartley Shawcross to Prime Minister, 3 November 1948).

565. Stathis N. Kalyvas, *The Logic of Violence in Civil War*, 2006.

566. *Corfu Channel (UK* v. *Alb.)*, Judgment, 9 April 1949, ICJ Reports 1949, p. 4 (hereafter *Corfu Channel*).

In the ICJ, the United Kingdom, seeking condemnation of Albania and damages, contended, among other things, that the passage of its squadron had been innocent. Now, Albania certainly should not have mined the channel or allowed emplacement of mines in its waters without notifying international users; that was a clear breach of international law. But was the passage of the British warships at the time "innocent"?

A document in a British submission to the Court made passing reference to an Admiralty document known as XCU, and the Court requested Britain to produce it [567]. The request ignited a secret debate at the highest levels of the British Government because it was feared that the XCU document might cast doubt on British motives in undertaking the passage at the moment it did. The Admiralty, which had not informed the Law Officers of the document prior to Britain's filing the case against Albania, steadfastly resisted allowing the document to be disclosed to the Court.

Sir Hartley Shawcross, the Attorney General, was leading the British legal team. He feared that the document might cast doubt on the British contention that the passage was innocent and was incensed that the document had not been disclosed to the Law Officers prior to the institution of proceedings [568]. If it had been, Shawcross said, he would have objected to filing the case. The internal Government debate was finally resolved at Cabinet level and XCU was not disclosed to the ICJ. Shawcross proceeded to argue the case without producing XCU. The Court said rather enigmatically:

> "These documents were not produced, the Agent pleading naval secrecy; and the United Kingdom witnesses declined to answer questions relating to them. It is not therefore possible to know the real content of these naval orders. The Court cannot, however, draw from this refusal to produce the orders any conclusions differing from those to which the actual events gave rise." [569]

The United Kingdom won the case.

After Shawcross had been overruled by the Cabinet, he sent a memorandum to the Prime Minister on 3 November 1948, stating that, in the circumstances, not discovering XCU violated Britain's duty to the Court.

---

567. *Corfu Channel*, *supra* footnote 566, at p. 32. The Admiralty was the UK Government department responsible for the command of the Royal Navy until 1964.
568. See *supra* footnote 564.
569. *Corfu Channel*, *supra* footnote 566, at p. 32.

> "It is a fundamental principle of the practice of the Courts of our country and of the conduct of our legal profession that parties to litigation are not entitled to use merely those documents which they think will assist their case and to suppress others which are inimical to it. I must make it clear that neither the Solicitor General, nor myself, nor, I am sure, any of the other members of the Bar who are assisting us in this matter, would for a moment contemplate being parties to the course of conduct now forced upon us by the Admiralty's failure to procure and produce these documents earlier *had our country's international position not been so gravely involved*. As it is, we retain great misgiving about the propriety of what is being done, which we can only justify on the principle 'my country . . . right or wrong, my country'. We all feel that we must insist that circumstances such as these are not allowed to recur." [570]

The memorandum was released more than half a century after the event.

Did Lord Shawcross, in his role as an international lawyer, do the right thing? As a critical actor in an international process, he complied with and, indeed, then implemented a national decision he believed to be internationally problematic, if not unlawful. His "act of conscience", his "speaking truth to power", consisted of submitting a confidential memorandum in which he expressed his disagreement and which he knew would not be released for at least fifty years.

That is not on the order of an act of conscience, akin, for example, to the release to the media by Daniel Ellsberg of the "Pentagon Papers", a secret report by the United States Department of Defense, which detailed the history of US engagement in the Vietnam War and, on its publication, intensified domestic opposition to the war. Ellsberg leaked the Pentagon Papers in 1971 while the United States was still embroiled in Vietnam, and he knew, when he did it, that he faced the very real possibility of a long prison sentence.

Section 2. The international lawyer's dilemma

Do international lawyers in the twenty-first century, in permanent or short-term Government service, have obligations to the international

---

570. Carty, *supra* footnote 564, at p. 11 (emphasis added).

community that transcend their obligations to their States? Do international lawyers who serve the great multinational corporations, the largest of which rival many States, have comparable obligations? Does international law then prevail over contrary national law?

Skilled lawyer that he was, Shawcross set out his reasons, so anyone in the twenty-first century who might be concerned with the type of dilemma he encountered could turn to them for whatever guidance they might provide. In Shawcross's view, what he did (and presumably similar things another lawyer in his position might be called upon to do) could be done if his "country's international position [was] gravely involved".

"Gravely involved". Does that mean that, for the international lawyer, international law prevails over inconsistent national obligations only when the issues concerned are of minor importance? That the *Grundnorm* of the international lawyer faced with a choice between international duty and national duty is not *de minimis non curat praetor juris gentium* but *de maximis non curat praetor*? Or, even more bluntly, as Shawcross put it, that the *Grundnorm*, for all purposes, is "my country . . . right or wrong, my country"? That principle, if a rule – or lawful *exceptio* – of international law, would affirm the supremacy of loyalty to the nation-State. If it is taken as a more general ethical principle, it would mean that – amid the Babel of identities in the twenty-first century which we have encountered throughout these lectures, my tribe, my caste, my clan, my family, my religion – whatever might be the speaker's primary identification – prevails over more inclusive loyalties.

Even if Shawcross's primary operative principle was more refined and came into operation only when his country's international position was "gravely involved", what is the gravitational tipping point of such a test? Is it the very existence of the State, "an extreme circumstance of self-defence, in which the very survival of a State would be at stake" [571]? If it is not existential, is it to be weighed against the gravity of the prospective violation of international law?

In the Corfu Channel incident, the survival of the United Kingdom was not at stake. Nor was the outcome of the Greek civil war itself. By then its outcome was clear. If XCU had been released to the Court, the worst that could have happened would have been that the United

571. *Legality of Nuclear Weapons*, *supra* footnote 113, at para. 105.

Kingdom might have lost the case at The Hague. That would hardly have endangered its national security or existence.

Indeed, if XCU had been disclosed, it probably would not even have cost the case. The United Kingdom, as applicant, had framed the issue before the Court as Albania's unpublished laying of mines in a channel used for international transit. Under any circumstances, Albania's action could hardly have been found lawful. The real "worst-case" consequence of producing XCU would have been a measure of embarrassment for the British Government: the Royal Navy, instead of seeming the hapless victim of the incident, as the UK portrayed itself, could have appeared to share responsibility for precipitating it. If truth be told, even that would have had minimal consequences, for no thoughtful observer could have doubted that the purpose of the Admiralty's decision to send the cruisers and destroyers through the straits at a critical moment in the Greek civil war had been to convey the UK's concern about Albanian support for ELAS and to communicate, by the presence of a powerful naval force, the ability, if push came to shove, to substantiate that concern.

If the consequences of producing XCU were so far from grave as to have been trivial and evanescent, is the international lawyer's "legal" principle to which Shawcross adverted actually an unqualified "my country, right or wrong"?

What is so poignant about Shawcross's actions and self-justifications here is that he had, by then, become a hero of the burgeoning human rights movement. As Britain's lead lawyer at the Nuremberg Trials, it was Shawcross who, in his two-day opening argument in November 1945, had demolished the defence that the proceedings at Nuremberg were "victors' justice" and had established that the laws which the defendants had transgressed, international treaties, prevailed over contrary national law. It was Shawcross who famously said to the Tribunal: "There comes a point when a man must refuse to answer to his leader if he is also to answer to his own conscience." The Nuremberg Tribunal ultimately confirmed that proposition. In what is popularly known as the *Justice Case*, sixteen German lawyers and judges were prosecuted for their actions in support of the Third Reich [572]. Judges and prosecutors who used their positions to implement Nazi programmes were allowed no legal sanctuary in German law, no matter how imperative that national

572. *United States* v. *Altstoetter*, Nuremburg Mil. Trib., 1947, 3 Trials of War Criminals Before the Nuremberg Military Tribunal Under Control Council Law No. 10.

law may have been. International law judged their actions against the standards of universal humanity, not those of a single State.

Now it would surely be invidious to equate the Nazis' crimes against humanity with the suppression of a relevant document in an essentially civil case in The Hague, but is not the principle involved the same? Is Shawcross's eloquent pleading at Nuremberg part of the myth system of international law, while his actual conduct and his memorandum to his Prime Minister in 1949 a reflection of the operational code of the international lawyer when a duty under international law conflicts with a duty under national law?

Many twentieth-century treatises on international law reserved a section for the "relation between international law and national or municipal law", which they variously described as "monist", "dualist" or "monist-dualist". None, however, viewed the relationship from the *operative* perspective – the Shawcross perspective – that of the individual international lawyer who is, at once, a member of the world community and a national community. Thus, the national judge seised of a case that centrally raises international legal issues will encounter a tension between the loyalty demands of the national legal system and those of the international legal system. The military officer in the field may find himself in the same crossfire. The Legal Adviser of the Department of State or a Ministry of Foreign Affairs may encounter a comparable tension as will a Minister of Justice or Attorney General presenting a case before the ICJ or another international tribunal.

In this regard, international lawyers differ from their domestic counterparts who are usually engaged in entirely internal transactions. Working, as they do, at the interface of their national legal system and international law, international lawyers are always exposed to the Shawcross dilemma.

Section 3. Bureaucracy and responsibility

Some of what may seem to be the complicity of lawyers in State actions which violate international law may be attributed to rank careerism, a willingness to do anything that promises to advance one's own career. Some of it may be attributed to moral mediocrity. Some of it may, indeed, be attributed to theories of "dualism" rather than "monism"; if Shawcross had thought in dualist terms, he would have faced no dilemma. But some of it is attributable to something so pervasive in contemporary life that it is less noticeable: I refer to bureaucracy, a constantly replicated technique of organisation in the public and private sectors.

Bureaucracy is decision-making's analogue to the factory assembly line of twentieth-century industry. By its techniques of creating hierarchies of authority and radically differentiating individual function in complex patterns of social coordination, bureaucracy permits the enormous amplification of the power of whoever is at the pinnacle of the bureaucracy. The consequences for information-sharing and decision in this form of organisation are radically anti-democratic, as Professor Robert Presthus explains:

> "The assignment of authority and status along hierarchical lines means that the conditions of participation in big formal organizations are determined by a minority. This characteristic of the bureaucratic model may be called *oligarchy*, which means 'rule by the few'." [573]

The possibilities of many small and seemingly innocuous decisions leading to wicked consequences are increased:

> "[T]he decision-making process becomes highly diffused, the product of an organizational mind. Organized irresponsibility follows. Decision making in the big organization becomes vague and impersonal, and the instrument of an anonymous, fragmented intelligence. Each decision is the result of various technical and personal considerations, the sum of the contributions of everyone involved in the deciding process. This diffusion means that 'everyone' (i.e. no one) is responsible. In extreme cases the condition may lead to arbitrary and immoral behavior, particularly when compounded by intense personal identification with the state, the party, the church, or the 'organization'. In every case, the probabilities that the organization may act unjustly are increased by the weakening of individual responsibility. Only 'the system' is responsible." [574]

In *The Trial*, Franz Kafka captured the psychology of the subordinate in this type of organisation. There, the jailer explains to his prisoner:

573. Robert V. Presthus, *The Organizational Society: An Analysis and a Theory*, 1962, at p. 39.
574. *Id.*, at pp. 53-54.

> "We are humble subordinates who can scarcely find our way through a legal document and have nothing to do with your case except to stand guard over you for ten hours a day and draw our pay for it. That's all we are, but we're quite capable of grasping the fact that the high authorities we serve, before they would order such an arrest as this, must be quite well informed about the reasons for the arrest and the person of the prisoner. There can be no mistake about that. Our officials, so far as I know them, and I know only the lowest grades among them, never go hunting for crime in the populace, but, as the Law decrees, are drawn toward the guilty and must then send out us warders. That is the Law. How could there be a mistake in that?" [575]

Centuries earlier, two of Shakespeare's nameless soldiers, more reflective than Kafka's jailer, acknowledged the possibility of a mistake and its potential moral consequences but limited their own moral responsibility to obedience: "We know enough if we know we are the King's subjects. If his cause be wrong our obedience to the King wipes the crime of it out of us" [576]. But the most chilling expression is surely Tom Lehrer's couplets satirising a nuclear scientist in governmental service: " 'Once the rockets go up, who cares where they come down. It's not my department', says Werner von Braun".

The pervasive anesthetisation of personal moral and legal responsibility inherent in this type of relationship was explored empirically in disturbing experiments conducted by Professor Stanley Milgram at Yale University. Professor Milgram found, in an experimental setting, that two-thirds of the people from ordinary walks of life he recruited could become torturers. Professor Milgram concluded:

> "The essence of obedience is that a person comes to view himself as the instrument for carrying out another person's wishes, and he therefore no longer regards himself as responsible for his actions. Once this critical shift of viewpoint has occurred, all of the essential features of obedience follow. The most far-reaching consequence is that the person feels responsible *to* the authority directing him but feels no responsibility *for* the content of the actions that the authority prescribes. Morality does not disappear – it acquires a radically different focus: the subordinate

575. Franz Kafka, *The Trial*, trans. Willa and Edwin Muir, Knopf Pub., 1972 (orig. 1925), at p. 10.
576. William Shakespeare, *Henry V*, Act 4, Scene 1.

person feels shame or pride depending on how adequately he has performed the actions called for by authority."[577]

There are two features here which are relevant to our discussion. The first is what we may call "task responsibility" as opposed to "outcome responsibility". The very complexity of the bureaucratic organisation means that most individuals operating at lower levels are unlikely to know with any certainty its major purposes or to be able to see or even conceive of its entire operation. They assume perforce that their superiors know what they are doing: hence they can hardly be deemed to be responsible for the "outcome-event" which the organisation produces, be it a service, a commercial product, a pattern of destruction, or whatever; in many cases they will not even know what it is.

Indeed, it would be most unlikely that those working on an assembly line or engaged in lower-level clerical activities will appreciate the environmental impacts of some of the products they are producing. It is even more unlikely that they will appreciate long-term ecological effects on the other side of the planet on which even experts may disagree. Where production processes are complex, many workers may not even know, let alone understand, the outcome-events or end products to which they are contributing. Where bureaucracy incorporates advanced technology, in the context of an industrial, science-based and technological civilisation, the difficulties for many of the people working in organisations even to understand *the implications* of the outcome-events to which they contribute increase enormously.

In such a setting, it is not surprising that the ethic of responsibility that Shakespeare and Kafka captured so brilliantly takes hold and is seized upon by participants, both at the pinnacle and below: a responsibility to discharge the particular task which crosses one's factory space, one's desk – or one's brief – but not some responsibility for the final outcome even though it could not be concluded without the contribution of the particular task. This is the ethic of "task" rather than "outcome" responsibility.

The moral implications of this ethic are obvious. People who would otherwise test the outcomes to which their own actions contributed in terms of their own moral calculus and hence retain the option of refraining from or changing those actions if that calculus was going to

577. Stanley Milgram, *Obedience to Authority*, 1974.

be violated, need not even face that question. Mark Green could not have summed it up more concisely:

> "One Covington and Burling associate explained that he didn't have to worry about ethical issues because he's the low man on the totem pole . . . [who] works for a great bunch of guys who really know their stuff." [578]

If the only relevant ethic is task responsibility, they may suspend their moral judgement. Task responsibility is, among other things, a moral anaesthetic.

Should any of this have relevance to the international lawyer serving a Government or other corporate entity?

Section 4. The complexity of international professional responsibility

"A profession", Harold D. Lasswell and Myres S. McDougal observed, "is best regarded as a group with both a special skill and a sense of responsibility for the consequences upon the community of the exercise of that skill" [579]. In that sense of profession, should not international lawyers in the twenty-first century assume, as one of their tasks, a responsibility to the most inclusive international community for the cumulative consequences to which their actions contribute?

Because the individual human being, acting alone or in concert with others, is the ultimate agent for securing and maintaining such a public order system and because international lawyers often find themselves in critical decision roles, this conception of international professional responsibility to the international community as a whole is critical to its achievement.

This approach obviously rejects theories of law in which professional and personal responsibility is confined to the meticulous performance of a narrowly defined role or task with no personal responsibility for the aggregate consequences to which that role or task contributes. We all recoil in revulsion from the *Beamter* in the Nazi genocide machine who focused narrowly on the production and supply of Zyklon B gas, while scrupulously ignoring its indispensable part in mass murder or the *apparatchik* who maintained the files in the Cheka, KGB or Stasi, or some contemporary analogue, and did not think of the consequences

578. Mark Green, *The Other Government: The Unseen Power of Washington Lawyers*, 1975.
579. Lasswell and McDougal, *supra* footnote 69, at p. xxiii.

of those files. And I would hope we view, with at least some discomfort, Shawcross's effort at self-justification that accompanied his complicity in a State action which he himself believed to be incompatible with international law and his professional role in it.

Virtually no significant violation of international law and major systemic violation of human rights will occur in the twenty-first century without legal specialists playing some role in organising, managing, justifying or defending it. But the dimension of professional responsibility in the approach recommended for the international lawyer is far from an easy one. Ernest Satow wrote that

> "the task of a diplomatic agent is to reconcile the interests of his own nation with those of others, and to preserve the honour of his own unblemished and devoid of selfish aims, in short, to cultivate what has been so well described as the international mind" [580].

At the minimum, the international lawyer should cultivate the "international mind". But that can be tested in real situations. The international legal system and the political environment within which it operates, which influences it and which it, in turn, tries to influence, presents some legal anomalies and intellectual and ethical problems which are more complex than those facing the domestic lawyer. I will mention only four, one of which is unique to international law, the others endemic to all law.

One of the anomalies of international law is that, as a system, it is and must be committed to allowing for creating and sustaining effective States. What are frequently referred to as failures of international law, especially in the human rights, economic and environmental areas, are failures of States. For all the laments of internationalists about exorbitant claims of sovereignty by State officials, international law, as a system, requires effective States. Yet States, as social organisations, cannot operate if their Governments are unable to command and rely upon the loyalty and obedience of their public services and of the citizenry at large; the legal specialists in these Governments are indispensable to their operation. In that sense, the faithful discharge of the international lawyer's duty to the State he or she serves contributes to the effectiveness of international law. This anomaly creates a genetic tension between Tom Franck's normative "pull" of different legal systems, and it is especially acute for the international lawyer: the

580. Ernest Satow, *Guide to Diplomatic Practice*, 2nd ed., 1922, at p. 6.

tension between national and international loyalties. Shawcross's pithy "my country, right or wrong" might have waffled by putting it more elaborately as "in this instance, a setback, like this, for my country will actually spell a setback for international law".

A second anomaly, characteristic of all decision-making, is found in the tension between the two modes of principled decision-making which we considered in Chapter VI: the textual-rule-based mode and the contextual-policy-based mode. The contextual-policy-based mode of decision engages outcome responsibility in the most comprehensive sense. The textual-rule-based mode of decision-making essentially involves task responsibility: the exercise of that responsibility is supposed to be confined to identifying and applying the proper rule without regard to its larger social consequences. The textual-rule-based mode of decision is vital for the coherence of certain types of social organisations and, as we saw, is the prescribed mode for certain roles. In other circumstances, lawyers function within institutions in which the role they have been assigned is a small part of a larger social mechanism which can only operate if they do what they are expected to do. Indeed, for *some* roles, there is nothing we want less than an expanded sense of responsibility for the aggregate consequences of an individual act. In our discussion of the application function in Chapter VI, Section 2, you will recall, we considered the case of the sergeant sitting in an ICBM silo and agreed that, in that role, at least, the last thing we might wish is for that person to do anything beyond making the binary choice he or she has been assigned.

A third anomaly arises from the very nature of the legal profession. The conception of professionalism that Lasswell and McDougal have espoused applies rather comfortably to physicians as a profession, but some of the professional functions that lawyers are expected to discharge involve the obligation to advance or defend special interests. An appropriate discharge of that type of role may require presenting, as forcefully and persuasively as possible, a position which the lawyer, in his or her heart, does not believe serves the common interest or, to put it simply and artlessly, knows is wrong. A corollary to the principle that everyone must be entitled to legal representation imports that lawyers must be prepared to defend unpopular causes. When concern for procedural integrity trumps substantive wrongs in the inner forum of the lawyer's heart, the lawyer says that it is "the legal system", "the constitution" and "human rights" which have prevailed.

A fourth anomaly goes to the varied conceptions of the public interest and the ways legal processes are expected to relate to them. A dialectical conception of what is right holds that in making complex social choices, which is the essence of the modern legal process, what is "right" can only be determined after an authoritative process of decision has determined it. In this thesis, you do not know what is right in a given legal system until a court has told you what is right. Thus, Abe Krash contended that "the 'public interest', unless it is defined more precisely, is a concept too nebulous – it is too ambiguous a standard – to serve as a basis for any practical action or judgement regarding a lawyer's professional conduct" [581]. From this perspective, Krash insisted "that lawyers best serve the public interest when they faithfully and competently represent the private interests of their clients" [582]. Certainly, much of modern law is a process of social choices in which different claims compete and any of a number of different patterns of prioritisation and accommodation of those claims may approximate the common interest of those claimants. It may be role-appropriate to press aggressively, in strict accordance with the procedural arrangements of the system, for one among these possible patterns of prioritisation and accommodation, no one of which is *a priori* "right". In this view, only an authoritative decision will determine what is "right". Even then, it may be entirely appropriate, from the perspective of professional ethics, to continue to press to secure an authoritative change according to the procedural arrangements of the system.

Some trends in contemporary international law undertake to establish limits to this accommodating relativism. By common accord, certain matters are always insulated from adjustment by other legitimate or procedurally correct processes of decision. I refer, of course, to the principles of *jus cogens*, not, however, in the narrow sense of the VCLT but in the broader sense of the contemporary human rights movement. Claims or actions that violate these principles are always wrong, and it is difficult to see how the performance of legal tasks that facilitate such violations can ever be professionally justified.

The problem, however, is not the great "NOs" of contemporary international law, the unequivocal prohibitions of genocide, mass murder and crimes against humanity. The problem is the lesser violations of

581. Abe Krash, "Professional Responsibility to Clients and the Public Interest: Is There a Conflict?", *Chi. B. Rec.*, Vol. 55 (1974), p. 31 *et seq.*

582. *Id.*

international law when they find themselves in competition with urgent national requirements.

These are the slippery "MAYBEs" of international law, the "SOMETIMES", the "ONLY THIS ONCEs", the international legal prescriptions which may, in some circumstances, entail adjustment and accommodation with other prescriptions. For Shawcross, the *Justice Case* was a NO, while the *Corfu Channel* case was a MAYBE, outweighed in the circumstances of that case by the concern "had not our country's international position not been so gravely involved". But other considerations *may* weigh in the balance.

Section 5. Some inspiring examples

There are innumerable examples of individuals who, while committed to the integrity of their own communities and their respective authority systems, deferred, in different ways, to a transnational rather than a national prescription. I shall mention only a few striking examples of officials, within a bureaucracy, and private citizens, mobilised by it, who elected to give priority to international rather than national prescriptions.

In 1979, General Mohammad Zia-ul-Haq, the President of Pakistan, put into law sharia criminal punishments – stoning, flogging and amputation of limbs – which he had established by military decree a year and a half earlier. Zia acknowledged that although two sentences of amputation of hands had been imposed, they had not been carried out. The *New York Times* report stated that "[t]he military courts reportedly were unable to find a surgeon willing to perform the operation" [583].

In some instances, the superordination of international law has been more subtle and even casuistic, as some judicial examples will show. Under Section 11 of the 1947 Headquarters Agreement, the United States agreed not to impose impediments to transit to or from the UN Headquarters District for representatives of UN members, UN officials, experts performing missions, media representatives, personnel from UN-recognised NGOs and "other persons invited to the Headquarters District by the United Nations" [584]. The PLO Observer Mission personnel were among the "other persons" invited into the

583. Robert Trumbull, "Pakistan Adopting Islamic Laws with Their Severe Punishments", *New York Times*, 11 February 1979, at A1.

584. Agreement Between the United Nations and the United States of America Regarding the Headquarters of the United Nations, 26 June 1947, 11 UNTS 11 (1947).

Headquarters District. Thereafter, in the Achille Lauro incident, Palestinian irregulars commandeered an Italian cruise ship and, among other acts of violence, threw an elderly wheelchair-bound American Jew overboard. Responding to public outrage, Congress passed the Anti-Terrorism Act of 1987. It provided that, if the purpose was the furthering of the interests of the PLO, it was unlawful

> "notwithstanding any provision of law to the contrary, to establish or maintain an office, headquarters, or premises, or other facilities or establishments within the jurisdiction of the United States at the behest or direction of, or with funds provided by the Palestine Liberation Organization or any of its constituent groups, any successor thereto, or any agents thereof" [585].

The obvious targets of the legislation were the PLO Information Office in Washington, DC, and the PLO Observer Mission in New York; the Reagan Administration duly ordered them closed.

When the PLO Observer Mission refused a Department of Justice order to leave, the Department of Justice filed suit in a federal district court, where the case of *United States* v. *Palestine Liberation Organization* was heard before Judge Edmund L. Palmieri [586]. He was a seasoned jurist who, by chance, had been the clerk to Charles Evans Hughes when Hughes was the American judge on the PCIJ. Judge Palmieri held that closure of the PLO Observer Mission would have been a clear violation of the Headquarters Agreement but that Congress had not explicitly indicated an intention to violate the agreement. That was quite a stretch given the Act's extensive legislative history in the Congressional record and the media and the unusual degree of clarity of the text. Judge Palmieri managed this conclusion by ratcheting up the requirements for showing intent to violate an international agreement to an unprecedentedly high standard. In effect, Congress would henceforth have to put in its legislation *expressis verbis* that its intention was to violate an international binding agreement. Thus, Judge Palmieri did not give effect to an Act of Congress but ensured US compliance with its international commitment [587].

---

585. Anti-Terrorism Act, Pub. L. No. 100-204, para. 1003, 101 Stat. 1406 (codified at 22 USC, para. 5202).

586. *United States* v. *Palestine Liberation Org*., 695 F. Supp. 1456 (SDNY 1988).

587. See W. Michael Reisman, "An International Farce: The Sad Case of the PLO Mission", *Yale J. Int'l L.*, Vol. 14 (1989), p. 412 *et seq.*

When Israel commenced construction of what was euphemistically called a "separation fence" – in many places a high wall surrounded by a cleared perimeter, reinforced with barbed wire and other exclusionary devices to insulate metropolitan Israel from belligerently occupied Palestine, the path of the wall deviated from the 1967 boundary, into Palestinian territory. The Wall appeared, in light of Israeli practices over several decades, to be a device, not simply for security but also for incrementally advancing the annexation of territory held under belligerent occupation. The lawfulness of the Wall was challenged in the UN General Assembly, the Israeli High Court of Justice and the ICJ under its advisory jurisdiction. While the ICJ opinion was pending, the Israeli High Court issued an opinion in *Beit Sourik Village Council* v. *Government of Israel*[588], a case in which Palestinian villagers challenged the lawfulness of seizures of their property by the Israeli military to erect a specific section of the Wall.

In an opinion by Aharon Barak, then President of the Israeli Supreme Court, the Court held that military commanders seizing land for construction of the wall must act within the scope of the international law of belligerent occupation, which provides for the protection of the lives and dignity of local residents. Thus, the security needs of the State must be balanced against international law obligations to civilians. Justice Barak proceeded to apply international law's proportionality test to determine the proper balance between military and humanitarian considerations, and he held that some sections of the Wall near Beit Sourik imposed harm to civilians that was disproportionate to the enhancement of security given by this particular route. Because these sections failed the international law requirement of proportionality, the Court nullified the property seizure orders that had been issued to allow the Wall's construction.

A final example is offered by the resignation of Elizabeth Wilmshurst, who was Deputy Legal Adviser to the Foreign and Commonwealth Office of the United Kingdom. In March 2003, Wilmshurst advised the Attorney General that an invasion of Iraq without a second, authorising Security Council resolution would be unlawful. The Attorney General offered this advice to the Prime Minister. The Government then decided to participate in the invasion, based on subsequent advice given by the Attorney General. In her letter of resignation, Ms Wilmshurst stated:

588. *Beit Sourik Vill. Council* v. *Gov't of Israel*, 30 June 2004, HCJ 2056/04, 43 ILM 1099 (2004).

> "I cannot in conscience go along with advice – within the Office to the Public Parliament – which asserts the legitimacy of military action without such a [Security Council] resolution, particularly since an unlawful use of force on such a scale amounts to the crime of aggression; nor can I agree with such action in circumstances which are so detrimental to the international order and the rule of law.
>
> I therefore need to leave the Office: my views on the legitimacy of the action in Iraq would not make it possible for me to continue my role as a Deputy Legal adviser or my work more generally." [589]

There are surely many more, unnoted examples.

Section 6. Alternative futures

We confront two alternative futures: in one, international law will take precedence, and in the other, it will not. The one that eventuates will depend, in some measure, on what we, as a profession, do. Those lawyers who are not engaged professionally by international law will be oblivious to the tensions discussed here, but international lawyers, who must operate at the interface of the two legal systems, will often face dilemmas, some of them acute. If the dominant trend in the future is one of loyalty to the State over the world community, the personal dilemmas will be dispelled but so, too, will the prospects for world order.

The example of physicians in Pakistan is of interest to students of international law because, there, members of a transnational profession which prescribes and applies its own prescriptive code gave that code priority in a conflict with the law of their State. Apparently, it occurred spontaneously, without guidance or direction from an external or international authority. It is sobering to note that no Government prosecutors appear to have refused, in a way parallel to their medical counterparts, to press for sharia punishments.

The VCLT adopted *jus cogens* as a principle of treaty law. But, coupled with other institutional developments in the field of international criminal law and the protection of human rights, *jus cogens* may be evolving into a general category of customary (as opposed to conventional) non-derogable obligations *imposed upon individuals*. The incorporation of

589. "Wilmshurst Resignation Letter", BBC News, last updated 24 March 2005, http://news.bbc.co.uk/2/hi/4377605.stm.

a more general concept of *jus cogens* into contemporary international law will have an impact on the role of the international lawyer in the twenty-first century even if it fails to effect a clear superordination of international law.

This is an interesting, even ironic, twist. In human rights conventions, a non-derogable obligation is one which *a State* may not suspend or otherwise evade, even in the gravest of circumstances. In the evolving broad concept of *jus cogens* in human rights law, an individual within a State may not lawfully execute an action sanctioned by national law but prohibited by international law on *jus cogens* grounds. Nor may the individual, whether acting as a State official or acting in a private capacity, claim immunity from the application of international law on the ground of superior orders or compliance with national law.

Will these developments be expanded in the twenty-first century into a wider body of international prescriptions that apply directly to individuals and trump inconsistent national law? In the twenty-first century, will international lawyers, as a profession, be subject to the same superordination of international over national law and accept to serve as officers of the vanguard of the international community?

John Maynard Keynes famously said:

> "The ideas of economists and political philosophers, both when they are right and when they are wrong, are more powerful than is commonly understood. Indeed the world is ruled by little else. Practical men, who believe themselves to be quite exempt from any intellectual influence, are usually the slaves of some defunct economist." [590]

Although these lectures have largely focused on a theory about international law, I do not want to claim too much for theory. But neither will I claim too little. Some part of the answer to the questions posed here will depend on how one thinks about law in general and international law in particular. Much will also depend, as in everything, on the courage of those who confront the choices presented by the Shawcross dilemma.

---

590. John Maynard Keynes, *The General Theory of Employment, Interest and Money*, 1936, at p. 383.

PUBLICATIONS DE L'ACADÉMIE
DE DROIT INTERNATIONAL
DE LA HAYE

PUBLICATIONS OF THE
HAGUE ACADEMY OF INTERNATIONAL
LAW

RECUEIL DES COURS

Depuis 1923, les plus grands noms du droit international ont professé à l'Académie de droit international de La Haye. Tous les tomes du *Recueil* qui ont été publiés depuis cette date sont disponibles, chaque tome étant, depuis les tout premiers, régulièrement réimprimé sous sa forme originale.

Depuis 2008, certains cours font l'objet d'une édition en livres de poche.

En outre, toute la collection existe en version électronique. Tous les ouvrages parus à ce jour ont été mis en ligne et peuvent être consultés moyennant un des abonnements proposés, qui offrent un éventail de tarifs et de possibilités.

INDEX

A ce jour, il a paru sept index généraux. Ils couvrent les tomes suivants:

1 à 101	(1923-1960)	379 pages		ISBN 978-90-218-9948-0
102 à 125	(1961-1968)	204 pages		ISBN 978-90-286-0643-2
126 à 151	(1969-1976)	280 pages		ISBN 978-90-286-0630-2
152 à 178	(1976-1982)	416 pages		ISBN 978-0-7923-2955-8
179 à 200	(1983-1986)	260 pages		ISBN 978-90-411-0110-5
201 à 250	(1987-1994)	448 pages		ISBN 978-90-04-13700-4
251 à 300	(1995-2002)	580 pages		ISBN 978-90-04-15387-7

A partir du tome 210 il a été décidé de publier un index complet qui couvrira chaque fois dix tomes du *Recueil des cours*. Le dernier index paru couvre les tomes suivants:

311 à 320	(2004-2006)	392 pages	Tome 320A	ISBN 978-90-04-19695-7

COLLOQUES

L'Académie organise également des colloques dont les débats sont publiés. Les derniers volumes parus de ces colloques portent les titres suivants: *Le règlement pacifique des différends internationaux en Europe: perspectives d'avenir* (1990); *Le développement du rôle du Conseil de sécurité* (1992); *La Convention sur l'interdiction et l'élimination des armes chimiques: une percée dans l'entreprise multilatérale du désarmement* (1994); *Actualité de la Conférence de La Haye de 1907, Deuxième Conférence de la Paix* (2007).

CENTRE D'ÉTUDE ET DE RECHERCHE

Les travaux scientifiques du Centre d'étude et de recherche de droit international et de relations internationales de l'Académie de droit international de La Haye, dont les sujets sont choisis par le Curatorium de l'Académie, faisaient l'objet, depuis la session de 1985, d'une publication dans laquelle les directeurs d'études dressaient le bilan des recherches du Centre qu'ils avaient dirigé. Cette série a été arrêtée et la dernière brochure parue porte le titre suivant: *Les règles et les institutions du droit international humanitaire à l'épreuve des conflits armés récents*. Néanmoins, lorsque les travaux du Centre se révèlent particulièrement intéressants et originaux, les rapports des directeurs et les articles rédigés par les chercheurs font l'objet d'un ouvrage collectif.

Les demandes de renseignements ou de catalogues et les commandes doivent être adressées à

MARTINUS NIJHOFF PUBLISHERS

B.P. 9000, 2300 PA Leyde Pays-Bas **http://www.brill.nl**

COLLECTED COURSES

Since 1923 the top names in international law have taught at The Hague Academy of International Law. All the volumes of the *Collected Courses* which have been published since 1923 are available, as, since the very first volume, they are reprinted regularly in their original format.

Since 2008, certain courses have been the subject of a pocketbook edition.

In addition, the total collection now exists in electronic form. All works already published have been put "on line" and can be consulted under one of the proposed subscription methods, which offer a range of tariffs and possibilities.

INDEXES

Up till now seven General Indexes have been published. They cover the following volumes:

1 to 101	(1923-1960)	379 pages	ISBN 978-90-218-9948-0
102 to 125	(1961-1968)	204 pages	ISBN 978-90-286-0643-2
126 to 151	(1969-1976)	280 pages	ISBN 978-90-286-0630-2
152 to 178	(1976-1982)	416 pages	ISBN 978-0-7923-2955-8
179 to 200	(1983-1986)	260 pages	ISBN 978-90-411-0110-5
201 to 250	(1987-1994)	448 pages	ISBN 978-90-04-13700-4
251 to 300	(1995-2002)	580 pages	ISBN 978-90-04-15387-7

From Volume 210 onwards it has been decided to publish a full index covering, each time, ten volumes of the *Collected Courses*. The latest Index published covers the following volumes:

311 to 320 (2004-2006) 392 pages Volume 320A ISBN 978-90-04-19695-7

WORKSHOPS

The Academy publishes the discussions from the Workshops which it organises. The latest titles of the Workshops already published are as follows: *The Peaceful Settlement of International Disputes in Europe: Future Prospects* (1990); *The Development of the Role of the Security Council* (1992); *The Convention on the Prohibition and Elimination of Chemical Weapons: A Breakthrough in Multilateral Disarmament* (1994); *Topicality of the 1907 Hague Conference, the Second Peace Conference* (2007).

CENTRE FOR STUDIES AND RESEARCH

The scientific works of the Centre for Studies and Research in International Law and International Relations of The Hague Academy of International Law, the subjects of which are chosen by the Curatorium of the Academy, have been published, since the Centre's 1985 session, in a publication in which the Directors of Studies reported on the state of research of the Centre under their direction. This series has been discontinued and the title of the latest booklet published is as follows: *Rules and Institutions of International Humanitarian Law Put to the Test of Recent Armed Conflicts.* Nevertheless, when the work of the Centre has been of particular interest and originality, the reports of the Directors of Studies together with the articles by the researchers form the subject of a collection published by the Academy.

Requests for information, catalogues and orders for publications must be addressed to

MARTINUS NIJHOFF PUBLISHERS

P.O. Box 9000, 2300 PA Leiden The Netherlands **http://www.brill.nl**

TABLE PAR TOME DES COURS PUBLIÉS CES DERNIÈRES ANNÉES

INDEX BY VOLUME OF THE COURSES PUBLISHED THESE LAST YEARS

Tome/Volume 399 (2018)

Kanehara, A.: Reassessment of the Acts of the State in the Law of State Responsibility, 9-266.
Buxbaum, H. L.: Public Regulation and Private Enforcement in a Global Economy: Strategies for Managing Conflict, 267-442.

(ISBN 978-90-04-41670-3)

Tome/Volume 400 (2018)

Chedly, L.: L'efficacité de l'arbitrage commercial international, 9-624.

(ISBN 978-90-04-42388-6)

Tome/Volume 401 (2019)

Wood, P.: Extraterritorial Enforcement of Regulatory Laws, 9-126.
Nishitani, Yuko: Identité culturelle en droit international privé de la famille, 127-450.

(ISBN 978-90-04-42389-3)

Tome/Volume 402 (2019)

Kinsch, P.: Le rôle du politique en droit international privé. Cours général de droit international privé, 9-384.
Dasser, F.: "Soft Law" in International Commercial Arbitration, 385-596.

(ISBN 978-90-04-42392-3)

Tome/Volume 403 (2019)

Daudet, Y.: 1919-2019, le flux du multilatéralisme, 9-48.
Kessedjian, C.: Le tiers impartial et indépendant en droit international, juge, arbitre, médiateur, conciliateur, 49-643.

(ISBN 978-90-04-42468-5)

Tome/Volume 404 (2019)

Rajamani, L.: Innovation and Experimentation in the International Climate Change Regime, 9-234.
Sorel, J.-M.: Quelle normativité pour le droit des relations monétaires et financières internationales?, 235-403.

(ISBN 978-90-04-43142-3)

Tome/Volume 405 (2019)

Paulsson, J.: Issues arising from Findings of Denial of Justice, 9-74.
Brunée, J.: Procedure and Substance in International Environmental Law, 75-240.

(ISBN 978-90-04-43300-7)

Tome/Volume 406 (2019)

Bundy, R.: The Practice of International Law, Inaugural Lecture, 9-26.
Gama, L.: Les principes d'UNIDROIT et la loi régissant les contrats de commerce, 27-343.

(ISBN 978-90-04-43611-4)

Tome/Volume 407 (2020)

Wouters, J. : Le statut juridique des standards publics et privés dans les relations économiques internationales, 9-122.
Maljean-Dubois, S. : Le droit international de la biodiversité, 123-538.
(ISBN 978-90-04-43643-5)

Tome/Volume 408 (2020)

Cançado Trindade, A. A. : Reflections on the Realization of Justice in the Era of Contemporary International Tribunals, 9-88.
González, C. : Party Autonomy in International Family Law, 89-361.
(ISBN 978-90-04-44504-8)

Tome/Volume 409 (2020)

Shany, Y : The Extraterritorial Application of International Human Rights Law, 9-152.
Besson, S. : La *due diligence* en droit international, 153-398.
(ISBN 978-90-04-44505-5)

Tome/Volume 410 (2020)

Koh, H. H. : American Schools of International Law, 9-93.
Peters, A. : Animals in International Law, 95-544.
(ISBN 978-90-04-44897-1)

Tome/Volume 411 (2020)

Cahin, G : Reconstrution et construction de l'Etat en droit international, 9-573.
(ISBN 978-90-04-44898-8)

Tome/Volume 412 (2020)

Momtaz, D : La hiérarchisation de l'ordre juridique international, cours général de droit international public, 9-252.
Grammaticaki-Alexiou, A. : Best Interests of the Child in Private International Law, 253-434.
(ISBN 978-90-04-44899-5)

Tome/Volume 413 (2021)

Ferrari, F. : Forum Shopping Despite Unification of Law, 9-290.
(ISBN 978-90-04-46100-0)

Tome/Volume 414 (2021)

Pellet, A. : Le droit international à la lumière de la pratique : l'introuvable théorie de la réalité. Cours général de droit international public, 9-547.
(ISBN 978-90-04-46547-3)

Tome/Volume 415 (2021)

Trooboff, P. D. : Globalization, Personal Jurisdiction and the Internet. Responding to the Challenge of adapting settled Principles and Precedents. General Course of Private International Law, 9-321.
(ISBN 978-90-04-46730-9)

Tome/Volume 416 (2021)

Wolfrum, R: Solidarity and Community Interests: Driving Forces for the Interpretation and Development of International Law. General Course on Public International Law, 9-479. (ISBN 978-90-04-46827-6)

Tome/Volume 417 (2021)

d'Argent, P.: Les obligations internationales, 9-210.

Schabas, W. A.: Relationships Between International Criminal Law and Other Branches of International Law, 211-392.

(ISBN 978-90-04-47239-6)

Tome/Volume 418 (2021)

Bollée, S.: Les pouvoirs inhérents des arbitres internationaux, 9-224.

Tladi, D.: The Extraterritorial Use of Force against Non-State Actors, 225-360.

(ISBN 978-90-04-50380-9)

Tome/Volume 419 (2021)

Kolb, R.: Le droit international comme corps de «droit privé» et de «droit public». Cours général de droit international public, 9-668.

(ISBN 978-90-04-50381-6)

Tome/Volume 420 (2021)

Perrakis, S.: La protection internationale au profit des personnes vulnérables en droit international des droits de l'homme, 9-497.

(ISBN 978-90-04-50382-3)

Tome/Volume 421 (2021)

Estrella Faria, J. A.: La protection des biens culturels d'intérêt religieux en droit international public et en droit international privé, 9-333.

(ISBN 978-90-04-50829-3)

Tome/Volume 422 (2021)

Karayanni, M.: The Private International Law of Class Actions: A Functional approach, 9-248.

Mahmoudi, S.: Self-Defence and "Unwilling or Unable" States, 249-399.

(ISBN 978-90-04-50830-9)

Tome/Volume 423 (2022)

Kinnear, M.: The Growth, Challenges and Future Prospects for Investment Dispute Settlement, 9-36.

Weller, M.: "Mutual Trust": A Suitable Foundation for Private International Law in Regional Integration Communities and Beyond?, 37-378.

(ISBN 978-90-04-51411-9)

Tome/Volume 424 (2022)

Asada, M.: International Law of Nuclear Non-proliferation and Disarmament, 9-726. (ISBN 978-90-04-51769-1)

Tome/Volume 425 (2022)

(ISBN 978-90-04-51770-7)

Printed in July 2022
by Triangle Bleu,
59600 Maubeuge (France)

Setting : R. Mirland,
59870 Warlaing (France)